THE EARLY MONARCHY IN ISRAEL:
THE TENTH CENTURY B.C.E.

Society of Biblical Literature

Biblical Encyclopedia
Leo G. Perdue, Series Editor

An English Translation of Biblische Enzyklopädie
Walter Dietrich and Wolfgang Stegemann, Editors

Volume 3

The Early Monarchy in Israel:
The Tenth Century B.C.E.

THE EARLY MONARCHY IN ISRAEL:
THE TENTH CENTURY B.C.E.

by

Walter Dietrich

Translated by Joachim Vette

Society of Biblical Literature
Atlanta

THE EARLY MONARCHY IN ISRAEL:
THE TENTH CENTURY B.C.E.

Library of Congress Cataloging-in-Publication Data

Dietrich, Walter.
  [Frühe Königszeit in Israel. English]
  The early monarchy in Israel : the tenth century B.C.E. / by Walter Dietrich ; translated by Joachim Vette.
      p. cm. — (Society of Biblical Literature biblical encyclopedia series no. 3)
  Includes indexes.
  ISBN: 978-1-58983-263-3 (paper binding : alk. paper)
      1. Jews—History—1200-953 B.C. 2. Palestine—History—To 70 A.D. 3. Bible. O.T. Samuel—Criticism, interpretation, etc. 4. Bible. O.T. Kings, 1st, I–XI—Criticism, interpretation, etc. I. Title. II. Series.
  DS121.55.D5213 2007b
  933'.020922—dc22   2007035238

15 14 13 12 11 10 09 08 07   5 4 3 2 1
Printed in the United States of America on acid-free, recycled paper
conforming to ANSI/NISO Z39.48-1992 (R1997) and ISO 9706:1994
standards for paper permanence.

CONTENTS

PREFACE

Following the guidelines for the Biblical Encyclopedia, this book is composed of four main sections:

I. In "The Biblical Account of the Time Period" we will trace how the biblical (and a few extrabiblical) witnesses describe this era. The main emphasis will be on the description of the older textual stratum in the books of Samuel and the beginning of the books of Kings. The content of these texts are retold, but we will also point out the high degree of artistry contained in these narratives, which is increasingly recognized by scholars.

II. "The History of the Early Monarchy" cannot be simply taken from the Bible, but it also cannot be written completely without or in opposition to these texts. Following a short introduction to methodology and a classification of the material and written sources, we will construct a picture of the history of Israel in the tenth century B.C.E.: this history will be presented in the various categories of societal and political development and grouped around the very different kingships of Saul, David, and Solomon.

III. "The Literature of the Time Period" can only be classified as contemporary literature to a very small degree. Only one generation ago, scholars still believed with great confidence that the early Israelite state led to a first blossoming of text production and historical writing that even preceded Greek historiography. Since then scholars have grown much more cautious but not completely skeptical. Literary and historiographical activity may have had very modest beginnings during the early monarchy, but we cannot postulate larger, more artistic works that were based on these early sources until much later.

IV. The "Theological Conclusions" are thus not drawn from material from the early monarchy itself but from literature about the early monarchy. After a large gap in time, Israel debated its understanding of God and its own identity within the context of their first kings. These questions continue to remain relevant for readers today. It is no coincidence that this last section is closely related to the first section: we are moved to theological thinking not by hypotheses on the historical setting and on the growth of the biblical texts but rather by these texts themselves.

I would wish for the readers of this book that these different sections come together as a whole. The table of contents and the indices may be of help in this. In the writing process, after all, I deliberately tried to make sure that I did not write only or mainly for experts in the field.

For the translation of the book into English, I have revised sections of the German version and expanded the bibliographies. This book should now serve well as a textbook reflecting the current state of scholarly discussion. I hope that readers will benefit from it and be motivated to intensify their study of the material discussed here.

I thank the publishers, especially Jürgen Schneider from Kohlhammer Verlag and Bob Buller from SBL Publications, for their helpful and dedicated support of this book and the whole series.

Special thanks goes to Dr. Joachim Vette, who worked with incredible care and diligence, showing not only great insight into my text but also excellence in expressing it in his mother tongue.

I would also like to thank Professor Leo G. Perdue, who is promoting and supporting the introduction of the "Biblical Encyclopedia" to an English-speaking audience with great intensity and skill.

I remain very thankful to my former and current teacher Rudolf Smend. I dedicated the original version of this book to him on the occasion of his sixty-fifth birthday and the end of his active university teaching. What I wrote about him in my dissertation twenty-five years ago has not changed and remains true: "He taught me how to love the Old Testament."

Bern, August 1997/September 2006   Walter Dietrich

Abbreviations

AASF	Annales Academiae scientiarum fennicae
AASOR	Annual of the American Schools of Oriental Research
ÄAT	Ägypten und Altes Testament
ABG	Archiv für Begriffsgeschichte
ABRL	Anchor Bible Reference Library
ACEBTSup	Supplements to Amsterdamse Cahiers voor Exegese en bijbelse Theologie
ADPV	Abhandlungen des Deutschen Palästina-Vereins
AJBI	*Annual of the Japanese Biblical Institute*
AnBib	Analecta biblica
Anton	*Antonianum*
AOAT	Alter Orient und Altes Testament
ATD	Das Alte Testament Deutsch
AThD	Acta Theologica Danica
BA	*Biblical Archaeologist*
BAR	*Biblical Archaeology Review*
BASOR	*Bulletin of the American Schools of Oriental Research*
BBB	Bonner biblische Beiträge
BEvT	Beiträge zur evangelischen Theologie
Bib	*Biblica*
BibInt	*Biblical Interpretation*
BiLiSe	Bible and Literature Series
BJS	Brown Judaic Studies
BK	*Bibel und Kirche*
BKAT	Biblischer Kommentar, Altes Testament
BN	*Biblische Notizen*
BO	*Bibliotheca orientalis*
BR	*Biblical Research*
BThSt	Biblisch-theologische Studien
BWANT	Beiträge zur Wissenschaft vom Alten und Neuen Testament
BZ	*Biblische Zeitschrift*
BZAW	Beihefte zur Zeitschrift für die alttestamentliche Wissenschaft

CaE	*Cahiers évangile*
CahT	Cahiers Théologiques
CBET	Contributions to Biblical Exegesis and Theology
CBQ	*Catholic Biblical Quarterly*
CBQMS	Catholic Biblical Quarterly Monograph Series
ConBOT	Coniectanea biblica: Old Testament Series
EdF	Erträge der Forschung
EHS	Europäische Hochschulschriften
ErIsr	Eretz-Israel
ETL	*Ephemerides theologicae lovanienses*
EvT	*Evangelische Theologie*
ExpTim	*Expository Times*
FAT	Forschungen zum Alten Testament
FB	Forschung zur Bibel
FCB	Feminist Companion to the Bible
FRLANT	Forschungen zur Religion und Literatur des Alten und Neuen Testaments
FzB	Forschung zur Bibel
HSM	Harvard Semitic Monographs
HUCA	*Hebrew Union College Annual*
IEJ	*Israel Exploration Journal*
Imm	*Immanuel*
Int	*Interpretation*
JBL	*Journal of Biblical Literature*
JBS	Jerusalem Biblical Studies
JBTh	Jahrbuch für biblische Theologie
JNES	*Journal of Near Eastern Studies*
JNSL	*Journal of Northwest Semitic Languages*
JSOT	*Journal for the Study of the Old Testament*
JSOTSup	Journal for the Study of the Old Testament: Supplement Series
LumVie	*Lumière et vie*
MDOG	*Mitteilungen der Deutschen Orient-Gesellschaft*
NEAEHL	*The New Encyclopedia of Archaeological Excavations in the Holy Land.* Edited by Ephraim Stern. 4 vols. Jerusalem: Israel Exploration Society and Carta; New York: Simon & Schuster, 1993.
NTS	*New Testament Studies*
OBO	Orbis biblicus et orientalis
OBT	Overtures to Biblical Theology
OLA	Orientalia lovaniensia analecta

OTE	*Old Testament Essays*
OTL	Old Testament Library
OTS	Old Testament Studies
PEQ	*Palestine Exploration Quarterly*
PJ	*Palästina-Jahrbuch*
RB	*Revue biblique*
RevExp	*Review and Expositor*
RSO	*Rivista degli studi orientali*
RTL	*Revue théologique de Louvain*
SBLDS	Society of Biblical Literature Dissertation Series
SBLSP	Society of Biblical Literature Seminar Papers
SBLSymS	Society of Biblical Literature Symposium Series
SBT	Studies in Biblical Theology
SBTS	Sources for Biblical and Theological Study
SDM	*Scripta et documenta*
SESJ	Suomen Eksegeettisen Seuran julkaisuja
SHANE	Studies in the History of the Ancient Near East
SJOT	*Scandinavian Journal of the Old Testament*
SSN	Studia semitica neerlandica
ST	*Studia theologica*
SWBA	Social World of Biblical Antiquity
TA	*Tel Aviv*
TAVO	Tübinger Atlas des Vorderen Orients
TB	Theologische Bücherei: Neudrucke und Berichte aus dem 20. Jahrhundert
ThSt	Theologische Studien
TLZ	*Theologische Literaturzeitung*
TRE	*Theologische Realenzyklopädie*. Edited by Gerhard Krause and Gerhard Müller. Berlin: de Gruyter, 1977–.
TRev	*Theologische Revue*
TUSR	*Trinity University Studies in Religion*
TynB	*Tyndale Bulletin*
TZ	*Theologische Zeitschrift*
UF	*Ugarit-Forschungen*
VT	*Vetus Testamentum*
VTSup	Supplements to Vetus Testamentum
WMANT	Wissenschaftliche Monographien zum Alten und Neuen Testament
WO	*Die Welt des Orients*
ZA	*Zeitschrift für Assyriologie*
ZAH	*Zeitschrift für Althebraistik*

ABBREVIATIONS

ZAW	*Zeitschrift für die alttestamentliche Wissenschaft*
ZDPV	*Zeitschrift des deutschen Palästina-Vereins*
ZTK	*Zeitschrift für Theologie und Kirche*

List of Figures

I. THE BIBLICAL ACCOUNT OF THE TIME PERIOD

Most individuals growing up in a Western cultural context have internalized certain images of Israel's first kings: Saul, David, and Solomon. These images are part of our cultural memory—surrounded by a plethora of additional characters: the queens and princesses Michal and Bathsheba, the princes Jonathan and Absalom, the prophets Samuel and Nathan, the generals Abner and Joab, the priests Eli and Zadok.

Three millennia lie between Israel's early monarchy and our present time. We have not forgotten this distant past, thanks to a complex and intricate chain of memories and traditions, of retellings and reinterpretations that time and again have attempted to introduce Israel's first kings and their times to new eras and new generations. All those who passed on the traditions—scribes without number, translators, interpreters, teachers and scholars, critics and propagandists, narrators and preachers, people of prayer and dreamers, poets and painters—they all created their own image of the early monarchy in Israel and passed them on to subsequent generations. Our images are not directly influenced by the ancient events themselves or by the oldest sources that speak to these events; rather, they are shaped by a long reception history that reaches into the present. The following overview can convey only a very incomplete impression of this reception history before we turn to the biblical material.

I.1. ASPECTS OF POST- AND INNERBIBLICAL RECEPTION HISTORY

Amsler, Samuel. *David, Roi et messie* (CahT 49; Neuchâtel: Delachaux & Niestlé, 1963). **Baldermann,** Ingo, et al., eds. *Der Messias* (JBTh 8; Neukirchen-Vluyn: Neukirchener, 1993). **Berger,** K. "Die königlischen Messiastraditionen des Neuen Testaments," *NTS* 20 (1973/74): 1–44. **Burger,** Christoph. *Jesus als Davidssohn* (FRLANT 98; Göttingen: Vandenhoeck & Ruprecht, 1970). **Couffignal,** Robert.

"*Le saint roi David*": *La figure mythique et sa fortune* (Paris: Lettres modernes Minard, 2003). **Delcor,** Mathias. "La reine de Saba et Salomon: Quelques aspects de l'origine de la légende et des sa formation, principalement dans le monde juif et ethopien, à partier des textes bibliques," *SDM* 47 (1993): 307–24. **Desrousseaux,** Louis, and Jacques **Vermeylen,** eds. *Figures de David à travers la Bible* (Paris: Cerf, 1999). **Dietrich,** Walter. *Von David zu den Deuteronomisten: Studien zu den Geschichtsüberlieferungen des Alten Testaments* (BWANT 156; Stuttgart: Kohlhammer, 2002). **Dietrich,** *David: Der Herrscher mit der Harfe* (Biblische Gestalten 14; Leipzig: Evangelische Verlagsanstalt, 2006). **Dietrich,** and Hubert **Herkommer,** eds. *König David, biblische Schlüsselfigur und europäische Leitgestalt* (Fribourg: Universitätsverlag; Stuttgart: Kohlhammer, 2003). **Dudden,** F. Homes. *The Life and Times of St. Ambrose*, vol. 2 (Oxford: Clarendon, 1935). **Eggenberger,** Christoph. "David als Psalmist im Lichte mittelalterlicher Bildpsalterien," *BK* 51 (1996): 23–27. **Frontain,** Raymond-Jean, and Jan **Wojcik,** eds. *The David Myth in Western Literature* (West Lafayette, Ind.: Purdue University Press, 1980). **Gosselin,** Edward A. *The King's Progress to Jerusalem: Some Interpretations of David during the Reformation Period and Their Patristic and Medieval Background* (Malibu: Undena, 1976). **Hentschel,** Georg. *Saul: Schuld, Reue und Tragik eines "Gesalbten"* (Biblische Gestalten 7; Leipzig: Evangelische Verlagsanstalt, 2003), 206–32. **Hourihane,** Colum, ed. *King David in the Index of Christian Art* (Princeton: Princeton University Press, 2002). **Kleer,** Martin. "*Der liebliche Sänger der Psalmen Israels*": *Untersuchungen zu David als Dichter und Beter der Psalmen* (BBB 108; Bodenheim: PHILO, 1996). **O'Kane,** Martin. "The Biblical King David and His Artistic and Literary Afterlives," *BibInt* 6 (1998): 313–47. **Pietsch,** Michael. "*Dieser ist der Sproß Davids...*": *Studien zur Rezeptionsgeschichte der Nathanverheißung* (WMANT 100; Neukirchen-Vluyn: Neukirchener, 2003). **Rosner,** Abraham. *Davids Leben und Charakter nach Talmud und Midrasch* (Oldenburg: Littmann, 1908). **Steger,** Hugo. *David rex et propheta: König David als vorbildliche Verkörperung des Herrschers und Dichters im Mittelalter* (Erlanger Beiträge zur Sprach- und Kunstwissenschaft 6; Nürnberg: Carl, 1961). **Steussy,** Marti J. *David: Biblical Portraits of Power* (Columbia: University of South Carolina Press, 1999). **Thoma,** Clemens. "David im Judentum," *TRE* 8:384–87. **Ullendorff,** Edward. "The Queen of Sheba in Ethiopian Tradition," in *Solomon and Sheba* (ed. James B. Pritchard; London: Phaidon, 1974), 104–14. **Waschke,** Ernst-Joachim. "The Significance of the David Tradition for the Emergence of Messianic Beliefs in the Old Testament," *Word and World* 23 (2005): 413–20. **Waschke.** "Die Beurteilung Sauls im Spannungsfeld des 'Gesanges der Frauen' (1Sam 18,6f) und der 'Klage Davids' (2Sam 1,17–27)," *Händel-Jahrbuch* 52 (2006): 105–17. **Zenger,** Erich. "David as Musician and Poet: Plotted and Painted," in *Biblical Studies/Cultural Studies* (ed. J. Cheyl Exum and Stephen D. Moore; JSOTSup 266; Sheffield: Sheffield Academic Press, 1998), 263–97.

A wave of novels dealing with characters from Israel's early monarchy has recently washed over the book market. Authors such as Stefan Heym, Torgny Lindgren, Joseph Heller, Grete Weil, and Allan Massie should be mentioned in this context.[1] They all benefit from the high profile and attractiveness of their biblical subject matter. Not all of these authors have acquired the same degree of expertise, not all of them are equally able to fascinate their readers, yet all display a high degree of imagination and creativity, adding further layers to the already complex picture that we in the present have of those in the past. In addition, the mirror of the past can also illuminate the present. It is stimulating, sometimes even exciting, to be led back to the present by journeying through Israel's early monarchy.

Similar observations are true in the area of visual or aural media: the variations on the gentle, music-making David in Marc Chagall's paintings, for example, or the much more dramatic, almost militant *King David Oratorio* by Arthur Honegger (1921). Following these tracks, we naturally arrive at earlier stages of biblical reception history: the composer Johann Kuhnau, the immediate predecessor of Johann Sebastian Bach as *Thomaskantor*, created the *Musicalische Vorstellung einiger biblischer Historien, in 6 Sonaten, auff dem Claviere zu spielen, allen Liebhabern zum Vergnügen* in 1700, the first two of which center on David: his battle with Goliath and his attempts to heal Saul through music (compare IV.3). The stained glass window in the center of the east choir of the Selby Abbey in middle England displays—in noticeable proximity to images of prophets and saints—portraits of all the kings of David's line (including the Maccabean rulers!); the transparency to English royalty is obvious. Michelangelo's David in Florence is much more than the depiction of the noble ruler; it is the epitome of the beautiful human being—not merely for the Renaissance period.

The path of reception history goes back even further, back to the ancient church and to early Judaism. Ethiopian Christians told the saga of Kebra-Nagast, which narrated how Abyssinian descendants of Solomon were the result of his (supposed) liaison with the Queen of Sheba (see 1 Kgs 10); this myth, which in a late rendition served to legitimate the rule of the Ethiopian emperor Haile Selassie even in our times (Ullendorff), has a long previous history, reaching from Flavius Josephus over the Targumim to Job and Esther and back to the famous frescoes in the Synagogue of Dura-Europos (Delcor).

Jewish tradition, however, generally focused on David with much greater intensity. Rabbinic tradition rarely portrays him as a political leader and hero; more often, he is used as a typecast for the expected Messiah. Most frequent, however, is his depiction as a spiritual example and identification figure for

---

1. These novels are introduced by Dietrich 2002. Two additional titles are less of a novel and more text or subject oriented: Hans-Martin Gauger, *Davids Aufstieg: Erzählung* (Munich: Beck, 1993); and Stefan A. Nitsche, *König David: Gestalt im Umbruch* (Zürich: Artemis, 1994).

devout Jews.[2] "Lord of the word," he is supposed to have prayed, "when I stand in prayer before you, may my prayer not be put to shame in your presence, for the eyes of Israel are on me and my eyes are on you" (*TRE* 8:385). The scandal between David, Bathsheba, and Uriah must have been a significant obstacle for this spiritualized image of David (2 Sam 11–12); precisely this event, however, became the ideal prooftext to show how even exemplary saints are fallible and in need of forgiveness. As a representative of Christianity on its way to becoming a state religion, Ambrosius, bishop of Milan, applied this idea to politics and confronted the eastern Roman emperor Theodosius with the penitent King David when the need arose.[3]

The New Testament Gospels tend to emphasize the messianic aspect of David. The Synoptic tradition presents Jesus as the "Son of David." This is why Joseph had to be a descendent of David and why the birth of Jesus had to take place in Bethlehem, the birthplace of David. The blind and the deprived call out to Jesus, "You, Son of David, have mercy on me!" This emphasis is also witness to Jewish messianic longings that saw their savior prefigured in David and at times even believed that the Davidic dynasty was present in secret, so that a descendent of David could arise at any time and reveal himself as the Messiah. Christianity accepted this expectation from Judaism, only immediately to claim its fulfillment in Christ.

Jesus Sirach, on the other hand, the great Jewish wisdom teacher of the second century b.c.e., never once presents the early monarchy in an eschatological context. In his so-called "Praise of the Fathers," a meditation on the exceptional individuals of salvation history, he extensively exalts David as a warrior and devout singer but also mentions that God "forgave his sins" and "made a covenant with him" (47:2–11); he portrays Solomon as a man of peace, as wealthy and extraordinarily wise, but also as one who became "a slave to his sensuality"[4] (47:12–22).

Without the least trace of criticism, Jesus conveys a similar understanding of Solomon. "I tell you, even Solomon in all his glory was not clothed like one

---

2. Compare the article of Thoma and some contributions in the volume edited by Dietrich and Herkommer. This aspect is also part of Christian reception history: medieval book illustrations portray David preferably as a devout prayer of psalms (Eggenberger). The Christian image of David can also take on activist-militant facets, as with American Puritans. See the contribution by Marie L. Ahearn in Frontain and Wojcik: "David, the Military Exemplum" (106–18).

3. See Ambrosius's work *De apologia prophetae David ad Theodosium Augustum* (CSEL 32/2:297–355) and also Dudden, 381ff.

4. An allusion to Solomon's many wives according to 1 Kgs 11. Ben Sira does not, however, refer to the issue of idolatry, the dominant motif in that context.

of these" (Matt 6:29). Solomon thus is the epitome of wealth and beauty—surpassed only by the flowers of the field. In all instances, wealth is one of the central motifs in this figure's reception history. The other motif, even more important, is wisdom. A whole score of Old Testament and intertestamental literature claims him as its author. No other author was respected as highly when it came to the issue of unsurpassable wisdom. The book of Proverbs is twice referred to as the "Sayings of Solomon" (1:1; 10:1). Even though 24:23 speaks of other nameless "wise men" and 25:1 refers to the "officials of King Hezekiah" (this would point to the end of the eighth century) as authors and collectors, Solomon is and remains the supreme author. Wisdom in the ancient Near East is the "science of life," including the study not only of nature in its manifold appearance (made accessible to wisdom teaching through extensive list-making) but also of human life, on an individual as well as a collective level. To be wise meant to understand the inner workings of things, to understand why something is the way it is or functions the way it does, to understand which actions lead to which consequences, and to understand how life may be best organized and managed. The one person who knew this best was—King Solomon. Surveying all and knowing all detailed inner workings, he is capable of advising and counseling all wise people for all times to come. The book Ecclesiastes (Qoheleth) is attributed to Solomon: the gentle and tired, resigned and realistic worldview and life confession of an immeasurably wise man. In addition, he supposedly wrote a few psalms and, not least, the Song of Songs. The so-called apocryphal writings add the apocalyptic Sapientia Salomonis (Wisdom of Solomon), which differs a great deal from the basic attitude of Qoheleth. It seems that the incredibly wide robe of the wise man, as worn by Solomon, could include many varied and even contradictory attitudes.

If Solomon embodies the wealth and wisdom of a ruler in biblical reception history, then David embodies the individual who remains successful with God's help, who is able to claim the gift of divine promise for himself and his dynasty, and, finally, who humbles himself in exemplary devotion before God. Prophetic promises of dynastic rule, promising life in freedom and justice to the people of God, all take their starting point with David (Isa 9:1–6; 11:1–8; Mic 5:14; Zech 9:9–10). In the consciousness of later generations, the image of David who rules and who will return in glory is only surpassed by the image of David who prays and sings psalms. More than half of the psalms are attributed to him. As the ultimate praying individual, who even authored deeply touching prayers of lament and repentance, he draws close—quasi on his knees—to Jewish (and no doubt also Christian) believers: a person who shares his fears and mistakes, desires and hopes; someone from high places, yet still one of us. He is a leader in prayer, an example, almost a heavenly figure, yet one with all too earthly human characteristics.

I.2. The Time Period according to Chronicles

Abadie, Philippe. "La figure de David dans le livre de Chronique," in *Figures de David à travers la Bible* (ed. Louis Desrousseaux and Jacques Vermeylen; Paris: Cerf, 1999), 157–86. Im, Tae-Soo. *Das Davidbild in den Chronikbüchern* (EHS 23/263; Frankfurt am Main: Lang, 1985). McKenzie, Steven L. *The Chronicler's Use of the Deuteronomistic History* (HSM 33; Atlanta: Scholars Press, 1984). Rad, Gerhad von. *Das Geschichtsbild des chronistischen Werkes* (Stuttgart: Kohlhammer, 1930). Van Seters, John. "The Chronicler's Account of Solomon's Temple-Building: A Continuity Theme," in *The Chronicler as Historian* (ed. M. Patrick Graham, Kenneth G. Hoglund, and Steven L. McKenzie; JSOTSup 238; Sheffield: Sheffield Academic Press, 1997), 283–300. Willi, Thomas. *Die Chronik als Auslegung* (FRLANT 106; Göttingen, Vandenhoeck & Ruprecht, 1972). Willi. "Das davidische Königtum in der Chronik," in *Ideales Königtum: Studien zu David und Salomo* (ed. Rüdiger Lux; ABG 16; Leipzig: Evangelische Verlagsanstalt, 2005), 71–87. Williamson, Hugh G. M. "The Accession of Solomon in the Books of Chronicles," *VT* 26 (1976): 351–61.

Certain elements of the late Old Testament portrayal of David and Solomon, as mentioned above, are also part of the books of Chronicles—presented, however, as historical narrative. Through extensive lists of genealogies, 1 Chr 1–9 presents a highly condensed history of the world from Adam and Eve to the conquest of the land and the tribal era. The final tribe listed and classified according to families (fathers) is the tribe of Benjamin. One of these families is the family of Saul (1 Chr 8). Following a short intermezzo on the population of Jerusalem—quite an anachronism, considering that David still had to conquer Jerusalem, but an important one for Chronicles, which was written in Jerusalem—we read the story of Saul. But what a story! There is nothing on his rise, his life, his successes and failures. We are informed only of his death (1 Chr 10). This presentation is radical and highly intentional: Saul comes from northern Israel, and northern Israel will continue to play a non-role in the Jewish Chronicles. Much more, Saul is no David, not even worthy to be his opponent; he is merely David's predecessor and dies before David appears on the scene. In the end, Saul is judged—a surprise, considering that we have been told nothing about him (the Chronicler clearly assumes that his audience is familiar with the books of Samuel): "So Saul died for his unfaithfulness; he was unfaithful to the LORD in that he did not keep the command of the LORD;[5] moreover, he had consulted a medium, seeking guidance, and

---

5. This probably alludes to 1 Sam 15; the Chronicler thus assumes that his audience is familiar with this text.

did not seek guidance from the LORD.[6] Therefore the LORD put him to death and turned the kingdom over to David son of Jesse." Chronicles loves decisive characterization.

Now David appears. His first actions are his coronation and his conquest of Jerusalem (1 Chr 11; see 2 Sam 5). There is no mention of the intricate path that led to this successful conclusion, even if we can read about this path in the books of the seers Samuel and Gad and the prophet Nathan (this peculiar source reference in 1 Chr 29:29 most likely refers to nothing but the canonical books of Samuel). David does not become king in stages, first over Judah, then over Jerusalem, then over Israel; instead, he becomes king once and for all over all Israel.

In much greater detail we are told about the transfer of the ark to Jerusalem and of Nathan's promise to David (1 Chr 12–17). This now is important: David moves toward God, and God turns to David. During this transfer, David leads his subjects in singing a psalm, the famous "Thanks be to God," most likely a popular song in the time of the Chronicler; this psalm is a mixtum compositum of Pss 105, 96, and 106. Already here David appears as a composer of psalms—but surprisingly not of those attributed to him in the biblical Psalter. Is the book of Chronicles a step further than the Psalter redaction, or is it (more likely!) a step before?

First Chronicles 18–20 minutely reports the wars of David (in which David, of course, was entirely victorious; compare 2 Sam 8 and 10). This report does not focus on David's heroism (why otherwise would the Goliath episode be missing?); instead, it aims to explain why David, as a "man of blood," was not able to build the Jerusalem temple himself as he had originally intended (McKenzie, 72). Once again we look for such famous narratives as Absalom's insurrection and death in vain. Chronicles has completely erased the trail of blood left behind by David that winds through Saul's royal family. This is an early stage of subsequent reception history that never dwells on these topics at great length. On the other hand, the Chronicler enjoys telling us how David (following a failed census to which not God but Satan tempted him; compare 1 Chr 21:1 with 2 Sam 24:1) found and purchased the location for the future temple. Here he has arrived at one of his most important topics: the temple. David immediately goes about arranging and preparing everything necessary for temple construction. He organizes material and artisans, instructs prince Solomon in the construction plans, and even allocates the respective guilds of priests, Levites, and singers to their service in the temple

---

6. Compare 1 Sam 28, although Saul did turn to YHWH in this context but did not receive any answer!

(in 1 Chr 23–26, perhaps a secondary addition to the text). In the end, he hands the models for construction and interior design over to his son and successor, exhorts and encourages him for the great task that lies ahead, and concludes with a public prayer, thanking God for granting his people such wealth and thus the ability to finance the temple construction. All of David's subjects are deeply moved and lift Solomon onto the throne with shouts of joy (1 Chr 28–29, with no word of confusion or strife over the succession to the throne!)

The second book of Chronicles presents the story of Solomon in chapters 1–11. Elements that will influence the future reception history of this ruler are already present here: he is wise, pious, and wealthy beyond compare. According to Chronicles, his entire focus and desire is directed toward building the temple. The Chronicler even omits what Ben Sira alludes to, that Solomon had an unhealthy love of women. We learn nothing of the structure and organization of his kingdom, of the taxes and tributes, of the conscription to forced labor for the large construction projects. As if by lightning, Solomon's kingdom is split after his death, because the northern tribes rebel against the harsh oppression and exploitation under Solomon (of which we have heard nothing previously; 2 Chr 10). What follows in Chronicles is a history of Judah alone; northern Israel is completely suppressed. The fact that the kingdom of Judah correlates closely to the Persian province Yehud, in which Chronicles was written, and the fact that northern Israel is analogous to the province Samaria and thus the (later?) Samaritans fully explain this narrow horizon.

Judah, Jerusalem, and the temple—this is what takes center stage for the Chronicler. The temple is the center of Jerusalem, Jerusalem is the center of Judah, and Judah as the undivided people of God represents the entire world before God (Willi). The history of David and Solomon is presented within this framework. As kings of Judah, they were rulers over all of Israel, they resided in Jerusalem, and they planned and built the temple. The temple (the First Temple, built by Solomon and subsequently destroyed by the Babylonians, as well as the Second Temple, which is the Chronicler's real concern), however, is the place where Israel can affirm the presence of its God and thus its own identity.

I.3. THE TIME PERIOD ACCORDING TO THE DEUTERONOMISTIC HISTORY

Blum, Erhard. *Studien zur Komposition des Pentateuch* (BZAW 189; Berlin: de Gruyter, 1990), 333–60. **Brueggemann,** Walter. *David's Truth in Israel's Imagination and Memory* (2nd ed.; Minneapolis: Fortress, 2002). **Carlson,** R. A. *David* *the Chosen King: A Traditio-Historical Approach to the Second Book of Samuel* (Stockholm: Almqvist & Wiksell, 1964). **Childs,** Brevard. S. *Introduction to the Old Testament as Scripture* (Philadelphia: Fortress, 1979). **Crüsemann,** Frank. *Die Tora* (Munich: Kaiser, 1992), 381–425. **Dietrich,** Walter. *David, Saul und die Propheten: Das Verhältnis von Religion und Politik nach den prophetischen Überlieferungen vom frühesten Königtum in Israel* (2nd ed.; BWANT 122; Stuttgart: Kohlhammer, 1992). **Dietrich.** "Martin Noth and the Future of the Deuteronomistic History," in *The History of Israel's Traditions* (ed. Steven L. McKenzie and M. Patrick Graham; JSOTSup 182; Sheffield: Sheffield Academic Press, 1994), 153–75. **Dietrich.** "History and Law: Deuteronomistic Historiography and Deuteronomic Law Exemplified in the Passage from the Period of the Judges to the Monarchical Period," in *Israel Constructs Its History: Deuteronomistic Historiography in Recent Research* (ed. Albert de Pury, Thomas Römer, and Jean-Daniel Macchi; JSOTSup 306; Sheffield: Sheffield Academic Press, 2000), 315–42. **Edelman,** Diana Vikander. *King Saul in the Historiography of Judah* (JSOTSup 121; Sheffield: Sheffield Academic Press, 1991). **Eslinger,** Lyle M. *Kingship of God in Crisis: A Close Reading of 1 Samuel 1–12* (BiLiSe 10; Decatur, Ga.: Almond, 1985). **Eslinger.** *Into the Hands of the Living God* (JSOTSup 89; Sheffield: Sheffield Academic Press, 1989). **Knoppers,** Gary N. *The Reign of Solomon and the Rise of Jeroboam* (vol. 1 of *Two Nations under God: The Deuteronomistic History of Solomon and the Dual Monarchies*; HSM 52; Atlanta: Scholars Press. 1993). **McKenzie,** Steven L. *The Trouble with Kings: The Composition of the Book of Kings in the Deuteronomistic History* (VTSup 42; Leiden: Brill, 1991). **Müller,** Reinhard. *Königtum und Gottesherrschaft* (FAT 2/3; Tübingen: Mohr Siebeck, 2004). **Niehr,** Herbert. *Herrschen und Richten: Die Wurzel špt im Alten Orient und im Alten Testament* (FB 54; Würzburg: Echter, 1986). **Noth,** Martin. *Überlieferungsgeschichtliche Studien I: Die sammelnden und bearbeitenden Geschichtswerke im Alten Testament* (3rd ed.; Tübingen: Mohr Siebeck, 1967). **Tanner,** Hans Andreas. *Amalek: Der Feind Israels und der Feind Jahwes* (Zürich: Theologischer Verlag Zürich, 2005). **Van Seters,** John. *In Search of History* (Winona Lake, Ind.: Eisenbrauns, 1997). **Veijola,** Timo. *Die ewige Dynastie: David und die Entstehung seiner Dynastie nach der Deuteronomistischen Darstellung* (AASF B/193; Helsinki: Suomalainen Tiedeakatemia, 1975). **Veijola.** *Das Königtum in der Beurteilung der Deuteronomistischen Historiographie: Eine redaktionsgeschichtliche Untersuchung* (AASF B/198; Helsinki: Suomalainen Tiedeakatemia, 1977). **Veijola.** "Geographie im Dienst der Literatur in 1Sam 28,4," in *David und Saul im Widerstreit: Diachronie und Synchronie im Wettstreit* (ed. Walter Dietrich; OBO 206; Fribourg: Academic; Göttingen: Vandenhoeck & Ruprecht, 2004), 256–71.

The narratives on Israel's first kings in 1 Sam 1–1 Kgs 11 are part of a large work of biblical historiography that in its final form reaches from creation (Gen 1) to the collapse of the kingdom of Judah in the year 586 B.C.E. (2 Kgs 25). A host of literary connections interconnects the various sections of this large historical work and create a coherent whole. A chronological system seems to form the backbone of the entire structure: one episode and one era more or less follows the previous one. In addition, a chronological structure of dates pervades the whole corpus: from the dates of birth and death of the first humans in the primal history (Gen 5, etc.), to those of the patriarchs (according to Gen 25:7, Abraham lived for 175 years), to the generations living in Egyptian slavery and, following the exodus, in the desert (Exod 12:40; Num 14:32–34; cf. Deut 34:7), then on to the generation of the conquest (Judg 2:10) and the period of judges, with its alternation of peace and turmoil and the dates of the so-called minor judges (e.g., Judg 3:11, 30; 12:7ff.), finally to the official dates of all of the kings of Israel and Judah, starting with Saul, David, and Solomon (1 Sam 13:1; 2 Sam 5:5; 1 Kgs 11:42) and ending with the last Davidic king who ruled in Jerusalem and was deported to Babylon (2 Kgs 24:18; 25:27).

We find an explicit retrospective connection to Israel's first beginnings in 1 Kgs 6:1: "In the four hundred eightieth year after the Israelites came out of the land of Egypt ... Solomon began to build the house of Yhwh." For twelve generations, this is what the text wants to tell us, Israel existed without the house of Yhwh in Jerusalem. According to the chronology of kings, 430 years will pass until the destruction of the temple by the Babylonians in the year 586 b.c.e. and about 50 more in exile, until the Persian king Cyrus orders the rebuilding of the temple (2 Chr 36:22ff.)—once again 480 years between the first and the second laying of the foundation stone: obviously a well thought out chronological architecture that spans almost one thousand years of Israelite history.

The canon as we know it today creates a significant break that interrupts this overarching structure: the five books of Moses, the Pentateuch (or Torah, according to Jewish terminology), claim a unity all their own. The Torah claims a twofold advantage against the following historical books (Joshua–2 Kings, referred to as Former Prophets in the Hebrew canon). In the historical development of the canon, these books were the first to be established as normative, as canonical; according to their subject matter, they enjoy unrivaled authority and dignity in the context of all canonical writings. The Prophets— the Former as well as the Latter—now appear as the interpreters of the Torah. When "prophetic" books narrate history, they narrate it within their canonical context as reception history of the Torah. Long before Israel became a state with kings to rule it, long before Israel even claimed its land and consolidated itself on it, the norms were already in place that determined how Israel would enter into its history. Theirs was a history destined to be a history with the god Yhwh—or against him, but never without him. The relational tension to Yhwh released enormous energy, driving Israel's history onward. Sure enough, other historical forces also play their part: political, sociological, economic, ecological, and anthropological; still, the decisive motor of biblical history is the relation of the people of Israel to its god Yhwh.

For the books Joshua, Judges, Samuel, and Kings, Martin Noth postulated a separate historiographic work, the so-called Deuteronomistic History. This work centers not on the entire Torah but only on Deuteronomy, which is also its starting point. It spans a time period from the conquest to the loss of the land.[7]

This is not the place to discuss the various hypotheses on the possible growth and intention(s) of the Deuteronomistic History. This much is clear: the period of the monarchy is hardly more than half of the time period covered by Deuteronomistic writers—this is also true for the amount of text that deals with this period. The time period before the establishment of the state is as important—in truth, even more important. From the very beginning, Moses, and thus actually God himself, lays out the criteria for Israel's life and history. In the ancient Near East, kings tend to decree and implement laws; the most famous example is the codex of the Babylonian king Hammurabi. This is not true for Israel—at least not according to the Deuteronomistic authors. Prior to any state organization, the god YHWH constitutes his people Israel by means of his Torah.

I.3.1 TOWARD ESTABLISHING A STATE

Moses has hardly proclaimed the Torah—according to Deuteronomistic fiction, in his 120th year, during a single day—when he must relinquish his leadership position; one glance at the promised land beyond the Jordan from Mount Nebo is all he is granted, then he dies and is buried east of the Jordan (Deut 34). Joshua assumes leadership of the people and receives instructions from YHWH to conquer the land (Deut 34:9; Josh 1). An immensely victorious campaign takes its course: from Gilgal and Jericho and then up to the mountains of Benjamin, Israel moves into the middle of Canaanite territory (Josh 2–9) and conquers first the southern, then the northern country (Josh 10–12) in two quick campaigns. This territory is subsequently divided among the tribes by lot (Josh 13–22). Yet already in Joshua's farewell address dark clouds line the cloudless blue sky of Israel's earliest history: the people who

---

7. The growth of the first two canonical sections can most likely be understood as follows: The Deuteronomistic History was completed first, and this means in exilic and early postexilic times. This was then extended into the past by a historical narration reaching back to the patriarchs, perhaps even to creation. The Sinai-Torah was added even later (Exod 20–Num 10) and turned into the middle of the Torah by separating the Former Prophets. Thus, Deuteronomy received the status of a "second Torah," interpreting the "first."

were given the gift of Torah and land might possibly alienate their God and (once again) turn to other gods.

This is precisely what occurs: the book of Judges describes a continual up and down, a continual turning to YHWH and turning away from YHWH. God reacts directly to this movement and causes an unremitting alternation between success and failure in the realm of politics as well as on the battlefield. Reading these texts, the reader gains a sense of an ever-increasing decline or a downward spiral motion: Israel's falling away to other gods becomes more and more brazen, the enemies allowed into the land by YHWH are more and more dangerous, the saviors sent to drive them away—after the people have repented—are less and less convincing. Gideon himself still rejects the kingship (Judg 8:22), but his (supposed) son Abimelech seizes the kingship with brute force (Judg 9); Jephtah is not able to prevent the tribes from engaging in civil war (Judg 12); Samson, a hero equipped with enormous physical prowess but limited moral standing burns out in skirmishes with the Philistines (Judg 13–16). Finally, bloody and brutal chaos breaks out in Israel (Judg 17–21); even the judge-priest Eli cannot lead the tribes (1 Sam 1–3) out of this conflict. On the contrary, the Philistines, Israel's continuously dangerous enemy, take advantage of Israel's agony and win a decisive victory (1 Sam 4).

The story of Israel prior to the establishment of a state appears to start gloriously under Moses and Joshua. Under the leadership of the judges, however, this story continues to become more erratic and agonizing. The question arises automatically: Will glory and salvation return under a new leadership, or will Israel drown in calamity and misery? Thus, the establishment of the kingdom, the founding of a state, occupies a key position in the entire scope of the Deuteronomistic History. Each of the first kings is shown in his attempt to consolidate Israel's inner and external order. Each of these kings uses different means, and each king is successful to a different degree. The overall question remains: Will Israel and its kings learn the most important lesson from the prior history, that Israel's fortune and demise fully depend on the adherence to or rejection of the Torah, most specifically the demand for exclusive commitment to YHWH?

As in all good historiography and also in history, it is never known in advance how it will all end. The Deuteronomistic Historians set the basic parameters for their depiction and evaluation of the monarchy in 1 Sam 1–12. These texts already contain a mixture of light and darkness, starting with the presentation of the era of judges in its final stages. Eli and Samuel are presented as the last representatives of this prestate era in the history of Israel.

Eli, the Deuteronomistic Historian tells us, "was שָׁפַט over Israel for forty years" (1 Sam 4:18). The term שפט oscillates between "to judge" and "to rule" (see Niehr). The Deuteronomistic book of Judges uses this term both for leaders who judged Israel for a number of years as a matter of domestic politics and for heroes who liberated Israel from external enemies (such as Ehud, Gideon, etc.). The Deuteronomistic Historian combines these functions and offices and depicts those who hold these offices as the leaders of Israel prior to the establishment of the state. Eli is such a leader. In the area of domestic policy, Eli is priest of Yhwh at the central sanctuary at Shiloh. In the area of foreign policy, he is the leader in the conflict with the Philistines. He fails miserably in both areas.

Eli himself is not an unworthy priest. There are no major failures or violations of which he is guilty. Even though he does not act quite correctly when confronted with Hannah, who is looking for help in the sanctuary (1 Sam 1) and when God speaks to Samuel in the night (1 Sam 3), he corrects his mistakes quickly. Hannah receives an oracle of promise, and Samuel receives instructions on how to react properly to God. Even when Samuel tells him about God's intentions, he reacts in exemplary fashion to the depressing divine message. Eli's actual weakness is his sons. He has legitimately appointed them as his successors in office, but he cannot prevent their continual grave misuse of that office (1 Sam 2:11–17, 22–25). In the end, he will lose them and his own life for this very reason (1 Sam 4).

Corresponding to his ineptitude to maintain order in his own house and country, he is also incapable of protecting Israel from its worst enemies, the Philistines. He officiates with both of his sons at the sanctuary of Shiloh. Here, in the holy of holies, is the location of the sacred ark, a cultic object with nationwide importance. As a palladium of war, it marks the presence and aid of Yhwh in Israel's war with its external enemies. Help exists, therefore, which Israel might also use against their present enemy, the Philistines. With great hopes, the Israelites take the ark along to the decisive battle. According to the Deuteronomistic point of view, the priest of the ark assumes the role of the hero-liberator, as we have come to know it from the book of Judges. This time, however, he is not able to liberate Israel. The fact that Eli himself is too old and inflexible to go to war himself and that he sends out an army that is much too small already gives little reason for hope; the fact that his sons, who are rotten through and through, go out in his place, confirms this deep-seated unease. And so the inevitable takes its course: Yhwh does *not* fight for Israel; the battle and the ark are lost to the Philistines (1 Sam 4).

A new hope has grown in Eli's shadow: Samuel. The Deuteronomistic Historian states that he too "judged Israel all his life" (1 Sam 7:15). Samuel is much better able to fulfill this role than Eli. Not only are his actions as Eli's successor in the priesthood above reproach (1 Sam 12:3–4), but unlike Eli, he is also a prophet to whom God speaks time and again (1 Sam 3:21). In addition, he travels in legal matters as a real judge throughout the land and speaks justice for the people (1 Sam 7:16). Matching his ability to maintain order within Israel, he also succeeds in protecting Israel against its external enemies. Under his leadership, Israel wins an important battle against the Philistines—exactly where the last battle was lost, close to Eben-ha-ezer (1 Sam 7:11–12; see 4:1). *As long as Samuel remains alive*, Israel actually wins back all the territories lost to the Philistines and enjoys a time of peace, not only with this dangerous enemy to the west but also with the Amorites, the non-Israelite inhabitants of their own land (1 Sam 7:13, most likely all secondary Deuteronomistic additions).

Samuel is close to being an ideal character; he is able to raise the office of judge to heights never known before—were there not the problematic issue he shares with his unfortunate predecessor: the inadequacy of his sons. He appoints them as judges, apparently as his successors, but they become active only in the far south, in Beersheba. There they prove themselves to be corrupt and pervert the law (1 Sam 8:1–3). Israel has already once sorely experienced what happens when an otherwise honorable leader is succeeded by his good-for-nothing sons. They do not want to go through this experience again—and ask Samuel to appoint a king (1 Sam 8:4–5).

According to the Deuteronomistic History, the repeated motif of two different judges with wayward sons becomes the motivating factor for the transition from the period of judges to the period of the kings. The more profound reason for this transition, however, is the inability of the various judges to secure reliable and durable order inside Israel and protection against the outside. This does not have to be the personal shortcoming of a particular judge; it can also be the result of external circumstances—to be more precise, of the structure of the office of judges itself. The charismatic deliverer stands down as soon as victory has been accomplished; the internal leader may not have the means and resources necessary to enforce his authority. In any case, Israel time and again falls into a state of disobedience and disloyalty toward YHWH and repeatedly causes its own misery: externally, it succumbs to the cruel oppression of foreign nations (with the Philistines as the climax of this development); internally, it sinks into rampant lawlessness and murderous conflict. The actions of Eli and Samuel's sons may seem more harmless, but they are made of the same horrendous stuff as the actions of the Israelite tribes in the so-called appendix to the book of Judges. It is no coincidence that the Deuteronomistic Historian interjects a refrain-like comment in that context that indicates the direction of the development: "In those days there was no king in Israel; all the people did what was right in their own eyes" (Judg 21:25; see 17:6; 18:1; 19:1).

Did the monarchy, which Samuel was supposed to help inaugurate, result in a new era in which Israel did what was pleasing to YHWH and YHWH what was helpful for Israel? Far from it. We will see that the kings did not always do, hardly ever did, what YHWH expected of them according to his will expressed in the Torah. And we have already seen that the judges were not all bad in comparison. Even in the book of Judges these individuals are the only highlights and bright spots we can find: the *people of Israel* themselves continue to fail. This is also true for the last two judges, Eli and Samuel. They are not crude transgressors of the Torah, especially not Samuel—on the contrary! Neither Eli nor Samuel, however, can compensate for the *system* of judges with all its shortcomings. The source of evil is the absence of continuity. With almost mathematical certainty, the people turn away from YHWH once a judge steps down. Eli's and Samuel's attempt to establish their sons in their place during their lifetime may be motivated by their attempt to correct this weakness. Constructive continuity, however, guaranteed by a stable institution of judgeship and ensuring correct behavior toward God, is not merely a matter of sheer willpower. It is therefore doubtful, whether the new institution of monarchy can accomplish such continuity, even if it is more stable in itself.

The Deuteronomists engage in a discussion, perhaps even an argument, on this topic right from the start, when the last judge, Samuel, inaugurates the first king, Saul. The arguments are presented in 1 Sam 8–12, most clearly in the very Deuteronomistic chapters 8 and 12. The one side argues that the office of judge cannot be a long-term solution, as the case of Samuel's sons clearly shows. Who will be able to protect Israel permanently from its own sins as well as from those of its leaders? Who will protect Israel from its enemies (in other words, from the divine punishment that follows from its sins)? The judges have not proven themselves capable of this task. The solution is to approbate a different type of tried and tested leadership from the surrounding nations: kings. "So that we may be like other nations and that our king may govern us and go out before us and fight our battles" (1 Sam 8:20).

The other side also presents strong arguments. The people had hardly uttered their request to Samuel, "Appoint for us a king to govern us [שׁפט!], like other nations" (1 Sam 8:5), when a Deuteronomistic theologian interjects an evaluation of this request: "And the thing was evil in the eyes of Samuel" (8:6)—and not only in the eyes of Samuel, but also in God's eyes. When Samuel bitterly turns to God and seeks advice, he receives this answer: "They have not rejected you, but they have rejected me from being king over them. Just as they have done to me, from the day I have brought them up from Egypt to this day, forsaking me and serving other gods, so also they are doing to you" (8:7–8). To desire a king is not only a rejection of Samuel; it is also a rejection of YHWH—it is, in fact, idolatry! The criticism could hardly be more devastating.

The vehement criticism of the monarchy reappears in subsequent passages. When the people are gathered to institute the king, Samuel rebukes them in the name of YHWH and reminds them that God had led them out of Egypt and subsequently delivered them from all sorts of kingdoms (!)—"yet you today have rejected your God" (1 Sam 10:18–19). In his farewell speech, held by Samuel following Saul's final coronation (1 Sam 12:1ff.), Samuel reviews the entire period of the judges as a time of guidance and deliverance by God (he makes no mention of the negative experiences!), in order to level his final criticism: "But you said: 'We still want a king to reign over us'—but YHWH, your God, is your king!" Then, with heavy sarcasm: "Now behold the king whom you have chosen, for whom you have asked" (12:12).

All this is Deuteronomistic commentary on older traditional material that reports the constitution of the state of Israel and Saul's inauguration as king in mostly positive, sometimes even emphatic, tones. We will turn to these traditions later; for now we can assert an ambivalent if not conflicting Deuteronomistic attitude toward the monarchy. In short, from a political point of view the office of judge was harmful; from a theological point of view it was beneficial. The monarchy threatens to be the other way around. Both organizational structures, however, also contain opposite tendencies: judges can on occasion be politically successful, and there is no general theological condemnation of kingship. History can show positive developments with both judges and kings; very often, however, it does not—and this with increasing frequency and consistency. Israel's relationship to YHWH and his Torah remains decisive for its welfare and downfall; civil institutions can merely influence this relationship positively or negatively; they cannot establish this relationship on their own.

Against the background of the monarchy's prior history, we start reading the description of the Deuteronomistic history of the monarchy with great expectation. This description is structured in three large segments: the time of the united monarchy over all of Israel (1 Sam 9 or 13–1 Kgs 11; dating from ca. 1000 to 926 B.C.E.); the time of the divided monarchy in Israel and Judah (1 Kgs 12–2 Kgs 17; dating from 926 to 722 B.C.E.); and the time when only Judah continued as a monarchy (2 Kgs 18–25; dating from 722 to 586/562 B.C.E.). These main sections are separated formally from each other. The first section presents the fate of the first kings Saul, David, and Solomon in expansive narratives and narrative cycles; the second section is shaped by synchronistic connections between the ruling dates of the northern Israelite and the Judaic kings ("…in this and this year of the reign of king X [in Israel or Judah], king Y became king [in Judah or Israel], and reigned for so many years…"); as can be expected, the third section presents only the ruling dates of Judahite kings.

In the following we will initially turn to the first of these time periods, the early monarchy (2.2), and then look at the following two time periods.

As a guiding criterion, we will focus on those passages and statements that can be classified as *Deuteronomistic* according to common consensus or with high probability.

I.3.2. THE PERIODIZATION OF THE EARLY MONARCHY

Coming from the Deuteronomistic depiction of the transition from the period of judges to that of kings, there is a high degree of anticipation as to how the hopes and fears that the Deuteronomistic Historian connects with the new institution will be fulfilled.

A brief retrospective is helpful in this context: going back beyond the era of the judges and conquest to the presentation of the Torah by Moses. Deuteronomy 17:14–20 contains a specific law for the monarchy, in which the great lawgiver prophetically anticipates subsequent developments and sets down basic guidelines for the institution to come. It seems that the entire passage is Deuteronomistic (i.e., not based on prior preexilic traditions).

> (14) When you have come into the land that the LORD your God is giving you and have taken possession of it and settled in it, and you say, "I will set a king over me, like all the nations that are around me," (15) you may indeed set over you a king whom the LORD your God will choose. One of your own community you may set as king over you; you are not permitted to put a foreigner over you, who is not of your own community. (16) Even so, he must not acquire many horses for himself, or return the people to Egypt in order to acquire more horses, since the LORD has said to you, "You must never return that way again." (17) And he must not acquire many wives for himself, or else his heart will turn away; also silver and gold he must not acquire in great quantity for himself. (18) When he has taken the throne of his kingdom, he shall have a copy of this law written for him in the presence of the Levitical priests. (19) It shall remain with him, and he shall read in it all the days of his life, so that he may learn to fear the LORD his God, diligently observing all the words of this law and these statutes, (20) neither exalting himself above other members of the community nor turning aside from the commandment, either to the right or to the left.

We have already encountered the request to *appoint a king over us, like all the people* in 1 Sam 8:6. It all happened as Moses foresaw. Now everything is dependent on whether the guidelines are met that Moses set in place for this very situation—or not. If Israel succumbs to its desire to appoint a king, then it at least should appoint a king, whom YHWH "chooses for himself"; and it should definitely be an Israelite and not a foreigner. This final criterion seems strange; a non-Israelite as king over Israel or Judah is at best a remote possibility. Perhaps the text refers to external potentates that Israel might accept as its own kings: the Pharaoh of Egypt, or the king of Babylon, who was the ruler of the known world during the time in which the Deuteronomistic History was written.

Saul, the first king, is an Israelite beyond doubt, more specifically a Benjaminite (1 Sam 9:1–2). He thus fulfills one of the Torah's criteria for being king. What about the criterion that he must be the one whom God himself has chosen (בחר)? The Deuteronomist's evaluation is not clear on this point. We have already mentioned the passage where Samuel emphasizes that *the people* have "chosen [בחר] and asked for" Saul (1 Sam 12:13). Other passages clearly refer to Saul as God's choice: when Saul is presented to the people after having been selected by lot, Samuel says, "See the one, whom YHWH has chosen" (בחר; 1 Sam 10:24; see also 9:16).

Saul's position, therefore, is ambiguous. Is he the people's choice or the chosen one of YHWH—or perhaps both, with differing intentions? In any case, we will have to observe whom Saul will follow: the people or YHWH. One thing seems clear: he does live up to the standards explicated in Deut 17:16–17; Saul does not gather an inordinate amount of horses, women, or treasures; on the contrary, the summary 1 Sam 14:47–52 reports only *one* wife, *one* high officer, and a small group of mercenaries. His kingdom as a whole has very humble proportions.

In spite of all this, the Deuteronomists soon allow dark shadows to fall on the figure of Saul. During a war against the Amalekites in Palestine's far south, Saul follows Samuel's, or better, God's, instruction only in part: instead of "banning" all living things, meaning their complete elimination, Saul spares a few choice animals and, more to the point, Agag, the king of the Amalekites. As a result, Samuel throws this judgment at him: "You have rejected the word of YHWH, and YHWH has rejected you from being king over Israel" (1 Sam 15:26). The verb "reject" (מאס), used twice in this context, has already appeared in the context of the people's request of a king (1 Sam 8:7) and constitutes the opposite of "choose, elect" (בחר). In immediate succession, the following narrative reports how God "chooses" David as the new king (1 Sam 16:1–13).[8]

Saul's fate is no longer determined by God's election but instead by his rejection. The final Deuteronomistic redaction leaves no doubt on this issue. It is fully aware that God has broken with Saul and chosen another as

---

8. The term בחר is not yet used positively of David, but only negatively of his brothers who are not chosen (1 Sam 16:8, 10). When Samuel, however, follows God's guidance and does not choose them but rather David, this term enters the context of David's election. See also 2 Sam 6:21.

king. We are soon told who this person is; Saul does not share this knowledge. In his insecurity he lashes out at many different supposed enemies, David among them, but he is unable to actually harm him. Not blind fate, not even an arbitrary or cynical God, is the source of his misery. According to the Deuteronomistic description, Saul himself is the cause of his turn to the worse; there is no need for false sympathy. We would have to read against the basic intention of the Deuteronomistic presentation if we were to excuse Saul and, instead, accuse God. Saul has transgressed God's command. This alone is the decisive factor, not how badly or how often he has transgressed. Already Israel's first king failed to live according to the Torah—and this YHWH could not accept. He regrets having made Saul king. This is what Samuel, or better a Deuteronomist, conveys to the readers (1 Sam 15:11). Another Deuteronomist objects: God is no human being that he would "regret" anything (1 Sam 15:29). Everything is in order: God had to reject Saul because Saul rejected God.

Against the ambiguous presentation of Saul's beginning and the dark conclusion of his story, David's figure appears in an almost blinding light. Referring back to the Deuteronomistic law for kings (Deut 17:14–20), David fulfills all of the demands listed there: he is an Israelite, more specifically, from the tribe of Judah, a son of the Ephrathite Jesse from Bethlehem (1 Sam 17:12); he does not amass horses and treasures and has only a limited number of wives (Michal and Bathsheba are to be added to those listed in 2 Sam 3:2–5). Most important, he is "chosen" by YHWH and, in contrast to Saul, is never rejected.

It thus comes as no surprise that David's biography shines as it takes shape in the biblical narratives, but also in so many works of art from Michelangelo to Chagall. In dream-like security, David first ascends the throne of Judah, then Israel, then Jerusalem (1 Sam 16–2 Sam 5); he must, indeed, overcome many obstacles as well as a whole score of powerful opponents and rivals, survive many attempts on his life, and, more often, resist the urge to do violence to the life of others and thus lose his standing with God and his contemporaries. In spite of all these challenges, he transcends all difficulties—truly with the help of God. As a result, God grants him his presence in Jerusalem, a promise of a continual dynasty, and victory over all his enemies (2 Sam 5–8). After all this has been accomplished, however, at the climax of his power, dark clouds line the horizon, and dark sides of his personality appear in connection with the issue of who is to succeed him (2 Sam 9–20): the scandal surrounding Bathsheba and Uriah, the matter of Amnon and Tamar, and the uprisings of Absalom and Sheba cause severe turbulence for himself and his reign. Even in these dark passages, however, the narrative maintains a certain degree of respect and sympathy and describes him as fallible and tempted but also, and particularly in his weakness and suffering, as a true human being. The final chapters of 2 Samuel essentially portray him as an individual who ends up as the purified and sanctified king, despite initial transgressions (2 Sam 21–24). In the description in the first two chapters of the book of Kings, David is at the mercy of various political interests, yet he remains the one who gives direction to the various power plays and, in the end, can watch with satisfaction how Solomon's ascension to the throne marks the beginning of the fulfillment of the divine promise (1 Kgs 1–2). David dies a peaceful death as an old man after ruling for forty years, during which he established an empire and a dynasty—truly the exemplary biography of a great leader.

The summary statement of David's kingdom in 1 Kgs 2:11 is clearly a Deuteronomistic passage. What else between 1 Sam 16 and 1 Kgs 2 is a product of Deuteronomistic writing remains a matter of controversial discussion. Perhaps it was a Deuteronomistic historian who portrayed a seamless, smooth, and divinely ordained transition from David to Solomon in 1 Kgs 1–2 (see Veijola 1975, who explicitly refers to the passages in 1:30, 35–37, 46–48; 2:1–10, 24, 32–33, 42–45 as Deuteronomistic additions). We are on relatively firm ground with extended passages of the Nathan chapters 2 Sam 7 and 12 as well as with the addition of the so-called appendix to the books of Samuel, 2 Sam 21–24.

In 2 Sam 7 David addresses an inquiry to the prophet Nathan whether or not he should build YHWH a temple in his new residence, Jerusalem. After first agreeing, Nathan then vetoes the project following God's disapproval. David is not to build a house for YHWH; instead, YHWH will build a house for David: the Davidic dynasty. Following this promise, David utters an extensive prayer of thanksgiving. The entire chapter is most likely a product of Deuteronomistic writing, with the exception, perhaps, of an older ceremonial text from the ritual surrounding the ascension to the throne in Jerusalem in 7:11–15 (Dietrich 1992). The Deuteronomistic writers make several things clear: the king is not obligated to return to God in accordance with what God has done for him; the principle *do-ut-des* does not apply. God does not require a temple as a trade-off for his blessings! On the contrary, David and all of Israel will continue to depend on God's blessings, by means of stable political circumstances guaranteed by a continual Davidic dynasty and God's continual guidance through history. (At a later point the Deuteronomists will have ample opportunity to emphasize the value of this guidance—in contrast to the non-Davidic northern kingdom.) David's pious prayer signals that he has understood the direction in which God is pointing him through the words of the prophet Nathan and that he is willing to follow this course. In Israel, God's will, as conveyed by God's emissaries, must be done first; the will of the king takes second place!

In 2 Sam 12 the divine will and the will of the king meet in a head-on collision. David has become an adulterer and murderer and, according to our sensibilities, has fallen much deeper into sin than his predecessor Saul. We would expect God to reject him immediately—were it the matter just of one person and not a dynasty. And who would not know that the successor to the throne would be the product of the liaison between David and Bathsheba? Once again, the Deuteronomistic theologians use Nathan to make the necessary explanations, this time, however, not as a promise, but as a hellfire and brimstone sermon (there are many Deuteronomistic additions in 12:7–12). Once confronted with his sin, the king bows down low before Nathan and God, and his repentance transfers the penalty of death from the adulterer to the child who was conceived in adultery, followed by the birth of a second child, free from the blemish of adultery: Solomon. By reinforcing tradition at this point, the Deuteronomists emphasize that David cannot sin against the Torah without punishment; they also emphasize that deep repentance can lead to forgiveness and a new future. Furthermore, even a David can stumble and fall, but this greatly blessed leader can profoundly humble himself and allow God once again to lift him up and guide him onward.

In 2 Sam 21–24 we encounter David caught in the consequences of sin: in 2 Sam 21 in connection with the inhabitants of the old Canaanite city Gibeon and the last living descendants of Saul; and in 2 Sam 24 in connection with a public census, which may be understandable from the point of view of a great political and military leader but is an affront to God, leading to a major catastrophe. In both cases David is able to find reconciliation with his subjects and with God. In between these two narratives we find lists of David's heroes and their heroic deeds and, exactly in the middle of this small oeuvre, two songs of David, in a sense, his spiritual legacy (2 Sam 22:1–23:5). It seems that the Deuteronomists have put this collection together (Veijola 1975) in order to complete David's portrait according to the old traditions but also according to their own interests, which have become clear in 2 Sam 7 and 12. Once more we are told that the king is fallible but that God stays with him and helps him out of various difficulties. David proves himself to be sensitive, introspective, and flexible (attributes that are not true of every ruler!). Most of all, he proves himself to be a pious man of prayer who is open to God; aside from David, there is only one other pious individual who utters two farewell prayers, according to the biblical text: Moses (Deut 32–33). By creating this parallel between these two figures, the Deuteronomistic writers clearly indicate whom they believe to be the greatest figures in the history of Israel.

The Deuteronomistic theologians of course also know of the problematic aspects of David's reign and his personality as they become apparent in the second half of 2 Samuel. This darker color in the portrait of the great king, however, is not a product of Deuteronomistic redaction (against Carlson) but respect for their sources. Especially the texts in 2 Sam 10–11; 13–20 show few traces of Deuteronomistic reworking, whereas freely composed Deuteronomistic sections show a clear intention to draw a positive picture of David.

The Deuteronomistic portrait of Solomon uses different shades altogether; here we once again find a mixture of light and dark colors—as in the case of Saul. Starting again with the law for kings in Deut 17:14–20, we quickly recognize the clearly drawn outline. The text never refers to Solomon as "chosen by Yhwh" (only David and Jerusalem are "chosen"; see 1 Kgs 8:16; 11:32, 34). Even though Solomon as the son of David is part of the promise of a Davidic dynasty in 2 Sam 7:11–16, the question arises: Why him and not a different son of David? The older texts clearly speak of other aspirants to the throne, the last one being Adonijah as a direct rival of Solomon (1 Kgs 1–2). The fact that Solomon wins the race is decided not so much in heaven as in David's bedroom, due to the massive support of a few "major players" in Jerusalem's court as well as the royal body guard, "Cherethites and Pelethites." Solomon's subsequent elimination of opposition leaders may be efficient, but it must come as a shock to sensitive readers, despite the attempts at justification contained in the text.

Solomon is definitely no foreigner (Deut 17:15), yet according to the biblical text he maintained many intensive contacts with foreign powers. At first glance, some of the respective information does not seem disrespectful: the connection with the Phoenicians, whose natural resources, trade relations, and artisans are needed for the construction of the temple (1 Kgs 5; 7); the highly lucrative transregional trade (1 Kgs 9:26–27; 10:28–29); the international exchange of wisdom (1 Kgs 5:14; 10:1–9, 24); and the marriage of supposedly hundreds of women from many surrounding nations—even including a daughter of Pharaoh—as a matter of foreign policy (1 Kgs 3:1; 9:16; 11:1, 3). All this information, however, also has a negative ring to it—and not only for Deuteronomistic ears! What are we supposed to think of the fact that Solomon relinquishes "twenty cities from the land of Galilee" to the Phoenician city-king of Tyre for services rendered (1 Kgs 9:10–12)? What of the fact that he owes his wealth directly to his cooperation with foreigners (1 Kgs 9:27–28; 10:10–12, 22)? Did not the law in Deut 17:17 explicitly forbid amassing great wealth? Did it not also warn against the danger that many wives could turn away the heart of the king? The information on Solomon's harem shows clearly what this warning alludes to: the danger lies not with women in general (e.g., on a moral level) but rather with the fact that foreign women might remain tied to their original non-Yahwistic religions. Indeed, the passage in 1 Kgs 11:1–11 is one of the passages where the Deuteronomistic style is most obvious and from which we can learn much of the

fears of alienation and foreign infiltration within Judaism during and following the exile.

The short passages on Solomon's foreign trade are also quite cryptic. The
text particularly emphasizes the trade with horses from Egypt to Syria and
Asia Minor (1 Kgs 10:28–29); much attention is also given to the purchase of
horses for the establishment of a personal brigade of chariots (1 Kgs 10:26;
9:19; 5:6). In Deut 17:16, however, the king is forbidden to "own many horses
and lead the people back to Egypt in order to multiply its horses." We cannot
avoid reading this statement as explicitly directed toward Solomon, or rather
the biblical narrative about Solomon. Solomon is *the* example of allowing
Egyptian influence to creep into Israel, for creating Pharaoh-like structures
within the people of God. Chariots were the very weapon that YHWH had
drowned in the sea to save his people (Exod 14:28; 15:21), and now Solomon
introduces this type of weapon in Israel on a large scale! From this perspective, the marriage to Pharaoh's daughter also no longer counts to Solomon's
credit. The forced labor, organized by the state and used to accomplish Solomon's large-scale construction projects (1 Kgs 5:27–32; 9:15–22; 11:28; 12:4),
now also appears in a negative light; the terminology used in these contexts is
the same that described the slavery in Egypt (מס, עבד) from which YHWH led
his people Israel, according to the Deuteronomistic creed. Solomon's rule thus
contains many Pharaoh-like elements and consequently breaks the (Deuteronomic-Deuteronomistic) law for kings on a massive scale; in general, against
YHWH's Torah for Israel. The punishment follows as expected: David's empire
crumbles (1 Kgs 11:14ff.) and finally falls (1 Kgs 12).

On the other hand, the Deuteronomistic depiction also credits Solomon
with great merits. He is the first individual to fulfill the promise of a dynasty
given to David (1 Kgs 8:15ff.). As an example to all, he initially requests (and
receives!) wisdom from YHWH at the onset of his rule, in order successfully to
accomplish his great and difficult task (1 Kgs 3). With great wisdom, he organizes his kingdom (1 Kgs 4); he carefully, single-mindedly, and generously
plans and completes the construction of the Jerusalem temple—the sanctuary that is so important for Deuteronomic-Deuteronomistic theology (1 Kgs
5–8)! In this manner, the Deuteronomistic Historians utilize very specific
traditions, adding commentary that mixes sympathy and criticism, in order
to create a unique picture of King Solomon that differs markedly from the
portraits of his two predecessors.

I.3.3. MIRRORING THE EARLY MONARCHY IN ITS CONTINUED HISTORY

According to the biblical depiction, the first three Israelite kings ruled over
a kingdom that included northern and southern Palestine. The Davidic nar-

ratives relate explicitly how David built up this kingdom (2 Sam 3–5). The narratives on the uprisings of Absalom and Sheba do convey the impression that the north tried to escape David's rule; nevertheless, David stifles these separatist movements and renews his rule over all of Palestine. The same is true for Solomon: an uprising does ignite in the north, but Solomon can strike it down and thus is and remains king over all of Israel (1 Kgs 11:26–28 … 11:40). At least the Deuteronomistic redactors seem to have assumed the same situation for Saul: his rule was accepted not only by the northern tribes (2 Sam 2:9)—who even accepted the weak rule of his son Eshbaal—but also by Judah. How else could Saul have dwelled and moved in the south with such great ease (1 Sam 15:23–26)?

We are told in 1 Kgs 12 how this combined rule broke apart following the death of Solomon. A separate kingdom was established in the north, while the Davidic dynasty merely ruled over the Judahite south, which did contain, however, the capital of Jerusalem. From a clearly Judahite perspective, the texts tell of the development of and reasons for this political catastrophe with many signs of great consternation. According to the books of Kings, Judah continued to work toward reunification of north and south; they even fought for it, all for nothing (1 Kgs 12:21–24; 14:30; 15:6, 16–22, 32). Even in the final stages of the monarchy, the Judahite Josiah seems to have attempted a new integration of the north into Davidic rule—with temporary success at most (2 Kgs 23:15ff., 30).

Following their division, the states of Judah and Israel followed their own paths through history, and the Deuteronomistic Historians accompany them with great interest and evaluating commentary. Already the fact that they report not only the history of Judah, their own home—quite in contrast to the book of Chronicles—but also the interlocking history of Israel shows their inner conviction that the two kingdoms in truth belong together. The synchronistic dates of the ruling kings, supported by the many reports on both peaceful and tension-laden relations between Judah and Israel, present us with the history of both states as a single history, separated only by artificial factors. Thus the unified northern and southern kingdom becomes an influential issue all throughout the period of the monarchy. In the end, we must assume that the reasons that motivated the Deuteronomists to emphasize the unity between the two kingdoms were theological instead of historical; together, the inhabitants of both kingdoms always were and continued to be the people of God, elected and chosen by YHWH.

On the other hand, the Deuteronomistic History leaves no doubt as to where to find historical as well as theological prevalence in this tension-laden unity, or rather inseparable duality: with Judah, more precisely with Jerusalem.

According to Deuteronomistic belief, the historical fact that northern Israel lost its political autonomy about 150 years before Judah can be explained by internal factors. In comparison with the south, the north was much more saturated with idolatry, with turning away from YHWH—described in general terms as the "sin of Jeroboam," the first king of Israel. According to the Deuteronomistic description, the cultic practices at the royal sanctuaries at Bethel and Dan centered on the worship of idols and calves (Judg 17–18; 1 Kgs 12–13). All the northern kings receive low marks simply for the fact that they were not able to serve God properly in Jerusalem, the only true and legitimate sanctuary, in Deuteronomistic eyes; not one king is praised without reservation for his religious practice. This is especially true after Omri and Ahab (1 Kgs 16), who erected a Baal temple in the new capital city Samaria; from this point on, the north is verily contaminated. The "revolution" of Jehu (2 Kgs 9–10) can change this situation only in part. In 2 Kgs 17:7–23 the highly negative final evaluation of the northern kingdom finds its clearest expression in a completely Deuteronomistic text: "The people of Israel had sinned against the LORD their God ... and worshiped other gods and walked in the customs of the nations whom the LORD drove out before the people of Israel" (17:7–8).

The south was a different matter. Jerusalem and the temple, and thus the starting point for a good relation to God, were located there. Those kings who showed concern for the temple, its construction, its accessories, and its care were recipients of Deuteronomistic praise; aside from David, who prepared the construction of the temple (2 Sam 7; 24), and Solomon, who carried out the construction, the temple renovators and cultic reformers were Asa, Jehoash, Hezekiah, and Josiah (1 Kgs 15; 2 Kgs 12; 18; 22–23). Jerusalem was Judah's chance. The danger for Judah lay outside of Jerusalem, primarily up on "the hills" with their own sanctuaries (במות), which were erected or tolerated by all southern kings who are criticized, starting with Solomon (1 Kgs 11:6–8) up to the epitome of the godless Davidic king, Manasseh (2 Kgs 21:3). This very king was also responsible for transplanting Baal worship and other idolatry from the perished northern kingdom Israel to Judah, even to the temple of Jerusalem itself (2 Kgs 23:26–27).

Both aspects, the preference for Judah and Jerusalem over against the north as well as its eventual, unavoidable collapse, are mirrored in how the Deuteronomistic Historians in the course of their narratives refer back to the first kings again and again. Saul, we should state first, is not mentioned anywhere in the book of Kings. Deuteronomistic historiography thus eradicates his memory. We nowhere find the perhaps obvious notion that the uprising against Davidic rule leading to the formation of the northern kingdom could be described as a revival of Saul's kingdom; perhaps this notion was even repressed. Solomon appears on four occasions in 2 Kings: three times as the temple builder (21:7; 24:13; 25:16) and once as the builder of the "hill sanctuaries" east of Jerusalem (23:13). This ambivalence exactly mirrors the twofold picture painted by the Deuteronomists in 1 Kgs 1–11.

After he disappears from the political scene, David is mentioned about fifty times—and only in positive contexts! Three aspects determine these passages. First, David is the carrier of God's promise. The history of the Davidic kingdom is ultimately based on the fact that God has promised loyalty to the "house of David" (1 Kgs 3:6; 8:15ff.). It is no accident that the Deuteronomistic History ends with the pardoning by Evilmerodach, the king of Babylon, of the deported king Jehoiachin (2 Kgs 25:27–30)—and thus with a Davidic glimmer of hope. Second, David in the Deuteronomistic evaluation is a model of Torah loyalty (1 Kgs 9:4–5; 14:8). On only one occasion do we encounter the critical commentary that God was displeased with the Uriah incident; otherwise, David did what God commanded throughout his life (1 Kgs 15:5). This is why the founder of the dynasty becomes the measure for the evaluation of all of his successors, whether positive (1 Kgs 15:11; 2 Kgs 18:3; 22:2) or negative (2 Kgs 14:3; 16:2). The third aspect of David's legacy is the *continued existence of Judah and Jerusalem.* David, not Solomon, gets credit for the fact that the kingdom of Judah survived the separation of the north (1 Kgs 11:12–13, 32–39). Later, when Jerusalem and Judah are threatened repeatedly by outside forces, the miraculous deliverance is explained as God's preference for his holy city (referred to in Hebrew as נר, lamp) as well as David's merits (1 Kgs 15:4–5; 2 Kgs 8:19; 9:34; 20:6).

The portraits of Israel's first kings, drawn by Deuteronomistic historiography in 1 Sam 9–1 Kgs 11, thus continue to influence the subsequent history of the monarchy.

I.4. The Time Period according to Pre-Deuteronomistic Sources

We have seen how the Deuteronomistic redaction adapted the history of the early monarchy for their literary opus by expanding and modifying the material. We can now turn to how the time period is depicted in the pre-Deuteronomistic sources. This is not (yet) the point at which a detailed theory of textual growth in the books of Samuel and Kings may be proposed. The following discourse is based on one basic literary-historical decision: before or underneath the Deuteronomistic text, dated roughly during the exile, there is an older and thus preexilic textual layer that was known to and used by the Deuteronomistic redaction. We will work with the basic hypothesis that this material was quite extensive and organized to a large degree as we find it now in the Hebrew Bible; the Deuteronomistic changes within the text of 1 Sam–1 Kgs 11 described above are significant, but they are neither very extensive nor structurally very significant. This fact explains why the pre-Deuteronomistic depiction of the early monarchy seems relatively complete and coherent and thus can be reconstructed and interpreted well, not only by novelists and writers (see I.1 above) but also by exegetes. The biblical depiction of the first kings provides rich material and satisfying work for the recent enterprise of "literary criticism," prevalent mainly in an English-speaking context; this is *not* the same as the *Literarkritik* popular in German exegesis but rather the holistic appreciation of the present text, its poetic structure, and its content.

The following will attempt to delineate the pre-Deuteronomistic depiction of the early monarchy based on observations on the textual surface by paying attention to the compositional elements and narrative intentions. The first thing that becomes noticeable is a certain degree of overlapping in the text between the biographies of the main protagonists: David is still alive when Solomon takes over (1 Kgs 1–2); David's rise occurs opposite Saul's demise (1 Sam 16–31); Samuel accompanies Saul's kingdom almost to the end (1 Sam 8–25, or rather 28); and Samuel himself takes over from Eli as Israel's priest and judge (1 Sam 1–3). None of these transitions from one leader to the next occurs logically by itself; none happens smoothly and without tension. The events take an unexpected turn every time. To use an analogy, it is almost as if the ship of Israel's history must fitfully sail around several cliffs before entering calm waters. The transition of the various leaders signals a change in historical eras. The movement from the time before the state to the period of the state was a very decisive and consequential process for Israel. The biblical narrators know this and ask not only about the changes themselves but also about their meaning; this meaning, for them, is the question of God's actions in history.

An additional compositional element is significant for the narrative: biographical portraits of the respective protagonists emerge from the text. They emerge in chronological order, but they do not comprehensively list every year or even every day, but rather important life stages and extraordinary events. In this manner, each of these "biographies" consists of different phases, each with its own compositional color. Following certain turning points, a character can grow dark, or new tasks and possibilities may emerge. If we pay attention to this structure, the textual material quickly loses every appearance of being unconnected and arbitrarily joined together; every anecdote, every list has its place in the respective life story and in the history of the early monarchy in general.

I.4.1. The Portrait of Samuel

Berges, Ulrich. *Die Verwerfung Sauls: Eine thematische Untersuchung* (FB 61; Würzburg: Echter, 1989). **Brueggemann,** Walter. "I. Samuel 1. A Sense of Beginning," *ZAW* 102 (1990): 33–48. **Buber,** Martin. "Das Volksbegehren," in *In Memoriam Ernst Lohmeyer* (ed. Werner Schmauch; Stuttgart: Evangelisches Verlagswerk, 1951), 53–66. **Buber.** "Die Erzählung von Sauls Königswahl," *VT* 6 (1956): 113–73. **Dietrich,** Walter. "Samuel—Ein Prophet?" *Sacra Scripta* 5 (2007): 11–26. **Donner,** Herbert. "Die Verwerfung des Königs Saul," in idem, *Aufsätze zum Alten Testament* (BZAW 224; Berlin: de Gruyter, 1994), 133–64. **Eslinger,** Lyle M. "Viewpoints and Points of View in 1 Samuel 8–12," *JSOT* 26 (1983): 61–76. **Eslinger.** *Kingship of God in Crisis: A Close Reading of 1 Samuel 1–12* (BiLiSe 10; Decatur, Ga.: Almond, 1985). **Fokkelman,** Jan P. *Vow and Desire* (vol. 4 of *Narrative Art and Poetry in the Books of Samuel: A Full Interpretation*; SSN 31; Assen: Van Gorcum, 1993). **Garsiel,** Moshe. *The First Book of Samuel: A Literary Study of Comparative Structures, Analogies and Parallels* (Ramat-Gan: Revivim, 1985). **Gitay,** Yehoshua. "Reflections on the Poetics of the Samuel Narrative: The Question of the Ark Narrative," *CBQ* 54 (1992): 221–30. **Miscall,** Peter D. *1 Samuel: A Literary Reading* (Bloomington: Indiana University Press, 1986). **Polzin,** Robert. "The Monarchy Begins: 1 Samuel 8–10," in *Society of Biblical Literature 1987 Seminar Papers* (SBLSP 26; Atlanta: Scholars Press, 1987), 120–43. **Polzin.** *Samuel and the Deuteronomist* (Bloomington: Indiana University Press, 1993). **Rendtorff,** Rolf. "Die Geburt des Retters: Beobachtungen zur Jugendgeschichte Samuels im Rahmen der literarischen Komposition," in idem, *Kanon und Theologie: Vorarbeiten zu einer Theologie des Alten Testaments* (Neukirchen-Vluyn: Neukirchener, 1991), 132–40. **Vette,** Joachim. *Samuel und Saul: Ein Beitrag zur narrativen Poetik des Samuelbuches* (Beiträge zum Verstehen der Bibel 13; Münster: LIT, 2005). **Wénin,** André. *Samuel et l'instauration de la monarchie (1S 1–12): Une recherche littéraire sur le personnage* (EHS 23/1342; Frankfurt am Main: Lang, 1988). **Willis,** John T. "Samuel versus Eli: I Sam. 1–7," *TZ* 35 (1979): 201–12.

I.4.1.1. Samuel Rises as Israel's Last Judge

The book of Judges concludes its narration of the chaotic situation in Israel's tribes with the sentence: "In those days there was no king in Israel. All the people did what was right in their own eyes" (Judg 21:25). The book of Samuel begins with the genealogy—not of the first king, Saul, but of Samuel, or rather of his father Elkanah (1 Sam 1:1). God's work of deliverance begins from an unexpected starting point—even with a human disappointment: the woman on whom everything depends, Hannah, is childless. With great care, the narrative in 1 Sam 1 describes this distressed and then triumphant female character. Surpassing all other characters—the cantankerous-egoistical rival Peninnah, the kind but helpless husband Elkanah, the grouchy, inattentive priest Eli—she achieves happiness with God: happiness for all of Israel! The leading motif of the entire passage is the verb שָׁאַל "to request." Hannah requests, Eli grants the request, and when the boy is born, she calls him Shemu'el. This name is derived from the verb שָׁאַל; the name Sha'ul, however, would have fit even better, all the more because this passive participle of the verb (1:28) is identical with the name of Israel's first king.[9] Mysteriously, the name of the first king is already present, even if it is not yet spoken out loud. Samuel, the man of God, must come first; only after him and through him the man of power!

The song placed in Hannah's mouth in 1 Sam 2:1–10 clearly defines the relation between divine and human power: just as God had helped her, the distressed and suffering women, he "strengthens those who stumble, satisfies the hungry, lifts up the lowly from the dust and the poor from the dirt," while "breaking the bows of the mighty" and ensuring that "those who were full hire themselves out for bread" and those who sit on the "seat of honor" must tolerate the needy, whom God lifted from the ashes. Hannah asks of this God that he will "give strength to his king and exalt the power of his anointed" (2:10). Thus, the new institution is already a major issue long before its first representative appears on the scene. From the very beginning, the text lays out the right relation between king and God: in Israel, a king never assumes power himself; rather, he is "exalted" by God. He derives his "power" not from himself or from his followers but from God. He does not represent the interests of the mighty but, like God, the interests of the "lowly" and "needy."

Samuel's rise starts at the sanctuary in Shiloh. There he serves the man whom he later will replace—as if Saul's displacement by David is already pre-

---

9. This identity has given rise to the hypothesis that 1 Sam 1–3 was originally the birth story not of Samuel but of Saul (Ivar Hylander, *Der literarische Samuel-Saul-Komplex [1 Sam 1–15]: Traditionsgeschichtlich untersucht* [Uppsala: Almquist & Wiksell, 1932], 11ff.; Jan Dus, "Die Geburtslegende Samuels I.Sam 1.," *RSO* 43 [1968]: 163–94; more recently, Robert P. Gordon, "Who Made the Kingmaker? Reflections on Samuel and the Institution of the Monarchy," in *Faith, Tradition, and History: Old Testament Historiography in Its Near Eastern Context* [ed. Alan R. Millard, James K. Hoffmeier, and David W. Baker; Winona Lake, Ind.: Eisenbrauns, 1994], 255–69). This suggestion cannot be proven, nor is it especially helpful. The etiology in 1:21 is well within the scope of Hebrew name etiologies (see M. Tsevat, "Die Namensgebung Samuels und die Substitutionstheorie," *ZAW* 99 [1987]: 250–54). It would also be difficult to explain שְׁמוּאֵל differently, especially if the name is derived not from שָׁמַע "to hear" but from an ancient divine name (such as "Shem is God") or from a Semitic word for "son" (thus "son of God"; see *HAL* 1,438)—neither option very appealing to Jewish ears.

figured here. It seems that God always lifts the lowly from the dust in order to set them on a royal or priestly throne! Samuel cannot yet imagine God's plan for his life. He innocently serves his master and contrasts positively with Eli's depraved sons (1 Sam 2:11–26; the mention of a nameless "man of God" in 2:27–36, foretelling the end of the priesthood in Eli's dynasty and predicting the rise of Josiah, is mainly Deuteronomistic). A dream revelation during the night turns Samuel unwillingly into a prophet with a message of doom for Eli; the narrators do not mention at all what Samuel himself feels and thinks in this situation (3:1–18). They only tell us that Samuel has now become the new intermediary between God and his people (3:19–21; 4:1a). Then the "requested" disappears from the narrative scene for more than two decades (1 Sam 7:2); the fulfillment of God's portentous will against Eli, his house, and Israel must first take its course.

The focus of the narrative now turns completely to the Elides and the ark of the covenant that is in their care. Suddenly, international politics enter the arena: the Philistines appear and immediately prove themselves as a vitally dangerous enemy. "Israel"—we are not told who supposedly gathers the people and leads them into battle—is thoroughly defeated (1 Sam 4:2). This occasions the decision to take the ark from Shiloh and to march into the next engagement with the God whose throne is above the ark. When the palladium, accompanied by Eli's sons, arrives on the battlefield, the Israelites rejoice and the Philistines tremble (1 Sam 4:5ff.). The outcome of the battle seems clear, but Israel is once again defeated. The Elides fall, and Eli himself dies when he receives the battle report (1 Sam 4:12–18). Thus, Samuel's prophecy to Eli is fulfilled.

Israel's defeat is not the defeat of the God of the ark. The sacred cultic artifact, dragged as a trophy through the land of those who were victorious, develops an interesting life of its own: in a temple of the Philistine agricultural god Dagon, where the ark was taken to demonstrate its inferiority, the statue of the god fell down overnight, breaking its neck, quite the same as Eli shortly before, except that Eli fell backward, whereas Dagon fell forward—as if bowing in worship (1 Sam 5:4; see 4:18). The ark of God inspires fear among the people, which is increased by the fact that strange epidemics break out in each city to which the ark comes (1 Sam 5:7–12). The people approach the appropriate spiritual leaders, asking for advice, and these leaders—pagan or not—are actually able to provide sound advice: the dangerous object must be allowed to travel where it (or rather, the divinity above it) wants to go. This clearly is the territory of Israel. Thus, the ark is accompanied with full honors first to Beth-shemesh, then to Kiriath-jearim, where it decides to remain (1 Sam 6)—until it can be transferred to Jerusalem at a later point (2 Sam 6).

The ark narrative in 1 Sam 4–6 is not about Samuel; still, several issues are clarified here before the main protagonist appears on the scene in 1 Sam 7. Eli and his sons have left the scene for good. None remain who could take over leadership in Israel—none except Samuel. Sooner or later he will assume leadership. For now, however, following defeat in battle and loss of the ark, the situation of the Israelites must seem hopeless. Unlike the reader, they were not informed of what had occurred in the land of the Philistines. They must have assumed that YHWH was weaker than the Philistine gods or that he had rejected the ark and Israel—all this, no doubt, because of the sinfulness of two priests!

Then, after a long time, Samuel gathers the people together at Mizpah, where he functions as priest and leader of the people, in short, as Eli's successor (7:6, 9; the beginning of the chapter seems to be redacted heavily by the Deuteronomists). The Philistines, of course, have no intention of allowing Israel to come together. They attack—and are thoroughly defeated. The events narrated in 1 Sam 4 are turned on their head: then the Philistines had defeated Israel and the ark at Ebenezer; now Israel defeats the Philistines at Ebenezer without the aid of the ark. What made the difference: that YHWH was present this time—or Samuel? It seems that both aspects work hand in hand: "the hand of YHWH was against the Philistines all the days of Samuel" (7:13b).

First the deliverer against outside forces, Samuel now also becomes judge in internal matters (1 Sam 7:15–17). It seems as if all problems are solved, as if the narrative has reached its conclusion. Such thinking is deceptive. In truth, several unsolved problems remain. The Philistines are still there, even though they have been temporarily humiliated. Even though the ark no longer dwells in Philistine territory, it remains at a temporary location, not worthy of its status. Even though Samuel's leadership nominally covers all of Israel, it practically only includes a small area in the very south of Israel, circumscribed by the place names Bethel, Gilgal, Mizpah, and Ramah. The most difficult problem is: What will happen *after* Samuel?

I.4.1.2. Samuel Appoints Israel's First King

Samuel, now old, tries to secure Israel's future by preparing his sons Joel and Abijah to succeed him as judge. These two, however, turn out to be complete failures. This is not merely a private family problem; after the experiences with Eli and his sons, the Israelites must fear the worst. The elders come to Samuel and request that he appoint a king over them (1 Sam 8:1–5).

At this point a Deuteronomistic redactor who is very critical of the monarchy interjects a commentary: "But the thing was evil in the eyes of Samuel when they said: 'Give us a king'" (8:6). Was it evil only in *Samuel's* eyes? And *why* was it evil in his eyes? The narrative allows us to assume for a moment that Samuel's reaction may have been motivated by personal violability and vanity. Some exegetes hear a silent struggle between Samuel and God at this point, even describing God as a character with unclear motives (Polzin; Eslinger). The harmony between Yʜwʜ and Samuel in 1 Sam 7 and the main thrust of 1 Sam 8 do not leave much room for such thinking.

Samuel hides his attitude toward the request for a king from the Israelites and first turns to Yʜwʜ for guidance. In prayer, he receives the information that his own evaluation was not harsh enough: "they have not rejected you, but they have rejected me" (8:7). Then follows the surprising instruction: "Listen to their voice" (8:9a). God seems to understand that he cannot prevent his people from "rejecting" him; perhaps they even have good subjective reasons for their request. Instead of preventing or disallowing the request, he resorts to argument and tries to make clear to Israel that nothing good can be expected of a king: "Solemnly warn them and show them the ways of the king who shall reign over them" (8:9b). The small but important difference between the elders' request for a king "to govern us," or rather "to judge us" (לשפטנו), and Samuel's warning against a king who will "rule over them" or even "be a king against them" must be emphasized. Following the divine instruction, "Samuel reported all the words of Yʜwʜ to the people who were asking him for a king." Coincidence or not, the verb שאל reappears here, the *Leitmotiv* of 1 Sam 1, echoing clearly the name of Saul as "the one asked for."

Samuel reveals the law of the king—more of a pamphlet than a legal text (8:11–17). He warns the people that a time will come when they will cry out to Yʜwʜ because of their king, yet he will not answer (8:18). "But the people refused to listen to the voice of Samuel; they said, 'No! But we are determined to have a king over us' " (8:19).

The request for a king is combined with the expectation that this king will provide internal and external security (8:20)—not surprising considering what had occurred previously. Samuel relates this request to God, who indicates to him: "Listen to their voice and place a king over them. And Samuel said to the men of Israel: 'Go, each to his own city!' " (8:22). Does this ending contain hidden antagonism coming from Samuel? Why does he not institute a king as he was commanded to do? The narrator's intention seems to go in a different direction: Samuel does not yet know *whom* he is to institute as king. Suspense builds for him, for the people, but also for us as readers: Who will be the one, who will be made king by Samuel?

The next narrative (9:1–10:16) initially takes us to Gibeah in Benjamin and introduces us to Saul. Coming from 1 Sam 1, we as readers suspect that this will be the "requested" king. We thus seem to know more than Samuel, whom the narrator has left behind in Ramah. Yet one day before, God had already told Samuel who will be coming and what he is supposed to do (1 Sam 9:15–16). Samuel and the reader know what is happening; Saul, however, does not. An artful change of perspectives ensues. We accompany Saul on a long journey where he hopes to find his father's donkeys; we observe him as he is about to give up but is persuaded by his servant first to consult the "man of God in that city" (probably Samuel in Ramah, but only the reader can draw this conclusion). In a short interjection, the narrator then takes us aside and explains that "man of God" and "seer" were interchangeable with "prophet" (now our last doubts disappear). We listen in when the two young men ask the maidens at the well where the house of the seer is and we hear the many-voiced enthusiastic answer. Suddenly, in the city gate, they stand in front of—*Samuel* (all of the sudden, the name is mentioned). The narrator reveals to us that God tells Samuel that this is the expected one at this very moment. We observe with amusement how Samuel heaps attention on his guest, who cannot understand what is going on. Then at last we see Samuel the next morning, outside the city alone with Saul, anointing him. Samuel is sure of what he is doing; he mentions a total of three signs to Saul by which Saul will recognize the hand of God in what is occurring. Finally, we leave Samuel behind in Ramah, wander home with Saul, discover how all of the signs occur—and observe how Saul says nothing at home of what happened to him. The secret of the anointment, the "messianic secret," must not be uncovered before the hour of the anointed (and of his mentor!) is at hand.

After these events, Samuel—once again—summons the people to Mizpah (1 Sam 10:17). Important events had occurred there previously (1 Sam 7:15ff.). Meanwhile the people had strongly voiced their desire for a king (1 Sam 8:1–5), and now Samuel gathers the people at this same location. Important events cast their shadow. Samuel orders preparations for ritually drawing lots (1 Sam 10:19b; the brusque accusations in vv. 18aβb, 19a were again inserted by the antimonarchic Deuteronomist who had already spoken in 1 Sam 8:6ff.). As readers informed by the narrator, we ask ourselves why this ritual is necessary: Saul has already been anointed. The people, however, do not yet know this and may have reacted with reservation to Samuel's announcement that Saul was to be the new king. Is it not also comforting for us and maybe even for Samuel that Saul's election is confirmed once again? The lot quickly determines the one whom Samuel and we know as "the one asked for." The people, too, seem satisfied and turn to crown the elected—but he cannot be found! This surprises everyone: the Israelites, Samuel, and us as well. A sense of insecurity arises: Perhaps something is not in order after all? The people obtain an oracle of YHWH. They find the man behind the baggage, bring him into their midst, and Samuel presents him to the people as YHWH's chosen one.

We are tempted to say: a happy ending for all. On several occasions it has been confirmed that God has chosen Saul ben Kish to be the first king of Israel. Samuel has prepared and executed his election; the entire people of Israel have affirmed and accepted this choice. It is now clear that Saul is not merely Samuel's candidate or the candidate of some of the people. Still, dissonance enters as Samuel disbands the gathering in Mizpah: some—Saul and "those warriors whose hearts God had touched"—go home with great joy; others—"worthless" or "anarchic elements" (בני בליעל, "sons of Belial")—complain: "'How can this man save us?' And they despised him and brought him no present" (10:26–27). The narrator's evaluation of the two groups is obvious: Saul's opponents are demonized, while his followers are connected with God's actions. Even so, a trace of bitterness spoils the unadulterated joy of Saul's coronation.

Saul's supporters and followers will be able to obliterate this dishonor. With the help of God and the Israelite-Judahite army, Saul is victorious against the neighboring Ammonites (1 Sam 11:1–11). This gloriously confirms Saul's abilities and clearly refutes his skeptics. When these are to be lynched by the people, Saul (Samuel, according to the Greek version) orders them to withdraw. After the victory granted by God, it is time for generosity toward adversaries on the home front. Initiated by Samuel, the people move to Gilgal, *renew* the kingdom, and confirm Saul— once and for all, we are tempted to add—in his royal position. A great celebration ensues, "and Saul and all the men of Israel rejoiced greatly" (11:12–15).

In Samuel's farewell speech (1 Sam 12), the (Deuteronomistic) critic of kingship speaks once more in the voice of Samuel. He asserts—and is confirmed by the people—that he has been blameless as a judge in Israel (1 Sam 12:1–5). He then reflects back on God's providential guidance in Israel's previous history up to the present (12:6–11). Success and failure in the future depend on the people's and the king's attitude toward God (12:12–15). A quickly staged natural miracle generates great fear among the Israelites; they appeal to Samuel to ask God for mercy (12:16–19). Samuel once more demands loyalty to YHWH and promises to remain loyal to the people (12:20–25). This speech displays once again the entire skepticism held by Deuteronomistic circles against the issue of the monarchy—but not specifically against its first representatives. Confirmed by God, but with grave misgivings and rejection, they have allowed Samuel to comply with the desire for a king (1 Sam 8:6ff.); now they let him look into the future after he has instituted a king against his own will. His loyalty to Israel does not yet allow him completely to disqualify the new king. Still, he already foresees how disbelief and misery will enter Israel through the portal of kingship.

I.4.1.3. Samuel Rejects Israel's First King and Designates a Second

After instituting Saul as king, Samuel does not retreat into privacy; he continues to act publicly. Now he no longer holds power in his own hand; instead, he watches over how the monarchy is executed by the king. He is thus the first to hold the office of prophetic observer, which the biblical account places as an accompaniment and corrective at the side of the ruling king. The counterparts of king and prophet determine much of the books of Samuel and even more so the books of Kings. Yet even the prophets themselves, as much as we can access from their own accounts, understood their role to be in opposition to the kings. This follows age-old ancient Near Eastern tradition.[10] In general, however, most of the prophets were in favor of the monarchy. This was also true in Israel. Samuel himself is described as having close ties to the monarchy and specifically to Saul. Yet nowhere else in the ancient Near East could we imagine that the institution of a king was solely dependent on a man of God such as Samuel and that this very Samuel would then reject the first king immediately after he had failed to listen to the prophet's word. In these texts we encounter the first indication of a fundamental battle over what or who takes prime position in Israel: the king and the constrictions of power or the prophet and YHWH's insistence on obedience by the people—including the king!

The Bible shows in two examples how the first king and his spiritual mentor carry out this basic conflict. When Samuel anointed Saul, he told him to execute a military strike against the Philistine governor and then to retreat to the Jordan Valley and to wait for Samuel for seven days in order to receive further instructions (1 Sam 10:5–8). Saul (or perhaps Jonathan; the text is not quite clear on the issue: 1 Sam 13:3–4) does indeed strike the Philistine governor and arranges the troops against Gilgal. When the Philistines make preparations for a counterstrike, the Israelites are beset with fear and desert in great numbers (13:5–7a). Saul should act but cannot because he must wait for

---

10. We should specifically take note of the prophetic texts of the eighteenth century B.C.E. from Mari on the Euphrates. See the edition in *TUAT* II/1:83–93, as well as the discussion in Edward Noort, *Untersuchungen zum Gottesbescheid in Mari: Die "Mariprophetie" in der alttestamentlichen Forschung* (AOAT 202; Kevelaer: Butzon und Bercker; Neukirchen-Vluyn: Neukirchener, 1977), and in Armin Schmitt, *Prophetischer Gottesbescheid in Mari und Israel* (BWANT 6/14; Stuttgart: Kohlhammer, 1982). Recent scholarship has paid increasing intention to prophets from the Neo-Assyrian period (during the eighth/seventh century B.C.E.), see Simo Parpola, ed., *Assyrian Prophecies* (SAA 9; Helsinki: Helsinki University Press, 1997) as well as Martti Nissinen, *References to Prophecy in Neo-Assyrian Sources* (SAAS 7; Helsinki: Helsinki University Press, 1998).

Samuel. He waits seven full days and then finally brings himself to offer the sacrifice that is seemingly needed before battle. Just then Samuel appears and asks accusingly: "What have you done?" Saul defends his action with great eloquence, almost with too much eloquence. Samuel shows no pity: if Saul had listened, his kingdom would have endured; now, however, YHWH has "found a man after his own heart" and appointed him to be the future leader of Israel (13:7b–15).

We are shocked by this harsh reaction. It is almost as if Samuel is making an example of Saul. (It was also probably relatively easy—given the major lapse in time[11]—once Saul and his house had become an obscure part of Israel's early history, whereas David and his house had made a long-lasting historical impact.) Israel's God made sure that Saul's kingship remained a mere episode in Israel's history.

Saul is afforded one last chance to prove himself. Samuel once again commands a military action in the name of YHWH—this time against the Amalekites. Already the phrasing present in Samuel's introduction should have made Saul pay attention; in any case, it makes us pay attention: "YHWH has sent me to anoint you king over his people Israel; now therefore listen to the words of YHWH" (1 Sam 15:1). The explicit, almost solemn recourse to the anointment foreshadows that we are faced with an all-or-nothing situation. Samuel informs the king that God still has an account to settle with Amalek, Israel's very first enemy following the exodus out of Egypt (15:2; cf. Exod 17:8–16). Now that Israel has grown strong and has united under its king, the time seems right to eradicate the primal enemy—more a cipher than real—of God's people: "Go and attack Amalek and utterly destroy all that they have; do not spare them, but kill both man and woman, child and infant, ox and sheep, camel and donkey" (15:3).

This is not the place to deal with the institution of a dedicated ban.[12] One thing is clear: Saul is called to lead a war *for God*, yet he has no interest in doing so. The justification for this war lies not in the realm of politics but in the realm of historical theology. Not even the most basic reason for battle, the loot, is supposed to play a role: the meager possessions of these

---

11. 1 Sam 13:7–15 is a relatively late redactional text; 1 Sam 15, which will be discussed below, has undergone strong Deuteronomistic redaction.

12. See the extensive article on חרם in *TDOT* 5:180–99 (Nobert Lohfink) as well as my article, "The 'Ban' in the Age of the Early Kings," in *The Origins of the Ancient Israelite States* (ed. Volkmar Fritz and Philip R. Davies; JSOTSup 228; Sheffield: Sheffield Academic Press, 1996), 196–210. Regarding the problem of the Amalekites see Hans Andreas Tanner, *Amalek—Der Feind Israels und der Feind Jahwes: Eine Studie zu den Amalektexten im Alten Testament* (Zürich: Theologischer Verlag Zürich, 2005).

steppe dwellers and they themselves are to be left for the deity (through execution of the "ban," i.e., by their total destruction). No king will find such a war particularly sensible, yet the king of Israel must undertake such a war by divine command. Saul does as told—almost. He allows a few choice animals and King Agag to live (15:3–9). God immediately tells Samuel of this, and Samuel becomes angry (at whom: Saul or God?) and "cries out to YHWH all night" (15:11). He had neither expected nor hoped for Saul's failure. Instead of abandoning his protégé, he wrestles with God over his fate. The next day he inspects the situation personally, noticeably once again in Gilgal, where the first clash between prophet and king had occurred and where Saul had gone after his victory. A kind of cross-examination ensues in which Samuel plays the role of the prosecutor or inquisitor (15:13–23). The final culmination is the expression: "Because you have rejected the word of YHWH, he has also rejected you from being king" (15:23b). Samuel abruptly turns away from the one he had once anointed. As Saul attempts to grasp him, he tears the prophetic cloak. The scene symbolizes not only the tear in a once-close relationship but also Samuel's torn inner self. He stands in a conflict of loyalties between the divine authority and his earthly protégé—we could almost say between duty and affection. He consequently cannot bring himself to undermine Saul's authority with the people; instead, he commences the victory celebrations with him and cooperates openly with him in the execution of the captured Amalekite king (15:31–33). Neither the king nor the people have any indication how deeply Samuel suffers from the torn relationship; merely we as readers are witness to how hard Samuel had previously wrestled with God and how deeply he later mourned Saul (15:11, 35).

God has to wrench Samuel from his pain. He should no longer suffer because of the rejected Saul but instead go and anoint a new king (1 Sam 16:1). Are we to understand Samuel's protest that this undertaking is too dangerous only on a literal level—or is this not also resistance against the change of course demanded of him? He does, however, journey to Jesse in Bethlehem, has him present his sons, and is repeatedly willing—to anoint the wrong one! God must first teach him "not to look on his appearance or on the height of his stature" (16:7). We cannot miss the reference to Saul's stature (1 Sam 9:2; 10:23). Samuel obviously can hardly suppress his sympathy for Saul and the image of a king represented by him. In the end, he anoints young David. It must have been a comfort to him that he at least had "handsome features" (16:12).

Samuel, Saul, and David—only once do the paths of these three men cross. The context is highly dramatic, the conclusion of this meeting highly revealing. David, having meanwhile ascended the ranks in Saul's court, has increasingly experienced Saul's jealousy and hatred. In the end, he barely saves his life by means of escape. His first path takes him to Samuel in Ramah (1 Sam 19:18). Saul hears of this and decides to arrest him there. Samuel, however, is not alone, but rather the leader of a group of ecstatic prophets. When the pursuers arrive, they are drawn into the vortex of group ecstasy and cannot execute their order. This occurs three times until Saul finally goes himself—and experiences the same fate as his men. This time David escapes for good (1 Sam 19:23–24; 20:1). Now it is completely clear that Samuel has switched sides: he has turned away from Saul and whole-heartedly supports David; he has saved the life of the future king from the current king.

While David is still on the run and Saul is desperately trying to maintain power, Samuel dies. "And all Israel assembled and mourned for him. They buried him at his home in Ramah" (1 Sam 25:1, cf. 28:3). Thus ends the period described in 1 Sam 7:13: "The hand of YHWH was against the Philistines all the days of Samuel." Will God now pull his hand away? David does, in fact, have to flee to the Philistines not much later (1 Sam 27), who arm themselves to strike a final blow to Israel (1 Sam 28:1). Saul is informed beforehand that this battle will end tragically for Israel and especially for his family—by the dead Samuel! In his fear of the Philistines and especially of God's silence, he goes to a necromancer. The woman is indeed able to conjure up Samuel from the dead (1 Sam 28). Saul is not able to see him but asks the woman to describe him. He recognizes him by his cloak. Samuel brusquely asks why his peace has been disturbed. Saul admits his helplessness and his fear. The answer is given with great abrasiveness: "Why, then, do you ask[13] me, since YHWH has turned from you and become your enemy? [textual emendation] … Tomorrow you and your sons shall be with me; YHWH will also give the army of Israel into the hands of the Philistines" (1 Sam 28:16, *19). Samuel substantiates this prophecy with Saul's failure to enact the ban against Amalek and he also does not forget to once again mention David as the one whom God has chosen to succeed him (28:17–18).[14] Saul falls to the ground, struck down by the harsh words, just as he already fell down before Samuel when the prophet rejected him (1 Sam 19:24). The next day he will fall in the battle against the Philistines and will finally be "with Samuel." The two men whose fate was so closely and tragically intertwined thus join again in death.

---

13. Is it coincidence that the verb שאל occurs here, the very same verb that determines so much of Samuel's birth narrative (1 Sam 1) and also forms the root for the name "Saul"?

14. This text, especially the passage quoted above, also seems to have been redacted heavily by the Deuteronomistic redactor.

I.4.2. The Portrait of Saul

Barrick, W. Boyd. "Saul's Demise, David's Lament, and Custer's Last Stand," *JSOT* 73 (1997): 25–41. **Barth**, Karl. *Kirchliche Dogmatik* (4th ed.; Zürich: Evangelischer Verlag, 1959), 2.2:404–34. **Berges**, Ulrich. *Die Verwerfung Sauls: Eine thematische Untersuchung* (FzB 61; Würzburg: Echter, 1989). **Couffignal**, Robert. Saül, héros tragique de la Bible: Étude littéraire du récit de son règne d'après les Livres de Samuel, 1S IX–XXXI et 2S I (Paris: Minard, 1999). **Dietrich**, Walter, ed. *David und Saul im Widerstreit: Diachronie und Synchronie im Wettstreit* (OBO 206; Fribourg: Academic; Göttingen: Vandenhoeck & Ruprecht, 2004). **Edelman**, Diana Vikander. *King Saul in the Historiography of Judah* (JSOTSup 121; Sheffield: Sheffield Academic Press, 1991). **Exum**, J. Cheryl. *Tragedy and Biblical Narrative: Arrows of the Almighty* (Cambridge: Cambridge University Press, 1992). **Fokkelman**, Jan P. *The Crossing Fates (I Sam. 13–31 and II Sam. 1)* (vol. 2 of *Narrative Art and Poetry in the Books of Samuel: A Full Interpretation Based on Stylistic and Structural Analyses*; SSN 23; Assen: Van Gorcum, 1986). **Garsiel**, Moshe. *The First Book of Samuel: A Literary Study of Comparative Structures, Analogies and Parallels* (Ramat-Gan, Israel: Revivim, 1985). **Gordon**, Robert P. "David's Rise and Saul's Demise: Narrative Analogy in 1 Samuel 24–26," *TynB* 31 (1980): 37–64. **Gunn**, David M. *The Fate of King Saul: An Interpretation of a Biblical Story* (JSOTSup 14; Sheffield: JSOT Press,1980). **Good**, Edwin M. *Irony in the Old Testament* (2nd ed.; BiLiSe 3; Sheffield, Almond, 1981). **Hentschel**, Georg. *Saul: Schuld, Reue und Tragik eines „Gesalbten"* (Leipzig: Evangelische Verlagsanstalt, 2003). **Humphreys**, W. Lee. "From Tragic Hero to Villain: A Study of the Figure of Saul and the Development of 1 Samuel," *JSOT* 22 (1982): 95–117. **Jobling**, David. "Saul's Fall and Jonathan's Rise: Tradition and Redaction in 1 Sam 14:1–46," *JBL* 95 (1976): 367–76. **Klein**, Johannes. *David versus Saul: Ein Beitrag zum Erzählsystem der Samuelbücher* (BWANT 158; Stuttgart: Kohlhammer, 2002). **Miscall**, Peter D. *1 Samuel: A Literary Reading* (Indiana Studies in Biblical Literature; Bloomington: Indiana University Press 1986. **Reis**, Pamela Tamarkin. "Eating the Blood: Saul and the Witch of Endor," *JSOT* 73 (1997): 3–23. **Vette**, Joachim. *Samuel und Saul. Ein Beitrag zur narrativen Poetik des Samuelbuches* (Beiträge zum Verstehen der Bibel 13; Münster: LIT, 2005).

I.4.2.1. The Chosen One

When the name Saul (שָׁאוּל) occurs for the first time (1 Sam 9:2), it has already been prepared for beforehand. From the beginning of the first book of Samuel we recognize that it has something to do with the one "asked for" by Hannah (1:28: שָׁאוּל). Shortly before Saul's name is mentioned, the elders of Israel have brought their request for a king before Samuel (1 Sam 8) and had their request basically affirmed by God. Now everyone—Samuel, the people, and the readers—is waiting for the person God has chosen for this high office. The first appearance of Saul ben Kish sounds promising: he was "chosen" (בחור) and "good" (טוב), "no one among the Israelites was better [טוב] than him. From his shoulders upward he was taller than all the people" (9:2). This is what heroes are made of. How will God bring this Saul together with Samuel?

Saul starts a quest: not for Samuel and the kingship, but for donkeys who have strayed from his father. In almost torturous detail, the narrative lists the areas that he traverses with his servant. We read how he intends to abandon the search (1 Sam 9:3–5). At this point the servant tells him of a seer whose reputation for good and reliable information is well known. We immediately suspect whose reputation the servant is talking about—thus we have a certain advantage over Saul. With amusement we observe the two young men in their encounter with maidens at a well; we hear their question and the multivoiced answer. Then we wander with them into the city, observe how they encounter Samuel and are invited to a festive meal; we stand with them in amazement as Samuel provides them unasked with information about the donkeys (they are found!) as well as about the mysterious aura of the festive meal (9:11–24). Unlike Saul, however, we know why Saul is accorded this honor. "Am I not a Benjaminite, of the smallest tribe of Israel and of the smallest of all families in the tribe of Benjamin?" (9:21) Saul does not have a clue what is going on; he displays congenial modesty and no trace of expediency. We, however, are able to see, with Samuel, Israel's future king.

The game continues until the next morning, when Samuel is alone with Saul on the outskirts of the city. Here Samuel anoints him as *nagid*—which probably means "designated king"—and offers him three signs of affirmation. In other call narratives (cf. Exod 4:1–9; Judg 6:14–24) these signs of affirmation serve the purpose of overcoming the doubts of the person called into office. This is most likely their function here as well—except that Saul is not even given the time to voice any doubts. Samuel predicts for him which people he will encounter when on his way home. At the end, and most importantly, he will encounter a group of ecstatic prophets who will infect him with their "spirited" enthusiasm (10:1–6). Everything happens as foretold, and "as he turns his shoulder to leave Samuel, God turns his heart" (10:9); he turns into "a different person" (10:6) and falls into ecstasy with the prophets (10:10–12). Yet all these events remain a secret. Not even his uncle discovers what has happened (10:14–16), not to mention the Israelite public. Except for God (and the narrator!) only Samuel and Saul know what will happen now—as well as the reader. We take note with great astonishment how Saul displays no outward emotion in reaction to all of the wondrous and groundbreaking events. He allows everything to happen without becoming active himself. It almost seems as if he journeys from the farm to the kingship as if in a dream.

In Mizpah, Saul also plays no active role. Quite the contrary: all activity lies in the hands of Samuel, who initiates a ritual drawing of lots. The first lot is cast between the different tribes; it falls on Benjamin (1 Sam 10:20). We are not too surprised, but the Israelites may have wondered, as this tribe (in Saul's own words) was "the smallest among all the tribes of Israel" (9:21). Among the families, the lot falls on the clan of Matri (10:21)—according to Saul "the smallest among the clans of Benjamin" (9:21). Among the men of Matri, the lot falls on Saul ben Kish—Did Saul think himself small as well? And now, at the very point where Saul should have become active and shown himself to the people—he has disappeared. God, Samuel, and the people have to work together to find him and bring him to the center. In reaction to his presentation by Samuel and the acclamation of the people, Saul does not utter a single word (10:19–24). He presents no contribution to the writing down of the royal law (10:25). And against the hostility of his internal opponents, he does nothing (10:27; 11:13). He does brilliantly confirm his role through his victory over the Ammonites (1 Sam 11)—but in this he does not really act himself, but rather God's spirit acts in him and through him.

These traits may make Saul likeable and endearing. If there ever was a potentate who did not push himself into a position of power, then it is Saul. God, Samuel, and the people have taken him out of his small, private world and then from his hiding place behind the baggage in order to lift him onto the throne. He is the perfect image of a reticent, almost shy individual. In the face of prevailing misgivings about the monarchy in general, we could say: if a king at all, then this one! But this is just one side of the issue. Are these misgivings truly put to rest, just because *one* representative of this institution shows no cause for alarm? More important, could the choice of this one be driven too much by these misgivings? Will Saul be man enough, will his personal power base be strong enough to succeed in the task he is given? Is he in the end perhaps too modest, too reticent in his dealings with power? Physical size is not the only important asset!

In addition to these personal problems that cast their shadow on Saul's ascension to the throne, the biblical depiction presents us with a grave conflict of loyalties. Saul is indebted both to God and to the people. This duality determines much of the narratives in 1 Sam 9–11: Samuel follows God's command and anoints the young Saul to be the future king, God's spirit moves from the prophet to Saul, God guides the process when Samuel initiates a ritual casting of lots, Samuel presents Saul as the chosen of YHWH, and Samuel redefines Saul's victory over the Ammonites as a "renewal" of the kingdom. On the other hand, a large group of "invited guests," most likely nobles from the surrounding area, pay homage to Saul (9:22–24), the people shout in acclamation (10:24), Saul quickly finds loyal followers (10:26), the people follow his call to arms "as one man" (11:7), and in the end "Saul and all men of Israel rejoice greatly" (11:15—important: "in the presence of Yhwh").

This constant emphasis on two authorities to which Saul owes his ascension to the throne can be comforting, if they are understood to affirm each other. We can also ask, however, what might happen when these authorities drift apart or collide. The relation between Yhwh and Israel is generally understood to be inseparable in the biblical account, but this relationship is never free from conflict and collision. Especially in the area of politics, Israel's (theological) history was again and again determined by the opposition of two principles: the rationally determined government of a state, guided by immanent laws of political leadership, and the faithful following of God in obedience to transcendent commandments. Will Saul, perhaps the first professional politician, be able to serve both masters? Whom will he follow in case of conflict: God or human beings?

The third problem that weighs heavily on Saul's kingship, according to the text in its final Deuteronomistic redaction, is situated outside of Saul as an individual or his personal decisions. Before he even appears as the candidate for this high office, there has already been a severe conflict between the people and Samuel, or better, between the people and God. The question at the center of 1 Sam 8 is whether Israel needs a king at all, whether this king will cause more harm than good. This issue is, of course, not a matter of any specific king but rather of kingship in general. Still, the fierce conflict, Samuel's resentment, and God's bitterness, as well as the severe warnings to the people and their obstinacy, do not bode well for any king to come out of this conflict. Samuel's resistance is not without reason (1 Sam 8; 12). It is almost strange how he welcomes Saul with open arms once he is sent to him and presents him hereafter to the people. The people's acclamation and their joy over Saul's election have an insipid aftertaste, considering all that has gone before. From this perspective, the fact that Saul allows all this to happen to him and in the end shows signs of contentment is not only understandable and appealing. Are we not dealing with someone who was carried up by ominous tides, someone who in hindsight perhaps should have stayed at the bottom? The final Deuteronomistic shape of the text describes an ill-omened event, no matter how positive it may seem at first glance.

What will become of Saul if aspects of his personality and the nature of his office are working against him?

I.4.2.2. Saul as a Failure

Examining all of the material on Saul and his kingship, the biblical portrait seems strangely incomplete, indecisive, unfavorable, and unfortunate. This impression begins with the first sentence introducing his reign, the well-known stock introductory phrase from the book of Kings that appears here in a modified form. Later kings are introduced in the manner of Solomon's successor: "Now Rehoboam son of Solomon reigned in Judah. Rehoboam was forty-one years old when he began to reign, and he reigned seventeen years in Jerusalem" (1 Kgs 14:21). In 1 Sam 13:1 we read, "Saul was ... years old when he began to reign; and he reigned ... years over Israel." It seems that the Deuteronomistic Historians did not have specific dates at hand. Later textual versions fill the first gap with the number "thirty" or "twenty-one"; the Hebrew (but not the Syriac) fills the second gap with the number "two." Many scholars consider it highly improbable that Saul reigned for such a brief period of time. There is no solution to this debate. We know with certainty only that the text aims to introduce the first king in a sequence of Israelite and Judahite kings and that those who handed down the text did not consider it necessary to provide Saul's reign with specific dates. In the case of Saul, the standard introductory phrase appears as a vessel without content, as a facade without a building behind it. This is symptomatic for the entire depiction of Saul's reign.

In the biblical depiction, Saul stands entirely in David's shadow. From 1 Sam 16 on, David clearly determines what is going on. Saul is merely the negative background against which David's light can shine brightly. Of the time before David's appearance, we hear very little. In brief summaries we are told of Saul's family and of several wars that he fought successfully (1 Sam 14:47–52). In addition to these lists, we merely have two narrative passages: one of a war against the Philistines (1 Sam 13–14), the other of a war against the Amalekites (1 Sam 15); both result in victory for Israel but in disaster for Saul.

The narrative on the Philistine war already describes Saul's basic dilemma. On the one hand, he is the rational and professional leader of the Israelite army. He conscripts three thousand soldiers, divides the command with his son Jonathan (which will lead to a further conflict!), stations his troops in strategic positions, opens the engagement with a strike against the Philistine governor (or is it Jonathan who strikes first?), and then withdraws to the Jordan Valley to Gilgal and calls his troops together (1 Sam 13:2–4). On the other hand, Saul is dependent on Samuel. The prophet had encouraged him to strike against the Philistines but at the same time had demanded that Saul wait for further instructions at Gilgal (1 Sam 10:7–8); indeed, Saul waits for Samuel a long time—too long from a military perspective (13:5–8). Yet he is faced with Samuel's rebuke that he did not wait longer. He even has to listen to Samuel's announcement that God has chosen another, a better man (13:9–14). Even though he is able to defend himself eloquently against Samuel with good arguments, he has *nothing* to say to the final verdict. He allows Samuel to depart without protest and enters into battle without his mentor (N.B. an experienced warrior against the Philistines!). His starting position is desperate: barely two hundred men remain under his command; their ordinance is miserable. The Philistines do as they please; they plunder and pillage the land of Israel without restraint (13:15–22).

Thus Saul is ground up between the millstones of political-military necessities and prophetic-divine demands even before he has become fully active as king. It is hard to decide which of the three problems described above is responsible for this outcome, perhaps all three together. Samuel appears as someone who is only waiting to correct a mistake, namely, the coronation of Saul. The Israelites do not seem fully to trust the abilities of their new king; they flee as soon as the Philistines start applying pressure. The prelude to Saul's first action as king is anything but impressive; his self-confidence cannot be very great as a consequence.

It is fortunate for Israel—but only very partially for Saul!—that Saul has an accomplished, courageous, and even pious son: Jonathan. When military fortune seems to depart from the father, he pushes himself with verve and success onto center stage. The entire fourteenth chapter of 1 Sam deals with *Jonathan's* victory over the Philistines. Saul plays at most a supporting role, if not the part of the antagonist. He starts participating in the action only after the victory has been guaranteed by Jonathan's heroic escapade—which was supported by God (14:1–15)! Yet participation to what end? He first demands to know who has thrown himself into battle without prior announcement. He believes an oracle to be necessary, yet aborts the ritual because of the developments on the field (14:16–19)—a strange combination of religious observance and religious (also military) inefficiency.

In the case of Saul, we can again and again observe such vacillating between fearful observance of religious rituals and opportunistic conformity to political necessity. Prior to the battle with the Philistines, he made his troops take an oath of abstinence, which only Jonathan broke. An unfortunate turn of events on the battlefield points the king to the fact that the oath has been broken. By casting lots, he pinpoints his son. Following correct jurisprudence, he passes the death sentence (1 Sam 14:24–31, 36–44). This time, it seems, he intends to obey God more than human beings—even at the cost of his own son! This may seem tragic-heroic, but we cannot forget that Saul has been told that a new ruler will soon replace him (13:13–14) and that Jonathan has spoken rebelliously against his father (14:29–30). The scary thought rises that the king might not be that unhappy about the death of the crown prince. *The people*—one of the two sides that determine Saul's conflict of loyalty—object to the death sentence and save the life of the hero of the day (14:45). Readers rejoice in this and note at the same time that Saul wordlessly accepts this affront by his soldiers and immediately discontinues the battle (14:46): not really what one might call a self-assured and assertive ruler.

The narrator of 1 Sam 14 guides us readers to side with and sympathize with Jonathan rather than with Saul. We intuitively feel that he is the next important figure. As we read on, we encounter endearing stories of the friendship between Jonathan and David (1 Sam 18:1, 3–4; 20) that lead to the rightful heir to the throne fully relinquishing his claim to his most severe (and finally successful) competitor (23:16–18). This line, from Saul over Jonathan to David, is foreshadowed in 1 Sam 14. Jonathan is the intermediary who legitimizes and legalizes the transfer of power from the house of Saul to the house of David (see Jobling). For Jonathan to be able to do this, he must replace his father already during his lifetime. This is exactly what happens in 1 Sam 14, where Jonathan, not Saul, vanquishes the Philistines. Saul even seeks to take his life. Later on, both Saul and Jonathan will lose their life together, but not before the crown prince has passed the scepter on to David. Saul, of course, knows nothing of this. He just feels the vague suspicion, planted by Samuel, that his reign will soon be over, passed on to someone else ....

The second major war is the battle against the Amalekites (1 Sam 15). Samuel gives Saul the order—not for political but for religious reasons— utterly to eradicate this tribe located in the far south of Palestine. Saul follows this order in pious obedience. He is not too pious, however, to allow his sense of pragmatism to spare the Amalekite king Agag and the best animals. On this point, he is fully in accord with *the people* (15:9). At God's command, however, Samuel bursts into the proceedings. The dispute between prophet and king (15:13–26) reveals much about Saul's character as seen by the biblical narrators. Reacting to Samuel's accusation, Saul is able to justify his actions (although not completely!): "The people have spared" choice animals. "We [!] executed the ban upon the rest." He cleverly adds that the animals were spared "to sacrifice them to YHWH, your God" (!); he says nothing of Agag. Samuel's answer exposes the real state of Saul's soul. He may be "small in his own eyes," but God had "anointed him king over Israel." Why, then, did he "swoop down on the spoil" and "not listen to the voice of YHWH" (15:16–19)? Samuel directly addresses Saul's feelings of inferiority and his conflict of loyalty between God and the people.

The following passage seems to contain an especially high degree of Deuteronomistic redaction. Saul defends himself once again by stating that he did "listen to the voice of YHWH" when he waged battle as ordered, captured the king, and executed the ban on the Amalekites; it was "the people" who took the choice animals in order to sacrifice them to YHWH at Gilgal—in response to which Samuel utters the famous saying "obedience is better than sacrifice" and pronounces judgment: "Because you have rejected the word of YHWH, he has rejected you from being king" (15:20–23).

Saul submits to Samuel's judgment without further objection: "I have sinned and transgressed against the comm nd of YHWH, for I feared the people and listened to their voice" (15:24). He thus admits to being torn between "listening to the voice of YHWH" and "fearing the people," precisely the basic conflict that has determined his kingship from the beginning. It is to his credit that Saul gains this insight himself and is able to put it in words. He is open to God's word to him and capable of self-criticism. On the other hand, Saul is not so devout that in the moment of his humiliation he would forget political pragmatism. He asks Samuel not to expose him now "before the elders of my people and before Israel" but to show himself publicly at his side instead (15:30). Even if God has rejected him, the people do not have to know! This means that Saul intends to hold on to power for as long as possible. The price for this will be high. The individuals who surround him will start to notice that something is wrong. For the biblical depiction from this point on, Saul is no longer merely a vacillating character but a sick and even dangerous man.

I.4.2.3. The Raving Saul

"The spirit of YHWH departed from Saul, and an evil spirit from YHWH tormented him" (1 Sam 16:14). The "evil spirit" is an expression for severe illness, which could only be understood as coming from God. When Saul encountered the group of prophets following his anointing and when he heard of the ignominious attack of the Ammonites against Israelite settlements, the "spirit of God" came upon him (10:10; 11:6). Now this spirit, which had driven him to accomplish great things, departed from him and *evil* possessed him. It seems that the narrators understood this process to have taken place in stages, resulting in different kinds of abnormal states of mind. Those surrounding Saul decided to counteract these fits with a kind of musical therapy. With Saul's consent, they brought a young man to the court who was not only handsome, intelligent, and courageous but also capable of playing a stringed instrument—David (16:15–22). The therapy was successful. "Whenever the spirit of God came upon Saul, David took the lute and played it with his hand, and Saul would be relieved[15] and feel better, and the evil spirit would depart from him" (16:23). The king "loved the young man, and he became his armor-bearer" (16:21).

---

15. The verb used in this instance is רוח, from which the noun רוּחַ "breath, wind, spirit" is derived.

Saul did not in the least suspect that the one who comforted his distress was in a certain sense the very reason for his distress. The reigning king had brought the one individual to his court and into his closest circle who had been designated to be the next king.

The next story (1 Sam 17) tells of the resurgence of the Philistines. It will become a question of fate whether Saul can defeat this enemy. He had only won the first great battle with the Philistines thanks to Jonathan (1 Sam 13–14). This time, again, he is in a precarious situation. The troops have risen up and stand in a stalemate opposite each other. Right then a giant of a warrior, Goliath of Gath, challenges the warriors of Israel to single combat. He specifically mentions Saul as his true opponent: "Am I not a Philistine—and you servants of Saul? ... And Saul and all of Israel with him heard the words of the Philistine and were dismayed and greatly afraid" (17:8, 11). No one dares accept the challenge, not even Saul.

As if coming from a different world, the shepherd boy David ben Jesse enters the tension-laden scene. He, who least seems capable of meeting the task, decides to accept Goliath's challenge. King Saul, whose permission he needs, raises several objections. The young boy David does not stand a chance against this heavily armored warrior. When David insists on his plan, Saul decides to at least arm him appropriately and clothes him with the royal (!) armor; this, however, is too large and heavy for David. Barely clothed, as one might expect of a shepherd boy, David confronts Goliath—and defeats him with a sling. We hear in amazement how king Saul asks his general Abner who this young man may be (17:55); once he has discovered his identity, Saul decides to take the son of Jesse into his service (18:2)—as if he had not all the while been his armorbearer. In this story, Saul seems not only hesitant and paralyzed but also small-minded and confused. Are these the effects of the "evil spirit"?

Saul soon feels that his fortunes are sinking whereas David's are rising. One day, as he hears the song of the women—"Saul has defeated thousands, David tens of thousands" (18:7)—anger, jealousy, and fear boil to the surface: "Saul was very angry.... He said, ... 'What more can he have but the kingdom?'" (18:8). Is Saul beginning to understand that this David may have something to do with Samuel's announcement of a new king? In any case, "Saul eyed David from this day on" (18:9).

The next day the "evil spirit from God" once again fell upon the king so that he "raved within his house" (18:10); the verb used here is often, also in the Saul narratives, used to describe prophetic behavior and probably refers to an ecstatic phenomenon. The people had once observed and probably admired that "Saul, too, was among the prophets," that is, could fall into ecstasy (10:12), this trait now proves to be a two-edged sword. As long as a "good spirit" is connected to the phenomenon (10:10), it remains a positive attribute; once an "evil spirit" is the cause, Saul moves toward madness. This very point is emphasized in the episode where Saul seeks to apprehend his opponent when he dwells with the prophets in Ramah (19:18–24). Here Saul's well-known closeness to the prophetic-ecstatic takes a turn toward the demented and insane. In this sense (!) "Saul is also among the prophets" (19:24).

As long as David still lives at Saul's court, his music is an antidote to the "evil spirit." Paradoxically, it seems to be David himself who causes most of these "spirit attacks." The king starts raving once when he hears the victory song of the women and once when he hears of David's victory over the Philistines (18:10; 19:9). He seems to understand intuitively what the narrator also suggests to us: there is a connection between the good fortune of the new upstart and Saul's own misfortune. On several occasions he tries to end this situation by making an attempt on David's life (18:11; 19:10). This action is marked by horrific brutality, even if we can understand it psychologically. It is, however, full of irony, especially on two levels: Saul uses his *spear* (חנית), which the narratives almost see as a part of him, not against the Philistines but against David, his best and most successful fighter (once even against his son Jonathan, also a proven warrior, 20:33). It must be even worse and quite depressing for Saul that he is not even able to kill an unsuspecting, unarmed man; each time David is able to avoid the attempt on his life. "And Saul feared David" (18:12).

The motif of Saul's *fear* of David is repeated on two further occasions: once when Saul must recognize that the disciplinary transfer of David away from his court only served to increase his popularity among the troops (18:14); and once when "Saul saw and recognized that YHWH was with David and that Michal, the daughter of Saul, loved him" (18:28–29). How is the deeply unbalanced king supposed to bear the fact that God and his daughter have sided with his opponent? Saul tries his best to prevent David from marrying into the royal family, or at least to use this situation as a deadly trap. He already owed a daughter to the one who vanquished Goliath (17:25), but David did not receive a wife. As trade-off for Saul's older daughter Merab, Saul demands David's full dedication in the wars against the Philistines—hoping that his opponent will be killed in the course of action. David remains alive, but he does not receive Merab (18:17–19). For the second daughter, Michal, Saul demands one hundred Philistine foreskins as the bridal price; David agrees to the eerie demand, stays alive once again—and presents Saul with two hundred foreskins. This time he gets the royal daughter; Saul, however, is gripped with fear and becomes "David's enemy from that time forward" (18:20–28).

Michal now becomes the person who rescues David from another attempt on his life, this time carried out openly with all the instruments of power at Saul's command (1 Sam 9:11–17). To her father's question, "Why have you deceived me like this and let my enemy go, so that he has escaped?" she coldly responds with the lie that David had threatened her life. Michal has switched loyalties: from her father to her husband, from Saul to David.

Jonathan does not go quite so far. He will remain at his father's side until the bitter end. On the other hand, he is David's most beloved friend. Already following the victory over Goliath, he fraternized with the young hero (18:1, 3–4). Now, after the open rift between Saul and David, he attempts twice to heal this rift by interceding with his father on his friend's behalf: once he is successful (19:1–7); the second time, his attempt almost costs him his life (20:33). This scene is quite revealing: Saul almost explicitly accuses Jonathan of sexual dependence on David (20:30) and warns him: "As long as the son of Jesse is alive on earth, you and your kingship will not be established" (20:31). Are these the hallucinations of a psychotic individual or the clear insight of a wounded soul?

It does not take long until the king, mortally wounded on the inside, can see only enemies around him. The entire world seems to have conspired against him to protect David in his flight from him. At one point, the narrative shows him "sitting at Gibeah, under the tamarisk tree on the height [textual emendation], with his spear in his hand" (1 Sam 22:6). He has just learned that David has escaped him once again. Then,

> Saul said to his servants who stood around him, "Hear now, you Benjaminites, will the son of Jesse give every one of you fields and vineyards, will he make you all commanders of thousands and commanders of hundreds? Is that why all of you have conspired against me? No one discloses to me when my son makes a league with the son of Jesse, none of you is sorry for me or discloses to me that my son has stirred up my servant against me, to lie in wait, as he is doing today." (1 Sam 22:7)

Thus, Saul assumes the existence of a conspiracy between Jonathan and David to kill him. He insinuates that the Benjaminites whom he appointed officers and granted land holdings support or at least tolerate this conspiracy.

The narrative seems to suggest that Saul is suffering from a severe persecution complex. This may be the only explanation for the most heinous deed the text accuses him of. In response to his bitter reprimand, an Edomite—not a Benjaminite!—steps up and denounces the priests of Nob to have helped David during his escape (1 Sam 22:9–10). Readers had previously encountered this scene in detail, and we know that the high priest Ahimelech acted in complete ignorance and subjective innocence when he gave David food for the way and Goliath's sword (1 Sam 21). Saul does not know this. He has Ahim-elech brought before him, initiates legal proceedings, and accuses the priest of being part of a conspiracy against the king. The priest does not deny the facts; he takes recourse, however, to the well-known close and loyal relationship between David and Saul. By this, he seals the fate for himself and his whole house. Even if the Benjaminites refuse to execute the death penalty pronounced by Saul (for the king, surely just one more indication of the conspiracy against him!), the Edomite informer is willing to commit mass murder (22:11–18). Now, at the very latest, it is clear that the narrators view Saul as an unbear-able burden and dangerous threat for Israel. The modest man who was once anointed by Samuel and enthusiastically acclaimed by the people has become an unpredictable despot who does not even hesitate to commit a bloody sac-rilege. His actions against the priests of Nob show depressing parallels to his actions against David (see Berges). His accusations have no foundation, his judgments are excessive, his arbitrariness without boundary. He utterly fails, not only in protecting against external enemies, but also in upholding internal order. This king has bitterly disappointed the Israelites' hope for a king who would "judge us and go out before us and fight our battles" (8:20).

On the other hand, we as readers cannot shake the feeling that Saul does not bear full personal responsibility for this development. From the very beginning, the narrators allow quiet doubts to creep into the narrative about whether Saul is the right person at the right time. As the narrative develops, they slowly build their case: he is not. His personal failings are not even the primary reason leading to this evaluation; he has made mistakes, no doubt, but not very large mistakes and, toward the end, hardly of his own volition. The primary reasons lie with circumstantial difficulties that Saul faces, dif-ficulties he can hardly influence or remove in any real sense. The first king is caught in a mire of political and psychological, religious and military opposi-tions; the more he tries to defend himself against this mire, the more he sinks into it; the more he strikes out, the more he hurts innocent bystanders and the more his guilt increases.

I.4.2.4. The Tragic One

The final narratives on Saul make sure that we do not feel rejection and revul-sion toward Saul as much as commiseration and compassion. The traditions narrating Saul's pursuit of David, for example, are told from the perspective of the latter so that we tremble with him and rejoice when he is able to escape once again. Yet Saul appears not so much astute and brutal but rather clumsy and really without realistic chances. In the two large narratives 1 Sam 24 and 26 the tide turns: the hunter becomes the hunted. On the first occasion,

Saul enters a cave to defecate. He does not know that David and his men are hiding farther back in the cave. This image has symbolic depth: one man, still pretty much in the light but blind to the dangers that lurk behind him, sits in a highly disadvantageous position, completely alone, defenseless, and helpless; the other man is in the back, still in the dark, but with a clear view of what is happening, surrounded by loyal men, truly master of his situation, ready to pounce and to fight. Saul will leave the cave unharmed without noticing that the corner of his cloak has been cut off. Once he has covered some distance, he suddenly hears a voice behind him: "My lord and my king." He turns around and sees David, submissively throwing himself to the ground. He hears how David protests his innocence against the king and sees how he holds up a corner of Saul's cloak to prove what he has said (1 Sam 24:9–16). As if he cannot believe what he is seeing, Saul asks: "Is this not your voice, my son David?" And then, without waiting for an answer, "Saul raises his voice and weeps" (24:17). This is the first and only time we hear Saul weeping. We cannot know why he weeps—deep emotion, gratitude, desperation, or anger—but he has lost control of himself. Obviously overwhelmed with the situation, he speaks:

> You are more righteous than I, for you have repaid me good, whereas I have repaid you evil. Today you have explained how you have dealt well with me, in that you did not kill me when YHWH put me into your hands. For who has ever found an enemy and sent the enemy safely away? So may YHWH reward you with good for what you have done to me this day. Now I know that you shall surely be king and that the kingdom of Israel shall be established in your hand. Swear to me therefore by YHWH that you will not cut off my descendants after me and that you will not wipe out my name from my father's house. So David swore this to Saul. (1 Sam 24:18–23)

It is no coincidence that the two terms "good" and "evil" (טוב and רע) are central to these passages. The "good" is on David's, the "evil" on Saul's side, as in the case of the "evil spirit." All this is voiced by Saul himself (or rather, the narrators voice it through him). The corner of Saul's cloak in David's hand is such clear proof of David's innocence that darkness is torn from Saul's eyes for one moment, and he sees the truth clearly. The necessary consequence would be to end his pursuit of David once and for all, the return of David to his court, and the transfer of authority to him soon after. The story, however, closes with a twofold ending: "Saul went to his house, and David and his men went up to their stronghold" (David's bastion during his stay in the desert; 1 Sam 24:23). It seems that the conflict between them is not over.

Soon thereafter, messengers come to Gibeah and report to Saul where David is currently hiding. Without hesitation, as if following an inner compulsion, the king departs with three thousand men to the Judean desert (1 Sam 26:1–2). This time, as if to emphasize further the inequality inherent in this conflict, there is not even a cave protecting the pursued and revealing the pursuer. Saul sets up camp somewhere in the desert without seeing David, but David is watching his every move. He then comes up with the daredevil plan to sneak into the camp with his comrade. Saul thus comes within reach of David a second time. This time he is not even attending to his digestion; he just lies there and sleeps. This time David is not surprised by Saul's sudden appearance in his hiding place; instead, he actively approaches the sleeping king, spares his life contrary to the advice of his comrade, and snatches Saul's water jar and his spear—as we recall, his most treasured possession (חנית)—and sneaks back out of the camp. From a safe distance, he first calls Saul's general Abner, mocks him, and triumphantly holds up the captured trophy. Saul reacts as he did before: "Is that not your voice, my son David?" Then, after David has protested his innocence once again and lamented his fate as a fugitive (a fate that will soon take him out of the country; 26:19–20), Saul cries out: "I have done wrong; come back, my son David, for I will never harm you again, because my life was precious in your sight today; I have been a fool and have made a great mistake" (26:21). This is a clear offer to rehabilitate David; the fugitive may return. Having been spared a second time, Saul is no longer out to kill him.

This could be the reconciliation, we might think, yet at the same time we could ask, like David, whether we can trust Saul's words. Saul repeatedly showed moments of lucidity and good intention, only to fall back into darkness and animosity on the next occasion. It is also hardly a coincidence that we are told that Saul "had given his daughter Michal, the wife of David" to a certain "Palti ben Laish" (1 Sam 25:44) just prior to the memorable encounter between pursuer and fugitive. This act had abruptly and single-handedly torn down a bridge that could have led David back to Saul and into the family. In this context, does Saul's offer to "return, my son David," not seem untrustworthy, perhaps even deceitful? Is the old hunter who could not catch the fox trying to lure him into a trap?

David does not accept Saul's offer. He tells Saul's men to come and pick up the king's spear, which was so important to him. As for himself and his men, he decides to fall back on Yhwh's protection rather than return to Saul (1 Sam 26:22–24). Saul does not seem overly surprised by this decision: "Blessed be you, my son David! You will do many things and will succeed in them." The episode closes again with a twofold ending; the two opponents separate one last time (26:25). There is a wistful element to Saul's final word to David. The king has finally understood that he cannot capture, stop, restrain, or bring back David. The rift has become irreparable. David will now move on to the Philistines (26:19), as indicated before. If Saul should be relieved by this development, his relief is shortsighted. On his own, without David and meanwhile also without Samuel, he will not be able to withstand the Philistines.

The long story in 1 Sam 28 brings us very close to Saul's end. The Philistines are marching in full force into the Jezreel Valley. In great fear "Saul inquired of Yhwh (וישאל שאול), but Yhwh did not answer."[16] None of the trusted tools of revelation—dreams, lots, prophetic oracles—work (28:2–6). The fact that there is no contact with the other world drives Saul to pursue illegal means of communication. The text clearly states that Saul had eradicated necromancers and fortunetellers from the land at an earlier point in time; now, however, he tries to find a necromancer (28:3, 7). We see a familiar pattern: Saul generally wants to do what is right but always does what is wrong in a time of crisis. Our rejection of this action is mixed with compassion for an individual who feels betrayed by the entire world, who has lost his most important supporters, and who now is also obviously abandoned by God.

Saul goes to the necromancer in Endor, at night and incognito, thus betraying his guilty conscience. He "swears in the name of Yhwh" to the fearful and distrustful woman: "As Yhwh lives, no punishment will come upon you for this thing" (1 Sam 28:10). He who is already burdened with guilt is willing also to take the blame in this matter.[17] The woman is actually able to call the prophet up from the realm of the dead. In response to Samuel's question as to Saul's motivation, Saul's entire desperation breaks out of him: "I am in great distress, for the Philistines are warring against me, and God has turned away from me and answers me no more, either by prophets or by dreams; so I have summoned you to tell me what I should do" (28:15). The king is as helpless as a child, waiting for someone to take his hand and lead him out of his desperate situation. He shows no more pride, no more self-assertion, not even anger. He is a tragic figure who had tried to be all things to all people, to God, to his surroundings, to himself, and who acted wrongly at every turn.

Saul receives the desired oracle, but it is not what he had hoped. It is so crushing that the king falls full length onto the ground. He also had not eaten for a very long time, the narrator tells us. Saul, weak and discouraged, is a symbol for his defenselessness and approaching death. He owes it to the nec-

---

16. Unlike Saul, two spiritual mentors support David: the priest Abiathar, son successor to Ahimelech, who was murdered by Saul; and Gad, a prophet. David is thus able to "inquire" of God anytime (שאל: 1 Sam 23:2, 4; cf. 30:8 and already 22:10, 13, 15).

17. The text is not clear on whether Saul allows the woman to lead him into idolatry (see Reis).

romancer that he is even able to rise again in order courageously to go into battle, to his certain death.

Saul's end as described in 1 Sam 31 is worthy of him. The Philistines attack the Israelite troops, drive them out the Jezreel Valley up to the hills of Gilboah, and cause heavy casualties. Then the Philistines pursue "Saul and his sons" and kill "Jonathan and Abinadab and Malchishua, the sons of Saul" (31:1–2). The narrator reports the events from a bird's-eye view. We cannot see details and do not know if or how Saul perceived and reacted to the death of his sons. But we do observe how the cruel events focus on him alone: "The battle pressed hard upon Saul; the archers found him, and he trembled before them."[18]

This final scene of Saul's life is quite revealing and can stand as a symbol for his entire life. Saul sees himself alone and defenseless, surrounded by enemies. His sword and spear do not reach far enough; his enemies can strike at a distance, wound him from afar, and kill him without him being able to strike back. Samuel, David, the priests, the Benjaminites, and the Philistines: an eerie and unseizable superiority places Saul in a state of isolation. He is fighting a desperate and hopeless battle that can end only with his death. Thus we hear him say to his armorbearer: "Draw your sword and thrust me through with it, so that these uncircumcised may not come and thrust me through and make sport of me." When his armorbearer refuses to comply, Saul falls onto his own sword, and his armorbearer follows his example (1 Sam 29:1; 31:1–6).

The behavior of this armorbearer, who stands by his lord until the end and then loyally follows him into death, is actually a faint ray of light in the tragic tale of Saul. But we are suddenly shocked by the thought that *David* himself fulfilled this role until his escape from Saul's court. What would have happened if *he* had stood beside Saul in this last hour? Would he have dealt the deathblow? In any case, he would have died at Saul's side, and not only Saul's but also his story would have come to an end. His story, however, is not over, because Saul had chased his former armorbearer into the Judean desert and finally *to the Philistines*. Once again we are struck by this fact: Would the Philistines have been able to beat Saul and Israel if David had been against them? Did they succeed only because David was *with* them? By his descrip-

---

18. The Septuagint reads ויחל not as חיל "be in anguish, tremble, writhe" but as חלה "be sick, weak, wounded" and adds the expression "under the ribs." Thus the archers would already have struck Saul, whereas the Hebrew text indicates that he feared being struck. Even if the latter version is correct, this does not mean that this depiction of Saul's death constitutes a pro-Davidic slander of Saul (see Barrick).

tion of Saul's death and David's involvement or noninvolvement, the narrator gives us much food for thought.

The death of Israel's first king and the way it is described confronts us inevitably with a feeling of trepidation. Saul's death is a heroic death. The hero has come to the end of his road, but he himself decides how he will go. By choosing his own death, he denies his enemies a cheap triumph. With great contempt, he denies them their revenge. The sorrow over the death of Saul, however, also includes the sorrow of the many who died with him, last but not least his sons. With great sadness, but without surprise, considering all that has gone before, we take notice that this king was not capable of protecting himself, his family, or his people from Israel's enemies. The narrators clearly spread out the entire scope of this defeat on Mount Gilboa: the Israelite population of all cities in the Jezreel Valley must flee and leave their land behind for the Philistines—a kind of "ethnic cleansing" (1 Sam 31:7). Even though the Philistines could not kill Saul themselves, they abuse his corpse. They cut his head off (just as David had done earlier with Goliath!), attach the body as a warning to the wall of Beth-shan, and send the head and the armor as "good news" to their idols and their people. Saul's armor (which David refused to wear in his battle against Goliath!) ends up in a pagan temple. Saul and Israel's humiliation could not have been worse. Behind all of these shocking events lurks the threatening question about the presence of God: Where was he when the Philistines defeated Israel? Is this the way he behaves when punishing the entire people for the mistakes and aberrations of an individual, even if it is the king? The same question came up in the context of Eli's evil sons and Israel's defeat at Ebenezer (1 Sam 4). The question has not yet been answered (and will not find an answer until David!).

It is but a small comfort when the narrators tell us that there were courageous men in the Transjordan area of Gilead who refused to accept the public display of Saul's corpse. They dared to go to Beth-shan, take the corpse, and bury it honorably near their hometown. During his lifetime Saul had rendered an outstanding service to Jabesh (see 1 Sam 11). He had also tried to be true to his people and their God. With his burial in Jabesh we see the end not of an evil person but of a tragic individual who had started tall and beautiful but who was not able to fulfill the high expectations and demands made upon him.

I.4.2.5. The Man without Heirs

Saul's story does not end with his death and burial. In ancient Israel, the story of a man was continued in his sons. Three of Saul's sons died with him in battle; a fourth son, Eshbaal, survived the family tragedy, however, and was placed on Saul's throne by the general Abner. Of greater importance is the fact that David was Saul's *son*-in-law according to the biblical account and that Saul had repeatedly referred to him as "*my son*" (1 Sam 24:17; 26:17, 21, 25). In addition, Saul had explicitly commended the fate of his bloodline to David (24:22). The biblical narrators thus set up an exciting play of perspectives between the heir designated by birth and the heir designated by God's predestination.

Following the death and burial of Saul, the narrative significantly shifts its attention to David. We are told in 2 Sam 1 how David reacted to the woeful report of Saul's death. An Amalekite is the messenger—together with Saul's crown and armlet. In response to David's questions, he states:

> I happened to be on Mount Gilboa, and there was Saul leaning on his spear, while the chariots and the horsemen drew close to him. When he looked behind him, he saw me and called to me. I answered, "Here sir." And he said to me, "Who are you?" I answered him, "I am an Amalekite." He said to me, "Come, stand over me and kill me, for convulsions have seized me, yet my life still lingers." So I stood over him, and killed him. (2 Sam 1:6–9)

This version of the tale deviates from the version told in 1 Sam 31 in several, but not in central, points. By placing the Amalekite's report in immediate succession to the version told in 1 Sam 31, the narrators probably intend to characterize the Amalekite as not quite honest—while simultaneously explaining how David came into possession of Saul's symbols of power. Regardless of the shady circumstances in which they were obtained, these artifacts point to Saul's true heir.

Before David gets ready to claim his succession, we observe how he pays final homage to the king and his biological heirs. He has the Amalekite who claimed to have dealt Saul his death blow killed (2 Sam 1:13–16). With his men he weeps "for Saul and for his son Jonathan, and for the people of Yhwh and for the house of Israel" (1:12). He composes a stirring elegy (1:19–27) praising Saul as a courageous and successful warrior, "swift" and "strong," who clothed "the daughters of Israel with crimson and gold." He further honors Saul by praising the people of Jabesh for their pious and loyal behavior toward Saul and promising them due reward (2:5–7).

Now the narrators shift our attention to those who claim Saul's throne by birth. "Abner son of Ner commander of Saul's army, had taken Eshbaal son of Saul and brought him over to Mahanaim. He made him king over … all Israel" (2 Sam 2:8–9). Eshbaal's reign is ill-fated from the beginning. In his ascent to the throne he seems like Abner's passive puppet; the text tells us, however, that he is not a child but a forty-year-old man (2:10). In the narratives that follow Abner is David's clear opponent, or rather the opponent of David's general, Joab. Eshbaal has nothing to say when his general wages war with the Judahite south (2:12–32). When the man in charge decides it is appropriate to have sexual relations with Rizpah, one of Saul's concubines, Eshbaal dares to protest; he obviously fears that this act is tantamount to claiming the throne. The following conflict between the two men is embarrassing for Eshbaal on a personal level; on a political level, it is a disaster. Abner rages at his king that he did not show "loyalty to the house of Saul" without reason, but now he himself would make sure that YHWH's promise to David would be fulfilled—an explicit announcement of high treason. "And Eshbaal could not answer Abner another word, because he feared him" (3:7–11). The creature bows before his maker.

Abner keeps his word. He sends messengers to David, saying, "To whom does the land belong? Make your covenant with me, and I will give you my support to bring all Israel over to you." As a service in return, David demands that "Michal, the daughter of Saul," be brought to him. Eshbaal meets this demand, which has at least as many political-dynastic implications as Abner's intercourse with Rizpah, without protest (2 Sam 3:12–16). He is as weak against David as he is against Abner.

We can summarize the rest of Saul's story quickly. Abner is killed by Joab, who sees in him a competitor and who still has a score to settle (2 Sam 3:20–30). Eshbaal is murdered by two of his officers who still have a score to settle with Saul (2 Sam 4). Other members of Saul's house are subsequently executed because the inhabitants of Gibeon still have a score to settle with Saul (2 Sam 21). After all the scores are settled,[19] only a cripple remains of the house of Saul, Jonathan's son Meribaal, yet he depends entirely on David's goodwill (2 Sam 9; 16; 19). In the end, Saul would indeed be without heir—except for David.

I.4.3. THE PORTRAIT OF DAVID

Bailey, Randall C. *David in Love and War: The Pursuit of Power in 2 Samuel 10–12* (JSOTSup 75; Sheffield: JSOT Press, 1990). **Bar-Efrat,** Shimon. "Literary Modes and Methods in the Biblical Narrative in View of 2 Sam 10–20 and 1 Kings 1–2," *Imm* 8 (1978): 19–31. **Berlin,** Adele. "Characterization in Biblical Narrative. David's Wives," *JSOT* 23 (1982): 69–85. **Brueggemann,** Walter. *David's Truth in Israel's Imagination and Memory* (2nd ed.; Minneapolis: Fortress, 2002). **Carlson,** R. A. *David the Chosen King: A Traditio-Historical Approach to the Second Book of Samuel*

---

19. Shimei and Sheba, both opponents to David (see 2 Sam 16; 19; 1 Kgs 2; 2 Sam 20), were Benjaminites and tied to Saul by tribal relations; moreover, Shimei was related to him by blood. Both of them met a violent death.

(Stockholm: Almqvist & Wiksell, 1964). **Clines,** David J. A., Tamara C. **Eskenazi,** eds. *Telling Queen Michal's Story. An Experiment in Comparative Interpretation* (JSOTSup 119; Sheffield: JSOT Press, 1991). **Coates,** William L. "A Study of David, the Thoroughly Human Man Who Genuinely Loved God," *RevExp* 99 (2002): 237–54. **Conroy,** Charles. *Absalom, Absalom! Narrative and Language in 2 Sam 13–20* (AnBib 81; Rome: Biblical Institute Press, 1978). **Dallmeyer,** Hans-Jürgen, and Walter **Dietrich.** *David—Ein Königsweg: Psychoanalytisch-theologischer Dialog über einen biblischen Entwicklungsroman* (Göttingen: Vandenhoeck & Ruprecht, 2002). **Deist,** F. E. "David, a Man after God's Heart? An Investigation into the David Character in the So-Called Succession Narrative," in *Studies in the Succession Narrative, OTWSA 27 (1984) and OTWSA 28 (1985): Old Testament Essays* (ed. W. C. van Wyk; Pretoria: n.p., 1986), 99–129. **Dietrich,** Walter. "Der Fall des Riesen Goliat: Biblische und nachbiblische Erzählversuche," in *Bibel und Literatur* (ed. Jürgen Ebach and Richard Faber; Munich: Fink, 1995), 241–58, repr. in idem, *Von David zu den Deuteronomisten: Studien zu den Geschichtsüberlieferungen des Alten Testaments* (BWANT 156; Stuttgart: Kohlhammer, 2002), 120–33. **Dietrich.** "Das biblische Bild der Herrschaft Davids," in idem, *Von David zu den Deuteronomisten: Studien zu den Geschichtsüberlieferungen des Alten Testaments* (BWANT 156; Stuttgart: Kohlhammer, 2002), 9–31. **Exum,** J. Cheryl. "Bathsheba Plotted, Shot, and Painted," *Semeia* 74 (1996): 47–73. **Fokkelman,** Jan P. King David (II Sam. 9–20 and I Kings 1–2 (vol. 1 of *Narrative Art and Poetry in the Books of Samuel: A Full Interpretation Based on Stylistic and Structural Analyses*; SSN 20; Assen: Van Gorcum, 1981). **Fokkelman.** *The Crossing Fates (I Sam. 13–31 and II Sam. 1)* (vol. 2 of *Narrative Art and Poetry in the Books of Samuel: A Full Interpretation Based on Stylistic and Structural Analyses*; SSN 23; Assen: Van Gorcum, 1986). **Gunn,** David M. *The Story of King David: Genre and Interpretation* (JSOTSup 6; Sheffield: JSOT Press, 1978). **Hagan,** Harry. "Deception as Motif and Theme in 2 Sm 9–20; 1 Kgs 1–2," *Bib* 60 (1979): 301–26. **Levenson,** Jon D. "1 Samuel 25 as Literature and as History," *CBQ* 41 (1978): 11–28. **Miscall,** Peter D. "Moses and David: Myth and Monarchy," in *The New Literary Criticism and the Hebrew Bible* (ed. J. Cheryl Exum and David J. A. Clines; JSOTSup 143; Sheffield: JSOT Press, 1993), 184–200. **Nicol,** George G. "Bathsheba: A Clever Woman?" *ExpTim* 99 (1988): 360–63. **Nicol.** "The Alleged Rape of Bathsheba: Some Observations on Ambiguity in Biblical Narratives," *JSOT* 73 (1997): 43–54. **Noll,** K. L. *The Faces of David* (JSOTSup 242; Sheffield: Sheffield Academic Press, 1997). **Polzin,** Robert. "Curses and Kings: A Reading of 2 Samuel 15–16," in *The New Literary Criticism and the Hebrew Bible* (ed. J. Cheryl Exum and David J. A. Clines; JSOTSup 143; Sheffield: JSOT Press, 1993), 201–26. **Polzin.** *David and the Deuteronomist: 2 Samuel* (Indiana Studies in Biblical Literature; Bloomington: Indiana University Press, 1993). **Schenker,** Adrian. *Der Mächtige im Schmelzofen des Mitleids: Eine Interpretation von 2 Sam 24* (OBO 42; Fribourg: Universitätsverlag; Göttingen: Vandenhoeck & Ruprecht, 1982). **Sternberg,** Meir. *The Poetics of Biblical Narrative: Ideological Literature and the Drama of Reading* (Bloomington: Indiana University Press, 1985), esp. 186–229. **Thompson,** J. A. "The Significance of the Verb Love in the David-Jonathan Narratives in 1 Samuel," *VT* 24 (1974): 334–38. **Trible,** Phyllis. *Texts of Terror: Literary-Feminist Readings of Biblical*

Narratives (OBT 13; Philadelphia: Fortress, 1984). **Yee,** Gale A. " 'Fraught with Background': Literary Ambiguity in II Samuel 11," *Int* 42 (1988): 240–53.

The biblical depiction of David's rise is closely intertwined with that of Saul's fall. Jan Fokkelman aptly titled his book on the subject *The Crossing Fates,* where the "crossing" refers to events not only on the horizontal plane but also on the vertical. With David, there is no fall after he has left Saul behind and won the kingship over Judah and Israel, at least not to the degree and depth as in Saul's case. True, David's star does not always shine with equal brightness; his later years especially are darkened by many shadows. But his light is never fully extinguished. No newcomer, not even a descendent of Saul, threatens his reign. What threats there are come from his own sons. David, however, remains on the throne almost until his death, at which time he sees the enduring dynasty promised to him take its course in his successor Solomon. He thus becomes the founder not only of a dynasty that lasted almost half a millennium but also of a never-waning myth of "eternal" rule that will shine again at the end of times in new glory: *David redivivus.*

I.4.3.1. Yнwн's Chosen One

When David enters the biblical narrative for the first time, he is described as "ruddy, with beautiful eyes and handsome" (1 Sam 16:12). Yнwн did not choose his older, taller brothers—on the contrary: as he did with Saul, he *rejects* them!—but rather this youngest and seemingly most tender of the sons of Jesse (16:6–11). We do not discover what David feels when Samuel anoints him (16:13), but we are told that "the spirit of Yнwн came mightily upon David from that day forward." With David, the "spirit" is not the fleeting, disquieting presence it was with Saul; in his life, the spirit is a reliable force to be reckoned with.

When David comes to Saul's court in order to alleviate the king's seizures brought on by the "evil spirit," he is characterized as "skillful in playing, a man of valor, a warrior, prudent in speech, and a man of good presence" (1 Sam 16:18)—in short, a noble knight in shining armor. The following statement closes this characterization: "And Yнwн was with him." This statement is a central motif that will occur throughout the following narratives. David's personal talents and abilities are not so important, but rather the fact that God goes with him. There is no other way that the narrators could understand this man's strangely convoluted yet goal-oriented life story; there is no other way in which the reader is supposed to understand it either.

The next narrative, telling us of David and Goliath, introduces David a second time (1 Sam 17:12–14)—as if the introduction in 16:12, 18 had not occurred. Following David's surprising victory, Saul asks long-winded questions about who this man is and calls him to his court—as if this had not already happened in 16:14–23. The biblical narrators surely noticed the differences between these three traditions, but they seemingly did not bother them. All of the traditions emphasize certain facets of David's character that we are supposed to view together and combine into one whole picture. First, he is the anointed of God (and noble and handsome as well); then, he is the gifted musician (and courageous, intelligent, and handsome); finally, he is the stout-hearted and pious warrior (and, once again, "a ruddy young man and handsome," 17:42).

David's victory over Goliath lays the foundation for his fame as warrior victorious over the Philistines. The way he is suddenly thrown into the decisive battle that determines Israel's fate, the way he is outraged at the impudence of the Philistine challenger, the way he does not allow anyone, least of all his older brother, to stand in his way, the way he works his way to Saul and gains his permission for single combat—all this characterizes him as an unselfconscious and high-spirited young man who has his heart in the right place and fears none. His victory over the heavily armed Goliath, and how he achieves this victory, is special even among heroic deeds. True, the biblical narrators do not suppress the information that a certain "Elhanan, son of Jaare from Bethlehem, killed Goliath of Gath, the shaft of whose spear was like a weaver's beam" (2 Sam 21:19). There can be no doubt that this Goliath and the warrior in 1 Sam 17 are the same,[20] yet we can doubt this in the case of Elhanan and David. This ambiguity is most likely intended and conveys to us that even David should not grow too large in our imagination.

The narrators expend much effort trying to portray David as a *shepherd*. Already in 1 Sam 16:11 and 19 Samuel calls him from the herd. In 1 Sam 17 he enters the action as a shepherd boy, tells Saul of his mighty deeds against wild animals (17:34–36), and defeats Goliath with a shepherd's sling. The metaphor of the shepherd is a standard element in the repertoire of ancient Near Eastern royal ideology. The victory over wild animals symbolizes the extensive power of the king as well as hi task to fight against the powers of evil and chaos in order to bring peace and wealth to his "herd." David's victory over Goliath already shows that this young man is capable of and predestined for royal office.

---

20. He, too, carries a spear, the shaft of which was like a weaver's beam (1 Sam 17:7). Is it a coincidence that Saul's favorite weapon was just such a spear (חנית), that Saul's armor (17:38–39) reminds us of Goliath's armor (17:5–6), and that both these warriors were known for their extraordinary size? The small and agile David is the antitype to both Saul and Goliath.

In his two speeches to Saul and Goliath, the narrators portray David as a deeply pious individual. To Saul he says: "Yhwh, who saved me from the paw of the lion and from the paw of the bear, will save me from the hand of this Philistine." As if saying his amen, Saul answers, "Go, and may Yhwh be with you!" (17:37). As the narrative continues, we see clearly that David believes that he owes everything he does to divine assistance—and not to his own courage or his expertise with a sling. To Goliath he says, "You come to me with sword and spear and javelin; but I come to you in the name of Yhwh of hosts ... and all this assembly may know that Yhwh does not save by sword and spear, for the battle is Yhwh's, and he will give you into our hand" (17:45, 47). The man who defeats Goliath is as much preacher as he is warrior, and he does not preach militarism but trust in God. God is not *with him* because he has weapons, but precisely because he does not.

The new hero begins almost magically to attract people from Saul's court and from all of Israel. *Saul loves* him (1 Sam 16:21), *Jonathan loves* him (18:1, 3; 20:17), *Michal loves* him (18:20), *all of Israel and Judah loves* him (18:16, 28; see also 18:22 and the women's song in 18:7). These are all unusual statements, unusual for the king, the crown prince, the king's daughter—for an oriental woman in general!—as for the subjects of the king. The Hebrew verb used here, אהב, can express different things: the emotional, erotic relationship between two lovers; or a functional, political connection to a valued and honored partner, such as the relation between a subject to his liege lord (see Thompson). The narrators do not tell us which meaning they intend in each particular case. It is noticeable that David receives "love" from all sides, but it is never stated that David himself loved someone. Is he modest—or self-centered or cold-hearted?

Nothing stands in the way of David's rise (1 Sam 18) from armorbearer to officer and finally to the son-in-law of the king. Very soon Saul is pretty sure that this is the one who was foretold to take over the throne. David knows that he was anointed and will be king someday, but he does not know if Saul is aware of this. He grows suspicious of Saul's harsh and hostile behavior; he can understand this behavior merely as a result of Saul's growing illness or the outcome of injured vanity—Saul's words and the narrative structure allow this possibility. He thus does not understand right away that his life is in danger. Otherwise he would not innocently continue to make music for Saul or accept the various tasks Saul gives him, as suicidal as they may be. More sensitive readers may be concerned, however, that David sheds blood all too easily. Or should we give him credit for thinking that this may be the path that God is leading him on toward the kingship? Does he interpret the love of Jonathan, Michal, and the people as promising harmony that will eventually lift him to the throne? Unlike David, the readers are fully informed of Saul's evil intentions and suspect that there will be no peaceful and uncomplicated transition from Saul's kingship to David.

I.4.3.2. Saul's Opponent

After Saul throws his spear at David and thus attempts to kill him for the second time, David flees from Saul's presence. He must realize by now that his relationship to Saul is a matter of life and death. According to the biblical depiction, this seems to have been a traumatic experience for David. The plan he had pursued until now and that had seemed to lead him to his goal cannot continue. Instead, "David flees the very same night" (1 Sam 19:10). These verbs—first נוס and מלט, later ברח—describe the central issue of the following chapters: David flees from Saul.

His first goal is the nearby house that he shares with his wife Michal. She, however, is also Saul's daughter, and we must ask the fearful question: Whose side will Michal prove to be on: her father's or her husband's? She sides with David and assists him when she notices Saul's men outside her door. "So Michal let David down through the window; he fled away and escaped" (1 Sam 19:11–12). The two separate quickly and wordlessly. The narrator will take careful note how they later come back together only to lose each other for good. We have a similar case with Jonathan and David. The biblical narrators show great art in how they weave different narrative strands into the story as a whole, submerging them for a while, only to have them resurface, develop, disappear again, resurface once more, and finally come to an end. In their narrative technique, the books of Samuel resemble an artful quilt. The overall structure is incredibly fascinating, and even though the various narrative strands are not distributed equally throughout, the effect of the whole is that of a well-balanced composition.

The narrator first accompanies David in his escape route. Leaving Michal, he "fled and escaped" to Samuel at Ramah (19:18). An old issue resurfaces here: the relation between Samuel and David, on the one hand, and the relation between Samuel and Saul, on the other. As soon as Saul hears where David has gone, he sends his men to arrest him. A failed attempt is followed by a second and a third attempt until Saul finally goes himself. Even the king, however, is unable to apprehend his adversary, because David is protected by Samuel, or more precisely by the "spirit of God" (19:19–24). "And David fled from Ramah" (20:1).

Now the narrators pick up a different narrative strand: the relation between Jonathan and David as well as the relation between Jonathan and Saul. The two friends meet, and David lets Jonathan know that Saul seriously intends to take his life (1 Sam 20:1). Jonathan finds it hard to believe what David is saying, but he is willing to follow David's request, investigate the situation, and report back to him. The speech given by Jonathan in this context is interesting (20:13–16). Should it become necessary that David flee for good, Jonathan wishes that "Yнwн be with you as he was with my father." This, too, is a well-known motif: God's presence with David, expressed by Jonathan of all people, who explicitly compares David to Saul. In an attempt to remain loyal to his father, he states that Saul's relationship to God *is* intact. He does not say more; he asks David for the future, however, that David show *loyalty* (חסד) to him and his descendents "once Yнwн seeks out the enemies of David." We have an idea who David's fiercest enemy is[21] and that Jonathan has thus pronounced judgment on his father without intending to do so. Shortly afterwards, he also learns that Saul wants David dead. His protest is useless, even dangerous (20:25–40). Jonathan warns David, and the two men say farewell with kisses and tears (20:41–42; finally David shows emotion!).

"David came to Nob" (1 Sam 21:1). He fabricates a story that he is on an urgent and secret mission from the king and in need of provisions and weapons. As nothing else is available, David receives the holy bread and Goliath's sword, which is apparently stored at this sanctuary. The Edomite Doeg, a servant of Saul, witnesses the transaction (21:8)—and shortly afterwards all of the priests of Nob are dead (1 Sam 22). A single son of Ahimelech, Abiathar, "escapes" the massacre and "flees after David" (22:20). David hears what has happened and confesses: "I knew on that day, when Doeg the Edomite was there, that he would surely tell Saul. I am responsible[22] for the lives of all your father's house" (22:22). David confesses something that he could never have been accused of. At the same time, he takes Abiathar under his protection, gaining a prominent priest among his followers. Even this disaster thus results in good fortune for David. Still, the fate of the priests of Nob throws a dark shadow over David.

David now adjusts to life as a fugitive and vagabond. He gathers around him "everyone who was in distress, and everyone who was in debt and everyone who was discontented gathered to him, and he became captain over them" (1 Sam 22:2). He soon commands about four hundred men. With their help, he liberates or occupies Keilah, a city in the southwest of Judah that had been occupied by the Philistines. Will he now settle down and become a city-king? Saul prevents this option by forcing David to retreat back into the

---

21. Saul, after all, has already called David his "enemy" (איב, 1 Sam 19:17). He is subsequently called "David's enemy," even if not by David himself (24:5, 20; 26:8; Saul is also included in 25:22, 26, 29; 2 Sam 7:9).

22. The text uses the same verb that was used for the action of Doeg the executioner (סבב בי)

Judean wasteland (23:1–13). Saul continues to pursue him there (23:14, 19–28). Like a *deus ex machina* Jonathan appears in the midst of this conflict and encourages his friend: "Do not be afraid, for the hand of my father Saul shall not find you; you shall be king over Israel, and I shall be second to you; my father Saul also knows that this is so" (23:17). David receives this statement silently, even though it contains important new information. No one yet has told him this explicitly that he will become *king*. He himself may have started to doubt this calling because of Saul's incessant pursuit. It is remarkable that he receives confirmation of his calling from a member of Saul's family. At the same time, this indicates clearly to David that Saul as well as Jonathan must know of his calling but that the king, unlike the crown prince, is not willing to accept God's plans. Jonathan's visit and statement make it very clear to David and to the reader that the situation is a matter of life and death. The two friends part in peace by making "a covenant before Yhwh" (23:18). They will never see each other again.

The three chapters 1 Sam 24–26 form a kind of triptych. The similar narratives relating how Saul is spared connect the outer texts (1 Sam 24; 26). The middle text consists of a portrait of David, Nabal, and Abigail (1 Sam 25). The text describes how David tries to secure a living for himself and his men—and gains insight and a wife. With deliberate politeness and yet noticeable pressure, David requests of Nabal a share of the profit from the sheep shearing; after all, he did make sure that nothing unfortunate happened to Nabal's herds and shepherds. We cannot deny a certain Mafiosi flavor when ten (!) men convey David's message to Nabal. Nabal, who is introduced to us as a stingy and foolish individual, reacts harshly: "Who is David, and who is the son of Jesse? There are many servants who have torn away from their master" (25:10). In David's case, this is not far from the truth and therefore all the more insulting. David hears this statement and leaves the camp with his four hundred men on a vendetta. On the way he swears that "until morning he will not leave anything of Nabal's that can piss against a wall" (25:21–22)—surely an unrefined sentiment even in the eyes of the narrators. He has hardly uttered this oath when Abigail, Nabal's beautiful and intelligent wife, confronts him. She has been warned by her servants, has gathered bountiful gifts for David, and has hurried to meet him. Now she speaks to him with an impressive display of rhetorical finesse, argumentative clarity, and prophetic illumination (25:24–31). Her three main points are: (1) God will make David king; (2) God will eliminate David's enemies (a very transparent reference both to Nabal and to Saul); (3) David should not become guilty by shedding innocent blood and live to regret this action. Abigail emphasizes her words not only with the gifts she presents to David—a kind of anticipated material tribute to the king—but by offering herself: "When Yhwh has dealt well with my lord, then remember your maiden" (25:31). David will accept this offer. As soon as Nabal has died—indeed, a natural death—and has been mourned appropriately by Abigail, David takes her as his wife. Thus the story concludes with a private happy end. More important for the continuing narrative, however, is the fact that Abigail has prevented David from massacring the men in her household, even teaching him a lesson in the incompatibility of divine election and guidance and personal lust for vengeance.

In the two surrounding narratives, 1 Sam 24 and 26, the biblical narrators demonstrate that David has understood this lesson. Following Abigail's lesson, David acts with less violence than in his earlier encounter with Saul. In 1 Sam 24 David does cut off a piece of Saul's cloak after his comrades encourage him to kill Saul—and is immediately plagued by a guilty conscience (24:5b, 6). In 1 Sam 26 his companion Abishai offers to kill the sleeping Saul. David responds: "Who can raise his hand against YHWH's anointed, and be guiltless? … As YHWH lives, YHWH will strike him down!" (26:8–10). The previous text had used this expression (נגף with God as subject) to denote the death of Nabal. We see: David has understood. He does not touch Saul, not even his cloak; instead, he only takes his spear and his water jar, which he needs to prove his innocence to Saul. David's last words to Saul state: "As your life was precious today in my sight, so may my life be precious in the sight of YHWH, and may he rescue me from all tribulation" (26:23–24). David no longer will rely on Saul, who has deceived and disappointed him so often, but only on God. This trust in God, so the narrators signal to us, allows him now to take an extremely risky and momentous step: the defection to the Philistines.

It is witness to the narrative art of the text that we have already once learned of a similar attempt. Following his brief stopover in Nob, David "rose" and "fled" from Saul to Achish, the king of Gath (1 Sam 21:11). There the Philistines remembered the victory song of the women according to which Saul had slain thousands and David tens of thousands of Philistines. David was quick-witted enough to feign madness, or rather epilepsy—with the result that Achish decided he had enough crazy men around him and had him deported (21:12–16).

After this experience, it must have been incredibly hard for David to try his luck again in Philistine territory. The narrator allows us an insight into his thoughts. "I shall now perish one day by the hand of Saul; there is nothing better for me than to escape to the land of the Philistines; then Saul will despair of seeking me any longer within the borders of Israel, and I shall escape out of his hand" (27:1). Saul's murderous rivalry does not leave him with a choice. He has to move from the frying pan into the fire. As readers, we are led to the conclusion that David does not side with the national enemy because of lack of character or pure opportunism but rather because of unmitigated adversity. "When Saul was told that David had fled to Gath, he no longer sought for him" (27:4). David's plan worked. Saul may have thought the same of his plans, but he was mistaken, as he was soon to find out.

Achish of Gath was also mistaken about David. We are surprised that this time he does not consider David to be dangerous or mad, but even grants him a city in which to live, Ziklag (1 Sam 27:6). Achish does not have a bad memory. Important developments have meanwhile changed the situation. The first time David came alone (21:11), but this time he brings six hundred men with him (27:2); back then David had just fled from Saul, but meanwhile he had proven himself to be a tough opponent. The Philistines may have thought that they had found a valuable combatant in their struggle against Saul and Israel. Instead of striking out into the Judean Negev (Saul's territory, in the eyes of the narrators), however, as Achish had told him to, David raids Israel's (and Judah's) enemies in the far south, never taking prisoners, in order to keep his actions hidden from Achish (27:8–11).

While the Philistine king "believed" that David "had become odious to his people," David was successful in spreading his fame as a successful and generous warlord among his people at home. In 1 Sam 30:26–31 we find a list of towns and alliances in the Judahite south who benefited from David's particularly successful raids. In this manner, the narrators show us that even in exile David was able to gain sympathy at home and shrewdly prepare his return. A further intention, even more important, aims to separate David from Philistine interests as much as possible. This becomes all the more important as the final battle between Saul and the Philistines is about to take place. The narrators take much care in driving home the point that David had *nothing* to do with this battle and Saul's death—even though he was a vassal and follower of a Philistine king during this time.

Chapter 29 addresses this precarious issue directly. Achish, along with the other Philistine kings, is arming his troops against Israel, and David is obligated to assist him. Then something interesting happens: it is not David who refuses to honor his obligation; the other Philistine kings refuse to go into battle with him. *They* now cite the victory song of the Israelite woman, according to which Saul has killed thousands and David tens of thousands (29:3–5), and persuade Achish to send David away to fight against Amalek instead of Israel. The readers must understand: while the final battle is taking place in the north of Israel, David is fighting Israel's hereditary enemy in the far south. The text also suggests something else: if David had marched north, who knows if he would not have turned against the other hereditary enemy, the Philistines, and thus changed the entire outcome of the battle of Gilboa! In this sense, David's protest against his exclusion from battle is ingeniously ambiguous: "But what have I done?" he asks. "What have you found against your servant...? Why can't I go and fight against the enemies of my lord the king?" (1 Sam 29:8). Achish has not *found* anything that David *has done*; Achish also does not know that David used to address Saul as his "lord the king" (1 Sam 24:9; 26:17), so he does not suspect that the *enemies* David wants to fight against might actually not be Achish's enemies, the Israelites, but Saul's enemies, the Philistines. David presents himself openly as a "fifth column" even though Achish does not realize what is happening. David's ruse, however, does not work. Achish generously affirms him: "I know that you have been as pleasing in my eyes as an angel of God"—what brilliant narrative irony!—but he insists that the mistrust of the other Philistine lords prevents him from taking David along. Thus, David is prevented from assisting Saul and Israel in the decisive battle against the Philistines. It is consequently not David's fault when Saul's worst fear actually comes true: he meets his doom because of his opponent David.

I.4.3.3. The Ruler of Israel

Saul and three of his sons die during the battle of Gilboa. A short time later Abner, Saul's uncle and the center of power in Saul's continuing kingdom, and Eshbaal, Saul's son and Abner's protégé on the throne, die a violent death. The (assumed) last member of the house of Saul, Jonathan's son Meribaal, is not capable of office due to an unfortunate accident. The biblical narrators do not conceal that all these factors contributed to David's rise as ruler over Israel. At the same time, they emphasize that David was not at all involved in or culpable of these events.[23] Several narratives in 2 Sam 1–9 deal with this issue.

---

23. It has become fashionable to blame David for all of these deaths (see, e.g., P. Kyle McCarter Jr., "The Apology of David," *JBL* 99 [1980]: 499–504; James C. VanderKam, "Davidic Complicity in the Deaths of Abner and Eshbaal: A Historical and Redactional Study," *JBL* 99 [1980]: 521–39; Steven L. McKenzie, *King David: A Biography* [Oxford: Oxford University Press, 2000]; Baruch Halpern, *David's Secret Demons: Messiah, Murderer, Traitor, King* (Grand Rapids: Eerdmans, 2001). In doing so, the biblical narratives are taken too quickly and, in the end, naïvely to be historical accounts. Blaming David also shifts the emphasis of the biblical intention to promote nonviolence (see below IV.5) to what is already all-pervasive in history and the present: violent action. Alexander A. Fischer criticizes such a "hermeneutics of suspicion" in his very noteworthy article, "David unter Tatverdacht—Zur Hermeneutik der Verdächtigung," in idem, *Von Hebron nach Jerusalem: Eine redaktionsgeschichtliche Studie zur Erzählung von König David in II Sam 1–5* (BZAW 335; Berlin: de Gruyter, 2004), 188–93; see also the wise objection by David A. Bosworth, "Evaluating King David: Old Problems and Recent Scholarship," *CBQ* 68 (2006): 191–210.

When a young man—of all people, an Amalekite!—comes to David with Saul's royal insignia and claims to have granted Saul his final wish and dealt him his death blow, David reacts on two levels: he mourns with heart-rending emotion and holds the Amalekite responsible. He lashes out at him, "Were you not afraid to lift your hand to destroy Yнwн's anointed?" What David never allowed himself or his men, this man (apparently) did; for this he must die (2 Sam 1:14–16).

Not long afterwards, two officers come to David with Eshbaal's severed head and hope to reap praise and a reward from David. He, however, makes an explicit connection to the Amalekite and has them killed immediately. Eshbaal's head receives a proper burial (2 Sam 4:8–12).

The narrators distance David from Abner's murder in several ways. Their background story tells of a breach between Abner and Eshbaal and Abner's attempts to persuade Israel to join David's kingdom (2 Sam 3:6–19). Abner then comes to David personally and promises to bring Israel under his leadership; "and David dismissed Abner, and he went away in peace" (בשלום, 3:21). We find out later that Joab was not present during these negotiations. When he comes back from a military action and discovers what has happened, he storms to David, accuses him bitterly, sends messengers after Abner, has him brought back, and knifes him in the belly (3:22–27).

David plays no part in these events; he is only the object of Joab's wrath. Now we notice, however, that he does not respond to the accusations of his general at all. Does he signal his silent assent to Joab's words and actions? Perhaps the narrators want to indicate that Joab may have interpreted David's silence along these lines; they do not allow the readers to follow this line of reasoning by placing the following words in David's mouth after he has learned of Joab's actions: "I and my kingdom are forever innocent before Yнwн concerning the blood of Abner son of Ner" (2 Sam 3:28). He follows this claim of innocence with an imprecation of Joab and "the house of his father." This phrase includes Joab's brother Abishai; both brothers, so the narrators inform us, had a score to settle with Abner, because he had killed their youngest brother Asael in battle, provoking a bloody vendetta (2:18–23). David explicitly blames Joab and Abishai, both referred to as "sons of Zeruiah" after their mother (and not their father!), once more at the end of the eulogy for Abner. "These men, the sons of Zeruiah, are too violent for me. Yнwн pay back the one who does wickedly in accordance with his wickedness!" (3:39). The blame for Abner's death is clearly shifted away from David onto Joab and Abishai. Both men play the violent part in subsequent narratives, a part that David definitely does not play. In this distribution of roles, we can clearly sense the apologetic desire of the biblical narrators.

David is outraged over these events. He demands that "Joab [!] and all the people" put on sackcloth, and he himself walks behind the bier to the burial; he weeps aloud at Abner's grave, and "the people wept also" (2 Sam 3:31–32). After David sings a brief and moving lament, "the people wept for him even more" (3:34). Then the people urge David to eat, but David decides to fast until nightfall. "And the people took notice and were pleased." This is repeated to make sure that nobody misses the point: "Indeed, everything the king did pleased them. So on that day all the people and all Israel knew that the king had no part in the murder of Abner son of Ner" (3:36–37).

David's own behavior toward members of the house of Saul is demonstrated in his treatment of Jonathan's son Meribaal. He asks first himself and then a servant of the house of Saul: "Is there anyone still left of the house of Saul to whom I can show kindness for Jonathan's sake?" (2 Sam 9:1, 3). Meribaal is brought to him, and David declares: "Do not be afraid"—the narrators indicate that Meribaal could indeed have been afraid after all that had happened—"I will show you kindness for the sake of your father Jonathan." His words are followed by action as he restores Saul's hereditary lands to Meribaal—this is the first time we learn that they were confiscated—and invites him to dine at the royal table from now on (9:7). Meribaal, who is paralyzed in both legs, accepts the offer with oriental politeness and remains henceforth at David's court, whether he likes it or not.

The situation, however, is not only filled with harmony. Meribaal and his estate manager Ziba will attempt to cause political upheaval at a later point (2 Sam 16:1–4; 19:25–31). Meribaal also has a young son, Mica, as the text explicitly states. His young and obviously healthy existence will definitely outlive David (9:12). We also find out from the appendix to the books of Samuel that David was more implicated in the deaths of at least seven more members of the house of Saul than supporters of David would care to acknowledge (2 Sam 21). Most important, there still remains a woman from the house of Saul. During the negotiations with Abner, the narrators have David demand that "Michal, daughter of Saul," be surrendered to him. Just as Saul had *given* Michal to Paltiel following David's escape, so Eshbaal now *takes her away* from him again (3:14–15). We hear nothing of her fate on David's side—until she reappears once more in 6:16, 20–23 in an emotional dispute with David, only then to disappear for good. David is about to bring the ark of the covenant into Jerusalem in a festive procession, "when Michal, daughter of Saul, saw king David leaping and dancing before Yhwh, and she despised him in her heart." She receives David with cutting sarcasm when he returns home. "How the king of Israel honored himself today, uncovering himself today before the eyes of his servants' maids, as any vulgar fellow might shamelessly uncover himself!" (6:16, 20). Michal's sarcasm is motivated by political and personal reasons that are not shared by the narrators. They have David retort with great acridness that he enjoys being regarded by the maids and rejoicing before Yʜᴡʜ, "who chose me in place of your father and all his household, to appoint me as prince over Israel, the people of Yʜᴡʜ" (6:21–22). Michal does not respond—and bears no children from David: one more blow against the house of Saul.[24]

The first part of 2 Samuel tells us not only of the fall of the house of Saul and David's innocence in this matter; it also reports positively David's activities leading to the establishment and consolidation of his kingdom. Guided by an oracle, he resettles his family and his troops from Ziklag to Hebron and allows the Judahites to anoint him king (2 Sam 2:1–4). According to the biblical account, his first official act consists of sending a diplomatic letter to the people of Jabesh-gilead, a city that has proven itself to be especially pro-Saul and is also situated in Eshbaal's territory (2:4–7). In a long and grueling war, David (or rather his general Joab) destabilizes Eshbaal's kingdom (2:12–32; the end of the war is summarized by the narrator: "David grew stronger and stronger, while the house of Saul grew weaker and weaker," 3:1). In negotiations with Abner, David attempts to draw the Israelite north into his sphere of influence (2 Sam 3). This proves successful, as one day the "tribes of Israel," or rather their "elders," come to Hebron, sign a contract with him, and anoint him to be their king (5:1–3). David then gains Jerusalem, lying between Israel and Judah, for himself, expands the city, builds a palace, and takes up permanent residence (5:6–12). Politically well-chosen marriage ties draw the various regions of his kingdom to him and bless him with many sons (3:2–5; 5:13–16)—not unimportant for someone who is to found a dynasty. An obstacle emerges through the Philistines. When they hear that David has been anointed king, they apply military pressure (5:17—it seems they are still strong enough!), as they had with Saul. David must withdraw to his "mountain stronghold" (see 1 Sam 24:23), but two battles, guided by an oracle, eliminate the Philistine threat once and for all (2 Sam 5:18–25).

As a result, David's kingdom is stable and secure. Three chapters follow, each quite different, but each of momentous importance.

---

24. The text does not explain why she remains without child. Did she refuse David, or did David refuse her? According to 2 Sam 21:8 (ᴍᴛ), Michal did have children: five sons—but hardly from David. The Septuagint replaces "Michal" with "Merab" in order to avoid the tension. Hypotheses regarding the relation between these two texts are found in Hans-Joachim Stoebe, "David und Mikal: Zur Jugendgeschichte Davids," in idem, *Geschichte, Schicksal, Schuld und Glaube* (BBB 72; Frankfurt am Main: Athenäum, 1989), 224–43; and Otto Kaiser, "David und Jonathan: Tradition, Redaktion und Geschichte in I Sam 16–20: Ein Versuch," *ETL* 66 (1990): 281–96.

(1) 2 Sam 6: According to the biblical account, David was keenly interested in bringing the ark as a symbol of Yhwh's presence to his new place of
residence. After an initial failed attempt, the plan succeeds by honoring the
cultic object with the appropriate rituals.

(2) 2 Sam 7: David entertains the understandable thought of building a
temple for the ark, which had been housed in a tent up to this point. After
all, Yhwh should not be living in worse conditions than the king (7:1–2).
The prophet Nathan first affirms David's plans but is moved to change his
mind by a nighttime revelation of God. Like Samuel with Saul, but not at all
as harsh, Nathan opposes David, yet with ultimately positive intentions. He
surprises the king with an oracle promising him a dynasty:

> When your days are fulfilled and you lie down with your ancestors, I will
> raise up your offspring after you, who shall come forth from your body, and
> I will establish his kingdom. He shall build a house for my name, and I will
> establish the throne of his kingdom forever. I will be a father to him, and
> he shall be a son to me. When he commits iniquity, I will punish him with
> a rod such as mortals use, with blows inflicted by human beings. But I will
> not take my steadfast love from him, as I took it from Saul, whom I put away
> from before you. Your house and your kingdom shall be made sure forever
> before me; your throne shall be established forever. (7:12–16)[25]

(3) 2 Sam 8: The chapter offers a summary of David's victories over the
surrounding nations. He consistently appears as the only actor; neither his
army nor Joab are mentioned. The text emphasizes twice, however, that
"Yhwh helped David wherever he went" (8:6, 14). God and the king work
hand in hand, thus making Israel the dominant power in Syro-Palestine. The
success on the outside is matched by success on the inside: "David was king
over all Israel, and David administered equity and justice to all the people"
(8:15). Almost as further emphasis, the text presents a list of David's most
important officials and their functions, most likely with the aim of showing
the high degree of organization in David's state (8:16–18). If we compare
these statements with the similar summary of Saul's reign in 1 Sam 14:47–
52, we see how much poorer and weaker Saul's kingdom was in comparison
to David's.

---

25. The question, deliberated at length before this oracle is pronounced, why David
did not already build a temple in Jerusalem (2 Sam 7:1–11a) seems to be a Deuteronomistic addition, just as is David's lengthy prayer that follows (2 Sam 7:18–29).

I.4.3.4. The Founder of a Dynasty

Of the seventeen sons of David who appear in the two lists 2 Sam 3:2–5 and 5:13–15, it will be the tenth who will succeed David on the throne. The circumstances surrounding his birth are told in 2 Sam 10–12. The political context is the military conflicts east of the Jordan; the description of these encounters (10:1–11:1, 12:26–31) forms a framework around the actual birth story of Solomon.

In 2 Sam 10, David is described as a king who is forced into battle by an upstart and aggressive neighbor (10:1–5). The Israelites are able to defeat the Ammonites and their treaty partners, the Arameans, in a succession of battles (10:6–19). In the following year, David sends Joab with the troops to force capitulation from the Ammonites (11:1). Their land is conquered, their capital city taken (12:26). Once the capitulation is a mere formality, Joab sends for David, who leads "all the people," takes the city, deposes the king, and enslaves its inhabitants (12:26–31).

This final campaign against the Ammonites alone is the context for Solomon's birth story. David can leave the weakened enemy to his general and stay behind with his duties in Jerusalem (2 Sam 11:1). This division of labor is not unusual or dishonorable (see 2:8–31; 3:22; 10:7–14). It does, however, lead to a fatal chain of events when David observes a beautiful woman bathing from the roof of his palace and discovers that she is the wife of an officer named Uriah, who is in the field with Joab. David sends for her, sleeps with her, and sends her back home (11:2–4).

This exposition, which will lead to a series of complications, is narrated as minimally as possible. There are no evaluations, the participants express no emotion. The narrator leaves it to the readers to decide whether David started burning with sexual lust once he had seen Bathsheba; the reader must conclude that David committed adultery and betrayed the loyalty of his officer as well; and the reader must realize that David took a grave private and political risk by engaging in this sexual escapade. We discover even less of Bathsheba. We only hear that she was beautiful, that she was washing herself, that the king *took* her, and that she went home and became pregnant.[26] Why was she washing herself in the sight of the king? What did she think when royal messengers came to get her? How did she interact with David when she was brought before him and he slept with her? What did she feel during and

---

26. According to verse 4 it seems that the pregnancy was a surprise ("she had started to purify herself from her uncleanness")—if the "uncleanness" does not refer to David's maculation but to her menstruation (see Lev 15:19ff.).

after? How did she react to the realization of her pregnancy? The question underneath remains: Is Bathsheba victim or clever perpetrator?

The narrative is minimalist on purpose. It leaves so many gaps that the reader is forced to fill in these empty spaces with reason and imagination—without ever knowing for sure how to decide between various interpretations. We hold the final responsibility for our understanding of the narrated events and for the conclusions we draw from it. The narrator, however, does give us subtle guidance. David *takes* Bathsheba (2 Sam 12:4); she is the object of his lust and his actions. We observe the fatal consequences of his actions (11:6–25; 12:15–23). We hear how God's harsh judgment (11:27) and the prophet's severe appearance are directed solely against David, not against Bathsheba. Eventually the text shows us how David's oldest son, Amnon, closely follows his father's example by luring a beautiful woman he loves and desires to him, rapes her, and sends her callously back home—except that Tamar does not get pregnant but is psychologically and emotionally shattered (13:1–20). By this point at the latest, we know who was victim and who was perpetrator in 1 Sam 11. And we (in this case especially we men) will have been convicted of assuming many things regarding David's affair that can only have come from inside ourselves.

When Bathsheba becomes pregnant, David tries to foist paternity onto the legal husband; he has him brought from the field for this very reason. Uriah, however, refuses to enjoy life and sleep with his wife while the troops and the ark and Joab must sleep on the open field (2 Sam 11:11). David dines with him the following evening until Uriah is drunk, but Uriah still does not go to his house (and to his wife) (11:13). The next morning the king sends him back to Joab to Rabbah Ammon and dispatches the infamous Uriah letter with him. Joab deliberately executes a strategically fatal campaign during which Uriah and several other soldiers die. David is unperturbed when he receives this report and moves to take Bathsheba as his wife (11:14–27a).

We can easily guess David's motivation in all of this, even though the narrator makes no explicit comment on it. The king is trying to foist the child he has fathered on the husband. Once this fails, he removes the bothersome rival in order to legalize his own parentage. These actions are as logical as they are dirty. It is much harder to understand the actions of the other characters. What does Bathsheba do all the days and nights her husband is in the city? Why does Uriah not go to her? Is he that honorable? Are his reasons explained in his relationship to Bathsheba, or has he understood what is going on and refuses to participate in the charade? What does David think of his officer's upstanding behavior? "What does David think that Uriah thinks?" (Sternberg). Also, why does Uriah transport the letter with his own death sentence to Joab—or does he not want to live any longer? Did he really not read the letter? How does Joab react to the letter? How much does the general suspect as reasons behind the murderous command? Why does he comply—but differently than David had ordered so that not Uriah alone was killed but several other soldiers as well? Were there no tactical alternatives, or did Joab aim to turn a private affair into a state affair? What kind of confusing game are the characters playing with each other and is the narrator playing with us that his account of how Uriah dies differs from David's command, which in turn differs from how the messenger reported the death to David (11:16–17, 19–21, 23)? What was known in Jerusalem of this affair? How could anyone have known what had happened? How does the narrator know what he claims to know: that Bathsheba was with David, that Uriah was not with Bathsheba, that Uriah's letter was a death sentence, that this letter explains Uriah's death, and so on? Questions and more questions arise that allow not just *one* answer, so that we as readers must take responsibility for our own readings. We are not informed objectively, but we are also not merely entertained; instead, we are thus drawn into a story and forced to draw our own conclusions from it such that in the end it becomes our story.

The ending contains God's direct and harsh judgment of what has happened: "The thing that David had done was evil in the eyes of YHWH" (2 Sam 11:27b). God sends his prophet Nathan to David. He tells the king, as if it were an actual legal case, the parable of the rich man who takes the only, beloved lamb from the poor man in order to spare his own herd. David feels called to pronounce judgment and reacts, as every decent human being must: he is outraged and condemns the perpetrator to fourfold compensation as well as to death. Nathan's reaction is short and brutal: "You are the man!" (12:1–7a). An extended speech follows in which Nathan remonstrates David and predicts difficult times for his house (12:7b–13). Now David turns inward, confesses his sin—and his punishment is eased: he will not have to die himself, but rather the child fathered in adultery (12:13–14). In prayer, David wrestles with God for the life of the child, but when it dies in the end, he surprises his surroundings with his ability to deal with death calmly and realistically (12:15–24). He comforts Bathsheba, sleeps with her, and she gives birth to a second son: Solomon. In all this, the king acts without blemish. It is almost as if he was intoxicated during the Bathsheba-Uriah episode and finally woke up. He cannot undo what has happened, this is true, and the death of the child and the expectation of future calamity for his dynasty are a burden on him and darken our attitude toward him. On the other hand, his sense of justice and his ability to accept criticism and punishment are impressive. His compassion for the dying child is moving, his ability to rise from his mourning admirable. The characterization of David is deepened by many profoundly human traits. Is it a coincidence that they are revealed just after he has failed so bitterly? The way David causes suffering and then suffers himself—this probably brings him closer to us than any victory over Goliath.

We also draw close to David on a personal level during the following conflicts between and with his children. Even though he plays no important role in the matter between Amnon, Tamar, and Absalom (2 Sam 13), nothing occurs without his presence in the background. Amnon becomes sick (as readers we know this is due to unrequited love); he asks his father, who has immediately come to visit, to send him his half-sister Tamar so that she can please him with her pastries. David fulfills this wish without further questions. Then the disastrous events take their course. Amnon grabs the unsuspecting Tamar and demands that she sleep with him (13:11). She refuses and requires that he ask the king for permission to marry her. Amnon, however, is beyond reasoning and rapes her. Following his act of violence, his love suddenly transforms into hate (13:15)—this is the central statement around which the narrative is composed as chiasmus (see Fokkelman)—and he casts her out. When David hears what has happened, his anger is kindled, just as it did earlier when Nathan told him his parable. This time, however, he says nothing and does nothing (13:21). Has he learned to hold himself back? Is he careful not to antagonize his firstborn?[27] Is he of the opinion that this matter is between his sons and none of his business? Is he afraid to throw the first stone after what he had done with Bathsheba and Uriah? When Absalom asks him two years later for permission to invite all of his brothers, and especially Amnon, to a celebration, David first hesitates but then grants his request (13:21–27). Amnon is promptly murdered (13:28–29). Was David unable to prevent this? Why did he not suspect anything? The narrator does not comment on the events, merely reports how the grim news reached David. The father is first afraid that he has lost all of his sons, then realizes that he must only mourn his firstborn (13:28–36); he is spared from taking any further action and punishing the fratricidal brother as Absalom flees the country (13:37–38).

The next large section of the Davidic narrative, 2 Sam 14–20, tells of two major uprisings: the first instigated by David's now eldest son Absalom, the second by the Benjaminite Sheba. We will continue to focus on David.

In 2 Sam 14 the king becomes victim of an intrigue in which Absalom is brought back to Jerusalem. The story starts with David himself: "And king David ceased to go out after Absalom [in war, perhaps weaker: ceased to

---

27. This is what the extended text of the Greek Septuagint and, apparently, a text fragment of the Samuel scroll from Qumran suspect.

be angry against], for he was now consoled over the death of Amnon. Now Joab son of Zeruiah perceived that the king's heart went out to Absalom" (2 Sam 13:39–40). The Hebrew words can also be translated quite differently: "And David longed to go out [in war] against Absalom, for he mourned that Amnon was dead. Now Joab the son of Zeruiah perceived that the king's heart went against Absalom." The unclear semantic structure and the problems of textual tradition may explain this ambiguity; the obscurity, however, could also be intentional. In any case, Joab notices a change in David's attitude and intends either to fulfill the secret desire of the king's heart or to prevent a war.

General Joab decides to obtain amnesty for Absalom. To this end, he uses a ruse that is strongly reminiscent of Nathan. A woman tells David a fictional legal case; the king as high judge pronounces judgment—and is surprised by the announcement that he has just judged his own case. As a matter of fact, he has judged in favor of Absalom's return (2 Sam 14:2–17). Her rhetorical and psychological virtuosity reminds us not only of Nathan but also of Abigail (1 Sam 25). When she states that the king is "like an angel," able to "distinguish good and evil," and that "God may be with him" (2 Sam 14:17), we are reminded of statements about David during the early years of his rise (see 1 Sam 16:18; 17:37; 19:28; 29:9). Thus the narrators are able to bridge the scope of the entire Davidic narrative.

David understands clearly who is behind the woman's clever action, and he allows Joab to bring Absalom back. He does not, however, want to see his son (2 Sam 14:24). Absalom succeeds in breaking out of his imposed isolation, once again helped by Joab, who serves as his advocate, initially without his knowledge. The prince may finally come before the king, Absalom prostrates himself before David (a gesture of loyalty and submission!), "and the king kissed Absalom" (14:33). The narrative has now reached a point that in music we might call a deceptive cadence.

The next large section, 2 Sam 15–20, shows a well-crafted symmetrical structure.[28]

A	15:1–12	Preparation and outbreak of Absalom's rebellion
B	15:13–16:14	David's escape; encounters with:
		(a) 15:13–37 loyal friends (Ittai, Zadok, Abiathar, Hushai)

---

28. See Conroy and Fokkelman; the outline above follows Walter Dietrich and Thomas Naumann, *Die Samuelbücher* (EdF 287; Darmstadt: Wissenschaftliche Buchgesellschaft, 1995), 271.

		(b) 16:1–4	the house of Saul (Ziba, indirectly Meribaal)
		(c) 16:5–13	the Benjaminite Shimei
C	16:15–17:23		Preparations for war (war council: 16:15–17:14)
C'	17:24–19:9a		The war (Absalom's death, David's grief)
B'	19:9b–41		David's return; encounters with:
		(c') 19:17–24	the Benjaminite Shimei
		(b') 19:25–31	the house of Saul (Meribaal, indirectly Ziba)
		(a') 19:32–41	the loyal friend Barsillai
A'	19:42–20:22		Emergence and repression of Sheba's rebellion

Already the first reports in 2 Sam 15:1–6 sketch the scope of the narrative that will enthrall us over several chapters. Absalom quickly displays far-reaching ambitions by acquiring a war chariot with horses and a bodyguard of fifty men. We are not told that David had ever done anything similar; further on, however, we hear of the same action undertaken by Absalom's brother Adonijah—and here the text adds that Adonijah "had proven his arrogance and said, 'I, I will be king!'" (1 Kgs 1:5). Absalom does not say this, but his intentions are the same. He subversively starts a propaganda campaign for himself; he does not even hesitate to denigrate his father in doing so. Strangely enough, we do not ever hear David reacting to his son's activities. Does he not know? Or must we interject another text from the Adonijah narrative: "And his father never rebuked him, saying, 'What are you doing?'" (1 Kgs 1:6). We can interpret this intentional silence in different ways: as self-assurance or as weakness, as negligence or as implicit consent, as hurt and whiny or as silent-threatening passivity. Absalom (as Adonijah after him) could in any case assume that the king did not object to his behavior.

David gives the crown prince free rein for four whole years, and when Absalom tells him that he wants to go to Hebron to fulfill an oath he took during his time abroad, the king says only, "Go in peace" (2 Sam 15:9). But should not the catchword "Hebron" have alerted David, just as he should have been suspicious when Amnon requested Tamar's presence and when Absalom asked for permission to invite the other princes to a celebration?! Hebron was the very place at which David himself had started his royal career. David seems to be completely surprised at the intensity of events that now move against him. After his initial shock he reacts decisively with lightning speed: he flees the city (just as he once fled Gibea from Saul [1 Sam 19] and Jerusalem from the Philistines [2 Sam 5:18]) and leaves his residence without resistance to the rebels (15:14). Absalom could understand this move either as tactical retreat or as an actual abdication.

The narrators shape the following scenes as gripping emotional stories about David's painful farewell from his residence and about the unquestioning loyalty of his remaining troops. David gallantly offers a Philistine mercenary the option of withdrawing with his six hundred men, but the mercenary stays (2 Sam 15:19–22). "The whole country wept aloud as all the people passed by" (15:23). "And David went up the ascent of the Mount of Olives, weeping as he went, with his head covered and walking barefoot, and all the people who were with him covered their heads and went up, weeping as they went" (15:30). Between these two highly emotional scenes, the narrators have placed short episodes that prove David to be not only a man filled with grief but also a man possessed of a very capable strategic mind. He sends the priests Zadok and Abiathar back to the city with the ark. He explains that God could help him even without this cultic artifact—and turns the two priests and their sons into spies against his son and rival (15:24–29). He follows the same plan with Hushai, planting the royal advisor in Absalom's inner circle in order to neutralize Ahithophel, who has defected to Absalom (15:31–37). The message is clear: David is not thinking of abdicating; he is planning his return.

The following narrative section introduces several important characters who provide us with case studies on the different reactions to David's departure and, in turn, David's response to them.

Ziba, the manager of the house of the Saulide Meribaal, pays homage to the fleeing king and denounces his master, who supposedly expects that he will receive the kingship over Israel (!). David immediately transfers all of Meribaal's possessions to Ziba (2 Sam 16:1–4). Later, when David returns to Jerusalem, Meribaal approaches him and insists that he had always been on David's side but that Ziba had dishonestly slandered his name. Once again, David is assured that he is wise "as the angel of God" and should do what is "good" in his eyes. David, without having heard Ziba's side, pronounces a Solomonic judgment: Meribaal and Ziba are to divide the heritage of the house of Saul.

The appearance of the Benjaminite Shimei is quite a bit more unpleasant. He berates the escaping David as a "man of blood" who is now receiving due punishment for his murders of members of the house of Saul; he also throws stones and dirt at the king. Abishai, the son of Zeruiah, offers to liquidate the man, but David restrains him with words of modest piety (2 Sam 16:11–12). This is once again the David whom we know from the episodes in which he spared Saul (1 Sam 24; 26). Upon returning to Jerusalem, Shimei hurries toward David to receive him with one thousand men from Benjamin and assists him in crossing the Jordan. He eloquently confesses his sin toward the king. Once again Abishai suggests killing Shimei because he "has cursed the anointed (משיח) of YHWH." This time David severely rebukes him: on a day such as this, nobody should die, and David swears to Shimei: "You will not die" (2 Sam 19:24).

Waiting for David on the other side is the Gileadite Barsillai, who had generously supplied David and his troops during their escape east of the Jordan (2 Sam 17:27–29). David intends to compensate him upon his return to Jerusalem (19:32–39). On the whole we see clearly: David does not forget the good done to him, and whoever has done evil must face sternness but not revenge.

The middle section of this narrative passage deals with the conflict between David and Absalom. The narrators describe in great detail how the young rebel makes preparations in Jerusalem and how David subverts these preparations without being present himself (2 Sam 16:15–17:23). His quickly erected network of espionage and subversion works superbly; most important, however, "Yhwh had ordained to defeat the good counsel of Ahithophel, so that Yhwh might bring ruin on Absalom" (17:14).

From the very beginning the entire battle report is aimed at Absalom's death. David's men first prevent the king from joining the battle. Their reasoning is noteworthy: the loss is not great if a normal warrior should fall, "you, however, are worth as much as ten thousand of us"; the king should stay behind with the reserves. David responds: "I will do what is good in your eyes." On one issue, however, David is very clear (or the words placed into his mouth by the narrators are very clear): the explicit commitment of every troop leader—especially and including Joab—to spare "the young man Absalom" (2 Sam 18:1–5).

The actual battle is described in a mere three verses: David's men defeat the "people of Israel" in the forest of Ephraim, the forest being more of an opponent than the army (2 Sam 18:6–8). This description—along with a seemingly passing remark much earlier on that the crown prince possessed a wealth of hair (14:26)—constitute the expositional material for the following narration of Absalom's death. The crown prince is stuck with his hair in the branches of an oak tree, his horse runs away from underneath him, and one of Joab's soldiers finds him in this dire situation. He immediately reports his discovery to his general; when Joab rebukes him for not liquidating Absalom right away, he appeals to David's order "to spare the young man Absalom" (18:12). Joab then initiates the execution but pays careful attention that not he but rather his bodyguards deal the final blow. After the rebellion has lost its head, the battle can be abandoned (18:9–18).

Now the narrative turns all its attention to the question as to how David will be informed of what has happened and how he will react to this information. Ahimaaz, who has already proven himself as a messenger in delicate situations (2 Sam 15:27, 36; 17:17–22), reports to Joab and offers: "I will run and bring the king the joyful news" (בשׂר, 18:19). The root of the verb בשׂר now becomes the central motif of the following passage; the basic problem consists in the fact that the "joyful news" of the troop's victory has to be brought to the king together with the "bad news" that his son is dead. Joab, who values Ahimaaz and wants to protect him, orders a Cushite, a mercenary from Nubia, "Go and report to the king what you have seen" (18:21); the order is deliberately unspecific, as if Joab wants to wait and see what happens. Ahimaaz, however, cannot be held back; he starts running and actually passes the Cushite. At this point the narrator changes the location of the narrative and tells us that David concludes, based on the fact that two single men (not a horde of fleeing soldiers!) were running toward the city, that these are "messengers of joy" with a "message of joy" (מבשׂר, בשׂורה, 18:25, 26; in 18:27 even בשׂרה טובה). He is only partly right. Ahimaaz arrives first and cries out: "Blessed be YHWH your God, who has delivered up the men who raised their hand against my lord the king" (18:28). His words are cleverly phrased to allude only to the victory in battle. David immediately asks, "What about the young man Absalom?" (18:29). Ahimaaz avoids a clear answer. He did observe a tumult around Joab, but he does not know what it meant. At this point the Cushite arrives and says, "Good tidings (בשׂר) for my lord the king! For YHWH has vindicated you this day, delivering you from the power of all who rose up against you" (19:31). This answer is also slightly obscure so that the king must ask once more about the fate of the young man Absalom. This time he receives a careful but nevertheless clear answer, "May the enemies of my lord the king, and all who rise up to do you harm, be like that young man" (19:32).

Thus David receives news of the death of his son together with news of victory. He breaks down, runs up to the chamber over the gate, and weeps and wails unceasingly: "My son Absalom, my son, my son, were I dead instead of you, Absalom my son, my son" (2 Sam 19:1). The father's grief could not be described with greater anguish. David had faced the reality of death many times in his life—this death undoubtedly hit him the hardest. Now we understand that when he started fighting he had intended to regain his kingdom but not lose his son. And it would have been possible, if there was not Joab....

Joab is the one who takes action once he realizes that the king is about to alienate his troops and loyal followers because of his bottomless grief. He makes David turn his tearful eyes to the hard political facts (2 Sam 19:6–8). We see reasons of state standing against humanity, cold calculation against emotion, power against love, and we are automatically drawn to David and repulsed by Joab. This is the brute responsible for Absalom's death and thus to blame for David's unbearable pain! On the other hand, seen objectively, Joab is not wrong: David's loyal followers are unsure of themselves (19:4–5). Was not the decapitation of the rebel force the least bloody way to end the rebellion? If Joab gets his way against David, will not Absalom's murder be justified in the end? The narrators describe a dilemma to us, almost a tragedy, from which all participants can only emerge harmed and broken.

David does not answer Joab—not with a single word; he silently gets up, goes outside and presents himself to his people, and they are satisfied (2 Sam 19:9). Did David cave in to Joab? Was this man too powerful, too threatening for him? Or were his arguments simply irrefutable? Or is David's silence an icy, threatening sign of ominous things to come? In any case, we discover not much later that David has replaced Joab with Absalom's general Amasa to be the leader of his troops (19:14). This act, however, is typical for David in that it is only a small part of a well-planned strategy to assure his former position of power following the conflagration caused by Absalom's uprising. After the rebellion has been put down, the biblical account tells us of a strange race between Judah and northern Israel to determine who will first reinstitute the victorious king to his former position. We are told that the north takes action first so that David prods his countrymen to move more quickly—and offers Amasa the position as his general. So he "swayed the hearts of all the people of Judah as one" (19:9–16). Now the Israelites are offended by the favoritism David is showing Judah, the Judahites defend themselves, and a bitter conflict ensues in which the text speaks in strange collective imagery of the "man of Israel" and the "man of Judah" (19:42–44). In the end, the north formally secedes from the Davidic kingdom. An "unruly person" (אִישׁ בְּלִיַּעַל) named Sheba ben Bichri from the tribe of Benjamin initiates the secession. He propagates the slogan: "We have no part of David and no heritage with the son of Jesse. Every man to his tents, Israel!" The slogan bears fruit, and "all the men of Israel went away from David and followed Sheba ben Bichri" (20:1–2). David realizes that this threat could become more dangerous than the threat posed by Absalom (20:5) and orders his new general Amasa to draft the Judahite troops within three days. When he is unable to comply with this deadline, the king gives orders, not to Joab but to his brother Abishai, to march against Sheba with professional soldiers (20:4–6). And who leads the campaign? "Joab's men went out after him, along with the Cherethites, the Pelethites, and all the elite warriors"—as if a Joab could be written off this easily (20:7)!

Joab is the central figure in the narrative that follows. He eliminates two opponents: first his own, Amasa; then David's, Sheba. Amasa's murder in many ways parallels the murder of Abner (cf. 2 Sam 20:8–10 with 3:27). This time the narrator also portrays Joab as the only perpetrator, but at the same time the question whether David knew about or consented to this action lurks in the background. Was the deadline of three days deliberately unrealistic?

Did David not know that Joab would definitely march with Abishai? Did he not realize that Joab would liquidate his rival (as he had liquidated Abner)? Was David really concerned that this might happen? After all, Amasa was the general who led the troops in Absalom's rebellion! In any case, we do not hear that David mourned the murder victim. In fact, the soldier charged with leading the troops past Amasa's corpse and on to battle brings both names together: "Whoever favors Joab, and whoever is for David, let him follow Joab" (20:11). Only much later, in 1 Kgs 2:5, will we read that David did not want Amasa murdered and that he never forgave Joab for his crime.

Sheba withdraws to the far north of Israel to Abel of Beth-maacah. Joab explains to a "wise woman" who enters into negotiations with him that he is not interested in taking the city but only in the surrender of "that Sheba ben Bichri who raised his hand against king David" (2 Sam 20:21). He does not apprehend Sheba alive, but his head is tossed over the wall, and thus the battle comes to an end: "Joab returned to Jerusalem to the king" (20:22); everything between the two seems to be in order. The next sentence thus reads: "Joab was [appointed] over the entire army of Israel" (20:23a). This is the beginning of a list of all of David's top officials that is quite similar to the earlier list in 8:16–18. There, too, Joab held the top military position. This time, however, a second name appears beside him that was at the bottom of the first list: "Benaiah son of Jehoiada was [appointed] over the Cherethites and the Pelethites" (20:23b). This small change indicates that the power structure has changed to the disadvantage of Joab; in the end, Benaiah will kill Joab and take his place as the highest military leader in Israel (1 Kgs 2:34–35).

This is not the only bridge that connects the books of Samuel to the beginning of the books of Kings. In 1 Kgs 1–2, many motifs reoccur that were a part of the narrative until 2 Sam 20. David, however, has now become so old that he can no longer "get warm," not even when lying beside a highly attractive girl named Abishag of Shunem, who was given to the king for his personal service (1 Kgs 1:1–4). This is a very drastic way of saying that the king is no longer able to rule, that his procreational powers have dried up, and that his sons must now take up the issue of his succession.

It is thus only logical when the next sentence states: "Adonijah, the son of Haggith, rose up and said, 'I, I will be king'" (1 Kgs 1:5). He thus follows the example of his half-brother Absalom—in itself a bad omen. He, too, has free reign; the king does not rebuke him. We have already discovered once that the king's silence is not automatically a sign of his benevolence, quite the contrary. The narrator then draws an explicit ominous connection: "He was also a very handsome man, and [his mother bore] him next after Absalom" (1:6). Adonijah is the next in line for the throne—and the next to lose his life. It will be of no help that he has been able to gain the support of Joab (of all people!) and Abiathar. We immediately discover that a group of powerful men (among them Benaiah, Zadok, and Nathan) has gathered in opposition (1:7–8).

The next scene doubly reminds us of Absalom. Adonijah invites "all of his brothers" as well as every Judahite official to a large sacrificial banquet (1 Kgs 1:9; cf. 2 Sam 13:23–29 and 15:7–12). What is Adonijah up to? Does he want to kill one of his brothers, or does he "only" want to start a rebellion? We are almost relieved to read that he "did not invite" Nathan, Benaiah, the elite soldiers, "and Solomon, his brother" (1 Kgs 1:10). As if by coincidence, the name "Solomon" occurs here for the first time since his birth narrative in 2 Sam 11–12. We realize intuitively: this is the future king!

The following scenes allow the reader to witness a succession of highly secret conversations between two protagonists that will become important in the story. (1) Nathan and Bathsheba (1 Kgs 1:11–14): Nathan informs Solomon's mother that Adonijah has become (!) king and instructs her how to save (!) her life and the life of her son by reminding David of his (supposed or real?) vow to make Solomon king. (2) Bathsheba and David (1:15–21): Bathsheba follows Nathan's instructions precisely, yet adds several statements of her own. She tells David of the large celebration that Adonijah is holding (and she of course reminds him of Absalom's actions!) and claims that "all Israel" is waiting for David to decide "who shall sit on the throne of my lord, the king, after him" (1:20). (3) Nathan and David (1:22–27): Nathan goes one step further and alleges that David has established Adonijah on his throne, for he is celebrating a large feast and the people are calling to him: "Long live the king!" Why did David not tell anyone who "will sit on the throne of my lord, the king, after him?"

David seems to be a puppet in the hands of those around him: Abishag, Adonijah, Nathan, and Bathsheba. Now he takes the initiative. He calls Bathsheba and swears to her: "As YHWH lives, who has saved my life from every adversity, as I swore to you by YHWH, the God of Israel, 'Your son Solomon shall succeed me as king, and he shall sit on my throne in my place,' so will I do this day!" Bathsheba thanks him with a pious wish: "May my lord, King David, live forever!" All of a sudden David returns to his former self and comes up with a wise and decisive course of action: Zadok and Nathan, protected by Benaiah and his troops, are to anoint Solomon.

> "Then blow the trumpet, and say, 'Long live King Solomon!' ... Let him enter and sit on my throne; he shall be king in my place, for YHWH has appointed him to be ruler [נגיד] over Israel and over Judah." Benaiah son of Jehoiada answered the king, "May YHWH, the God of my lord the king, say amen. As YHWH has been with my lord the king, so may he be with Solo-

mon and make his throne greater than the throne of my lord King David."
(1 Kgs 1:34–37)

God's presence with David and David's status as נגיד was a constant theme
in the narratives of David's rise. Then, the absence of God from Saul was the
sharp contrast to this theme. Now there is no contrast between the king and
his successor, only continuity. If at all, Adonijah and his followers are the contrast, but they are overwhelmed and wiped away by the events to come.

We cannot be sure if they understood their festive celebration to be a
coronation ceremony, since the narrator does not say this directly. We do
not even know if Nathan, who is the first to draw the picture of an imminent
uprising, truly believes this himself. Bathsheba is also intent only on making
sure that David will establish Solomon, not Adonijah, on the throne *after*
him. It is David himself, who turns the *after* (אחר) into *in my place* (תחת);
David himself decides—seemingly under the impression that an uprising is
imminent— not only to make plans for the time after him but to change the
status quo immediately. Has he been deviously tricked? Or has he—as well
as Nathan—recognized the signs of the time and barely preempted Adonijah's plans?

Everything happens as David has ordered (1 Kgs 1:38–40). The question
is now how the festive gathering around Adonijah will react to the changed
status quo. As soon as they become aware of the tumult in the city and Joab's
trained ear perceives the sound of the shofar, Jonathan ben Abiathar, whom
we know well from his previous missions,[29] appears on the scene. Adonijah
welcomes him with words that also sound familiar: "Come in, for you are
a worthy man and surely you bring good news" (בשר טוב, 1:42; cf. 2 Sam
18:27). It is very bad news, however, that Jonathan has for Adonijah. He
describes once more what the reader has already learned, but adds:

---

29. Compare 2 Sam 17:17–21. It is a highly artistic twist that Jonathan operates together with Ahimaaz in that passage, whereas Ahimaaz operates alone in 2 Sam
18:19–21, and that Jonathan (as if in return) appears alone in our passage above. The separation of the two sons of priests who appear almost as twins signals a general shift in the
character constellation. Whereas Ahimaaz followed Joab's order and reported Absalom's
uprising to David, Jonathan now reports to Joab that David and Solomon have put an
end to Adonijah's uprising. Joab has switched sides—most likely without realizing what he
has done; on the contrary, he could have assumed that he learned the right lessons from
David's boundless grief over Absalom when he sided with the new crown prince. Abiathar,
Jonathan's father, also stood at Adonijah's side. Zadok, however, the father of Ahimaaz,
stood at Solomon's side. As those of old have sung, it is rather risky in such situations to
sing the *wrong* song.

Solomon now sits on the royal throne. Moreover the king's servants [which king? Solomon?] came to congratulate our lord King David, saying, "May God make the name of Solomon more famous than yours and make his throne greater than your throne." The king bowed in worship on the bed [before Solomon, in a sense!] and went on to pray thus, "Blessed be YHWH, the God of Israel, who today has granted one of my offspring to sit on my throne and permitted me to witness it." (1 Kgs 1:46–48)

David has fully agreed to the transfer of power occurring already during his lifetime. This news seals the fate for Adonijah's party. Adonijah flees to the "horns of the altar" and only dares let go after Solomon promises to spare his life—if only "nothing evil is found in him" (1:49–53).

In the next scene the dying David conveys his last will to his son Solomon. Readers witness how the old king gives his successor advice in how to deal with certain individuals who have crossed David's path in the past. He mentions Joab (2:5–6), Barsillai (2:7), and Shimei (2:8–9).[30] Why these three? David still has a score to settle with each of them: a positive score with Barsillai (see 2 Sam 19:32–41), a negative score with Joab and Shimei. These last two, coincidence or not, were among Adonijah's followers, among whom Solomon will clean up in the near future (1 Kgs 2:13–46). David basically gives him his blessing for Joab's and Shimei's execution (2:28–34, 36–46). Liquidating Adonijah and exiling Abiathar (2:13–25, 26–27) is Solomon's own decision.

Any negative word about his son Adonijah and his long-standing friend and companion Abiathar that the narrator might place in David's mouth would only implicate David himself. As readers, we are supposed to accept that David severely accuses Joab and Shimei and takes the burden of responsibility for their deaths. He accuses Joab of murdering the two military leaders Abner and Amasa and of taking revenge during peacetime for blood spilled in battle (referring to the death of Asael by Abner in 2 Sam 2:18–23). Strangely enough, he does not mention the murder of his son Absalom. Is this only because Joab's guilt could not be proven completely or because this death was unavoidable? In any case, Solomon "in his wisdom should not allow Joab's gray head to go down to Sheol in peace" (1 Kgs 2:6). David accuses the Benjaminite Shimei of his harsh curses during David's escape from Jerusalem (2 Sam 16:5–13), but he also reminds Solomon that he had sworn an oath to this man: "I will not kill you by the sword." In all truth, his oath had been more profound: "You will not die" (19:24). Now he recommends to Solomon not to let Shimei's crime "go unpunished." There must be a way to make sure that his gray hair will go down with blood to Sheol.

---

30. The spiritual admonishment in 1 Kgs 2:1–4 is a Deuteronomistic addition.

I.4.3.5. Yhwh's Proven One

The entire section 2 Sam 21–24, most likely intended to separate the Davidic story from the Solomonic narratives, consistently follows a chiastic structure. The beginning and end consist of *narratives* that tell how David becomes guilty and how God shows him a way to atone for what he has done (2 Sam 21:1–14; 24:1–25). Immediately after and before these narratives are *lists* of names and deeds performed by important fellow warriors of David (21:15–22; 23:8–39). The center consists of two sections of *poetry* in which David turns to God. The axis of reflection is the ending of the first poem: "[God] is a tower of salvation for his king and shows steadfast love to his anointed, to David and his descendants forever" (22:51).

This construction was put in place by the final Deuteronomistic redaction (see above §I.3.3). It has already been observed that the two psalms provide a direct comparison between David and Moses (Deut 32–33). This comparison lends itself to different interpretations. The political sphere is connected to the Torah and perhaps subordinated to its importance, or, vice versa, the spiritual sphere is concretized by a specific political reality. Perhaps the portrait of David contains messianic elements already in these texts so that we could postulate a convergence of Torah theology and messianism that will become a determining factor for late Old Testament thinking. A further aspect is the fact that 2 Sam 22 is essentially identical to Ps 18; already here David is the important psalmist we will come to know in the so-called Davidic Psalters (Pss 3–41; 51–72; 101–103; 108–110; 138–145). Both songs are songs of praise and thanksgiving: the first situated during the time after David's rise (2 Sam 22:1), the second shortly before his death (23:1). Accordingly, the first song describes the king in his dangerous situation (22:5–7: "The waves of death encompassed me" [22:5]) and how God appeared—in a theophany! (22:8–16: "Then the earth reeled and rocked" [22:8])—in order to seek redress for his anointed ("I was blameless before you," textual emendation) and lead him from victory to victory (22:17–49: "By my God I can leap over a wall" [22:30]) so that the king is able to praise him now (22:50–51). The second song has the king express the various tasks of a ruler in Israel. Standing in the (Davidic) "covenant" means to seek "justice" (23:3) and to withstand "evil men" (23:6). Apparently, the reader is given a key by which to understand the story of David properly.

We find a much smaller degree of piety in the lists of David's men and their exploits that are placed around these songs. We are informed of several outstanding individual achievements of David's men in the context of various battles with the Philistines (2 Sam 21:15–22). We also are told the names and some of the deeds of two groups within his following: the Three (23:8–

17) and the Thirty (23:18–39). The Three are reported to have accomplished victorious deeds, and twice we read that "Yhwh brought about a great victory" (23:10, 12). This evaluation, as well as the fact that these texts continually focus on conflicts with the Philistines (21:15–22; 23:9–17), connects these texts closely to the description of David's rise in 1 Sam 16–2 Sam 8. In these earlier texts, however, all interest lies with the person of David (most notably in 2 Sam 8); here David's men who fought for him are the center of attention. Are we faced with subtle criticism and correction of the main corpus of the David traditions? One especially noticeable fact is the mention of "Elhanan, son of Jaare-oregim from Bethlehem," who "killed Goliath the Gittite, the shaft of whose spear was like a weaver's beam" (2 Sam 21:19)—a subtle hint not to read David's victory over Goliath as a factual report. In several anecdotes David does not appear as a victorious hero but as someone whose life is threatened by his enemies and is saved at the last moment by one of his men (21:16–17; 23:13–17). The long list of the Thirty does not even refer to David but mentions prominently in last position "Uriah the Hittite" (23:39). It is almost as if these texts form a mirror in which the story of David is reflected with a high degree of criticism.

The two large narratives 2 Sam 21 and 24 are connected by a common topic: both deal with a crisis situation in Israel. One is a famine brought on by Saul's blood guilt against the inhabitants of Gibeon (21:1); one is a plague brought on by David's desire to hold a public census (24:1–15). Both times God's wrath can be turned away: once by means of a ritual killing and subsequent burial of seven members of the house of Saul; once by erecting a sacrificial site and the presentation of a large sacrifice outside the Jerusalem gates. The present order of these narratives is hardly coincidental. The first narrative still deals primarily with Saul, the second with David only. In the first case, the sin must be expiated by human blood; in the second case, the blood of sacrificial animals suffices. The first narrative retroactively demands the eradication of an entire royal family; the second narrative proleptically points to a constant means of atonement for the new royal family and the people as a whole. The site "found" by David outside the gates of Jerusalem is the future site of the temple on Mount Zion. Today's readers (and probably earlier readers as well) will shudder at the archaic worldview of these texts. What kind of a God are we dealing with who subjects the entire people to famine and plague because of the sin of the king? What kind of kings are we dealing with who are responsible for bringing such suffering upon their people? What kinds of mechanisms are we dealing with that are used to placate the divinity?

The narrative in 2 Sam 21 surprises us with the news that there were more members of the house of Saul than had been mentioned previously and that David's problem with the house of Saul was even greater—and solved with even more blood—than reported thus far. David hands over seven members of the house of Saul to Gibeon, a non-Israelite enclave that up to this point was not known to have suffered under Saul. Five of these seven are sons of Michal (Merab, according to a different textual witness), daughter of Saul; the other two are sons of Rizpah, one of Saul's concubines. The sad story of their execution brings us closer to these women than the entire previous David tradition that knew these women only as objects of male ownership—and that in the case of Michal emphasized mainly that she conceived *no* children from David. David appears more reactive than active. His people and thus he himself suffered from a famine. After three years—we want to ask, why not earlier?—David turns to Yhwh, and God (most likely by means of an oracle) points him to the transgression against the Gibeonites. As if they were a superior power, the king must ask them what they desire. When they state their wish for revenge on the house of Saul, David concedes immediately (21:6). The fate of the sacrificed men and their mothers does not seem to trouble David—until Rizpah's desperate loyalty to her children moves him to bury the remains of these men in the family grave of the house of Saul. Now, finally, the rain falls and the story can state: "God heeded supplications for the land" (21:14).

The second narrative ends with the same statement: "Yhwh heeded supplications for the land, and the plague was stopped in Israel" (2 Sam 24:25). But what preceded this statement! David makes the decision (or rather is tempted to do so by a wrathful Yhwh) to enact a public census. General Joab, who is instructed to supervise the process, strongly advises against this action and proves much more perspicacious than the king. The process has hardly been completed when God through the prophet Gad faces David with the choice between three punishments: three years of famine (see 2 Sam 21:1!); three years of oppression by enemies; or three days of death by plague. David chooses the last option. The reasoning he expresses to Gad is quite astonishing: "Let us [!] fall into the hand of Yhwh, for his mercy is great, but let me [!] not fall into human hands" (24:14). God sends the plague, and seventy thousand people die in a few days. Faced with this result, both God and David change their attitude: God "repents" from what he has done and orders the angel of affliction to cease his action—just before he enters Jerusalem (24:16). David sees the angel and cries out: "I alone have sinned, and I alone have done wickedly, but these sheep, what have they done? Let your hand, I pray, be against me and against my father's house" (24:17). The "smelting furnace of compassion" (Schenker) has changed those in power, God as well as the king.

I.4.4. The Portrait of Solomon

Bloch-Smith, Elizabeth M. "'Who Is the King of Glory?' Solomon's Temple and Its Symbolism," in *Scripture and Other Artifacts: Essays on the Bible and Archaeology in Honor of Philip J. King* (ed. Michael D. Coogan, J. Cheryl Exum, and Lawrence E. Stager; Louisville: Westminster John Knox, 1994), 18–31. **Brettler,** Marc. "The Structure of 1 Kings 1–11," *JSOT* 49 (1991): 87–97. **Frisch,** Amos. "Structure and Its Significance: The Narrative of Solomon's Reign," *JSOT* 51 (1991): 3–14. **Parker,** Kim Ian. "Repetition as a Structuring Device in 1 Kings 1–11," *JSOT* 42 (1988): 19–27. **Rost,** Leonhard. *Die Überlieferung von der Thronnachfolge Davids* (BWANT 42; Stuttgart: Kohlhammer, 1926), repr. in *Das kleine Credo und andere Studien zum Alten Testament* (Heidelberg: Quelle & Meyer, 1965), 119–253, trans. as *The Succession to the Throne of David* (trans. Michael D. Rutter and David M. Gunn; Sheffield: Almond, 1982). **Talstra,** Eep. *Solomon's Prayer: Synchrony and Diachrony in the Composition of 1 Kings 8,14–61* (CBET 3; Kampen: Kok Pharos, 1993). **Veijola,** Timo. *Verheissung in der Krise: Studien zur Literatur und Theologie der Exilszeit anhand des 89. Psalms* (Helsinki: Suomalainen Tiedeakatemia, 1982).

Once again we will focus on passages that are assumedly pre-Deuteronomistic. Because the Deuteronomistic redaction is not only responsible for individual passages (especially 1 Kgs 8–9 and 11), but also for the final composition of 1 Kgs 3–11 (with the temple at its center), we will not follow the biblical order of the texts in all cases.

I.4.4.1. How Solomon Was Born and Attained the Throne

Solomon's birth narrative is anything but honorable, not for him and also not for his parents. The tradition is barely able to distance him from the David-Uriah-Bathsheba scandal. His departed brother is portrayed as the fruit of adultery, not Solomon himself, since Solomon is described as the outcome of a legitimate relationship between David and Bathsheba (2 Sam 12). But considering how strongly each individual was tied to a collective in those times (first and foremost to the family) and how carefully other rulers emphasize an immaculate lineage, if possible even containing transcendent elements, we realize how much Solomon is burdened by this birth narrative. The value judgment added by the narrators following his birth and naming ("And YHWH loved him," 12:24) almost has a defiant ring to it.

Over a stretch of almost endless narrative material, Solomon seems completely forgotten. We hear nothing of his youth and adolescence, his plans, or his character. Yet when he reappears on the scene in 1 Kgs 1, his portrait quickly becomes more defined. In the beginning he still remains in the background. Adonijah determines the foreground by gathering followers and establishing an opposing faction—Solomon does not appear yet (1:8). Only after Adonijah invites his followers to a state banquet and ignores his rivals does Solomon appear as the leader of these rivals (1:10). Solomon remains silent in response to this affront; the prophet Nathan and his mother Bathsheba state his case all the more emphatically. Solomon continues to remain silent when he is established as the claimant to the throne, during his anointing at the Gihon Spring, and when he is brought to the royal residence among shouts of joy from the people. Only his adversary Adonijah is accorded a few short sentences—once he has submitted to Solomon's authority (1:52–53). Solomon is silent when he hears David's last will; the narrators do not even tell us whether he nodded in assent (2:1–10). Until his father's death (2:11–12), Solomon remains completely in his shadow.

Then he steps into the spotlight. In a quick succession of events he arranges the elimination of several prominent individuals. Adonijah is the first on the list. He is foolhardy enough to ask Bathsheba (who has proved herself a schemer of the first order!) for the hand of Abishag of Shunem, who had serviced David toward his end—not without mentioning that he would have been first in line to claim the throne but that Solomon has "now gained the kingship from Yhwh." Bathsheba omits this last statement when reporting Adonijah's request to Solomon. He immediately suspects his *elder brother* of dishonest motivations and has him killed (1 Kgs 2:13–25). Solomon then exiles the priest Abiathar, who belonged to Adonijah's faction, from Jerusalem to the nearby town of Anathoth. Now Solomon's follower Zadok occupies the highest spiritual office on his own (2:26–27). Joab is next in line. The old lion perceives that the net is closing in around him and flees to the tent sanctuary, hoping to find political asylum within its confines. Without hesitation, however, Solomon gives Benaiah the order for Joab's execution. Surprisingly, Benaiah hesitates to comply with the order, a clear indication of how monstrous the narrators thought this action to be. Solomon does not relent; Joab must die beside Yhwh's altar. Benaiah, the henchman, receives Joab's position as a reward (2:28–35). Last on the list is Shimei ben Gera. On his deathbed David had specifically reminded his son of Shimei's infamous actions (1:8–9). Now Solomon places him under strict house arrest, and Shimei complies with this arrest for three years (!), only to break it in order to retrieve two slaves who fled to the Philistine town of Gath. He thus transgresses Solomon's order—even if unintentionally and with no political motivation—and is liquidated by Benaiah by order of the king (2:36–46).

If we read these episodes only for their plot content, we may conclude that Solomon is purposefully eliminating political opponents in cold blood without necessity and in some cases without good reason. We gain the impression that readers are to be biased against the new king instead of siding with him. We must not overlook the fact, however, that the text justifies each of Solomon's actions with explicit and detailed arguments and that many of his arguments match the arguments David gave him in his last will. The narrators try to give us the impression (or they at least let David and Solomon promote this understanding) that the actions described are *not* purely a political purge but rather justified and necessary steps Solomon had to take for the sake of the royal house and the kingdom, even for the sake of God! The rationale operates on two levels: (1) if anyone questions Solomon's claim to the throne, they rebel against the decision made by David and God and thus lose their right to live (1 Kgs 2:24: Adonijah; 2:26a: Abiathar); (2) if anyone has committed an unforgivable sin during David's lifetime, he must be called to account in order to prevent his unatoned sin from polluting the entire house of David (2:5, 31–33: Joab; 2:8, 44: Shimei). On the other hand, those who rendered outstanding services to David must be rewarded or spared (2:7: Barsillai; 2:26b: Abiathar).

Today's readers may consider these arguments to be of limited value; for ancient times we should at least consider that changes on the throne were often accompanied by conflict and confusion and often settled with violence (most often with much more violence than described in 1 Kgs 2).[31] In any case, by justifying the context of Solomon's birth and ascension to the throne, the narrators pave the way for a largely glorious description of Solomon's reign.

I.4.4.2. How Solomon Organized His Kingdom

Two large narratives stand at the beginning of the description of the Solomonic era (1 Kgs 3:4–15, 16–28). The aim is to show that Solomon's proverbial wisdom was a gift from God that allowed him to master even the most complicated situations. In Israel's memory, Gibeon was a pagan city (see Josh 9; 2 Sam 21:2) and the location of a large sacrificial cave or rather a temple where YHWH and perhaps also the sun-god Shemesh was worshiped (see Josh 10:12–13). Solomon stages a large sacrifice at this location and spends the night in the sanctuary, perhaps with the intention of producing a theophany. The divinity indeed appears and grants him a wish. Solomon proves himself to be remarkably modest and insightful: he wishes for wisdom to guide his ruling. Solomon is granted his wish—and he is given everything else he did

---

31. We have only to recall the large narrative in 2 Kgs 9–11 as well as the short notes in 12:20; 14:5, 18; 21:23–24, and others.

not wish for as well, providing him with all the attributes that are a part of the traditional picture of Solomon. The narrative's positive description continues in the following narrative of Solomon's judgment. With astonishing insight the king as judge is able to solve an unsolvable case. The praises of Solomon in verses 12–13 and 28 show the intention of the final narrator quite clearly.

More informational lists follow these vivid narratives in 1 Kgs 4:1–5:14. The list of Solomon's officials in 4:1–6 in comparison to the Davidic lists in 2 Sam 8:16–18 and 20:23–36 shows the continuity and discontinuity of the young monarchy. Several cabinet posts have not changed (Adoniram for forced labor, Jehoshaphat as recorder); Joab and Abiathar are missing; Beniah now is the only military official, but his ranking has dropped somewhat. Some posts have been reassigned, others have been added: the administration is growing! The list of provinces in 4:7–19 describes the twelve regions of northern Israel, the weightiest part of the Davidic-Solomonic kingdom. Not included is the city-state of Jerusalem and the land of Judah as well as foreign holdings. The provinces are obligated to supply the royal court in ordered rotation and to supply quotas of forced labor (9:23). The governors are taken partially from the immediate inner circle of the king (the names Ahilud, Ahimaaz, Nathan, and Hushai are well known from the Davidic-Solomonic tradition), partly also from individuals of whom we do not even know their parentage. The summary description of wealth and stability during the time of Solomon culminates in the sentence that sounds like true utopia: "During Solomon's lifetime Judah and Israel lived in safety, from Dan to Beer-sheba, all of them under their vines and fig trees" (5:5; cf. Mic 4:4). Now the narrative focuses not only on (northern) Israel but on the entire united kingdom that Solomon took over from David. All the inhabitants of the heartland enjoy an equally high standard of living, claims the narrator. He discretely points out that Israel did not have to bear the burden of Solomon's court alone but that the subjected nations "from the Euphrates to Egypt" shared this burden. Then the text describes in detail what the subjects invested in their king: ten thousand kilograms of flour a day and ten thousand head of cattle a year. Left unclarified is whether this included only the Jerusalem residence or the provincial administrations as well. Added to this were feed and straw for thousands of warhorses. The section ends with a description of Solomon's wisdom in 5:9–14, thus closing the circle that started with 3:1–15. Now, however, the text does not emphasize wisdom for ruling and judging but rather scholarly wisdom. The reporter makes it quite clear that scholarship was already then an international enterprise and that he believes Solomon embodied the height of international scholarship: "He was wiser than anyone else" (5:11).

The section described above is connected thematically on various levels with 1 Kgs 9–10. Between these two passages the temple construction stands as the centerpiece. The question of whether 1 Kgs 3–10 as a whole describes a "golden age" that is framed by the darker chapters of 1 Kgs 1–2 and 11–12 (Frisch) or whether Solomon's fall is already prepared from 1 Kgs 9 onward (Parker) is difficult to decide. The final redactional stage seems to emphasize the latter more strongly. Whether the material was arranged differently in its original form must remain unanswered.

Solomon had to pay with several northern Israelite villages for the aid received by the Phoenicians for his large construction projects (1 Kgs 9:10–14). This embarrassing fact is only tempered slightly by the claim that the king of Tyre was unhappy with this deal (the Chronicler, who turns these villages into gifts from Hiram to Solomon [2 Chr 8:2], is more thorough). Then 1 Kgs 9:15–19 lists the names of those cities that Solomon is supposed to have fortified and expanded (the list is supplemented by the claim in 9:20–23 that only Canaanite, not Israelite, forced labor was used, thus contradicting 5:27–30—probably a Deuteronomistic addition). The passage in 9:24–28 lists several administrative decisions that are credited to Solomon: the construction of a house for the daughter of the pharaoh who supposedly belonged to his harem (9:24; cf. 3:1; 9:16; 11:1); the staging of large sacrificial celebrations three times a year (9:25); and the construction and assembly of a shipping fleet, which Solomon initiated with the help of the much more experienced Tyrians, who then shared in the profit (9:27–28).

In characteristic fashion for the Solomon tradition, a large narrative follows the lists: the story of the Queen of Sheba (10:1–13). As indicated earlier, this particular story led to an extensive reception history (see §I.1). Like 1 Kgs 3, this story basically aims to praise Solomon's wisdom by describing a noble and wise ruler who is highly impressed by it. (The theologically well-versed speech that she gives in 10:6–9 is a typical Deuteronomistic composition; the immense wealth described in the text is most certainly an exaggeration that may praise the king or criticize him; cf. Deut 17:17.)

The summary statement about Solomon's wealth in 1 Kgs 10:14–29 may have caused the original readers to rejoice: "silver and gold were worth nothing during the time of Solomon" (10:21)—a fantastic, perhaps also traumatic, vision. Everything around Solomon glitters. All the objects mentioned, however, are only "covered" in gold and "decorated" with ivory. The short notices about the significant armament increase and the profitable weapons trade in 10:26–29 deserve special attention. This is mentioned regarding a time for which the text does not mention a single military conflict. Solomon is described as a ruler of peace; perhaps Solomon's army had a similar representative function in the minds of the narrators as did the fairy-tale dimension of the king's harem (11:1–3). The list of the home countries of these women shows clearly the diplomatic-political purpose of these marriages; later redac-

tors connected the subsequent division of the kingdom with the temptation
that went out from these many foreign women to serve foreign gods and
added an appropriate declaration (11:4–8, 9–13).

Two detailed stories dealing with matters of foreign policy during Solomon's reign (11:14–28 … 40) mark the end of the Solomon narratives. These
narratives are connected by the term שׂטן (satan), which does not yet refer to
a supernatural being but rather to an earthly agent of God's punishment. The
details concern the Edomite prince Hadad; Rezon, the founder of the Dama-
scene dynasty; and the northern Israelite rebel (and subsequent founder of
his own empire) Jeroboam. These three have in common that they attack
Solomon's sphere of influence described earlier and attempt to or succeed
in diminishing its size. The story of the rise and fall of the Edomite prince
Hadad is told with special empathy. Perhaps this was originally also true in
the case of Jeroboam—significant in that he is a man connected to the quotas
of forced laborers supplied to Solomon by the provinces—but now the narrative is shaped by a prophetic scene of Deuteronomistic origin at its center that
focuses on explaining the division of the kingdom that was so traumatic for
Judah (11:29–39).

I.4.4.3. How Solomon Built the Temple

The biblical narrators cannot conceal that Solomon depended on foreign know-how and resources in order to realize his construction projects,
including the construction of the Yhwh sanctuary in Jerusalem. As cosmopolitan tradespeople with a rich culture and rich natural resources, such as
the extensive forests of the Lebanon, the Phoenicians were a perfect partner.
Apparently Hiram of Tyre, who is already reported to have cooperated with
David (2 Sam 5:11), approached Solomon first. Nevertheless, Solomon is the
petitioner. The earliest source for the biblical text seems to be a very prosaic
contract governing the shipment of wood by the Phoenicians and Israel's payment with domestic natural resources; the Deuteronomistic redaction adds a
theological discussion between the two kings during their economic talks.

The text then proudly reports how a massive amount of forced labor was
brought in from "all of Israel" (contrast 1 Kgs 9:20–23). By presenting large
numbers and describing a gigantic rotational system that fed the construction sites with a continual supply of rested laborers, the text aims to impress
its readers. The entire country was on the move in order to realize Solomon's
high-flying plans. Wood had to be brought in from the Lebanon, whereas
stones came in abundance from the mountains around Jerusalem. The stone-
cutters also supposedly included the Gebalites, artisans from Byblos (today's
northern Lebanon), not a surprising fact, considering the context.

As 1 Kgs 6:1–10 describes the structural work, we can begin to visualize the building rather clearly. Indeed, this description has often served as the basis for reconstruction attempts. The temple is conceived as a long house; with a size of about 30 by 10 by 15 meters, it is spacious but not over-dimensioned.

A late Deuteronomistic redaction dates the laying of the cornerstone in the 480th year after the exodus, thus connecting it to *the* central event of biblical salvation history (1 Kgs 6:1). This number is full of mystery and symbolism: it can be divided by many other numbers, but (more importantly) it is the product of twelve generations of forty years. The fact that construction begins exactly in this year is significant. The Deuteronomists were also careful to make sure that the construction of the temple did not appear as an achievement that obligated God in any way. They have God himself convey clearly to Solomon that the fortune and misfortune of the dynasty and the land depends entirely on adhering to the Torah (6:11–13).

The interior of the temple is described in 1 Kgs 6:14–36, starting with the woodwork. All of the inner walls of the sanctuary are encased in wood panels and woodcarvings. Noticeably, the decoration lacks figural elements. With many elements from the animal and plant worlds, however, it represents living creatures and thus reminds the observer of the creator (Bloch-Smith). The cherubim (6:23–27) belong in part to the earthly, in part to the heavenly, realm. They are winged chimeras, part animal, part human, and part angel. The cherubim were probably thought to carry YHWH the king, who was throned invisibly above them. The technically and artistically elaborate doors are described separately (6:31–35). Later redactors probably added the fiction that the entire temple and its interior were encased in gold.

Almost as an aside, the biblical narrators let us know that the temple was part of a larger area that included several administrative buildings (1 Kgs 7:1–12). The description of these buildings, however, is not at all as detailed as the description of the temple. The "House of the Forest of the Lebanon," named after the vast amount of precious wood sheeting from the Lebanon built into it, seems an especially monumental construction. According to the numbers in the text, it measures 50 by 25 meters and contains an enormous ceremonial room. Forty-five pillars support the ceiling and a partial upper floor. Added to this building is a separate throne hall as well as several residential and administrative buildings. The entire description conveys the impression that palace and temple are designed in the same architectural style and use the same materials; the reader (or the viewer!) thus faces an imposing architectural complex.

According to the biblical description, a Phoenician artisan with the same name as his king, Hiram, crafts the metalwork in the temple interior (1 Kgs 7:13–51). Two pillars standing in front of the entrance to the temple are described first. They are decorated with strange and inscrutable names. It seems that we must imagine them to be huge stylized lotus plants, decorated with pomegranates, symbolizing God-given, creative life (7:15–22). The text then describes in great detail astonishing large bronze sculptures. The "molten sea" (7:23–26), perfectly round with a diameter of 5 meters and a height of 2.5 meters, perhaps reminded the ancient viewer of the primordial sea from which creation took its course (see Gen 1:1–10). The oxen symbolize fighting power and fertility. The ten identical tank wagons (7:27–39) each contain over 900 liters, according to the description: an image of the sweet water so important in nature but also necessary for many cultic practices (see 1 Chr 4:6). The original readers connected their own visual impressions with the descriptions in the text, probably adding many unknown facets to biblical description.

Everything described is listed once more in 1 Kgs 7:40–47, which adds that Solomon erected his own foundries in the Jordan Valley in order to supply the necessary copper. One redactor missed a list of the sacred implements and royal offerings, so he added these and covered everything liberally with gold (7:48–51).

The narrators describe the dedication of the temple as a huge celebration (1 Kgs 8:1–21). From all corners of Israel (and surely Judah as well), the elders and honored people (8:1, 3)—not all the men—came to the capital. At the beginning of the celebration, a procession carried the ark from its tent in David's city, where it had been previously located (see 2 Sam 6), up to the temple complex. We do not know what was originally contained in the wooden "box" (the original meaning of אָרוֹן); the Deuteronomistic redaction added both tablets containing the Decalogue (see 8:9 and Exod 25:21). The new location for the ark is the holy of holies in the temple, underneath the cherubim's spread wings. If they are the carriers of the throne, then the ark is perhaps the footstool of Yhwh the king. He himself is not portrayed—as a statue perhaps—only his royal implements are visible. The ark retains the signs of its former mobility, the carrying staffs; this may indicate that Yhwh is not bound to one location. The description is carried by the conviction, however, that he has voluntarily bound himself to this location. He moves into the impenetrable darkness of the holy of holies, becomes invisible on two levels, and yet remains within reach. The solemn temple dedication speech correlates God's mysterious nature with the bright light he was surrounded with in the sight of Israel. The next item of the ceremony is the blessing—by the king, not a priest!—given to the assembled congregation (8:14).

Then the Deuteronomistic redaction places a short sermon in the mouth of Solomon (1 Kgs 8:15–21). Ever since the exodus from Egypt (see 6:1!), God intended to take residence in Jerusalem. David's successes and Solomon's succession to the throne find their goal in the temple on Mount Zion: we can start to understand how important this building was to later generations—especially to those who stood before its ruins.

Solomon's entire prayer for the dedication of the temple (1 Kgs 8:22–53) seems to be Deuteronomistic or post-Deuteronomistic. The introduction to the prayer densely reflects the relation between the promise to David and obedience to the Torah (8:23–26) as well as between God's immeasurable greatness and his residence on Zion (8:27–30). A statement such as that found in 8:27 fends off a common temple ideology. God is too great to be contained by anyone in anything, yet he still allows himself to be found at a specific location and becomes accessible to his chosen people. The actual prayer contains Solomon's request to answer all prayers that rise up from this temple to heaven in the future: in the case of difficult court cases (31–32), threat of war (33–34), drought (35–36), and misfortunes of any kind (37–40). Toward the end of the text, the postexilic situation becomes clear: prayers are included for the proselytes coming to Jerusalem (41–43) and for the Israelites and Judahites who dwell in foreign lands (44–45, 46–51). Zion should create a common identity for all who belong to Yhwh's "own people" (52–53). The text can hardly have been written as one piece; it seems to contain the needs of different times and carrier groups. Talstra proposes textual layers: a pre-Deuteronomistic layer (8:31–32, 37–40*, 41–43*), an initial Deuteronomistic layer from the time of Josiah (14–20, 22–25*, 28–29*), a second Deuteronomistic layer written during the exile (44–45, 46–51*), and a post-Deuteronomistic layer (33–36, 52–53, also 57–61). This dating as a whole seems quite early. Veijola (1982) divides the text into three Deuteronomistic, that is, exilic-postexilic layers: (1) 8:14, 15*, 17–21, 62–63, 65–66; (2) 8:16, 22–26, 54a, 55–58, 61, 66*; (3) 8:29–30, 31–51*, 52–53, 59–60.

In 1 Kgs 8:54–61 Solomon blesses the gathered congregation once more. In moving images, he declares the fulfillment of all the promises given to Moses, such as the full possession of the entire land, a stable existence for the entire people, and the continual presence of God in the land and with this people. The important word "rest" (compare Josh 21:43–45; 2 Sam 7:1, 11) brings together the dreams and hopes of postexilic times. The prayer that God may not reject his people but prepare their hearts to keep his commandments speaks clearly to the fear of God's judgment and to the insight into one's own imperfection. Israel knows that it owes its existence to the grace of God, and it knows that this existence is not an end unto itself but a means of revealing the one and only God to all peoples.

The celebrations are followed by a seven-day banquet (1 Kgs 8:62–66). Solomon sacrifices hecatombs of offerings, many more, of course, than sacrificed at Gibeon (3:4) and many more than the regular altar could have managed (8:64 is a rationalizing addition). All of the numbers go beyond any rational scope.

The narrators want to convey to their readers that Solomon is anything but stingy, here and elsewhere, and does his utmost to please God and his people.

The entire passage describing the theophany in 1 Kgs 9:1–9 is late Deuteronomistic. The author explicitly refers to the Gibeon episode (9:2): now God no longer must meet with Solomon in such a questionable location! God assures Solomon of his goodwill for the dynasty and the temple, but he ties his promises to the condition of adherence to the commandments. If the king and the people do not keep the commandments, especially the first commandment, and turn to other gods, then loss of the land and destruction of the temple become a real threat. We clearly see how the events of 587/86 B.C.E. influence these statements. The text provides us with a guide for our reading of the entire era of the monarchy: under David and Solomon, Israel and Judah took off with a great start, yet the end will be miserable. The temple will fall into ruin, David's dynasty will be forced off the throne, and Judah as well as Israel will lose their land. What will remain, however, is God's love for his people and the possibility that his people might still learn to be loyal to their God. This passage is thus both the justification of calamity and the promise of salvation.

II. THE HISTORY OF THE EARLY MONARCHY

II.1. BASIC ISSUES

II.1.1. BIBLICAL HISTORY AND FACTUAL HISTORY

Amit, Yairah. "The Dual Causality Principle and Its Effects on Biblical Literature," *VT* 37 (1987): 385–400. **Baum,** Armin D. "Zu Funktion und Authentizitätsanspruch der *oratio recta*: Hebräische und griechische Geschichtsschreibung im Vergleich," *ZAW* 115 (2003): 586–607. **Carreira,** José Nunes. "Formen des Geschichtsdenkens in altorientalischer und alttestamentlicher Geschichtsschreibung," *BZ* NS 31 (1987): 36–57. **Dentan,** Robert C., ed. *The Idea of History in the Ancient Near East* (New Haven: American Oriental Society, 1983). **Dever,** William G. *What Did the Biblical Writers Know and When Did They Know It? What Archaeology Can Tell Us about the Reality of Ancient Israel* (Grand Rapids: Eerdmans, 2001). **Edelman,** Diana Vikander, ed. *The Fabric of History: Text, Artefact and Israel's Past* (JSOTSup 127; Sheffield: JSOT Press, 1991). **Kitchen,** Kenneth. "The Controlling Role of External Evidence in Assessing the Historical Status of the Israelite United Monarchy," in *Windows into Old Testament History: Evidence, Argument, and the Crisis of "Biblical Israel"* (ed. V. Philips Long, David W. Baker, and Gordon J. Wenham; Grand Rapids: Eerdmans, 2002), 111–30. **Kofoed,** Jens Bruun. "Epistemology, Historiographical Method, and the "Copenhagen School," in Long, Baker, and Wenham, *Windows into Old Testament History,* 23–43. **Krecher,** Joachim, and Hans-Peter **Müller.** "Vergangenheitsinteresse in Mesopotamien und Israel," *Saeculum* 26 (1975): 13–44. **McKenzie,** Steven L., and M. Patrick **Graham,** eds. *The History of Israel's Traditions: The Heritage of Martin Noth* (JSOTSup 182; Sheffield: Sheffield Academic Press, 1994). **Millard,** Alan R., James K. **Hoffmeier,** and David W. **Baker,** eds. *Faith, Tradition, and History: Old Testament Historiography in Its Near Eastern Context* (Winona Lake, Ind.: Eisenbrauns, 1994). **Oeming,** Manfred. "Bedeutung und Funktionen von 'Fiktionen' in der alttestamentlichen Geschichtsschreibung," *EvT* 44 (1984): 254–66. **Seeligmann,** Isaac Leo. "Erkenntnis Gottes und historisches Bewußtsein im alten Israel," in *Beiträge zur alttestamentlichen Theologie: Festschrift für Walther Zimmerli zum 70. Geburtstag* (ed. Herbert Donner, Robert Hanhart, and Rudolf Smend; Göttingen: Vandenhoeck & Ruprecht,

1977), 414–45. **Smend,** Rudolf. *Elemente alttestamentlichen Geschichtsdenkens* (ThSt 95; Zürich, EVZ-Verlag,1968), repr. in idem, *Die Mitte des Alten Testaments* (BEvT 99; Munich: Kaiser, 1986) 160–85. **Soggin,** J. Alberto. "Geschichte als Glaubens-bekenntnis—Geschichte als Gegenstand wissenschaftlicher Forschung," *TLZ* 110 (1985): 161–72. **Weippert,** Manfred. "Fragen des israelitischen Geschichtsbewusst-seins," *VT* 23 (1973): 415–42.

II.1.1.1. The Historical Picture of the Early Monarchy in the Bible

The biblical narratives about the early monarchy start as the period of judges draws to a close. Judgeship ends with its last leaders: Eli and Samuel and their wayward sons. Israel is utterly defeated by the Philistines, the sacred ark is stolen, and the future seems very precarious, despite Samuel's obvious merits. In this context we can easily understand the people's desire for a king who may be able to stabilize the situation (1 Sam 1:1–8:5). Saul seems to be the right person for the job. He wins major battles with the help of Samuel, or rather YHWH (1 Sam 11, also 13–14). On the other hand, we hear highly criti-cal voices (8:6–19; 10:17–19, 27; 12:1–25), not just against Saul himself but also against the institution of the monarchy in general. These voices proclaim the monarchy to be a latent threat against Israel, or rather against faith in YHWH. Thus only minimal mistakes suffice to have Saul rejected soon after he has been instituted as king (13:7–15; 15:1–35).

God has found a new man "after his own heart" for the kingship: David (1 Sam 13:14). Samuel must anoint him, and David is soon loved by the royal family and the people as a whole (16:14–18:30). Nothing, not even Saul's des-perate persecution, can stop his rise. In the end, the kingdom falls to him almost by itself (1 Sam 19–2 Sam 5). David transfers the sacred ark to his new residence in Jerusalem but is not permitted to build YHWH a "house"; instead, he finds out that God intends to build a "house" for him (2 Sam 6–7). God grants him military success against all peoples around him (2 Sam 8) and guides him in numerous different and threatening temptations and hostilities, crises, and dangers (2 Sam 9–20). In response to his life story, David reacts with thanksgiving and praise (2 Sam 21–24). In the end, he remains alive long enough to witness and contribute to the fulfillment of the promise of a con-tinual Davidic dynasty with Solomon's ascension to the throne (1 Kgs 1–2).

Solomon's rule (1 Kgs 3–10) is a time of power and glory, of success and fame. The temple stands at the center (1 Kgs 5–8), surrounded by many reports of Solomon's wisdom and wealth. A certain amount of skepticism, however, is mixed into this abundant praise: Does Solomon not have and do too much? Toward the end of his reign, his many wives lead him to apostasy, and the fringes of his kingdom immediately start crumbling as the first uprisings shake the center of power. Following Solomon's death, the united kingdom breaks apart into a northern and a southern kingdom (1 Kgs 11–12).

This is a brief summary of the biblical account of the early monarchy. As in all other periods of biblical history, God is clearly a main character. He does not, of course, determine history completely on his own; he must deal with Israel, especially with the kings, with several individuals and groups within Israel, and with non-Israelite nations. But human actions and their consequences are always more or less clearly connected to a relationship with God. Even if he is not always explicitly present to evaluate ongoing events and take action—most noticeably in 2 Samuel and the beginning of 1 Kings—he nevertheless is thought to be there and influence what is happening. Time and again people will speak of him, or he will speak himself and take action, as if from behind the scenes. This may seem strange or edifying, depending on one's point of view; in any case, it confronts us with a serious problem if we want to write the history of the early monarchy.

II.1.1.2. Historical Deconstruction

Our ideas about what we call "historical" and what deserves the name "historiography" are hardly influenced by biblical history writing, slightly more by ancient Greek and Roman histories, more again by what the Renaissance and the Romantic era thought "classical" and "ancient" to be, and mostly by the paradigms proposed during the Enlightenment. We are used to perceiving and organizing our reality rationally, to penetrate and master the laws that govern it, to understand causal connections and evaluate and act accordingly. Even if the modern period, following gigantic failures and catastrophes, has lost much of the optimistic belief that we eventually will be able to "enlighten" all things and protect humanity from unpleasant surprises, even if the popularity for the irrational and the transcendent is growing today, we cannot and we do not want to turn back from the decisions and achievements of the modern age. This is true for how we manage the present and plan the future as well as for how we perceive our past. We may be willing to see death as more than a purely biological phenomenon, for example, but we will not believe that a dead person can be conjured from the realm of the dead, as the Bible reports of the dead Samuel (1 Sam 28).

Despite all reflections on the inevitability of subjective preunderstanding and involuntary normative value judgment, we still pursue the positivist ideal that we must find out *what actually happened back then* when we study history. Our assessment of various sources from the past and on the past is strongly influenced by whether they promise to help us with this task, whether they can provide us with *objective* information. We thus trust material artifacts to a greater degree than verbal sources that bear witness to a certain culture, dry lists of facts more than legends or narratives that remind us of fairy tales, statements on human actions more than reflections on God's actions. The credibility of historical sources and historiographic works is measured by the degree to which they describe processes that can be understood and reconstructed rationally and report events that we might be able to verify. Within the category of credible sources, we discern various nuances: from objectively verifiable conditions and suppositions to those with a low degree of probability. Statements about God are above historical evaluation—except as information about those who made these statements. In the modern age, history must be understood and described *etsi deus non daretur* ("as though God did not exist").

From this perspective, the biblical narratives on Israel's first kings will not find it easy to gain the trust of the historian. As mentioned above, the first problem is presented by the fact that God plays an active role. Again and again he speaks to individual human beings: to Samuel and Solomon in a dream (1 Sam 3; 1 Kgs 3—we can only interpret these statements as auto-suggestion if we deliberately go against the intention of the text), to Nathan and Solomon directly (2 Sam 7:4; 1 Kgs 6:11–13; 9:1–9); God even engages Samuel in a real conversation (1 Sam 8:6–22; 16:1–13). God grants reliable oracles upon request (1 Sam 10:22; 23:2, 14; 2 Sam 5:19, 23; 21:1). God holds strong opinions on specific human actions, and, more to the point, the narrators claim to know these opinions (e.g., 1 Sam 15:10; 2 Sam 11:27; 12:24; 1 Kgs 11:9ff.). Most important, God gets personally involved in events on earth. He sends prophets (2 Sam 12:1; 24:12). He moves events along desired paths (2 Sam 17:14). He makes people sick (1 Sam 5:9) or even kills them (1 Sam 5:19; 25:38; 2 Sam 12:15). He allows a woman to become pregnant (1 Sam 1:20). He grants wisdom to a king (1 Kgs 4:9). His spirit results in courage (1 Sam 11:6) or depression (1 Sam 16:14). He personally defeats enemy armies and peoples (1 Sam 5–6; 14:15), demands the eradication of entire tribes (1 Sam 15), and aids the king in subjecting the surrounding nations (2 Sam 8:6, 14).

The biblical account of history does not only reckon with God's activities but also believes human beings to be capable of many, even superhuman accomplishments. In 1 Sam 2:27–36 a nameless "man of God" prophesies future events to Eli that occur either in the near future (1 Sam 4), after several decades (1 Kgs 1:26–27), or after several centuries (2 Kgs 23:8–9). We might prefer to interpret such miraculous foresight as the hindsight of later generations. A similar situation exists when Solomon already refers to the situation following the destruction of the temple in 587/6 B.C.E. and the subsequent exile in his prayer for the dedication of the temple (1 Kgs 8:46ff.). Even Abigail displays such a prophetic gift, even if not to the same degree, when she foretells David his entire future (1 Sam 25)—not to mention the magical abilities that allow the "witch of Endor" to conjure Samuel from the dead (1 Sam 28). Samuel can do almost anything: he is prophet, priest, judge, military leader, tribune, and kingmaker. David is good and successful beyond measure, Solomon wise and wealthy beyond compare. What enlightened person can accept all these things as historical accounts?

Many aspects of biblical historiography seem credible to a modern observer, even if they cannot be verified. Very often the narrative describes what happens inside various people (e.g., Saul's jealousy toward David or David's feelings during Absalom's rebellion), or the narrative reports direct speech that no one could have overheard (e.g., the conversations between Eli and Samuel in the middle of the night [1 Sam 3]; Uriah and David after the latter's adultery [2 Sam 11]; princess Tamar and her rapist, prince Amnon [2 Sam 13]; David and Bathsheba and David and Nathan during the events surrounding the succession [1 Kgs 1]). There are specific names, but no one can say whether or not they are fictitious (e.g., the names in Elkanah's family or of the priests of Shiloh [1 Sam 1]; the names of places where David is supposed to have been during his escape from Saul [1 Sam 19ff.]).

Certain things that we read we may classify as possible but unlikely: that Samuel persuaded his people to reject their non-Yahwist idols (1 Sam 7:3–4); that a casting of lots actually found the one who was supposed to be found (1 Sam 10:20–21; 14:40ff.); that the crown prince Jonathan loved David enough voluntarily to resign his claim to the throne (1 Sam 23:16–18); that King Saul was so vulnerable that the vagabond David could have easily killed him (1 Sam 24; 26); and much more.

Several events that are reported as facts seem utterly impossible: that the ark spread disease and death wherever it was taken in Philistine territory (1 Sam 5–6); that Saul raised 210,000 men for a military campaign and that Solomon sacrificed 22,000 cattle and 120,000 sheep during the dedication of the temple (1 Sam 15:4; 1 Kgs 8:62); that Solomon's harem included one thousand women (1 Kgs 11:3); that the location of the Jerusalem temple was determined by the spot at which the angel of doom ceased spreading the plague (2 Sam 24:16); that David, a tender shepherd boy, could have defeated and killed an elite warrior who was armed to the teeth (1 Sam 17).

We conclude that the description of history in the Bible followed different dictums than those governing modern historiography. This, of course, is not a new insight. Many scholars have expressed this truth before, most often and with a certain degree of malice against the Chronistic History. The same is true, however, for Deuteronomistic historiography and even for the books of Samuel, which were often regarded as reliable historical witnesses. The prime objective of biblical historians never was to discover and report *how it actually occurred.* They did not write about the past as much as for the present. They were concerned with informing and edifying and teaching their *current* readers.

This becomes especially clear in narratives that seem to have the primary intention of fulfilling the expectations of their original readers. We know of many similar stories with similar content, whether in the Old Testament itself or in the literature of the ancient Near East. A woman is without child but becomes pregnant by a miracle and gives birth to—of course—a son who will become famous all throughout the land (1 Sam 1; cf. Gen 18; 30; Judg 13). When a brave young man sets out to accomplish a task given to him by his father, he is confronted by mysterious events—and ends up in a position of leadership (1 Sam 9:1–10:16). Two men are anointed to be king by a man of God without being predestined for this position or even desiring it or suspecting that it may happen (1 Sam 10:1ff.; 16:1ff.; see 2 Kgs 9:1ff.). The spirit of God overwhelms a courageous farmer lad after he hears that disaster fell upon his countrymen; he sets out to do battle with the enemy and becomes the liberator of his people (1 Sam 11; see also the book of Judges). A king tries to arrest a bothersome prophet; after three attempts fail miserably, the king himself tries and fails (1 Sam 19:18ff.; see also 2 Kgs 1). Two armies encounter each other, but instead of engaging in battle an elite warrior challenges an opponent to single combat (1 Sam 17; 2 Sam 2:12ff.).[1] The narratives tell of the miraculous and unstoppable rise of a leader: the youngest of several brothers, that is, without much future in his own house, without royal blood, but of royal spirit, pursued by the jealousy of the current ruler and exiled from his home country, but, despite all, arriving at his final goal by fate or rather with the help of God (1 Sam 16–2 Sam 5)—a classic story of justification for a ruler who unexpectedly came to power.[2] And there is more: the king responds in thanksgiving to his heavenly benefactor for his many blessings by building a temple dedicated to him—or at least making the plans for such a construction (2 Sam 7; 1 Kgs 5–8).[3] King David is known as *the* pious man of prayer, not

---

1. The motif of substitutionary single combat can also be found in the Egyptian Sinuhe narrative as well as in Mari and Hittite texts; see Roland de Vaux, "Single Combat in the Old Testament: The Bible and the Ancient Near East," in idem, *The Bible and the Ancient Near East* (trans. Damian McHugh; London, Darton, Longman & Todd, 1972), 122–35; Jack M. Sasson, "Reflections on an Unusual Practice Reported in ARM X:4," *Or* 43 (1974): 404–10; F. Charles Fensham, "The Battle between the Men of Joab and Abner as a Possible Ordeal by Battle?" *VT* 20 (1970): 356–57.

2. See P. Kyle McCarter Jr., "The Apology of David," *JBL* 99 (1980): 489–504; the so-called Apology of the Hittite king Shuppiluliumash III is the most interesting parallel.

3. Siegfried Herrmann ("Die Königsnovelle in Ägypten und in Israel," in idem, *Gesam-*

only to the redactors of the Psalter but already to the authors of the books of Samuel (1 Sam 16:14–23; 2 Sam 1:17–27; 7:18–29; 22–23); on a smaller scale, the same is true for King Solomon (compare 1 Kgs 8:22–52 with Pss 72; 127). In terms of subject matter, the famous Solomonic judgment (1 Kgs 3:16ff.) is also a common topic in world literature.[4]

If we subject the biblical accounts of the early monarchy to a rigorous historical-critical analysis (as we must with all documents from the past!), then their credibility as historical accounts grows even smaller. It would go beyond the present context to discuss this in detail; a few indications must suffice. If we discover that the Bible is not a collection of eyewitness accounts, or only to a very small degree, then the claim that it reports *how it actually occurred* suffers greatly. Instead, we seem to be faced with a conglomeration of texts that developed over centuries and that were finally—most would claim, decisively—redacted half a millennium after the events themselves occurred. We can certainly assume a highly developed ability to memorize even complex matters and pass them on orally. We can even assume the transmission of written sources. We nevertheless cannot assume that a process of tradition covering centuries will be without breaks and reinterpretations, especially as it is not at all clear that the reporting of historical facts was ever the prime concern of those who wrote and handed down these texts.

A few examples may clarify the matter. There are clear indications that the "seer" in the original text who anointed Saul according to 1 Sam 9:1–10:16 was *not* Samuel and that Samuel was *not* present at Saul's battle with the Ammonites, assuming that this battle was historical at all (contrary to 11:12–14). What does this imply for the role of the historical Samuel for the founding of the Israelite state? What does it mean when we encounter two stories of David's battle with Goliath the Gittite hidden in the biblical account—and

---

melte *Studien zur Geschichte und Theologie des Alten Testaments* [TB 75; Munich: Kaiser, 1986], 120–44) and Manfred Görg (*Gott-König-Reden in Israel und Ägypten* [BWANT 105; Stuttgart: Kohlhammer, 1975]) have analyzed Egyptian analogies. Victor A. Hurowitz (*I Have Built You an Exalted House: Temple Building in the Bible in the Light of Mesopotamian and North-West Semitic Writings* [JSOTSup 115; Sheffield: JSOT Press, 1992]) has gathered material from Mesopotamia and Syria.

4. Hugo Gressmann ("Das Salomonische Urteil," *Deutsche Rundschau* 130 [1907]: 212–28) gathered twenty-two analogies from the Mediterranean area and also from the southern and eastern Asian regions. See also Martin Noth, "Die Bewährung von Salomos 'Göttlicher Weisheit,'" in *Wisdom in Israel and in the Ancient Near East: Presented to Professor Harold Henry Rowley by the Society for Old Testament Study in Association with the Editorial Board of Vetus Testamentum, in Celebration of His Sixty-Fifth Birthday, 24 March 1955* (ed. Martin Noth and D. Winton Thomas; VTSup 3; Leiden, Brill, 1955), 225–37. Bertolt Brecht's "Kaukasischer Kreidekreis" could also be mentioned in this context.

then find out from 2 Sam 21:19 that a certain Elhanan ben Jaare from Bethlehem defeated Goliath the Gittite, the shaft of whose spear was like a weaver's beam? How are we to explain that David was supposedly anointed three times as king: once by Samuel (1 Sam 16:1–13), once by the men of Judah (2 Sam 2:4), and once by the elders of Israel (2 Sam 5:3)? How must we understand that one of the songs that David supposedly composed toward the end of his life (2 Sam 22) is almost identical with Ps 18 and that only David and Moses say farewell to the readers with two psalm-like songs (cf. 2 Sam 22–23 with Deut 32–33)? What does it mean for the historicity of the Absalom material that its composition forms a perfect chiasmus stretching over five chapters (2 Sam 15–19) in which the individual episodes mirror each other exactly? How are we to evaluate from a historical point of view that Solomon once is supposed to have used conscripted labor from all parts of Israel and once is supposed to have recruited his labor force only from Canaanite inhabitants (1 Kgs 5:27–32; 9:15–23)? How can it be that all three kings, Saul, David, and Solomon, all begin as brilliant leaders, only to fall deeper and deeper into partly self-inflicted, partly tragic, unavoidable tragedies? Why do the positive sides of Saul's career disappear into the abyss of history whereas David and Solomon are assured of eternal fame? Why do the sacred accomplishments of establishing a dynasty and building a temple glorify their names for centuries to come even though their life stories took a turn for the worse?

We may no doubt be able to find answers to all of these questions, but they do not strengthen the case for the historical reliability of biblical texts—we must emphasize: not of *all* biblical texts. The examples listed above already contain textual layers that can claim a certain degree of credibility, not to mention the many other texts where historical credibility can hardly be questioned. The concept of "credibility" used thus far in connection with the historical reliability of texts can, however, also be defined along completely different lines. To this we will now turn.

II.1.1.3. History and Faith

The authors of the books of Samuel and Kings undoubtedly intend to write *history*—and this is what they actually do. They clearly perceive the temporal distance between themselves and the narrated events, indicated by the consistent use of past tense. Their description follows chronological order—not an absolute but a relative order that is highly memorable: Samuel is born and raised by his mother; he is trained by Eli and grows up (1 Sam 3:19); he witnesses how the ark is lost and his mentor dies; twenty years pass during which the ark remains unnoticed in Kiriath-jearim (7:2), after which time Samuel gathers the people at Mizpah and leads them triumphantly against the Philistines; he then grows old (8:1), plays an important part in installing the first king (1 Sam 9–10), guides this king with advice and criticism, and must finally reject him (1 Sam 11; 13; 15) and anoint another (1 Sam 16); he appears on the scene once more (19:18ff.) before he dies (25:1), only to be conjured from the realm of the dead once more (1 Sam 28). Meanwhile, other chronological or biographical developments have started: the narrative of Saul, who will die just shortly after Samuel, and especially the Davidic narrative that extends into the book of Kings. Aside from these large biographies there are several others that are less conspicuous but nevertheless well crafted and interwoven with the large narratives: the stories of Michal, Jonathan, Joab, Absalom, or Adonijah. Each of these individuals is introduced, accompanied on his or her path (even if only during certain periods), and finally bid farewell. *Time* thus passes before our eyes: the lifetime of individual human beings, but also a time period in the history of Israel.

This does not intend to be anything but and it is nothing but history writing—and not a reflection or a treatise *on* history or an unsorted collection of histories, legends, or even fairy tales. It seems that the Old Testament authors thought it correct and important to portray the history of the early monarchy with its origins prior to the establishment of the state and its continuation in the development of the state as a temporal development, that is, as a contingent and irreversible process. The early monarchy appears as a time period that finds its continuation in the time period of the authors and their audience. The readers are instructed to understand their own present on the basis of the past.

The most important fact that must be perceived is the interconnection between human activities with their consequences and the actions of God. This is a unique quality of Old Testament history writing, not necessarily in the context of ancient historiography, but definitely when compared to modern historiography. Even if the previous interaction between God and human beings is not the only way to describe the relationship between God and human beings, it is the most adequate way—this is the assumption behind Old Testament historiography. For Old Testament faith in God, what happened in the past is not secondary or unimportant. Traces of the divine have left tracks in the lives of the forefathers—for good and for bad. History, at least when described with the belief that God is active in history, presents us with models for appropriate and inappropriate behavior toward God as well as with models for God's actions among human beings and his reactions to their behavior. This is not intended as a description of continual repetitions of the same patterns, as if we could assume regular cycles of divine–human interaction. The earlier actions of God and human beings are rather a part of the past, described along a linear timeline, that have become determinative for the development of history up to the present.

David received a promise that includes not just his times, not just the early or the entire monarchy, but all times. Yet David almost caused the ruin of his kingdom and his dynasty through his transgression in the affair of Bathsheba and Uriah. Every one of his actions had consequences beyond their immediate context—because historians deemed them worthy of being handed down; thus, they influenced readers of later time periods up to today. The same is true for what God did to and with David according to the biblical depiction: it was important in its own context, but it also remained important for later authors and every reader of their writings.

Biblical historiography is explicitly oriented to the recipient. It makes no secret of the fact that it explicitly addresses its readers, and the authors do not hide that history speaks meaningfully to them. History speaks—this is the main reason why history most often takes on the form of narratives that culminate in dialogue: *history* is a succession of *stories*. Stories, at least good stories, are attractive. They draw their readers into the events, make past events relevant for the present, and turn history into current, even urgent, communication. If the Old Testament historians were primarily story writers, storytellers who used the medium of text, and if their works are less historiography and more narrative—in modern terms we would call them *novels* or *fiction*—then their intention and goal in writing the history of the early monarchy is to turn this history into the history of its readers. Of course, *what actually occurred* is important, not necessarily as *it precisely happened* but rather as *what it intended to become.*

Thus, biblical historians do not want to depict past reality; instead, they intend to communicate the truth of history to their readers (which also includes communicating the truth *through* history). This truth is the truth about God and human beings and their mutual interaction. This definition, of course, is too abstract. The subject matter of the Hebrew Bible is not just any human beings and just any god; neither are we dealing with abstract concepts of humanity and divinity. The subject matter is the people of Israel and the God YHWH. Those who wrote about the early monarchy have taken sides before they even started to write: for their people and their God. Even during those passages where they write only about individual members of the royal family and seem to stay silent about God, they are still writing the history of Israel with YHWH. They inform their readers who Israel was and who YHWH was—from history. Their parents, their teachers, as well as generations of Israelites before them and Jews after them told the stories of what the people of Israel and what their God YHWH had done in history. This shaped and continues to shape a picture that still determines the attitude and worldview of humans who live as members of this people in God's presence. In this manner, the biblical authors and storytellers and all who have been influenced by them also tell the story of

Israel's first kings: both in knowledge and in faith—and with the hope that they will increase the knowledge and rouse the faith of their readers and listeners.

II.1.1.4. Basics of Historical Reconstruction

Historical scholarship today is interested not in faith (or should not be, in any case) but in knowledge. It should, however, not only be interested in *what actually occurred* but pay attention to two additional aspects: the historical context and determination of the sources used; and the prejudices of the present observer in respect to the object of inquiry. This necessarily leads to a twofold responsibility. On the one hand, the modern historian must analyze the situation of current historical scholarship by making the location and interests of historical observers as transparent as possible; this does not always have to be expressed in grand and detailed declaration but can occur *en passant* through occasional remarks on the side. On the other hand, modern historians must evaluate and emphasize the witnesses of the past as pillars of historical research by showing their limitation, bias, and dependency but also by understanding their own insights, attitudes, and intentions.

As a result, even current historiography will never be "objective." It cannot ignore the subjectivity of the individual scholar as well as the intersubjective network of contemporary scholarship and past existence. History cannot be understood as the succession of transsubjective facts. Historiography that attempts to write history in such a manner would bypass its objects—in the past and in the present. Historiography is never merely the neutral description of events; it will always include interpretation and evaluation. Otherwise it would be pale and boring in the best case, half-true and dishonest in the worst.

Thus Old Testament history writing is perhaps not as far away from modern attempts as it may seem at first sight. We can understand the framework in which it presents history, we can recognize the principles used by them and by us, and we can value their keen insights without sacrificing modern paradigms of historical scholarship. Old Testament historians wanted to rouse faith. This cannot be the goal of modern historiography. Where Old Testament historians pursued their goal by rational means and by using historical knowledge, and where we do history not as an *art pour l'art* but as a *human* science, aiming to enlighten human nature and expression (thus also the expression of faith!) in the past and present, there our interests and even our methods are the same to a large degree.

For modern—and with some limitations also for ancient—historiography, there are basically three methods that can be used to enlighten historical occurrences (see further Smend): using direct witnesses; drawing conclusions from the comparison with previous and subsequent time periods; and utilizing sometimes even distant analogies. I would like to briefly clarify these three methods by applying them to Israel's early monarchy.

Direct witnesses to the early monarchy can be written sources, biblical and extrabiblical, Israelite as well as non-Israelite. Other material witnesses from this time, especially from the area of Palestine but perhaps even from other areas of the ancient Near East, can supplement the written documents. The *comparison* with the era *prior* to the state as well as the era *subsequent* to the early monarchy follows a simple basic pattern: if there was no state before and two distinctly separate states after, then we must have somehow moved from one to the other in the intervening time. *Analogies* to the formation of the state in Israel may be found preferably in close temporal and geographical proximity, but they may also be found at a much greater temporal and geographical distance. Causal connections are not important; instead, the search for analogies is the search for comparable situations and processes.

It is clear that the conclusiveness of insights gained from these three methods tends to follow a declining plane of plausibility. An analogy is limited in its argumentative value because the occurrences can only be compared with limitations—not to mention the problem that the events would have to already have enough of a profile that they can be compared at all; otherwise inaccuracies and incorrect conclusions will grow exponentially. Comparisons between previous and subsequent time periods also require a high degree of knowledge of the respective periods. Even where this knowledge is present— and there is much doubt whether this can even be possible for the era prior to the formation of the state in Israel—averaging the insights from either side for the era in between is a very tentative enterprise. Direct witnesses clearly deserve most of our trust; if only they too did not present us with manifold difficulties, as already indicated above. How contemporary, how reliable, how comprehensive, and how detailed are the literary sources? How should they be understood and interpreted? How precisely can we contextualize material witnesses, and how much do they actually tell us? Their weakness by nature is their lack of words, leaving them open to the danger of misinterpretation.

In the face of these questions we must proceed carefully and prudently in our reconstruction of the early monarchy in Israel without allowing ourselves to become discouraged or overcautious.

II.1.2. Indirect Witnesses to the Formation of the State

Alt, Albrecht. "Der Anteil des Königtums an der sozialen Entwicklung in den Reichen Israel und Juda," in idem, *Kleine Schriften zur Geschichte des Volkes Israel*

(3 vols.; Munich: Beck, 1953–59), 3:348–72. **Bartlett,** John R. *Edom and the Edomites* (JSOTSup 77; Sheffield: Sheffield Academic Press, 1989). **Crüsemann,** Frank. *Der Widerstand gegen das Königtum: Die antiköniglichen Texte des Alten Testamentes und der Kampf um den frühen israelitischen Staat* (WMANT 49; Neukirchen-Vluyn: Neukirchener, 1978). **Galling,** Kurt, ed. *Textbuch zur Geschichte Israels* (2nd ed.; Tübingen: Mohr Siebeck, 1968). **Halpern,** Baruch. "The Uneasy Compromise: Israel between League and Monarchy," in *Traditions in Transformation: Turning Points in Biblical Faith* (ed. Baruch Halpern and Jon D. Levenson; Winona Lake, Ind.: Eisenbrauns, 1981), 59–96. **Hecke,** Karl-Heinz. *Juda und Israel: Untersuchungen zur Geschichte Israels in vor- und frühstaatlicher Zeit* (FB 52; Würzburg: Echter, 1985). **Hübner,** Ulrich. *Die Ammoniter: Untersuchungen zur Geschichte, Kultur und Religion eines transjordanischen Volkes im 1. Jahrtausend v.Chr.* (ADPV 16; Wiesbaden: Harrassowitz, 1992). **Levin,** Christoph. "Die Entstehung der Rechabiter," in *"Wer ist wie du, Herr, unter den Göttern?": Studien zur Theologie und Religionsgeschichte Israels: Für Otto Kaiser zum 70. Geburtstag* (ed. Ingo Kottsieper et al.; Göttingen: Vandenhoeck & Ruprecht, 1994), 301–17. **Klengel,** Horst. *Zwischen Zelt und Palast: Die Begegnung von Nomaden und Seßhaften im alten Vorderasien* (Leipzig: Koehler & Amelang, 1972). **Knauf,** Ernst Axel. *Midian: Untersuchungen zur Geschichte Palästinas und Nordarabiens am Ende des 2. Jahrtausends v.Chr.* (ADPV; Wiesbaden: Harrassowitz, 1988). **Knauf.** "The Cultural Impact of Secondary State Formation: The Cases of Edomites and Moabites," in *Early Edom and Moab: The Beginning of the Iron Age in Southern Jordan* (ed. Piotr Bienkowski; Sheffield Archaeological Monographs 7; Sheffield: J. R. Collis Publications in association with National Museums and Galleries on Merseyside, 1992), 47–54. **Lipiński,** Edward. *The Arameans: Their Ancient History, Culture, Religion* (OLA 100; Leuven: Peeters, 2000). **Liverani,** Mario. "The Collapse of the Near Eastern Regional System at the End of the Bronze Age: The Case of Syria," in *Centre and Periphery in the Ancient World* (ed. Michael Rowlands, Mogens Larsen, and Kristian Kristiansen; Cambridge: Cambridge University Press, 1987), 66–73. **Na'aman,** Nadav. "The Contribution of the Amarna Letters to the Debate on Jerusalem's Political Position in the Tenth Century B.C.E.," *BASOR* 304 (1996): 17–27. **Noort,** Edward. *Die Seevölker in Palästina* (Palaestina antiqua 8; Kampen: Kok Pharos, 1994). **Tadmor,** Hayim. "Traditional Institutions and the Monarchy: Social and Political Tensions in the Time of David and Solomon," in *Studies in the Period of David and Solomon and Other Essays: Papers Read at the International Symposium for Biblical Studies, Tokyo, 5–7 December, 1979* (ed. Tomoo Ishida; Winona Lake, Ind.: Eisenbrauns, 1982), 239–57. **Timm,** Stefan. *Moab zwischen den Mächten: Studien zu historischen Denkmälern und Texten* (ÄAT 17; Wiesbaden: Harrassowitz, 1989). **Weippert,** Manfred. "Edom: Studien und Materialien zur Geschichte der Edomiter auf Grund schriftlicher und archäologischer Quellen" (diss. ev. theol., Tübingen, 1971). **Welten,** Peter. *Die Königs-Stempel: Ein Beitrag zur Militärpolitik Judas unter Hiskia und Josia* (Wiesbaden: Harrassowitz, 1969). **Wiseman,** Donald J., ed. *Peoples of Old Testament Times* (Oxford: Clarendon, 1973).

II.1.2.1. Comparisons to Earlier and Later Periods

It is not possible to give a detailed account of the period before and after the early monarchy in this context; this is done in detail in the previous and following volumes of the Biblical Encyclopedia series. For our current purposes, a brief overview of the main issues relevant for a comparison with the early monarchy must suffice.

We can be sure that no continual state existed in Israel, or rather Palestine, up to the first millennium B.C.E. In the year 1887 a library containing about 350 clay tablets was found in Tell el-Amarna (in central Egypt on the eastern shore of the Nile at about the latitude of the southern tip of the Sinai peninsula). These clay tablets were produced in Canaan and sent to Amenophis III and IV, pharaohs at that time. They present us with a very colorful picture of Palestine in the early fourteenth century. There existed several city-states, such as Jerusalem, Lachish, Hebron, Ashkelon, Shechem, Megiddo, Akko, Sidon, Tyre, Byblos; all were subject to Egyptian rule but shaped in their daily administration much more by mutual and internal strife, jealousy, skirmishes, and rebellions. Aside from this mosaic of small power centers in ancient Canaan, the following point is important for our discussion: all of the communities mentioned above are centered around cities located in the plains of Palestine; the hill country is largely unimportant and mostly uninhabited (with the exceptions of Jerusalem and Shechem). We find no traces of the Philistines in the cities of the plains, not to mention in the hill country. In contrast, we frequently encounter so-called Apiru or Habiru, who have often been connected with the Hebrews of the Bible. In the Bible, the Hebrews refer to the people of Israel, whereas the Amarna letters do not seem to refer to an ethnic group but rather to a social class. Perhaps they were refugees, perhaps also dropouts from the cities who went about their daily lives on the fringes or in service to the city kings. In any case, they were a clear cause of turbulence in a society that was already restless, lacking clear rule from Egypt and torn between the claims and aspirations of various different city-states. One character does appear in the central Palestinian city of Shechem who could be seen as a ruler over a larger territory, a certain Labaiah: on the one hand, ruler of the city of Shechem; on the other hand, lord over a fairly widespread territory in the mountain and hill country of central Palestine.

It is interesting that the biblical book of Judges credits a first, albeit failed, attempt at establishing a territorial state to a Shechemite, Abimelech: first lord of the Canaanite city of Shechem, then ruler over a larger territory of the Israelite tribe Ephraim. According to the biblical account, Abimelech failed due to inner imbalances in his domain and due to his own impetuosity in expanding his territory. The book of Judges otherwise portrays the period following the conquest of the land as a time of relative tribal sovereignty. Regardless of how historical the narratives of liberation and the lists of judges may be, regardless of how legendary the material may be, and regardless of how the texts should be interpreted in detail, there is no doubt that the picture of life in separate tribes, organized not as a state but along lines of blood relation (in a wide sense!), builds on a historical core. We can perhaps assume a tribal confederation as a precursor to a state: hardly as a sacred union (as Martin Noth assumed) but rather a segmentary structure (Crüsemann), for which we find analogies in different areas of the world, not least in the Swiss Confederation. The tribal constitution does not necessarily imply complete equality in the sense that hierarchical structures are completely absent; it does, however, imply that there is no central rule by one political leader over all other members. The system is acephalous and decentralized; social and, if the need arises, also military hierarchies may exist, but these are not centralized and institutionalized in concrete structures.

If we assume that Israel prior to establishing a state was such a loose union of tribes, then two changes become apparent in comparison to the Amarna period. First is the presence of rich human and material resources in the *hill country,* where these tribes seem to have primarily settled and from where they engaged in skirmishes with the Canaanite cities of the plains (Judg 4–5); in the following section (1.3.2) we will examine the archaeological witnesses for the early Iron Age that speak of intensive settlements of the Palestinian hill country in the early Iron Age. We also encounter the *Philistines* on the fringes of the narratives of liberation; they have meanwhile settled in the southwestern coastal plains and become a powerful and threatening factor who have slowly pushed the Danites, an Israelite tribe, out of the southwest to the far north of Palestine (Judg 13–18). Both factors will become important for subsequent developments.

We do not have to glean any more information about Israel prior to the establishment of a state from the literary sources, nor would it be appropriate to do so in this context. In contrast, we can say much about the era that follows the early monarchy in Israel.

Once again, the Bible—particularly the books of Kings but also a few prophetic books—serves as the main source; in light of its basic literary and theological character we must use it with great caution. According to the accounts in the books of Kings, the historical era that began following the death of Solomon was determined by the parallel existence and competition between two states on Israelite soil: the southern kingdom, ruled continually by members of the Davidic dynasty; and the northern kingdom, ruled by changing dynasties. The capital in the south was Jerusalem; the capital of the north (from the time of the dynasty of Omri, i.e., from the first half of the ninth century onward) was Samaria. We can continually trace the history of these two royal cities and their domains until their destruction in the eighth and sixth century, respectively—not just in biblical sources but also in extra-biblical sources.

Regarding the northern kingdom, Assyrian inscriptions dating to the middle of the ninth century mention the Omride ruler Ahab by name and also make reference to the rebel Jehu as a member of the "house of Omri" (*ANET*, 278, 280; Galling 1968, 50, 51). At about the same time, a stela of the Moabite king Mesha laments that the Israelite Omri and his son (most likely Ahab) oppressed his people for decades before he, Mesha, was able to throw off the Israelite yoke (probably against Jehu) with the help of the god Chemosh (*ANET*, 320; Galling 1968, 52). We have Assyrian texts from the second half of the eighth century that mention Israel's tribute duty, its participation in rebellions, its military "punishment," and its final destruction (*ANET*, 282–85; Galling 1968, 55–60). We can read the biblical prophetic books Amos, Hosea, and Isaiah in parallel and glean information from their oldest layers on the northern kingdom Israel, the conditions on the inside, but also its involvement in international conflicts, especially in regard to subjection to or liberation from Assyrian domination. Archaeological excavations and the finding of many lettered clay shards ("ostraca") have not only given further evidence for the royal city of Samaria and its function as a metropolis for this very time period but also provide witness to the existence and expansion of several other Israelite cities to administrative and military centers during this time (such as Megiddo, Jezreel, and Kinneret, to name just a few—more in §II.1.3.1).

There are at least as many sources on the southern kingdom of Judah and its capital Jerusalem. Aside from Assyrian and Babylonian references from the middle of the eighth century down to the sixth century, of which the report on the encirclement of Jerusalem by the Assyrian king Sennacherib in 701 B.C.E. is particularly noteworthy (cf. 2 Kgs 18), we also have Judahite inscriptions: a commemorative plate on occasion of the completion of the Siloam Tunnel (*ANET*, 321; Galling 1968, 60–61) or the marking of storage jars with the stamp *l^e-melek* "to the king" (P. Welten). In addition, archaeologists have identified several public buildings in Judahite cities (such as Arad and Beersheba as well as a score of forts in the Negev from the seventh century onward) that were most likely also used by the royal administration. The findings have at least been able to establish Jerusalem, which can only be excavated partially for practical and political reasons, especially in the area of the temple (and the palace), as the center of Judah—a function for which it was expanded considerably between the eighth and the seventh centuries. In terms of biblical sources, we can add the book of Deuteronomy and the

Psalter with their preexilic material to the already-mentioned books of Kings and prophetic books (Jeremiah, Ezekiel, Micah, Nahum, Habakkuk, Zephaniah—in addition to those mentioned above). All these texts display a high regard for the temple and the dynasty that ruled there.

All this shows conclusively that the northern kingdom of Israel existed at least from the middle of the ninth century, the southern kingdom of Judah from the eighth century. Both kingdoms were centrally ruled territorial states that included primarily hill regions but also some territory in the plains (such as the Jezreel or Jordan Valleys and parts of the coast). Cities continued to exist in the plains, but now there were also cities in the hill regions. The entire territory was integrated on a political, military, and economic level. Ruled by the will of the respective dynastic member, they faced the outside as a unity and developed coherence on the inside that was no longer threatened by any secession movements. Even though change and agitation was possible—in Judah more subsurface than in northern Israel—the identity of either state was not questioned until its final downfall.

Because we are faced with a gap in extrabiblical witnesses for this time, it is difficult to make definite inferences from the time of the divided kingdoms to the early monarchy. Inscriptions witness to northern Israel from the middle of the ninth century, to Judah from the middle of the eighth century. Did these monarchies not exist prior to this time? Were they only established at this point? Two factors speak against this assumption. First is a contrary account in biblical texts that are supported in their basic (!) credibility for the divided kingdom by extrabiblical sources. We can also assume such credibility for the early monarchy. Second and more important is the consideration that the political stability of the divided kingdoms did not grow overnight. In all likelihood, there was a prior phase of establishing and consolidating the monarchy. At least for the northern kingdom, this phase would most likely have to be dated in the tenth century—the traditionally assumed and biblically supported time period for the early monarchy.

We are confirmed in this conclusion by the realization that Israel, as stated earlier, developed from a nonmonarchical, nonstate existence. We are thus not dealing with reconfiguring an already-existing territorial state (or even several states) into a new state organization. The state had to be molded from the clay of tribal structures. There certainly were examples, such as the Philistines, even forerunners, such as with the Canaanites, yet both these nations had only developed city-states, not territorial states. The territorial states of Israel and Judah were, with the possible exception of the tentative attempts of Labaiah and Abimelech of Shechem, a new phenomenon in Palestine. Everything points to the fact that the major conversion from an acephalous to a monarchical system could not have occurred without a powerful stimulus and that this stimulus could not have been provided only by the hereditary rulers who by coincidence are the first to appear in extrabiblical inscriptions.

In this context, it strikes us as quite believable when the Bible portrays Israel's first king Saul with the contours of a "liberator," a well-known figure from the era prior to establishing the state. He wages his first battle, according to the biblical account, in the style of a Gideon (1 Sam 11); his army is like the armies of the old "liberators," a group of volunteers from the various tribes, or like the armies of the ancient city kings, a small band of mercenaries (14:52). His administration is that of a tribal leader, in this case the tribe of Benjamin; that is, he hardly has any administration at all. On the other hand, however, he is a true king in the sense that he cannot be deposed but remains in office until the end of his life with the expectation that his son will succeed him: a dynasty is formed *in nuce*, but this dynasty is prevented de facto by the Philistines—and by David. David is a true founder of a dynasty. In many ways, he is a much more established king than Saul. With his son Solomon, the monarchy stands on firm ground. The idea of describing such a period of transition between two highly different historical periods is either the result of an incredible degree of historical insight and imagination on the part of the biblical authors—or historical reality.

II.1.2.2. Analogies

The entire history of the ancient Near East is characterized by the tension and the alternation between noncentralized, tribal societies and hierarchical societies organized in a state (see especially the first volume of the Biblical Encyclopedia series). The large centers of culture and power on both sides of the Fertile Crescent, in the river valleys of the Nile and Mesopotamia, were almost always organized as states; this was a result of large population density, agriculture that was dependent on regular flooding and irrigation, and regional and supraregional trade of goods. Yet even here we encounter decentralized tendencies and movements. These states were subject to undermining and threatening forces from the fringes: from Ethiopia, Libya, and the Sinai, on the one hand, and from the mountains and plains surrounding Mesopotamia, on the other hand. Ethiopian dynasties and extensive border fortifications in northeastern Egypt and the threat to the Hittite and Assyrian empires from mountain tribes, as well as the founding of the Neo-Babylonian Empire by originally Aramean tribal members, the so-called Chaldeans, are particularly noteworthy examples of this fact.

Tribal societies were of even greater importance in the small and relatively impassable central regions of the Fertile Crescent, in Syro-Palestine. The first two volumes of the series give examples of this; later volumes add further examples. A few brief points will suffice in this context. The kings of Mari on the Euphrates (eighteenth century) were continually occupied with registering and controlling tribal groups, among them the Benjaminites (*sic!*)—only to fail in the end. According to the Amarna Letters, tribal groups, often referred to as Habiru, caused much disturbance for smaller and greater potentates in Canaan of the late Bronze Age. The Philistines who established themselves in city-states in the Palestinian coastal region toward the end of the late Bronze Age encountered "Hebrews" who settled there and who caused them more and more difficulties. The biblical prehistory raises a monument to the nomadic tribes through its mention of the Kenites, a monument that expresses distance and respect at the same time. According to the liberation narratives of the biblical book of Judges, "Israel" prior to statehood consisted of several tribes organized acephally along family lines and independent of one another in principle. These tribes gathered only in defense against immediate external danger and only for a temporary time period and never in totality; monarchic structures were rejected by honorable individuals and desired only by dishonorable characters who always failed in the end (Judg 8–9). According to the biblical account, once the monarchy succeeded in gaining a foothold in Israel, the first kings had to contend not only with opposition from the tribes along the southern border of the cultivated land (1 Sam 15; 27; 30) but also with inner-Israelite "opposition against the monarchy" (10:27; 25; 2 Sam 20; see Crüsemann 1978) originating from tribal traditions and ideals. Interestingly, when the powerful dynasty of the Omrides was overthrown in Israel, the rebels included prophetic groups operating on the fringes of the cultivated land (2 Kgs 2; 4:38–41; 9:1–13) as well as the Rechabites, who generally opposed an agricultural lifestyle (2 Kgs 10:15–16; cf. Jer 35; Levin's arguments for assuming that these groups are purely imaginative creations are not convincing).

These facts support the assumption of a basic dualism between tribal and state-centered tendencies for the Syro-Palestinian region. In Israel, as with all of its surrounding neighbors, the state-centered tendencies prevailed.

The *Philistines*, after their arrival in the Levant, took over the existing Canaanite city-states in southwestern Palestine, or rather, they established themselves as the new ruling elite in these city-states. Unlike their predecessors, they succeeded in preventing a large-scale fragmentation and presented—at least against the Israelites—a unified front. This focus of power may have been responsible for the fact that the monarchy was never challenged as a form of government, as far as we can see. Certain oppositional forces seem to have been pushed into the hill regions and derided as "Hebrew," that is, as un-Philistine (see 1 Sam 14:11). The Hebrew Bible tells many stories that highlight this flexible yet efficient and powerful system of government.

Three kingdoms developed in the Transjordan region over time: the Ammonite, the Moabite, and the Edomite—most likely also in this order. The wealth of natural resources decreased towards the south (as is the case today); thus, the social development led first to the establishment of a territorial state in *Ammon*. A widespread collapse of economic structures in the Levant and the eastern Mediterranean regions around 1200 B.C.E. led to the demise of the city-states in the tablelands of the Transjordan and the region west of the Jordan (Hübner 1992, 164). Unlike the Mediterranean coast, however, no waves of new immigrants filled the vacuum to build a centralized government, so more tribal structures developed around small village settlements (165). In the tenth century a more centralized form of government grew out of these structures. According to the biblical witness, the Ammonites were not yet led by a king during the time of the judge Jephthah (Judg 11) and King Saul (1 Sam 11); David was the first to encounter such a king and to remove his crown (2 Sam 12:30, where we should probably read *malkam* instead of *milkom*: the crown of "their king"). Among his many wives, Solomon seems to have had an Ammonite wife as well, a woman of royal blood and the mother of Solomon's successor Rehoboam (1 Kgs 11:1; 14:21, 31). After this we hear nothing of the state of Ammon for a long time. Was it subject to Israel? An inscription of the Assyrian king Shalmaneser III on the battle of Qarqar (853 B.C.E.) mentions a possible Ammonite king named Ba'asa as part of the Syro-Palestinian alliance. Amos accuses the Ammonites of war crimes (around the middle of the eighth century) committed in Gilead, an ancient Israelite settlement in the Transjordan region; the text is not clear on when these crimes are supposed to have occurred (Amos 1:13–15). Soon after Ammon—like Israel—fell under Assyrian rule. Even though there are many gaps, we can at least trace a history of the state of Ammon that seems to run parallel to Israelite history in many ways.

We can state similar things about *Moab*. A foundation for the reconstruction of Moabite history is an autobiographical inscription of the Moabite king Mesha on which he proclaims his great deeds, the most important of which was the liberation of his people from Israelite rule. This text was written in the second half of the ninth century B.C.E. and witnesses to the existence of the state of Moab for this time at the latest. Did such a state exist even earlier? In order to answer this question, we depend on biblical texts, and these are once again laden with the many difficulties mentioned above. When we read in Num 22–24 of a seer named Balaam who made predictions about Israel for the Moabite king Balak, or when we read in Judg 3 that the "liberator" Ehud stabbed the Moabite king Eglon to death in his private chambers, then we cannot be sure whether these stories contain legendary material, projecting the status quo of a much later time into an ancient narrative context, and we also cannot be sure whether these individuals (if they existed at all and with these names) were only local rulers whose power did not extend beyond a city and its immediate surroundings. There are certain unpretentious indications that kings did exist in Moab when the state took shape in Israel, however large their territory may have been. Of the young David fleeing from Saul, the text reports in a side comment that he brought his parents to the "king of Moab," to "Mizpeh in Moab" (an otherwise unknown location; 1 Sam 22:3), probably in order to protect them from Saul. In 2 Sam 8:2 we read that David defeated "the Moabites," massacred two thirds of all prisoners of war, and demanded tribute from the people. These texts are not colorful legends; they are short and quite credible notes that make reference to a territorial state of Moab—however small—and to a king who ruled that state. The temporal gap between these statements and those of the Mesha Stela covers about 150 years, during which we would have to assume the liberation of Moab from Jerusalem's rule and the returning oppression by the northern Israelite Omrides.

This historical development would closely match the fate of *Edom* during this time period. For Edom, we are completely dependent on the biblical witness for this early time period. Original Edomite material that could be evaluated historically has not yet been found, but we may still reconstruct a somewhat plausible picture. In 2 Sam 8:13–14 we find the annalistic note that David had killed eighteen thousand Edomites in battle. Regardless of how we evaluate this number, the event itself is confirmed in a second text: 1 Kgs 11:14–22 tells of a "Hadad the Edomite, of royal lineage," who escaped from a massacre committed by David's general Joab, rose to become the pharaoh's son-in-law, and finally returned to Edom following the death of David and Joab in order to become king in his home country. The Bible gives this man the unflattering title *satan*, which does not necessarily speak against his real existence. We thus would have an Edomite king during the time of Solomon who must have had at least one predecessor on the throne. We do not know how large their territory may have been. The information is hardly sufficient to claim a hereditary dynasty (Bartlett 1989). We do, however, have a list of "kings" in Gen 36:32–39 who are supposed to have ruled in Edom before there was a king in Israel. Without recognizable ideological intent, but perhaps with great temporal separation (Knauf 1992), this list clearly establishes a relation according to which Edom formed a state before such a development occurred in Israel. The list contains eight names, and these are ordered chronologically as if each name was the heir of his predecessor. Two facts, however, speak against a hereditary government: the regents all come from different towns; and the name of each father does not match the name of the preceding king. We should probably not interpret this data as a type of elected monarchy but rather as pointing to the existence of several regional chiefdoms.

There were regents or chiefs in different locations who were remembered by posterity; they may have ruled at the same time or been separated by larger intervals of time. Whatever the case, those who passed on the traditions in Judah interpreted the material in their own fashion: in analogy to the lists of the so-called lesser judges (Judg 10:1–5; 12:7–15) they fashioned a majority of regional or local nobility into a continual row of territorial rulers (Weippert 1971). Edomite rulers thus probably existed before Hadad and his father, contemporaries of Solomon, who possibly only had local influence. We cannot find any indication for an Edomite territorial state before the eighth century (Knauf 1992).

It thus seems that monarchies developed around the turn of the millennium everywhere in the southern Levant. Whereas Philistia and the territories east of the Jordan developed city-monarchies or regional monarchies, the territorial monarchy was present from the beginning in the Israelite and Judahite mountain areas.

II.1.3. MATERIAL WITNESSES FROM IRON AGE IIA

Albertz, Rainer. *A History of Israelite Religion in the Old Testament Period* (2 vols.; OTL; Louisville: Westminster John Knox, 1994), 1:105–14. **Albright,** William F. *Excavations and Results at Tell el-Ful (Gibeah of Saul)* (AASOR 4; New Haven: American Schools of Oriental Research, 1924). **Alt,** Albrecht. "Die Staatenbildung der Israeliten in Palästina," in idem, *Kleine Schriften zur Geschichte des Volkes Israel* (3rd ed.; 3 vols.; Munich: Beck, 1964), 2:1–65, trans. as "The Formation of the Israelite State in Palestine," in idem, *Essays on Old Testament History and Religion* (trans. R. A. Wilson; Garden City, N.Y.: Doubleday, 1968), 223–309. **Arnold,** Patrick M. *Gibeah: The Search for a Biblical City* (JSOTSup 79; Sheffield: JSOT Press, 1990). **Bieberstein,** Klaus, and Hanswulf **Bloedhorn.** *Jerusalem: Grundzüge der Baugeschichte vom Chalkolithikum bis zur Frühzeit der osmanischen Herrschaft* (3 vols.; TAVO B/100; Wiesbaden: Reichert, 1994). **Boaretto,** Elisabeth, A. J. Timothy **Jull,** Ayelet **Gilboa,** and Ilan **Sharon.** "Dating the Iron Age I/II Transition in Israel. First Intercomparison Results," *Radiocarbon* 47 (2005): 39–55. **Busink,** Theodor A. *Der Tempel Salomos* (vol. 1 of *Der Tempel von Jerusalem von Salomo bis auf Herodes: Eine archäologisch-historische Studie unter Berücksichtigung des westsemitischen Tempelbaus*; 2 vols.; Leiden: Brill, 1970–80). **Cohen,** Rudolph. "The Fortesses King Solomon Built to Protect His Southern Border," *BAR* 11/3 (1985) 56–70. **Cohen** and Yigal **Yisrael.** "The Iron Age Fortresses at 'En Haseva," *BA* 58 (1995): 223–35. **Coote,** Robert B., and Keith W. **Whitelam.** "The Emergence of Israel: Social Transformation and State Formation Following the Decline in Late Bronze Age Trade," *Semeia* 37 (1986): 107–47. **Coote** and **Whitelam.** *The Emergence of Early Israel in Historical Perspective* (SWBA 5; Sheffield: Almond, 1987). **Dever,** William G. "Monumental Architecture in Ancient Israel in the Period of the United Monarchy," in *Studies in the Period of David and Solomon and Other Essays: Papers Read at the International Symposium for Biblical Studies, Tokyo, 5–7 December, 1979* (ed. Tomoo Ishida; Winona Lake, Ind.: Eisenbrauns, 1982), 269–306. **Dever.** "Monumental Art and Architecture in Ancient Israel in the Period of the United Monarchy," in idem, *Recent Discoveries and Biblical Research* (Seattle: University of Washington Press, 1990), 85–117. **Dever.** "Ceramics, Ethnicity, and the Question of Israel's Origins," *BA* 58 (1995): 200–213. **Finkelstein,** Israel. *The Archaeology of the Israelite Settlement* (trans. D. Saltz; Jerusalem: Israel Exploration Society, 1988). **Finkelstein.** "The Emergence of the Monarchy in Israel: The Environmental and Socio-Economic Aspects," *JSOT* 44 (1989): 43–74. **Finkelstein.** "On Archaeological Methods and Historical Considerations: Iron Age II Gezer and Samaria," *BASOR* 277/278 (1990): 109–19. **Finkelstein.** "The Archaeology of the United Monarchy: An Alternative View," *Levant* 28 (1996): 177–87. **Frick,** Frank S. *The Formation of the State in Ancient Israel: A Survey of Models and Theories* (SWBA 4; Sheffield: Almond, 1985). **Frick.** "Social Science Methods and Theories of Significance for the Study of the Israelite Monarchy: A Critical Review Essay," *Semeia* 37 (1986): 9–52. **Fritz,** Volkmar. *Die Stadt im alten Israel* (Munich: Beck, 1990). **Fritz.** "Where Is David's Ziklag?" *BAR* 19/3 (1993) 58–61, 76. **Fritz** and Philip R. **Davies,** eds. *The Origins of the Ancient Israelite States* (JSOTSup 228; Sheffield: Sheffield Academic Press, 1996). **Gottwald,** Norman K. "The Participation of Free Agrarians in the Introduction of Monarchy in Ancient Israel: An Application of H. A. Landsberger's Framework for the Analysis of Peasant Movements," *Semeia* 37 (1986): 77–106. **Hauer,** Chris, Jr. "From Alt to Anthropology: The Rise of the Israelite State," *JSOT* 36 (1986): 3–15. **Herzog,** Ze'ev, and Lily **Singer-Avitz,** "Redefining the Centre: The Emergence of State in Judah," *TA* 31 (2004): 209–44. **Hopkins,** David C. *The Highlands of Canaan: Agricultural Life in the Early Iron Age* (SWBA 3; Sheffield: Almond, 1985). **Keel,** Othmar, and Max **Küchler.** *Der Süden* (vol. 2 of *Orte und Landschaften der Bibel*; Zürich: Benziger; Göttingen: Vandenhoeck & Ruprecht, 1982). **Kenyon,** Kathleen M. *Archaeology in the Holy Land* (3rd ed.; New York: Praeger, 1970). **Lapp,** Paul W. "Tell el-Fûl," *BA* 28 (1965): 2–10. **Master,** Daniel M. "State Formation Theory and the Kingdom of Ancient Israel," *JNES* 60 (2001): 117–31. **Mazar,** Amihai. *Archaeology of the Land of the Bible: 10,000–586 B.C.E.* (ABRL; New York: Doubleday, 1990). **Mazar,** Benjamin, Yigal **Shiloh,** and Hillel **Geva.** "Jerusalem: The Early Periods and the First Temple Period," *NEAEHL* 3:698–716. **Mazar,** Eilat. "Did I Find King David's Palace?" *BAR* 32/1 (2006): 17–27, 70. **Na'aman,** Nadav. "Cow Town or Royal Capital? Evidence for Iron Age Jerusalem," *BAR* 23/4 (1997) 43–47, 67. **Neu,** Rainer. *Von der Anarchie zum Staat: Entwicklungsgeschichte Israels vom Nomadentum zur Monarchie im Spiegel der Ethnosoziologie* (Neukirchen-Vluyn: Neukirchener, 1992). **Niemann,** Hermann Michael. *Herrschaft, Königtum und Staat: Skizzen zur soziokulturellen Entwicklung im monarchischen Israel* (FAT 6; Tübingen: Mohr Siebeck, 1993). **Rupprecht,** Konrad. *Der Tempel von Jerusalem: Gründung Salomos oder jebusitisches Erbe?* (BZAW 144; Berlin: de Gruyter, 1977). **Soggin,** J. Alberto. *Das Königtum in Israel: Ursprünge, Spannungen, Entwicklung* (BZAW 104; Berlin: de Gruyter, 1967). **Steiner,** Margreet. "Jerusalem in the Tenth and Seventh Centuries BCE: From Administrative Town to Commercial City," in *Studies in the Archaeology of the Iron Age in Israel* (ed. Amihai

Mazar; JSOTSup 331; Sheffield: Sheffield Academic Press, 2001), 280–88. **Thompson,** Thomas L. *Early History of the Israelite People: From the Written and Archaeological Sources* (Leiden: Brill, 1992). **Ussishkin,** David. "Notes on Megiddo, Gezer, Ashdod, and Tel Batash in the Tenth to Ninth Centuries B.C.," *BASOR* 277/278 (1990): 71–91. **Vaughn,** Andrew G., and Ann E. **Killebrew,** eds. *Jerusalem in Bible and Archaeology: The First Temple Period* (SBLSymS 18; Atlanta: Society of Biblical Literature, 2003). **Weippert,** Helga. *Palästina in vorhellenistischer Zeit* (Handbuch der Archäologie, Vorderasien 2/1; Munich: Beck, 1988). **Wightman,** G. J. "The Myth of Solomon," *BASOR* 277/278 (1990): 5–22. **Wright,** G. R. H. "The Monumental City Gate in Palestine and Its Foundations," *ZA* 74 (1984): 267–89. **Zwickel,** Wolfgang. *Eisenzeitliche Ortslagen im Ostjordanland* (Wiesbaden: Reichert, 1990).

II.1.3.1. City Architecture and Administrative Buildings

If we ask the question of what material artifacts remain from the early monarchy, we almost immediately associate material artifacts with large royal constructions that remain as ruins and that can be found by the archaeologist. The biblical reports on Israel's first kings, especially the reports on their building activities, provide us with a compass for our search. The texts tell us where the kings resided: Saul in Gibeah; David in Ziklag, Hebron, and Jerusalem; Solomon also in Jerusalem. The texts explicitly report that David built a palace for himself in Jerusalem (2 Sam 5:11; also 7:2; Neh 12:37). Solomon is also described as a prolific builder. We read that he built not only a (new? expanded?) palace and the YHWH temple in Jerusalem, as well as the "Millo" and the wall (1 Kgs 5–7; 9:15), but also "storage cities" (ערי המסכנות), "cities for horses and cities for chariots" (1 Kgs 9:19), as well as the cities Hazor, Megiddo, Gezer, Lower Beth-horon, Baalath, and Tamar (1 Kgs 9:15–19).[5] According to the books of Kings, all of the kings in the Davidic dynasty, starting with David up to King Ahaz, were buried "with their fathers," so there obviously must have been a royal necropolis (see also Neh 3:16).

---

5. Most scholars believe the list of cities in 1 Kgs 9:15, 17–19 to be an old source. The separate notice on Gezer in 9:16 was obviously added because the city was mentioned in 9:15; by mentioning Gezer again in 9:17, the narrator moves back to the old list. Ernst Axel Knauf, in contrast, postulates the existence of *two* lists ("Le roi est mort, vive le roi! A Biblical Argument for the Historicity of Solomon," in *The Age of Solomon: Scholarship at the Turn of the Millennium* [ed. Lowell K. Handy; SHANE 11; Leiden: Brill, 1997], 81–95): an old and historically reliable list in 9:17–18; and a younger list of little historical value in 9:15–16 and 19.

In the past, "biblical archaeology" assiduously and naively followed these texts and set out to find the remains of these early royal constructions. A great many difficulties arose in several cases where the location could hardly be determined (such as Gibeah and Baalath) or where archaeological excavation could not proceed (in densely populated Hebron, for example, or in Jerusalem with its sacred sites and delicate political situation). In other cases, however, the archaeologists were successful—at least at first sight.

Some general methodological comments should be made at this point. The direction of inquiry associated with and often willingly accepted by "biblical archaeology"—a movement from the biblical texts to their confirmation—is problematic for several reasons. (1) The biblical passage serving as the starting point must first be examined regarding its place in the historical development of the text and its historical credibility. (2) The biblical notices could be quite coincidental, even if they are historically reliable; much of what the archaeologists find has no correlation with a biblical text and cannot be confirmed by the text. On the other hand, much of what the Bible states is meaningless or even a source of misdirection for archaeology. (3) The urge to find confirmation for biblical statements or positively to identify archaeological findings with the help of biblical texts can cause a prejudice that distorts the perception of both. (4) Archaeological findings are often not as unambiguous as desired; they can easily be misinterpreted. (5) The attraction of large royal constructions and large findings for an archaeologist may obstruct his or her view for smaller findings that are less spectacular but equally important for archaeological research.

The following section will nevertheless discuss the traditional findings dated to the time of the early monarchy. We will see that noticeable and interesting excavations were made but that the interpretation of these excavations was fraught with the problems mentioned above. The next section (§II.1.3.2) will then pay attention to a different mode of inquiry that moves from large-scale archaeological findings of Iron Age IIA to social structures that may be connected to these findings. Only as a last step will this inquiry take biblical texts into consideration.

Until recently, the allocation of archaeological eras and absolute dates was not a matter of controversy. The large compendium by Helga Weippert lists the following numbers: Iron Age I, ca. 1250–1000 B.C.E.; Iron Age IIA, ca. 1000–900 B.C.E.; Iron Age IIB, ca. 925/900–850 B.C.E.; Iron Age IIC, ca. 850–586 B.C.E. This list is fraught with the problem that concrete events from the history of Israel are used to delineate any eras (925, 586). For our purposes, however, it is sufficient to state that the early monarchy coincides basically with Iron Age IIA. Israel Finkelstein, however, has recently submitted good reasons for a "low chronology" that pushes all archaeological time periods that concern us here about one hundred years lower.[6] This has serious consequences especially for the time and the portrait of Solomon. Until now, scholars have tended to connect archaeological evidence for the fortification of Israelite cities in the Iron Age IIA to Solomon; with the "low chronology," however, this evidence would point to the Omride dynasty, which is not favored with a great reputation by the biblical texts! Scholars are divided over this issue: many follow Finkelstein, whereas others—probably still the majority—continue to favor the old dates.[7] The following account will take this situation into consideration.

Let us start with the location that according to the biblical account was the residence of Israel's first king: Gibeah (see, e.g., 1 Sam 9:1; 10:26). We are faced with the problem that the name is actually just a description for a—very common—landscape feature: "hill, elevation." This term thus occurs frequently and describes very different locations. The database expands drastically once we include such synonyms as "Geba" and "Gibeon," not to mention the possibility that the biblical text may mistake certain similar-sounding locations with each other. Additions to the name such as "Gibeah in Benjamin" or "Gibeah of God" or "Gibeah of Saul" are of little help because these labels often do not correspond to each other and are frequently connected to a specific literary historical background. We at least know that the residence of the Benjaminite Saul is to be found in the territory of the tribe of Benjamin, that is, slightly north/northeast of Jerusalem. William F. Albright identified Tell el-Ful, approximately 5 km north of Jerusalem, with Saul's residence. At that location he found a small square stronghold (35 x 40 m) surrounded by casemate walls and fortified by four corner towers. He dated the stronghold to the eleventh century and believed to have found "Saul's rude fortress." A later emergency excavation (Paul W. Lapp) revealed a much later date for the casemate fortress but confirmed a dating in the eleventh (or tenth) century for a previous stronghold (fig. 1). It is, however, very doubtful whether this

---

6. See Israel Finkelstein, "The Archaeology of the United Monarchy: An Alternative View," *Levant* 28 (1996): 177–87; idem, "The Rise of Jerusalem and Judah: The Missing Link," in *Jerusalem in Bible and Archaeology: The First Temple Period* (ed. Andrew G. Vaughn and Ann E. Killebrew; SBLSymS 18; Atlanta: Society of Biblical Literature, 2003), 81–102.

7. A bibliography on the controversy initiated by Finkelstein's hypothesis is found in Gunnar Lehmann, "The United Monarchy in the Countryside: Jerusalem, Judah, and the Shephelah during the Tenth Century B.C.E.," in Vaughn and Killebrew, *Jerusalem in Bible and Archaeology*, 117–62, here 120 n. 6. A more detailed account of the debate is found in Thomas E. Levy and Thomas Higham, eds., *The Bible and Radiocarbon Dating* (London: Equinox, 2005).

stronghold was really built by Saul—and not perhaps by the Philistines or the Jebusites or David or a later ruler. In the face of these uncertainties, Patrick M. Arnold suggests identifying Gibeah with Geba, a location that in his view can be identified with the contemporary village of Ğeba, 5 km northeast of Tell el-Ful (or 9 km northeast of Jerusalem). For obvious reasons, there has been no extensive excavation at this location to date; a surface analysis has produced only clay shards from Iron Age II and the Persian era (which would complicate a connection to Judg 19–21 but not to the Saul and David narratives). In Tell el-Ful we at least had a small stronghold, in Ğeba we merely have a few shards, none of which is imprinted with Saul's name.

Readers familiar with the biblical texts may find this meager evidence disappointing but bearable, as these texts hardly present Saul as the success-

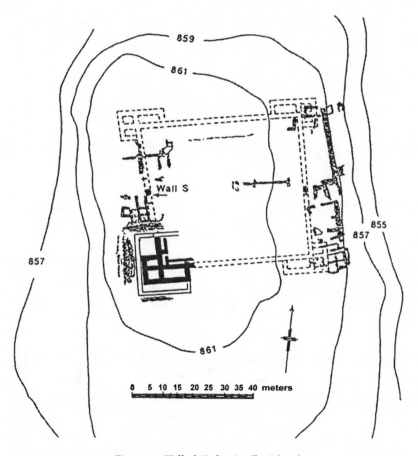

Figure 1: Tell el-Ful—Saul's Gibeah?

ful king and prolific builder. But the archaeological remains that point to his famous successor King David are unfortunately no more definite. According to the Bible, the first royal office held by David was the office of city ruler of Ziklag, which was granted to him by the Philistines. No less than four different locations have been identified with this city: Tell el-Farʿa South, Tell eš-Šeriʿa, Tell el-Chuwēlfe, and Tell es-Sebaʿ—all four quite close together about 25 km southwest of Hebron. None of these locations present us with impressive public buildings for the relevant time period; it is more honest to speak of small country villages. Tell es-Sebaʿ (the newest candidate for Ziklag; see Fritz 1993) was a noteworthy, even if not very large, royal center of administration

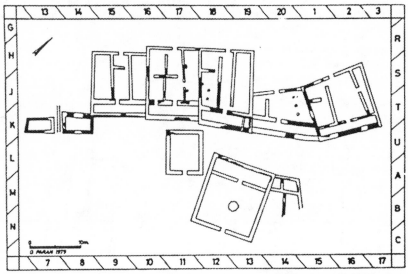

Figure 2: Tell es-Sebaʿ (Stratum VII resp. Stratum VI)—David's Ziklag?

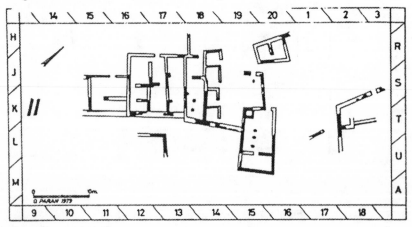

from the ninth century onward (strata III–V). But during the Iron I and IIA periods (strata VI–IX) it was no more than a sleepy little hamlet. We can at least observe that some of the houses were arranged to form a defensive belt (fig. 2). Yet this is not what we imagine when we speak of a royal residence, even if David was only a regional ruler and warlord during his residence here.

Hebron, according to 2 Sam 2:1–4 the seat of David's government during his rule over Judah, has been permanently settled from ancient times to the present; large excavations have not taken place for this reason. The Ǧebel er-Rumēde, west of the so-called Graves of the Patriarchs, which seems to contain the remains of the ancient city, was partially excavated in the 1960s. There have been no extensive excavation reports so far. We can at least state that an extensive wall existed during the Bronze Age and that the location was also settled during Iron Age II; beyond this we know very little.

In the case of David and Solomon all expectations are centered on Jerusalem, but the most interesting area of research, the so-called Haram (the temple

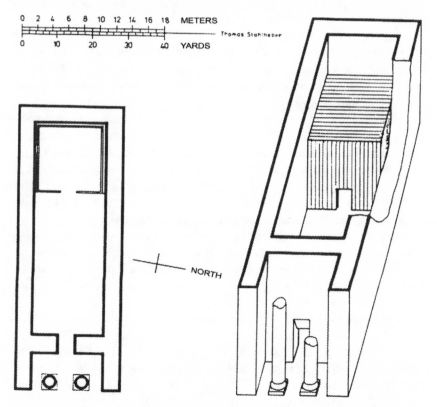

Figure 3: Solomon's temple—an attempted sketch and reconstruction

area refashioned and massively expanded by Herod, now the site of the Dome of the Rock and the Al-Aqsa Mosque), is closed to archaeological curiosity. This was the ancient location of the Solomonic temple and Solomon's palace, which according to a credible biblical statement was much larger than the temple. In this case we have no choice but to reconstruct the layout and construction solely from the biblical sources: from an archaeological-methodological point of view a grave error, but forgivable considering the circumstances (fig. 3).

In 1 Kgs 6, the temple's external dimensions are given as 30 x 10 x 10 meters, a stately but not exorbitant building. There have been various different attempts at reconstructing the external facade and interior design, yet all agree on the basic elements: the temple was a so-called long-house temple that faced east and was surrounded on three sides by a three-storied gallery, most likely used to reinforce the stability of the building and create storage space. The sanctuary itself was divided along its length into three rooms: an anteroom flanked by two monumental freestanding pillars; a main room (the holy area); and the cella (the holy of holies). The cella was characterized by a low ceiling, either because the ceiling was lowered or because the floor was raised; the latter option would likely point to the existence of a previous sanctuary located at the highest point, of the approximate size of the holy of holies, and incorporated intentionally into the new structure (see Rupprecht 1977). The cella apparently did not contain the statue of a god, as was common in most of the Near East temples; instead, it contained the ark, a portable sanctuary in the shape of a box originally designed as a war palladium and conceived of as the seat or footstool of the god enthroned above it (certain critical scholars believe that the ark actually contained a small statue of a deity). The ark was flanked by two large winged cherubs, images of supernatural creatures portrayed as a crossover between the human and animal realms. The biblical text describes the interior design of the temple, basically the result of Phoenician artistry, in great detail that is not fully understandable at every point; more important, the description contains several exaggerations regarding the splendor and costliness of the building and its contents. It is definitely noteworthy that all the decorations are nonfigurative, a fact that is hardly the result of later conformance to the command not to make an image (Exod 20:4–6, even less in combination with Gen 1:26–27).

Following the Six Day War, archaeologists were at least able to examine more closely the hill adjoining the temple area to the southeast, often referred to as the City of David. Considering that this was the center of an empire, the external dimensions of this city are quite small: roughly 100 by 400 meters. David's palace may have stood at the highest point, perhaps above the Gihon Spring. Eilat Mazar has recently claimed to have found remains of the palace's foundations. Underneath the particular location, archaeologists have excavated an impressive bouldering that extends from the spring upward to the ridge and that could date to the Iron Age IIA or, rather, to an earlier period. It may have served as the substructure for the palace that presumably stood on top of it. Perhaps this is the "Millo" that is mentioned on several occasions in the Bible (most likely derived from the Hebrew verb מלא "to fill up," thus "landfill, filled area"; see also 2 Sam 5:9; 1 Kgs 9:15, 24). The exact course of a wall erected by Solomon (1 Kgs 9:15) has not yet been confirmed. There is not much more archaeological information for the Jerusalem of David and Solomon. We might still mention caves that were found close to the southern tip of the hill and that are sometimes identified with the necropolis of the Davidic dynasty. Networks of various tunnels underneath the City of David that are mostly of natural origin remain a source of controversy. Probably they were used as a water supply for Jerusalem of the Bronze Age and also the Iron Age. Some scholars think they played a role in David's conquest of the city (see 2 Sam 5:6–9; 1 Chr 11:4–6).

Of the many cities explicitly named in 1 Kgs 9:15–18 and credited to Solomon, Gezer, Megiddo, and Hazor have been excavated and positively identified. These three cities remain a source of intense controversy regarding Solomon's real or supposed construction activities.

The issues surrounding Tamar, the "city of palm trees," are less controversial but also less productive. Cohen and Yisrael build on a suggestion by Aharoni and identify this city with 'En Ḥaṣava, located about 30 km south of the Dead Sea in the Arabah. They date the oldest stratum identified by excavations at that site with somewhat exaggerated confidence to the tenth century; the identification with the Solomonic Tamar most likely influenced this decision. The findings allocated to this stratum are quite meager: a rectangular structure of about 13 x 11 meters, that is, the remains of a wall that consists in part of silex stone, and—a cooking pot! We can only hope that, if Solomon built anything at this site, it went beyond what now remains, otherwise Tamar would have been a desert stronghold, the size of a single-family dwelling.

Gezer (Tel Gezer), toward the exit of the Valley of Aijalon on the coastal plain, about two-thirds of the way from Jerusalem to the Mediterranean, was excavated at the beginning of the twentieth century by R. A. S. Macalister and subsequently with more modern methods under the supervision of the American archaeologist William G. Dever in the 1960s and 1980s. Macalister excavated the first half of what he referred to as a "Maccabean fortress" but what later turned out to be a six-chamber gate; as this gate was also connected to a casemate wall, Dever (following Yigael Yadin) classified the structure as a Solomonic construction. The situation is further complicated by the fact that the casemate wall is surrounded along the entire length of the city hill by a second ring wall (see fig. 4). Several different suggestions exist for dating this wall to the Hellenistic period, to the Iron Age, or to the Late Bronze Age. Dever suggests the latter: Solomon continued to use the "old" wall but fortified and supplemented it with the inner wall and the six-chamber gate. Ussishkin (1990) suggests instead that both walls were built at the same time and that the lower wall served as a substructure for the upper wall and that both served as a complex defensive system especially in the area of the gate. This assumption would certainly make the comparability of Gezer with other "Solomonic" cites much more difficult. In addition, the ceramics found with the stronghold can possibly be dated (at the earliest) in the tenth century but could also originate in the ninth century. Dever believes he has a fixed point for his early dating: the destruction of Gezer with its defensive systems—in his view by Pharaoh Sheshonq I on the occasion of his Palestinian campaign in about 920 B.C.E. We read of this event in 1 Kgs 14:25–28, but only from the perspective of the threat to and liberation of Jerusalem as well as the institution of a heavy tribute that King Rehoboam, successor to Solomon, had to pay to Pharaoh Shishak (as he is referred to in the Bible). We also cannot be certain that Gezer is mentioned in the so-called Sheshonq list (see §II.1.4.1 below and *ANET*, 242–43). We thus cannot prove that Sheshonq destroyed Gezer; the destruction—and thus also the construction or expansion of Gezer—could have occurred at a later point than Dever suggests. A completely different and open issue is how to connect the notice in 1 Kgs 9:16 to all of this, according to which "the pharaoh" (most likely not Sheshonq I) conquered and destroyed Gezer and presented it (as ruins?) to Solomon as a dowry for his daughter. What remains is a degree of probabil-

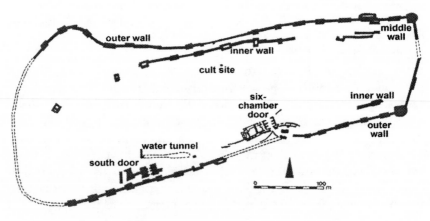

Figure 4: Gezer (excavation W. G. Dever, 1964)

ity, but not full certainty, that the defensive structures in Gezer were actually built by Solomon.

Hazor (Tell Waqqās), located 14 km north of the Sea of Chinnereth in Upper Galilee, was one of the most important cities in Palestine during the Bronze Age. Even today the hill with its approximately 80 acres of ruins is an impressive sight. The city is clearly divided into an upper city in the south (ca. 150 by a maximum of 500 m) and a lower city (ca. 700 x 1,000 m). The upper city is particularly interesting in our context. This was the only place where a possibly Solomonic construction was found in stratum X, again in the western area. Compared to the Bronze Age, during which the city was fully populated, Hazor was quite a bit smaller during Solomon's time. It is no surprise that the Bible (Judg 14–15), as well as the Amarna texts of the fourteenth century (EA 227, 228), the Egyptian cursing texts (inscribed clay figurines that were meant to be destroyed in order to bring a curse over rebellious vassals), and the Akkadian texts from Mari (the latter two from around 1800 B.C.E.), all refer to Hazor as the most powerful Canaanite center. Following its complete destruction around 1200 B.C.E., however (an accomplishment claimed by later Israel; see Josh 11), the ruins were hardly populated until the upper city was partially rebuilt in the tenth century (according to the conventional chronology). It was surrounded by a casemate wall that was interrupted by a three-chamber gate on the east side and contained a palace area of roughly 20 x 40 meters on the highest point on the western side; later on, in the ninth century, this was the location of a very impressive palace; by then the city had also expanded to the east to twice its size (see figs. 5–6). Whatever we can plausibly identify in Hazor as a Solomonic (or, according to the low chronology, as an Omridic) construction is not unremarkable, but compared to what was built later on, and even more earlier on, it remains quite modest.

Megiddo (Tell el-Mutesellim), located on the southwestern fringe of the Jezreel Valley where the Via Maris coming from the Mediterranean cuts through the foothills of Mount Carmel, was excavated at the beginning of the twentieth century by a German expedition and in the 1920s and 1930s by an American expedition. Unfortunately, these expeditions not only excavated the site but completely removed one stratum after another. All the same, the expeditions discovered up to twenty different strata in certain locations, strata that go back to the fourth millennium B.C.E. with walls, gates, palaces, and temples—a city of supraregional yet not continual importance. In regards to the times of Solomon, many claims were made, some of which were falsified later on. The city was supposedly entered by a monumental three-chamber gate in the north and surrounded by a ring-shaped casemate wall that enclosed a palace and a temple area; a large complex within the walls and close to the gate was interpreted as large stables for war horses, an inter-

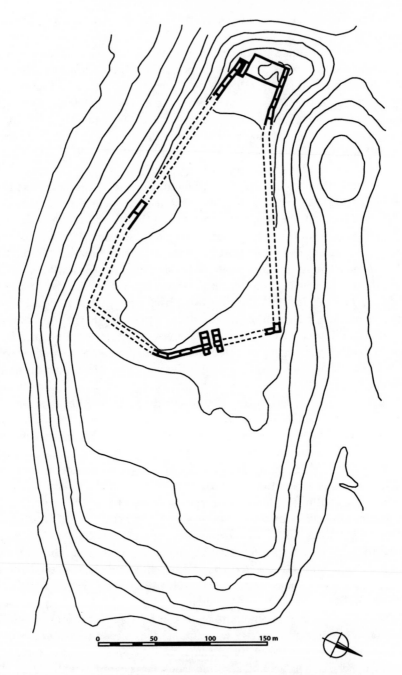

Figure 5: Hazor (Stratum X, general view)

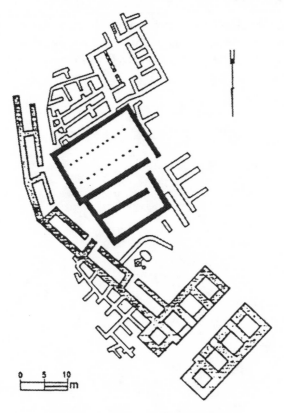

Figure 6: Hazor (Stratum X, detail)

pretation that closely matched the biblical data. In these early excavations, however, the stratigraphy of the location and of individual buildings had become muddled, a situation that was rectified in part by an Israeli excavation in the 1960s. The head of this excavation, Yigael Yadin, reconstructed a construction history (supported also by parallel phenomena in Gezer and Hazor) that still allotted much construction activity to the Solomonic era. Solomon had expanded a small village from the time of David (stratum VB) to a large city covering about 10 acres (strata VA–IVB); the three-chamber gate and the casemate wall were built during this time. Of this casemate wall, only a few remains were found in the northeast. We have to postulate the rest hypothetically. An extensive palace area was located directly across from the gate (building 1723); its main building measured 23 by 21.5 meters and was surrounded by a large square, about 60 by 65 meters, that itself was enclosed by a separate wall with a small gate again in the north. A much larger building was discovered in the northeast leaning against the city wall (the so-called palace 6000)—the apparent stables, however, were not stables but probably storage houses that belonged to a later stratum altogether. Yadin's reconstruction is hampered by one major gap: he could not conclusively show how the casemate wall was connected to the city gate; there has therefore been a recent

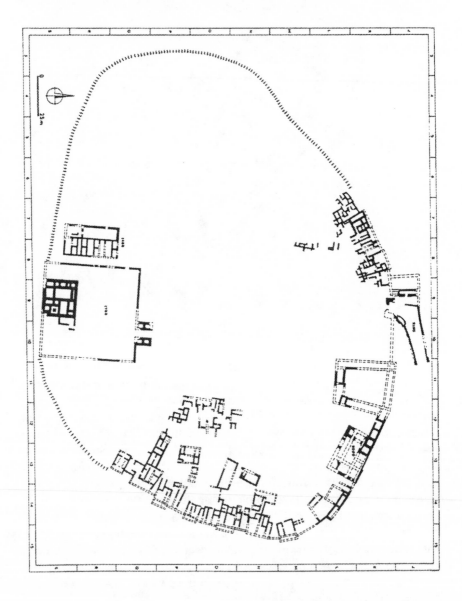

Figure 7: Megiddo (Stratum VA)

suggestion (Fritz 1990, 72) that the gate belonged instead to the later massive inset-outset wall that belongs to the above-mentioned storage buildings into the ninth century, the time of the Omride dynasty.

This specific issue is not without importance, as both the casemate wall and the three-chamber gate (or the four-entry gate) were previously seen as clear characteristics of Solomon's city construction. The gate constructions in Gezer, Megiddo, and Hazor are indeed remarkably similar (Dever 1982 and fig. 8). Meanwhile, however, very similar gates have been found outside of Israel (in Ashdod, in a Philistine context) and during later periods (in Tell ed-Duwēr [Lachish] and Tel Batash [Timnah]; see Ussishkin 1990). These findings severely weaken the case for Solomonic origin. On the other hand, we find not only casemate walls but also massive city walls in Iron Age II A (again in Ashdod or in Tell es-Sebaʻ [Ziklag?] and Tell el-Farʻa North [Tirzah]; see Weippert 1988, 436ff.). Casemate walls already existed during the Middle Bronze Age, disappeared for a long time, and came into use again during Iron Age IIA, probably based on fortified villages of Iron Age I, in which the houses were attached to each other so that their outer walls formed a kind of protective ring (see Finkelstein 1988, 238ff.). Once the farmhouses were no longer needed as fortification, because the state erected a wall, the missing houses may have been replaced by casemate structures that stabilized the outer wall without requiring the amounts of material necessary for a massive wall. In contrast to a massive wall, the casemate structures also provided space for storing various goods (for civil or military use).

We should also mention several strongholds in the Negev in this context. These strongholds served no urban purpose and were designated for military use only (such as Tell Arad and Tell el-Chlefe, close to the Gulf of Aqabah; see Weippert 1988, 480ff.). Here we find unadulterated examples of casemate building style: with straight lines and without regard for any city architecture, determined solely by military needs. The architectural and technical connection with the city structures mentioned above, however, is still recognizable (see fig. 9).

Even if we do not follow the most skeptical of all presumptions on Solomon's city-building activities and grant that he was responsible for constructions in Jerusalem, Gezer, Hazor, and Megiddo, perhaps even in the Negev, then we would still have to agree with the evaluation of the grand old lady of archaeology in Palestine, Kathleen M. Kenyon, when she says, "Archaeology has therefore provided us with little direct evidence of the glories of Solomon's court, and has shown that, away from the capital, the civilisation was not of a very high order, nor are there striking signs of economic prosperity" (1970, 255–56). What is true of Solomon is most definitely true for David and even more so for Saul.

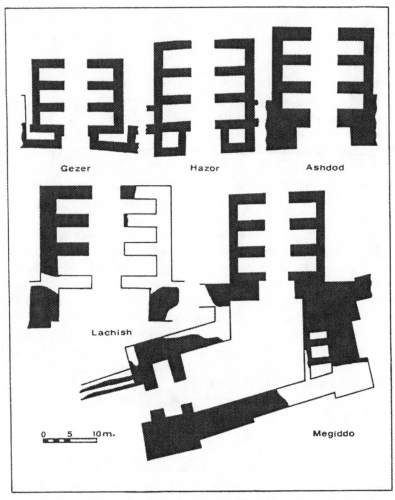

Figure 8: City gates of the building style frequently attributed
to the Solomonic period

Despite all this, the archaeological facts (as much as we can evaluate them according to the conventional chronology) do allow us to conclude that a coordinated, state-controlled construction of cities occurred throughout Palestine already during the tenth century (or at least at the beginning of the ninth century). The excavated wall remains do not reveal to us, however, who was responsible for this advance in urbanization that halted the long-standing demise of the cities in Canaan and where the resource came from that made this advance possible. They also do not reveal to us how a centralized government could have come into existence and organized such building projects in

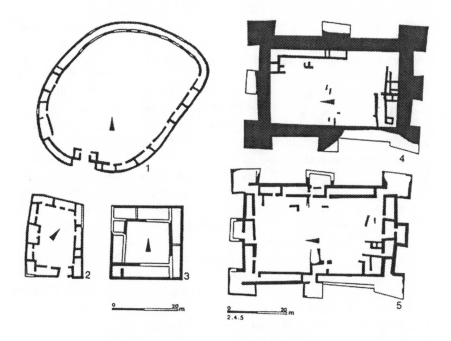

Figure 9: Negev fortresses

a region that had only ever known city-states. The Israelite monarchy has left its most concrete remains in these cities, but the key to how the monarchy originated in Israel seems to lie in rural regions.

II.1.3.2. Settlement Structures in the Country and the Formation of the State

According to the Bible, the Israelite state was formed because the institution of judgeship that had previously organized internal social structures and guarded against external threats proved more and more inadequate as time passed. The tribes refused to be "judged" any longer (Judg 17–21), the enemies, particularly the Philistines, could no longer be held at bay (Judg 13–16; 1 Sam 4), and the last "judges," Samson, Eli, and Samuel, could no longer guarantee a secure and organized way of life despite all their competence and piety. All this led to the desire for a king, brought to Samuel by the elders of Israel (1 Sam 8).

For critical historical scholarship, only one of these factors has long been accepted as historical fact: scholarly consensus held for a long time that the Philistines alone triggered the formation of the state in Israel. This ethnic group had immigrated into the southern Palestinian coastal region not much earlier, organized themselves into a union of cities, and expanded toward the hill country. Israel was able to withstand the pressure brought on by this movement only by deciding to form a state (Albrecht Alt was the first strongly to suggest this theory). Many different suggestions exist as to the motives that led the Philistines to expand their territory toward the east: they offensively reacted to Israelite expansionist tendencies or at least Israelite raids along the Via Maris; they desired to control all of Palestine, especially also the trade routes leading through the interior; they were forced to expand and acquire new territory, or at least control other settlements and exploit their resources, because of a population explosion. There are enough motives for the conflict between the Philistines and the Israelites that the biblical depiction whereby Samuel claimed a triumphant victory over this dangerous enemy just before the election of a king (1 Sam 7) seems rather out of touch with reality.

Many of these suggestions are based on the idea that a state comes into being because a fragmented polity is threatened from the outside. In order to defeat an enemy in battle, national unity results from external pressure. This is not the place to discuss where this idea originates, but it is hard to shake the suspicion that it is heavily influenced by European and especially German nationalism, particularly by ideals popular during the Enlightenment and Romanticism. These ideals are clearly seen in Friedrich Schiller's portrayal of the Swiss Confederation in their fight against Habsburg nobility in his play *Wilhelm Tell*. Other disturbing examples are the misleading myths surrounding the formation of the German Reich as the result of the Franco-Prussian war.

In general, we can assume that the formation of a state can indeed be initiated by external factors but that it cannot take place without the internal willingness of a society to give up their decentralized organizational structures. What may the internal factors have been that led Israel to install the monarchy? The basic insight we must work with is that the movement toward a territorial state was not driven by the cities (i.e., by the densely populated regions in the Palestinian plains with their city-states) but rather by the hill and mountain regions of central and southern Palestine. It is certainly no coincidence that the first king, Saul, had his place of residence and center of power in the Benjaminite hill town Gibeah, that David first became king of Judah in Hebron (most likely a relatively small Canaanite city located in the southern hill country), and that he had to deal with Saul's son and successor Eshbaal, who had established a power base in Mahanaim in the hill country east of the Jordan. It is also no coincidence that the royal residences of the monarchies in Judah and northern Israel, Jerusalem (first Hebron) and Samaria (first Shechem, Penuel, and Tirzah), were not located in the coastal area or in the Jezreel Valley but in the mountain regions. The Israelite monarchy established its roots and secured its resources in the Palestinian mountain regions before it incorporated the valleys and cities into its territories.

The Palestinian mountain regions, in the south and the central and northern areas, were sparsely or not at all populated during the Bronze Age. This changed drastically in the Iron Age. In earlier times archaeologists who concentrated on sensational findings in large cities (partially with success) were not even aware of this drastic change. Archaeologists have just recently started to focus on smaller settlements in the mountain regions that, in part, could be identified with biblical locations (e.g., Shiloh, Giloh, and Mizpah). Most of these settlements, however, are located in the far corners of the country and cannot be connected to biblical locations; they continue to be referred to by their modern Arabic names (such as Khirbet el-Mšaš and several other locations in the Negev or 'Izbet Ṣarṭah, an important excavation in the Ephraimite mountains). Aside from such individual excavations, the survey method has recently been intensified: the surface examination of smaller and larger regions aimed at finding material remains, especially clay shards, that coincidence or climate have brought to light over the course of the centuries. Such surveys are of course insufficient for the precise study of individual locations, but they do provide us with a reliable picture of settlement densities and durations at specific locations, in specific districts, and, finally, in whole regions (for the Samarian mountains, see Finkelstein 1988; for the mountain regions east of the Jordan, see the attempt of Zwickel). Much will depend in the future on how well the various findings from excavations and surveys can be interrelated so that the stratigraphy of a single location may provide information on the settlement history of an entire region.

We already know enough to state that the Samarian mountains were the first territory west of the Jordan to be covered by a large number of very small settlements, villages, hamlets, and single homesteads that started in the east and spread west toward the foothills and south past Jerusalem into the hills of Judah and the Shephelah. This process began during the early Iron Age I and came to an end toward the late Iron Age I. The population in the Samarian mountains increased during this time from 20,000 to 55,000: this is a significant increase but still small compared to the fact that the population reached 135,000 in the eighth century.

The types of settlements and thus the way of life of the people who lived in the hills were markedly different from the Canaanite cities. Most of the settlements were not just small; they were also unfortified (at least in the beginning). The so-called four-room house dominates the housing types: a fairly modest dwelling consisting of a main room (sometimes with two floors) and two side rooms attached perpendicularly and enclosing an inner court. Early speculations that this housing type imitated a nomadic tent and was "imported" from this lifestyle have not been substantiated; we also find the four-room house in the plains during the Iron Age, although not quite as frequently as in the mountain settlements of the Iron Age. Most important, we find no structure that may represent public buildings or even a palace. The houses are not exactly but almost the same size, each providing shelter for a small family of farmers with their tools, animals, and supplies. In certain locations (e.g., 'Izbet Ṣarṭah) these houses are arranged in a circle so that their main rooms join each other in creating a defensive ring around the village (see fig. 10).

These settlements, or settlements similar to this, proliferated in the Palestinian mountains between 1200 and 1000 B.C.E., and it seems that the formation of the state was connected to this process. In the following we will trace this connection between the settlement of the Palestinian mountains and the formation of the state in Israel.

This is not the place to discuss who the new settlers in the mountains may have been. Anyone willing to follow the biblical depiction even in part and taking the later history of the land into consideration will almost automatically think of the Israelites. The biblical depiction, however, of how the land was conquered—communally, violently, and comprehensively (including the plains!)—could be more axiomatic than realistic. Recent scholarship has entertained other models: the Israelites trickled slowly into the area, nomads

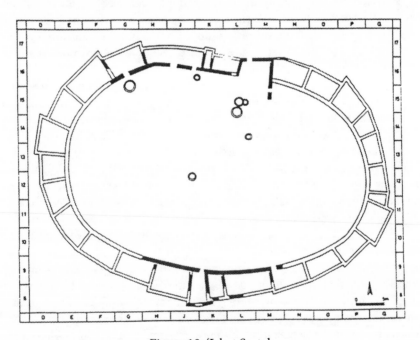

Figure 10: 'Izbet Ṣarṭah

following the grazing habits of their animals (Alt); they were "outlaws" and fringe members of society that withdrew from the Canaanite cities to the mountains in order to establish a revolutionary countersociety (Mendenhall, Gottwald); or they were the descendants of Canaanites who had reverted to a nomadic life style during the Bronze Age and now returned to farming, this time, however, not in the plains but in the mountains (Finkelstein). Perhaps the various models do not exclude each other.

What may have motivated and equipped these new settlers to establish a firm foothold in the mountains (and not simply move through the area as nomads and shepherds had always done)? Scholars have suggested technical innovations and increasing craftsmanship, such as the ability to produce and use iron. At the beginning of the Iron Age, however, the new metal was still very coarse and porous. Bronze, manufactured as an alloy from copper and tin, was of much higher quality and more useful for civil and military purposes. The transition from bronze to iron was probably occasioned by the lack of tin; during the Late Bronze Age, all international travel and trade routes (all the way up to Wales!) had become very insecure. The much cheaper iron may quickly have become useful for farmers as the "bronze for the poor," especially as people soon learned to process it with greater precision. Equally important, however, was the ability to construct terraces and lined cisterns capable of holding water. All of this together provided the necessary conditions for farming and gardening in an area where continual springs were rare. Of course, these technologies had not just been invented and thus cannot be the sole initiator for this mountain settlement; in the foothills, these technologies had already been used for a while, but their widespread use was likely not profitable on a large scale and also not necessary, as there were easier means of feeding the population. It is also logical to assume that the people were compelled to install terraces and cisterns—and capable of doing so—and to produce and to use iron once they settled in large numbers in the mountains.

By these means it became possible to engage in extensive as well as intensive agriculture in the mountain regions. Once the settlers were able to work and irrigate the hard and dry soil, they were able to secure a basic standard of living. The necessary investments in work and material, however, exceeded the capabilities of an individual family. Large-scale terraces on the slopes and spacious cisterns cannot be built by a father and two sons; this requires the solidarity and communal work of an entire village. It also requires the societal organization of work and material. The arduous living situation and the high degree of communal effort necessary to survive in such a situation depended from the beginning on strong political structures that combined the efforts of many individuals. The larger the project a group dared take on—whether the connection between several villages through difficult territory or the supply of water for a large region—the more important it became to develop a political system that all were willing to accept.

Despite the use of all means possible and the combination of all forces, the stony and meager soil did not allow a carefree existence but demanded ongoing efficiency and the use of every possible resource in every possible area. Not every farmer could grow what he wanted, or at least what he might have needed, to make his family economically autonomous. The arable land was limited, not every piece of land could be used to its full extent, and not every location was suitable for terracing. Some regions were more suited to grow grain on a large scale; some were suited only for small-scale gardening operations. One area might be suited for vegetables, another for fruit or wine. One area might have been suited for raising cattle, another for the fabrication of pottery. The diversity and limitations of the ecological framework led to economic specialization and social differentiation. There certainly were farmers in more advantageous surroundings who thus became wealthier; others were disadvantaged and thus poorer. The latter were solely concerned with securing their existence, whereas the former had enough leisure to pursue higher goals and to look at larger contexts. Political interests and economic efficacy thus were likely not distributed equally.

The specialization of individual farm operations, as well as also of entire villages and even regions, led to active local and regional trade. Trade occurred not only between the farmer and the shepherd: the grain farmer requires olive oil; the family with a surplus of vegetables or fruit requires grain for bread; the vineyard cannot sustain life by wine alone. Trade routes are established and maintained, and markets are created; some people live at the market, others in the mountains. Conflict may arise and rules become necessary, laws are fixed, and someone is needed to enforce law and order. Thus a service sector comes into being, if only a small one: traders, artisans, judges, and armed forces.

If all this is successful enough, economic prosperity and social well-being increases for all. The discussion above already mentioned the increase in population density during the Iron Age. The demographic and economic weight slowly shifted from the plains, clearly dominant in earlier times, to the mountains. This does not mean that the cities suddenly grew impoverished or were abandoned overnight; they did, however, see a marked decline during the Late Bronze Age and Iron Age I. The mountain regions did not suddenly turn into the economic center of the country; they did, however, undergo a decisive economic boom during the early Iron Age.

Once the population starts growing in an area not blessed with resources and limited in space, this leads to further economic intensification and consequent social differentiation—while some rise, others sink in social standing—on the one hand, but also to the search for new areas to be settled, on the other hand. A family member, or perhaps an entire family or clan, emigrates once the area becomes too crowded and there is no long-term prospect. From the heights of the Palestinian mountain regions, it is virtually impossible to go east; the migration will move west—and thus draw close to the plains. These were still densely populated, and, more important, the Philistines ruled them. The Philistines had extended their sphere of influence from their heartlands in the southwest to the entire coastal region, including the most fertile inland areas. Thus a conflict developed that found diverse reflections in biblical texts that seem fully credible on this issue in general.

The clash between the Philistines and Israelites was all the more unavoidable since both were greatly interested in regional and transregional, even international trade, which flourished among each adversary. Once local markets had been established, merchants were drawn in from far away. The local population, especially the wealthy segments, grew more interested in imported goods: merchandise from Egypt, Phoenicia, or Arabia. The Phoenicians were engaged in international maritime trade; to the northeast, trade routes ran right through or at least along Israelite territory—trade routes frequented by Arabic and Mesopotamian merchants peddling their wares. Apart from the Via Maris, there also was the more arduous, but not as strictly controlled, high route through the Palestinian mountains, and there also was the so-called King's Highway east of the Jordan. It too was not out of reach of the Israelites who also settled along and east of the Jordan; it was not even out of reach for the Philistines who apparently had a base in Beth-shean.

While the settlement activity in the Palestinian mountains had originally been limited to the Samarian hill region, it eventually became denser and expanded to the west, south, and north, reaching beyond the hill regions into the plains.[8] These settlements now had a clear view of the cities and trade routes located in the plains; at the same time, these settlements were now in clear view of the Philistines, who covetously looked east and north. In cultural, military, and political terms, the Philistines had great advantages over the mountain settlers. It is quite plausible that a gathering of forces and a combined effort was required to match this adversary and eventually overcome it. These forces and the will to use them did not fall from heaven; they had existed for a long time and continually grew stronger.

Finkelstein draws a similar multicausal picture (1989) that is much more plausible than assuming a single reason for the move into statehood,

---

8. See Finkelstein 1988 for the Ephraimite hill country. For the Judean hill country, see Lehmann, "The United Monarchy in the Countryside," 117–62. See 124 n. 7 above.

whether this reason was military, nationalistic (see the Philistine theory above), or something else, such as presented by Hopkins's *The Highlands of Canaan*. According to Hopkins, the farmers in the Palestinian mountains originally engaged only in subsistence agriculture during Iron Age I. Every small enterprise was basically self-sustaining and provided everything necessary from gardening to farming to livestock—the mountains primarily supported small livestock, sheep, and goats—to guarantee their existence. This structure, of course, allowed only a very basic standard of living. Everything that was produced barely met the basic requirements of a very meager existence; in times of crisis, solidarity became very necessary. The people were not wealthy, there were few prospects, but they were satisfied with a small house and the basic necessities of life—they were proud and free individuals. The great collapse of this rough and healthy lifestyle occurred with the formation of the state. The kings pursued far-reaching interests that went beyond protecting the existence of mountain farmers. They desired an army and an administration, palaces, temples, and city walls; they sought wealth for themselves and their followers. All this depended on taxation. Even if the tax rate was not very high, it did tear a significant hole in the farmer's limited budget. All of a sudden they were required to produce something they did not need themselves but was required by others: a surplus. This necessitated the introduction of new and efficient agricultural methods. Olives, wine, and similar products were now required, products consumed only to a small degree by the farmers themselves but sold instead at the markets for money—tax money—or traded for other luxury items. Some farmers were better equipped to deal with these new circumstances, others less so. Social inequality was the result, and social strata developed for the first time—now not only in the cities but also in the rural areas. The kings turned the subsistence economy of the mountain farmers into a surplus economy (which definitely was prosperous, just not for everyone). The monarchy thus became the economic and social "original sin" (a "sin" that also had its attractive aspects). This description also provides an explanation for how the state was established: power-hungry elements took advantage of the human and material resources present in Palestine to create and expand a "modern" communal structure. Two issues remain problematic for this hypothesis. First, there hardly ever was a true subsistence economy in the mountains of Palestine. The ecological circumstances did not really allow individual families to be self-sufficient. More important, it is highly doubtful that the state was a foreign element forced upon the farmers; it was, in fact, supported by the farmers, at least in part. From where in Canaan, which had always only known city-states, should the impetus to establish a territorial state and its success have come from, if not from the settlers themselves?

II.1.4. Written Evidence for Israel's First Kings

Barstad, Hans M., and Bob **Becking.** "Does the Stele from Tel-Dan Refer to a Deity Dôd?" *BN* 77 (1995): 5–12. **Biran,** Avraham, and Joseph **Naveh.** "An Aramaic Stele Fragment from Tel Dan," *IEJ* 43 (1993): 81–98. **Biran** and **Naveh.** "The Tel Dan Inscription: A New Fragment," *IEJ* 45 (1995): 1–18. **Birch,** Bruce C. *The Rise of the Israelite Monarchy: The Growth and Development of 1 Samuel 7–15* (SBLDS 27; Missoula, Mont.: Scholars Press, 1976). **Cohen,** Ronald. "State Origins: A Reappraisal," in *The Early State* (ed. Henri J. M. Claessen and Peter Skalník; The Hague: Mouton, 1978), 31–75. **Cryer,** Frederick H. "On the Recently-Discovered 'House of David' Inscription," *SJOT* 8 (1994): 3–19. **Cryer.** "King Hadad," *SJOT* 9 (1995): 223–35. **Davies,** Philip R. "'House of David' Built on Sand: The Sins of the Biblical Maximizers," *BAR* 20/4 (1994): 54–55. **Dietrich,** Walter. "*dāwīd, dôd* und *bytdwd*," *TZ* 53 (1997): 16–32, repr. as "Der Name 'David' und seine inschriftliche Bezeugung," in idem, *Von David zu den Deuteronomisten: Studien zu den Geschichtsüberlieferungen des Alten Testaments* (Stuttgart: Kohlhammer, 2002), 74–87. **Dietrich,** and Thomas **Naumann.** *Die Samuelbücher* (EdF 287; Darmstadt: Wissenschaftliche Buchgesellschaft, 1995). **Knauf,** Ernst Axel. "Le roi est mort, vive le roi! A Biblical Argument for the Historicity of Solomon," in *The Age of Solomon: Scholarship at the Turn of the Millennium* (ed. Lowell K. Handy; SHANE 11; Leiden: Brill, 1997), 81–95. **Knauf,** Albert de **Pury,** and Thomas **Römer.** "**BaytDawīd* ou **BaytDôd*," *BN* 72 (1994): 60–69. **Margalit,** Baruch. "The Old-Aramaic Inscription of Hazael from Dan," *UF* 26 (1994): 317–20. Hans-Peter **Müller.** "Die aramäische Inschrift von Tel Dan," *ZAH* 8 (1995): 121–39. **Noth,** Martin. "Die Wege der Pharaonenheere in Palästina und Syrien," in idem, *Aufsätze zur biblischen Landes- und Altertumskunde* (ed. Hans Walter Wolff; 2 vols.; Neukirchen-Vluyn: Neukirchener, 1971), 2:3–118. **Rainey,** Anson. "The 'House of David' and the House of the Deconstructionists," *BAR* 20/6 (1994) 47. **Thompson,** Thomas L. "'House of David': An Eponymic Referent to Yahweh as Godfather," *SJOT* 9 (1995): 59–74. **Thompson.** "Dissonance and Disconnections: Notes on the Bytdwd and Hmlk.hdd Fragments from Tel Dan," *SJOT* 9 (1995): 236–40. **Ussishkin,** David. "Notes on Megiddo, Gezer, Ashdod, and Tel Batash in the Tenth to Ninth Centuries B.C.," *BASOR* 277/278 (1990): 71–91.

II.1.4.1. Extrabiblical Evidence

Unfortunately, we have not yet discovered a single appreciable piece of writing from tenth-century Palestine. Extra-Palestinian textual material is also scarce. There was no prospering empire in the north, such as the former Babylonian or Hittite Empires; no collections of texts have been found in Syrian cities of the period comparable to those found from earlier times in Ugarit or Mari. The early Iron Age seems to have been a period that was as poor in text production as it was poor in general and hardly capable of high cultural achievements.

One exception must be mentioned: Egypt. Even this empire along the Nile had grown weak after the truce with the Hittites, which had been established with great difficulty, had been broken and after the maritime peoples had been driven back. This weakness resulted in the division of the empire into an Upper and Lower Egyptian monarchy and a quick succession of different dynasties. But then a pharaoh ascended to the throne who was able to rekindle the former glory of the empire for a brief time and once again establish an Egyptian presence in Palestine and Syria: Sheshonq I (ca. 945–924 B.C.E.), founder of the Twenty-Second, the so-called Libyan, Dynasty.

The Bible tells us that this pharaoh, whom it refers to as Shishak, threatened Jerusalem in the fifth year of Rehoboam, the son and successor of Solomon (following accepted chronology, in the year 922 B.C.E.), but that the city was ransomed by paying a heavy tribute (1 Kgs 14:25–28). Sheshonq himself eternalized the successes of one of his northern campaigns in the temple of Karnak. In this he followed the tradition begun by several of his predecessors (e.g., Thutmose III and IV, Amenhotep II and III, Ramesses II and III): they listed the names of Syrian and Palestinian cities that the pharaoh had conquered or subjected or claimed to have subjected. These lists seem shaped by strict conventions, but they often appear chaotic and are thus historically reliable only to a certain degree. It is possible, however, to distinguish three groups in this list. Two groups refer to cities conquered during the advance and return marches of the Egyptian army through southwestern Palestine, and a third refers to the "successes" during the stay in central Palestine (see Noth). This list mentions, among others, Beth-shean, Gibeon, Mahanaim, Shunem, Taanach—not Jerusalem (which indeed was not conquered, according to the Bible)—and Megiddo.

Excavations in Megiddo in turn discovered an Egyptian stela—or at least a fragment of it! The valuable find was first tossed as debris into a rubble pit, from which it emerged by coincidence twenty years later. In a daring but well-justified reconstruction, given known analogies, this piece of debris was identified as an edge piece of a monumental stela that likely was more than 3 meters high, 1.5 meters wide, and up to .5 meter thick (see fig. 11). It seems that this monument was shattered at a certain point and that the individual pieces were reused as separate building blocks, of which only one has reappeared—and this very one is inscribed with the name Sheshonq! This is not the place to speculate regarding what else may have been inscribed on the stela. It should be stated only that the monument was probably erected following the subjection of the city in order clearly to demonstrate the pharaoh's claim to power. Sheshonq wanted to be known as the ruler of Megiddo from that point on. Whom did he replace: a Canaanite city king? Solomon himself? or, in the meantime, Jeroboam? Unfortunately, the inscription fragment does not tell us. We can conclude only that Sheshonq I was indeed in Palestine and subjected (among others) the city of Megiddo during his time there. His efforts, however, did not meet with enduring success. He died shortly after his Palestinian campaign, after which Egyptian dominance over Palestine disappeared for a long time.

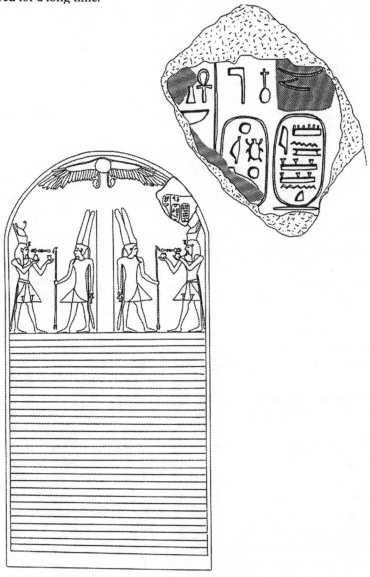

Figure 11: Sheshonq Stela
(fragment found in Megiddo and an attempted reconstruction)

One other extrabiblical inscription must be mentioned. It was likewise not written by Israelites but by Arameans and is also quite a bit later than the Sheshonq list. But it was found on Israelite soil and seems to be the earliest extrabiblical witness to David's name, as was triumphantly proclaimed following its discovery. It is an inscription that was found during excavations at Tel Dan, the hill of ruins identified with the northern Galilean city of Dan mentioned frequently in biblical texts (located at the foot of Mount Hermon at the Jordan springs). During the excavation of the defensive systems erected during the Iron Age, archeologists discovered a wall that was destroyed 733/2 by the Assyrian king Tiglath-pileser III. In the context of this wall, several fragments of a stone inscription were found. The letters were carved with a blunt chisel into a sanded basalt stone block. This inscription would be about a century later than the early monarchy.

The first fragment of the inscription, found in 1993 (A in fig. 12), has an inscribed surface area of around 22 by 32 cm and probably belonged to the right edge of a much larger stela. Most of the remaining thirteen (partial) lines are the beginning of lines, but it remains unknown how long the lines were to the left and how many lines existed above and below the fragment. As much as the fragmentary character allows, we can understand the following. Writing from a first-person perspective, an Aramean ruler tells of his "father," then of the former occupation of his land by Israel, then of a military conflict in which the author, supported by the god Hadad, had killed thousands of charioteers and horses. In lines 8 and 9 we find two important statements: "... king of Israel" and *bytdwd*. The latter statement was translated as "house of David" in the first publication of the fragment by the archaeologist Avraham Biran and the epigraphist Joseph Naveh.

This is unusual, as one would expect "Judah" to be parallel to "Israel" or a dynastic name parallel to "house of David." But Assyrian inscriptions do provide us with the expression *bit-ḫumri*, "house of Omri," which in context means the same as "Israel"; the dynastic name could thus also refer to the country, in our case "house of David" to Judah. Because the sequence of letters *bytdwd* is preceded by a *kaph*—the final letter of the word "king" (*mlk*), which also precedes "Israel"—Biran and Naveh supplemented the letters and translated "king of the house of David," an unusual construction in Semitic languages that does not occur in this form in the Bible. It is also strange that the text in line 6 seems to speak of "my king" (*mlk* with the suffix *y*). How could an Aramean king say this? The two scholars concluded that the speaker was a vassal king—perhaps from the small Aramean principality of Maacah or Beth-rehob—who spoke devotedly of his superior in Damascus in this manner.

For Biran and Naveh, a plausible historical picture emerged: the Aramean victory stela in Dan presumed that this northern Galilean border town had

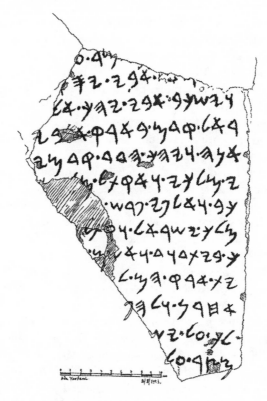

Figure 12: Tel Dan inscription, fragment A

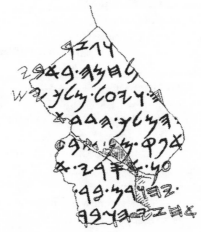

fragments B1 and B2

been conquered by the Arameans but that the Israelites had reconquered the town, shattered the stela, and reused its pieces in building a new wall, which in turn was destroyed in the eighth century. Thus, we can state a *terminus ad quem*. The *terminus a quo* is the beginning of the divided kingdom. The ninth-century context of this inscription, determined by paleography and epigraphy, coincides with the fact that the Bible dates almost all of the Aramean wars to this very century. Three options present themselves for a more precise dating (the first of which Biran and Naveh and many after them considered most plausible). First, according to 1 Kgs 15:18–20, the Aramean king Ben-hadad I started a campaign against Baasha in Israel in 885, during which Dan (among other cities) was conquered. The stela would then refer to this Aramean victory. According to the Bible, however, during this time the Judahite kings were enemies of the Israelite kings but allies of the Arameans. The fact that the stela polemicizes against both is a definite blemish on this theory.

Second, others (e.g., Emile Puech) try to connect the stela to the Aramean wars waged by Ahab (870–851), according to 1 Kgs 20 and 22. The name of the king, however, is probably a secondary and ideologically motivated insertion into this text, whereas the historical Ahab was an ally of Arameans against the approaching Assyrians. In the so-called Monolith Inscription (lines 90–92), the Assyrian king Shalmaneser III mentions the Aramean Adad-idri (= Hadadezer) and the Israelite Ahab in first and third place of a long list of enemies who had challenged him in the battle of Qarqar (853 B.C.E.) and whom he had naturally defeated (in truth, these enemies probably held out successfully against him).

The third possible historical location of the stela would be the war between Aram and Israel that enabled Jehu's uprising in 845 B.C.E. and continued long after this event (compare the list of Israelite losses in 2 Kgs 10:32). During this time, Israel and Judah indeed fought together against Aram. The respective Aramean king was Hazael, a general who according to 2 Kgs 8:7–15 rose to power under somewhat dubious circumstances and whom the Assyrians themselves referred to a "man without ancestry." But how can an insurrectionist without ancestry refer to his predecessor as his "father," as the author of the inscription does? Now, "father" in Semitic languages is not merely a term of kinship (see, e.g., 2 Kgs 2:12), and a successor might have every interest in portraying his relationship to his predecessor as intimate, especially when the former king was famous and now dead and the successor of questionable legitimacy.

A group of scholars, however (see the contributions by Knauf, de Pury, and Römer and the so-called deconstructionists Davies, Cryer, and Thompson), consider these arguments overburdened and in general inappropriate.

The more they reject any early dating and thus the historical reliability of the Bible, the more intensively they voice their criticisms. Their historical challenges are aimed at different issues—the methods used during excavation and publication, and the epigraphic, linguistic, and historical premises and claims of the first publishers—and they argue for a completely different context and interpretation of this text. According to these scholars, the text is probably not nearly as old as claimed (Thompson dares to move the date to the seventh century, thus into the time of the late monarchy). Biblical sources are in general not helpful when interpreting archaeological findings, as the Bible is clearly a religious and also certainly a late book. Most important, however, the translation of *bytdwd* as "house of David" is said to be incorrect on several points. Why should the Arameans have had anything to do with Judahites in the south of Palestine? Why should the name of a state (Israel) be used parallel to the name of a dynasty (see above)? Why are the words "house" and "David" not separated by a dot in the line, as all other words are? Why was it not considered that the sequence of letters *dwd* can also be read as *dôd* ("uncle, beloved") in biblical Hebrew and that *dwd* in the inscription of the king of Mesha in Moab obviously refers to an Israelite (!) deity whose sacred artifacts supposedly had to be robbed by the king of Moab? Why should *bytdwd* in the Dan Inscription not refer to the "house of the beloved (god)," especially since we have archaeological and even biblical evidence for sanctuaries in Dan? And were there not even more divine place names that, in contrast to personal names, were written as one word, such as As*dôd* (an error!) and *Bet*-El?

If we followed all of these arguments, then the mention of David, or rather the house of David, would dissolve in the incense of a local sanctuary and the inscriptional confirmation of large Israelite-Aramean wars in the ninth century would mutate to the mere reflex of a local skirmish. The debate provoked some almost spiteful reactions against this reductionist view (Rainey). Before the scholarly world ended this religious battle, however, the next sensation shook the academic world. In 1995 Biran and Naveh published two newly found smaller fragments of the same Aramaic inscription that clearly belonged together (B1 and B2 in fig.12). These text fragments also speak of battles and refer to the god Hadad as "king" (but hardly to the appointment of the respective king by Hadad, as Biran and Naveh assumed; this also solves the riddle of the expression "my king" in fragment A, line 26: the earthly king pays homage to the heavenly king). The most exciting aspect, however, is the appearance of two names on fragment B2. It is clear from the beginning that names on a monumental stela do not refer to "nobodies" but only to individuals of political importance, most commonly to kings. The names are, unfortunately, not fully preserved; we have only the last consonant

of each proper name, followed by *br* (= Hebrew *ben,* "son of"), which must
have continued with the name of the father. The two name fragments read ...
-rm br ... and ... *-yhw br.*... In the first case we should likely vocalize *-ram,*
in the second case *-yahu;* the second name is a YHWH composite, most likely
referring to Israel or to Judah. The electrifying analogy almost suggests itself:
if "Israel" and "house of David" (in the sense of Judah) follow each other in
fragment A (lines 8 and 9), then the names in fragment B2 (lines 6 and 7) are
likely the names of an Israelite and a Judahite king—probably in this order!
The Bible knows of only one such case when Israel was ruled by a king whose
name ended with *-ram* while Judah was ruled by a king whose name ended
with *-yahu.* We are dealing with J(eh)oram of Israel (850–845) and Ahazia(hu)
of Judah (845). Both were killed in 845 B.C.E. as a result of the uprising that
the Israelite officer Jehu staged on the occasion of a war with the Arameans
(2 Kgs 9). Biran and Naveh thus confidently supplemented the fragment to
read: "Joram, son of Ahab, king of Israel" and "Ahaziahu, son of Jehoram,
king of the house of David."

It is hard to disagree with this conclusion. True, the same constellation of
biblical names exists in reverse five years before 845 B.C.E., when the northern Israelite Ahaziahu (851–850) and the Judahite J(eh)oram (850–845) were
kings. There is no indication, however, that these two kings ever cooperated
in a joint action against Aram. It would also be very surprising that the order
(unlike the order in fragment A!) would first mention the Judahite and then
the Israelite king. All the same, even with this less probable suggestion, we
would still end up in the same time period.

What does the Tel Dan stela reveal about the events that occurred during
the middle of the ninth century? To maximize their information potential,
it would be very advantageous to bring fragments A and B into some sort
of relation and thus gain a clearer picture of the content of the entire text.
Biran and Naveh believed that they could join the two fragments in such a
fashion that both shared a common edge, that the country names and the
names of the kings could be related to each other, and that this alignment of
the fragments revealed the full width of the entire stela—a very tempting but
also risky operation that also led to the assumption that the rebel Jehu might
have been an agent of the Aramean king Hazael. This king, too, had risen to
power following a coup against the Adad-idri (Hadadezer) mentioned in the
Shalmaneser inscription or against the Ben-hadad (II?) mentioned in 2 Kgs
8:7–15. In the fragment, this king would be boasting that he killed Joram and
Ahaziah. This reading, however, is possible only if we follow the alignment of
the fragments suggested by Biran and Naveh.

Despite the second discovery and its interpretation by Biran and Naveh,
several objections have been raised (Cryer, Thompson): Do fragments B1 and

B2 really belong together? Do they belong to the same inscription as fragment A? Why must the names ending in -*rm* and -*yhu* be royal names and why the names of an Israelite and a Judahite king? Did the YHWH cult not also exist outside of Israel and Judah? Is this interpretation not influenced by too much faith in the Bible? Even if these attempts at refuting a clear issue may seem slightly desperate, the arguments raised against the hypothetical alignment of fragments A and B must be taken seriously. Does this alignment really result in straight lines of text? Is the assumed width of the stela not an arbitrary decision? How can we supplement letters and words if we do not know the size of the gaps to be filled? Who says that B did not relate to A quite differently?

Because the fragments of the Tel Dan inscription were found successively, a great degree of caution and restraint is advisable in all conclusions and propositions on this issue. For our context, we can at least make the following statement: during the second half of the ninth century, an Aramean king knew of both Israelite states and the kings who ruled there. Whereas he referred to "Israel" by this name, he referred to Judah (the reference is hardly to the ruling dynasty) as the "house of David." Interestingly, he or his scribe wrote the word for house, *byt,* with a diphthong; in other inscriptions of this time, "house" is simply written as *bt,* to be read as *bit* (a simple vowel inside a word is not written in this ancient script). The unusual *y* in *bytdwd* seems to indicate a specific Judahite diphthong that the Aramean scribe intended to represent as correctly as possible: *bayt* instead of *bit*—which is how the inhabitants in southern Palestine pronounced this word! They obviously referred to their land after a ruling dynasty whose eponym was called *dwd.* This succession of consonants should probably be vocalized as *Dawid,* as it is vocalized in the Bible (an alternative would be the attempt to indicate another special diphthong: *Daud, Doud,* or similar possibilities; the simple vowel *o* would not have been written). Based on this information, a certain David would have founded a dynasty that had already become a household name with its own specific pronunciation even in foreign countries during the time in which the Tel Dan inscription was written. This does not occur overnight; it takes generations.

This opens up a space that can be somewhat illuminated only by biblical information. If the inscription's ...-*yahu, son of...* really is Ahaziah of Judah, then this man ruled for less than a year; his predecessor Joram managed five years. For a dynasty to become such a stock phrase, as the inscription indicates, we must assume a longer passage of time, perhaps including Jehoshaphat (867–850) and Asa (907–867). We thus move into the tenth century and come very close to the early monarchy as depicted in the Bible. There are no substantial arguments against and many arguments for the assumption that the man whom the Bible refers to as *Dawid* was the very founder of a dynasty and a state indicated by the expression *bytdwd* on the Aramean Tel Dan stela.

If this is the case, then the Tel Dan stela is the first extrabiblical evidence for the name David and a not unimportant support for the existence and importance of this ruler from the tenth century B.C.E.

II.1.4.2. Biblical Sources

The Bible tells us of Israel's first three kings in unusual detail. The text takes sixty-six full chapters to describe their deeds and their fates (whereas the Bible writes of the last six kings of Judah in only five chapters and of the last six kings of Israel in only three). At first sight, we are unusually well-informed about Saul, David, and Solomon; once we take a closer look, however, problems arise. There are quite a few contacts between biblical and extrabiblical references for the later monarchy, even for the middle period of the monarchy. This is not the case for the early monarchy; the Palestinian campaign of Pharaoh Sheshonq I (§II.1.4.1 above) is the first such contact, and it is quite obscure. Following the biblical account, even this contact does not really fall into the times of Solomon. In the case of the Bible, it seems clear that the greater the gap between the events reported and the postexilic completion of the texts, the longer and more complex the growth process of these texts must have been. Even if we do not equate the first kings of Israel with legendary figures such as the Nibelungen (legendary kings of Burgundy) or King Arthur (see P. R. Davies), then we will have to admit that someone like Saul (not to mention Samson or Gideon) does remind us of an archetypal hero of old. In addition, the biblical narratives obviously do not intend to inform us objectively about the past.

The archaeological evidence, even in its most cautious interpretation, and at least the Tel Dan stela, warn us against throwing all the material overboard. Our task must not be to discard all of the biblical texts as historically useless but to examine them step by step with regard to their historical credibility. This requires a differentiated, methodically controlled analysis. The means are provided by the tried and tested historical-critical exegesis. Despite disagreement about its status and its clear weaknesses, it is quite capable of reconstructing the historical context of a text.

The most important questions that must be asked of a text in this context are:

➤ Is the text part of a late or a relatively old literary stratum? Textual material belonging to the Deuteronomistic or an older redaction are much less historically credible than source material used by these redactors—this also makes it clear that the distinction between the two is an important and possible exegetical operation. Caution is still required, since we cannot immediately classify even the older "sources" as contemporary and credible historical reports.

➤ What genre does the text belong to? A short dirge composed for a specific person can be linked to David with much greater certainty than an artificial psalm composition containing highly reflected theology. A short list or a dry report may gain our trust as historical sources much more quickly than an extended, decorated narrative, all the more if it contains redactional interjections and reflections.

➤ Does the communicative intent of a text fit the bias of the later biblical authors? If a text contains contradictory material and stands against its literary surroundings, it is more likely that we can assume historical credibility. Information that would have opposed the interests of the Davidic court, Judahite "common sense," or "orthodox" theology—such as David's residence with the Philistines or Solomon's questionable origins or the size of his palace when compared to the temple—deserves positive historical evaluation.

These are the main criteria that govern the following list. This list does not claim to be fully exhaustive, and single aspects may need revision, but it seems appropriate to unfold the biblical evidence alongside the extrabiblical evidence for the following historical reconstruction.

BIBLICAL SOURCES FOR THE HISTORY OF THE EARLY MONARCHY
(from left to right with decreasing historical credibility)

In Reference to Saul and His House

1 Samuel

9:1			genealogical information
9:2			body size
	9:1–10:16		Saul as the son of a wealthy farmer; a seer nominates Saul in a subversive gathering
10:20–21			Saul's "kinship"
	10:22		Saul does not thrust himself into power
	10:23		body size
10:24			acclamation by the people
10:25			the royal covenant deposited at the sanctuary in Mizpah
10:26–27			immediate opposition against the monarchy

		11	military conflict with the Ammonites; special connection to Jabesh in Gilead
	11:15		acclamation of the people in Gilgal
		13–14	military conflict with the Philistines; the name "Hebrews" for the Israelites; the Israelites are inferior to the Philistines in battle; vow of abstinence as a possible battle strategy; differences between Saul and Jonathan
	13:2, etc.		place names Michmash, Gibeah, Geba
	13:3		Philistine official in Geba
13:4			Saul's surprise attack against the Philistine official
13:19–20			Philistine monopoly in iron
	14:18		the ephod as an oracle
14:47			summary: wars against Moab, Ammon, Edom, Zobah, the Philistines
	14:48		war against Amalek
14:49			Saul's sons: Jonathan, Ishvi, Malchishua
	14:49		Saul's daughters: Merab, Michal
14:50			Saul's wife: Ahinoam bat Ahimaaz; Saul's general: his cousin Abner ben Ner
14:51			Ner and Kish = brothers, sons of Abiel
14:52			lifelong war with the Philistines; creation of a mercenary unit
		15	successful campaign in the Negev against the Amalekites; sparing of the Kenites; erection of a memorial in Carmel (Judah); victory celebration in Gilgal; capture and execution of Agag
		16:14ff.	Saul's depression
		18:17ff.	Saul's daughter Merab is married to Adriel of Mehola
		18:20ff.	Saul's daughter Michal is married to David
		19	Saul expels David from his court; Michal and Jonathan help David
		20	Jonathan befriends David; this provokes Saul's anger
13:22; 22:6			Saul's spear
		21–22	Saul massacres the priests of Nob
	22:7–8		the Benjaminites are Saul's power base
		23ff.	Saul chases David in the Judean desert
	25:44		Michal is married to Palti ben Laish of Gallim

29:1			places of departure for the decisive battle: Aphek und Jezreel
31:1			battle in the mountains of Gilboa
31:2			Saul and his sons Jonathan, Abinadab, Malchishua in final battle
	31		Saul, cornered by the Philistines, dies at his own hand; Saul's corpse is defiled
31:10			his armor is publicly displayed in an Astarte temple; his corpse is publicly displayed on the Beth-shean wall
31:11–13			Saul and his sons are buried in Jabesh/Gilead

2 Samuel

1:19ff.			Saul and Jonathan's death in battle against the Philistines at Gilboa
	1:24		Saul ensured Israel's wealth
2:8			Abner appoints Eshbaal as king in Mahanaim
2:9			Eshbaal's kingdom: Gilead, Asher, Jezreel, Ephraim, Benjamin = "all of Israel"
		2	military conflict between Judah and Israel
		3	Abner changes sides to David because of Rizpah
	3:11		Eshbaal is afraid of Abner
	3:15–16		Michal is taken from Paltiel and given [back] to David
		3:22ff.	Joab murders Abner; he is buried in Hebron
		4	officers of Beeroth murder Eshbaal; David executes the murderers
		6:20ff.	fight between Michal and David; Michal remains without child
		9	restoration of Saul's estates to Merib-baal ben Jonathan; Ziba is appointed estate manager; Merib-baal is suspended in Jerusalem
		16:1ff.	Merib-baal apparently desires kingship
		16:5ff.	David is berated by the Saulide Shimei
		19:17ff.	Shimei and Merib-baal submit to David
		[20	Israel's defects under the leadership of the Benjaminite Sheba]
		21	execution of the sons of Rizpah and Michal [or Merab] in Gibeon
		21:12–14	burial of the executed men as well as Saul and Jonathan in Zela

In Reference to David

1 Samuel

		16:14ff.	David as mercenary with Saul (16:18: son of Jesse from Bethlehem)
			18	rise through the ranks and son-in-law of Saul
		19		David leaves Saul's immediate surroundings
		21–22		the priest of Nob must die because of David
		22:20ff.		the priest Abiathar becomes David's follower
22:1–2				David is the leader of a militia of 400 Judahites from the fringes of society
22:3–4				David brings his parents to safety in Moab
	22:5			David finds a prophetic advisor in Gad
			23ff.	David is persecuted by Saul
	23:1ff.			inquiries of the oracle (cf. 2 Sam 2:1–2; 5:19, 23)
	25			David earns a living "protecting" local cattle breeders
	25			Abigail, the wife of Nabal, becomes David's wife
25:43				Ahinoam of Jezreel is another wife of David
	21:11ff.; 27			David enters the services of the Philistine king Achish of Gath
27:6				David receives the city of Ziklag as fiefdom
			27:8ff.	David engaged in raids against nomadic tribes in southern Palestine
		30		David leads a vendetta against the Amalekites
30:26ff.				list of Judahite villages that received battle spoils from David

2 Samuel

1:19ff.			David's lament of Saul and Jonathan
	2:1–3		David and his entourage relocate to Hebron
2:4a			the men of Judah anoint David king
	2:4b–7		David tries to win over Saul's supporters from Jabesh
2:11			David resides seven and a half years in Hebron
		2:12ff.	David leads a civil war against Eshbaal's Israel
		2:18ff.	the three sons of Zeruiah, the death of Asahel

3:2–5			list of the sons of David who were born in Hebron and their mothers
	3:12ff.		David negotiates with Abner
	3:31ff.		after Abner's murder, David gives him a state burial
	4:9ff.		David has the murderers of Eshbaal executed
5:3			the elders of Israel anoint David king in Hebron and negotiate a covenant with him
	5:6ff.		David wins Jerusalem
	5:11		David builds a palace [with the help of Hiram of Tyre]
5:14			list of David's sons who were born in Jerusalem
	6		David brings the ark to Jerusalem and places it in a "tent"
		7:11ff.	an oracle of Nathan on the Davidic dynasty
	8:1–14		brief summary of the wars and victories of David against the Philistines, Moabites, Arameans, and Edomites
		9	David "deals with" the remaining members of the house of Saul
		10	David's war against the Ammonites and the Arameans
	11–12		mercenary war against Ammon, led by Joab
	11		David commits adultery with Bathsheba
	11		Uriah dies at Rabbah Ammon
11:27			Bathsheba becomes pregnant
12:24			Bathsheba gives birth to a son and calls him Solomon
12:25			David gives the child the second name Jedidiah
	12:29–31		David conquers and subjects the Ammonites
	13		David's oldest son, Ammon, loves, rapes, and casts out his half-sister Tamar; he is murdered by her brother Absalom, who then flees to Geshur
	14		Absalom succeeds [with Joab's help?] in returning to Jerusalem
14:25			Absalom's beauty, especially his long hair
	14:26		royal weights and measures are used
14:27			Absalom has three sons and a daughter named Tamar

	15	Absalom starts a rebellion against David; the starting point is Hebron, and members of both Israel and Judah are involved; the mercenaries remain loyal to David (among them Ittai of Gath, a Philistine); David withdraws from Jerusalem but leaves a spy network behind
15:24		the ark as a palladium of war
	16	David is rejected and hated by the house of Saul and by the Benjaminites
	16–17	the advisor Ahithophel, who had sided with Absalom, is neutralized by David's trusted follower Hushai; Ahithophel kills himself; Absalom hesitates about going after David, who is well-informed of the events in Jerusalem and moves on to Mahanaim
	17:25	Amasa ben Ithra is Absalom's general
	18	David's mercenaries defeat Absalom's militia in the hills of Ephraim; Absalom is liquidated by Joab's men
	19	David returns to Jerusalem; the house of Saul submits to him; tensions exist between Judah and Israel; David replaces Joab with Amasa
	20	David's mercenaries subdue a separatist movement in the north led by Sheba; Joab murders Amasa
20:23–26		list of David's officials
	21:1ff.	David gives the Gibeonites free reign in executing seven members of the house of Saul
	21:15ff.	special accomplishments in the wars against the Philistines
	23:8ff.	heroic act of the "three" against the Philistines
	23:18ff.	heroic acts of Abishai and Benaiah
23:24ff.		list of the Thirty
	24:1ff.	report of a public census executed by Joab (with description of the kingdom's borders)
	24:10ff.	the later location of the temple belonged to the Jebusite Araunah

1 Kings

	1:1ff.	David old and weak; Abishag of Shunem serves him
	1:5ff.	in the succession to the throne, David sides with Solomon
1:39		a horn of oil for anointing in the "tent"

| 2:10 | | | David dies and is buried in the City of David |
| 2:28 | | | Joab flees to the altar in the "tent" |

In Reference to Solomon

2 Samuel

		11	marriage of Bathsheba bat Eliam, the wife of Uriah, with David
12:24–25			birth of Solomon as the second [or first] son of David and Bathsheba
12:25			the child has a special relationship to the prophet Nathan

1 Kings

	1		Solomon supported by Benaiah, Nathan, Zadok, and Shimei as candidate to succeed David to the throne
		1	Nathan and Bathsheba plead Solomon's case with David
	1		anointment by Zadok, Nathan, Benaiah; Solomon is king while David still lives
	2		Solomon's adversaries are eliminated: Adonijah, Abiathar, Joab, Shimei
	3:1		marriage with a daughter of Pharaoh
	3:4		large sacrifice in Gibeon
4:1ff.			list of officials (somewhat longer than with David)
4:7ff.			list of provincial governors (only in northern Israel)
	5:2		great expenditure at court
		5:6	4,000 [?] horse stalls [?]: 12,000 [?] war horses
	5:7–8		the provinces supply the court
	5:9ff.		Solomon's great wisdom
		5:15ff.	covenant with Hiram of Tyre: wood for grain and oil
	5:27ff.		forced labor for all of Israel
		6	construction (or expansion) of a temple (30 x 10 x 10 m)
		7:1ff.	construction of a (much larger) palace
		7:13ff.	the temple is furnished with the help of Phoenician artisans
	8		transfer of the ark from the "tent" to the holy of holies in the temple
	8		inauguration of the temple

9:11-14	twenty Galilean villages are ceded to Hiram of Tyre
9:15, 17-19	list of cities constructed under Solomon
9:16	Gezer as dowry given by Pharaoh to his daughter
10:14	tax revenues
10:15	endowments on behalf of the temple
10:16-17	ivory throne with lions
10:22	maintenance of a fleet of Tarshish ships
10:26	unit of chariots: 1,400 wagons, 12,000 horses
10:28-29	trade with horses and chariots
11:1-3	internationally staffed harem
11:14ff.	Edom becomes independent
11:23ff.	Aram-Damascus becomes independent
11:26-28, 40	Jeroboam leads an uprising of the Israelites
11:43	Solomon is buried in the City of David
14:21	Solomon's son Rehoboam ascends the throne at age 41; the Ammonite Naamah is mother of the king

II.2. THE HISTORY OF ISRAEL DURING THE EARLY MONARCHY

ON SAMUEL AND SAUL

Ahlström, Gösta W. *The History of Ancient Palestine from the Palaeolithic Period to Alexander's Conquest* (JSOTSup 146; Sheffield: JSOT Press, 1993), 429–54. **Arnold,** Patrick M. *Gibeah: The Search for a Biblical City* (JSOTSup 79; Sheffield: JSOT Press, 1990). **Bettenzoli,** Giuseppe. "Samuel und Saul in geschichtlicher und theologischer Auffassung," *ZAW* 98 (1986): 338–51. **Begg,** Christopher T. "Samuel Leader of Israel according to Josephus," *Anton* 72 (1997): 199–216. **Blenkinsopp,** Joseph. "Did Saul Make Gibeon His Capital?" *VT* 24 (1974): 1–7. **Cohen,** Martin A. "The Role of the Shilonite Priesthood in the United Monarchy of Ancient Israel," *HUCA* 36 (1965): 59–98. **Conrad,** Joachim. "Samuel im Alten und Neuen Testament," in *Von Gott reden: Beiträge zur Theologie und Exegese des Alten Testaments: Festschrift für Siegfried Wagner zum 65. Geburtstag* (ed. Dieter Viewger and Ernst-Joachim Waschke; Neukirchen-Vluyn: Neukirchener, 1995), 83–93. **Dalen,** L. van. "Samuel and Saul," in *Unless Some One Guide Me: Festschrift for Karel A. Deurloo* (ed. J. W. Dyk et al.; ACEBTSup 2; Maastricht: Shaker, 2001), 115–28. **Dietrich,** Walter, and Stefan **Münger.** "Die Herrschaft Sauls und der Norden Israels," in *Saxa loquentur: Studien zur Archäologie Palästinas/Israels: Festschrift für Volkmar Fritz zum 65. Geburtstag* (ed. Cornelis G. den Hertog, Ulrich Hübner, and Stefan Münger; AOAT 302; Münster: Ugarit Verlag, 2003), 39–59. **Edelman,** Diana Vikander. "Saul's Rescue of Jabesh-

Gilead (1 Sam 11:1–11): Sorting Story from History," *ZAW* 96 (1984): 195–209. **Edelman.** "The 'Ashurites' of Eshbaal's State (2 Sam. 2.9)," *PEQ* 117 (1985): 85–91. **Edelman.** "Saul's Journey through Mt. Ephraim and Samuel's Ramah (1 Sam 9:4–5; 10:2–5)," *ZDPV* 104 (1988): 44–58. **Edelman.** "Saul ben Kish in History and Tradition," in *The Origins of the Ancient Israelite States* (ed. Volkmar Fritz and Philip R. Davies; JSOTSup 228; Sheffield: Sheffield Academic Press, 1996), 142–59. **Evans,** W. E. "An Historical Reconstruction of the Emergence of Israelite Kingship and the Reign of Saul," in *More Essays on the Comparative Method* (ed. William Hallo, James C. Moyer, and Leo Perdue; Scripture in Context 2; Winona Lake, Ind.: Eisenbrauns, 1983), 61–77. **Flanagan,** James W. "Chiefs in Israel," *JSOT* 20 (1981): 47–73. **Fritz,** Volkmar. "Die Deutungen des Königtums Sauls in den Überlieferungen von seiner Entstehung I Sam 9–11," *ZAW* 88 (1976): 346–62. **Gillet,** Michel. "La folie de Saül," *LumVie* 39 (1990): 5–21. **Gordon,** Robert P. "Saul's Menengitis according to Targum I Samuel XIX 24," *VT* 37 (1987): 39–49. **Gordon.** "Who Made the Kingmaker? Reflections on Samuel and the Institution of Monarchy," in *Faith, Tradition, and History: Old Testament Historiography in Its Near Eastern Context* (ed. Alan R. Millard, James K. Hoffmeier, and David W. Baker; Winona Lake, Ind.: Eisenbrauns, 1994), 255–69. **Haelewyck,** Jean-Claude. "David a-t-il régné du vivant de Saül? Etude littéraire et historique de II Sm2, 1–11," *RTL* 26 (1995): 165–84. **Hayes,** John H. "Saul—the Unsung Hero of Israelite History," *TUSR* 10 (1975): 37–47. **Humphreys,** W. Lee. "The Tragedy of King Saul: A Study of the Structure of 1 Samuel 9–31," *JSOT* 6 (1978): 18–27. **Kaizumi,** Tatsuhito. "On the Battle of Gilboa," *AJBI* 2 (1976): 61–78. **Kreuzer,** Siegfried. "'War auch Saul unter den Philistern?': Die Anfänge des Königtums in Israel," *ZAW* 113 (2001): 56–73. **Long,** V. Phillips. *The Reign and Rejection of King Saul: A Case for Literary and Theological Coherence* (SBLDS 118; Atlanta: Scholars Press, 1989). **Long.** "How Did Saul Become King? Literary Reading and Historical Reconstruction," in *Faith, Tradition, and History: Old Testament Historiography in Its Near Eastern Context* (ed. Alan R. Millard, James K. Hoffmeier, and David W. Baker; Winona Lake, Ind.: Eisenbrauns, 1994), 271–84. **McKenzie,** John L. "The Four Samuels," *BR* 7 (1962): 3–18). **Miller,** J. Maxwell. "Saul's Rise to Power: Some Observations concerning I Sam 9:1–10:16; 10:26–11:15 and 13:2–-14:46," *CBQ* 36 (1974): 157–74. **Mayes,** A. D. H. "The Rise of the Israelite Monarchy," *ZAW* 90 (1978): 1–19. **Mommer,** Peter. *Samuel: Geschichte und Überlieferung* (WMANT 65; Neukirchen-Vluyn: Neukirchener, 1991). **Scheffler,** E. "The Game Samuel Played: A Psychological Interpretation of the Relationship between Samuel and Saul," *OTE* 3 (1990): 263–73. **Schunck,** Kurt-Dietrich. "König Saul—Etappen seines Weges zum Aufbau eines israelitischen Staates," *BZ* NS 36 (1992): 195–206. **Soggin,** J. Alberto. "The Reign of 'Eshba'al, Son of Saul," in idem, *Old Testament and Oriental Studies* (BibOr 29; Rome: Biblical Institute Press, 1975), 31–49. **Weiser,** Artur. *Samuel: Seine geschichtliche Aufgabe und religiöse Bedeutung: Traditionsgeschichtliche Untersuchungen zu 1 Samuel 7–12* (FRLANT 81; Göttingen, Vandenhoeck & Ruprecht, 1962). **White,** Marsha. "'The History of Saul's Rise': Saulide State Propaganda in 1 Samuel. 1–14," in *"A Wise and Discerning Mind": Essays in Honor of Burke O. Long* (ed. Saul M. Olyan and Robert C. Culley; BJS 325; Providence, R.I.: Brown Judaic Studies, 2000), 271–92. **Wildberger,** Hans. "Samuel und die Entstehung des israelitischen Königtums," in idem, *Jahwe und sein Volk, Gesammelte*

Aufsätze zum Alten Testament: Zu seinem 70. Geburtstag am 2. Januar 1980 (ed. Hans Heinrich Schmid and Odil Hannes Steck; TB 66; Munich: Kaiser, 1979), 28–55.

On David

Ahlström, Gösta W. "Was David a Jebusite Subject?" *ZAW* 82 (1980): 285–87. **Ahlström.** *The History of Ancient Palestine from the Palaeolithic Period to Alexander's Conquest* (JSOTSup 146; Sheffield: JSOT Press, 1993), 455–501. **Alt,** Albrecht. "Das Großreich Davids," in idem, *Kleine Schriften zur Geschichte des Volkes Israel* (3rd ed.; 3 vols.; Munich: Beck, 1964), 2:66–75. **Ben-Barak,** Zafrira. "Meribaal and the System of Land Grants in Ancient Israel," *Bib* 62 (1981): 73–91. **Bosworth,** David A. "Evaluating King David: Old Problems and Recent Scholarship," *CBQ* 68 (2006): 191–210. **Dietrich,** Walter. *David: Der Herrscher mit der Harfe* (Biblische Gestalten 14; Leipzig: Evangelische Verlagsanstalt, 2006). **Elliger,** Karl. "Die dreißig Helden Davids," *PJ* 31 (1935): 29–75, repr. in idem, *Kleine Schriften zum Alten Testament: Zu seinem 65. Geburtstag am 7. März 1966* (ed. Hartmut Gese and Otto Kaiser: TB 32; Munich: Kaiser, 1966), 72–118. **Fohrer,** Georg. "Der Vertrag zwischen König und Volk in Israel," *ZAW* 71 (1959): 1–22. **Gordon,** Robert P. "In Search of David: The David Tradition in Recent Study," in *Faith, Tradition, and History: Old Testament Historiography in Its Near Eastern Context* (ed. Alan R. Millard, James K. Hoffmeier, and David W. Baker; Winona Lake, Ind.: Eisenbrauns, 1994), 285–98. **Green,** Alberto R. "David's Relations with Hiram: Biblical and Josephan Evidence for Tyrian Chronology," in *The Word of the Lord Shall Go Forth: Essays in Honor of David Noel Freedman in Celebration of His Sixtieth Birthday* (ed. Carol L. Meyers and Michael O'Connor; Winona Lake, Ind.: Eisenbrauns, 1983), 373–97. **Halpern,** Baruch. "The Construction of the Davidic State: An Exercise in Historiography," in *The Origins of the Ancient Israelite States* (ed. Volkmar Fritz and Philip R. Davies; JSOTSup 228; Sheffield: Sheffield Academic Press, 1996), 44–75. **Halpern.** *David's Secret Demons: Messiah, Murderer, Traitor, King* (Grand Rapids: Eerdmans, 2001). **Hentschel,** Georg. "Die Kriege des friedfertigen Königs David (2 Sam 10,1–11; 12,26–31)," in *Überlieferung und Geschichte: Gerhard Wallis zum 65. Geburtstag am 15. Januar 1990* (ed. Helmut Obst; Wissenschaftliche Beiträge d. Martin-Luther-Universität Halle-Wittenberg A/125; Halle: Martin-Luther-Universität Halle-Wittenberg, 1990), 49–58. **Levenson,** Jon D., and Baruch **Halpern.** "The Political Impact of David's Marriages," *JBL* 99 (1980): 507–18. **Malamat,** Abraham. "Aspects of the Foreign Policies of David and Solomon," *JNES* 22 (1963): 1–17. **Master,** Daniel M. "State Formation Theory and the Kingdom of Ancient Israel," *JNES* 60 (2001): 117–31. **Mazar,** Benjamin. "David's Reign in Hebron and the Conquest of Jerusalem," in *In the Time of Harvest: Essays in Honor of Abba Hillel Silver on the Occasion of His 70th Birthday* (ed. Daniel Jeremy Silver; New York: Macmillan, 1963), 235–44. **McCarter,** P. Kyle. "The Historical David," *Int* 40 (1986): 117–29. **McKenzie,** Steven L. *King David: A Biography* (Oxford: Oxford University Press, 2000). **Na'aman,** Nadav. "In Search of Reality behind the Account of David's Wars with Israel's Neighbours," *IEJ* 52 (2002): 200–224. **Olyan,** Saul. "Zadok's Origins and the Tribal Politics of David," *JBL* 101 (1982): 177–93. **Rofé,** Alexander. "The Reliability of the Sources about David's Reign: An Outlook from Political

Theory," in *Mincha: Festgabe für Rolf Rendtorff zum 75. Geburtstag* (ed. Erhard Blum; Neukirchen-Vluyn: Neukirchener, 2000), 217–27. **Schäfer-Lichtenberger,** Christa. "David und Jerusalem: Ein Kapitel biblischer Historiographie," in *Sefer Avraham Malamat* (ErIsr 24; Jerusalem: Eretz-Israel, 1993), *197–*211. **Schunck,** Klaus-Dietrich. "Davids 'Schlupfwinkel' in Juda," *VT* 33 (1983): 110–13. **Skehan,** Patrick W. "Joab's Census—How Far North (2Sm 24,6)?" *CBQ* 31 (1969): 42–29. **Thompson,** J. A. "The Significance of the Verb *Love* in the David-Jonathan Narratives in 1 Samuel," *VT* 24 (1974): 334–38. **VanderKam,** James C. "Davidic Complicity in the Deaths of Abner and Eshbaal: A Historical and Redactional Study," *JBL* 99 (1980): 521–39. **Veijola,** Timo. "Salomo—der Erstgeborene Bathsebas," in *Studies in the Historical Books of the Old Testament* (ed. J.A. Emerton; VTSup 30; Leiden: Brill, 1979), 230–50, repr. in idem, *David: Gesammelte Studien zu den Davidüberlieferungen des Alten Testaments* (Helsinki: Finnische Exegetische Gesellschaft, 1990), 84–105. **Veijola.** "David in Keïla: Tradition und Interpretation in 1 Sam 23,1–13," *RB* 91 (1984): 51–87, repr. in idem, *David,* 5–42. **Weinfeld,** Moshe. "The Census in Mari, in Ancient Israel and in Ancient Rome," in *Storia e tradizioni di Israele: Scritti in onore di J. Alberto Soggin* (ed. Daniele Garronne and Felice Israel; Brescia: Paideia, 1991), 293–98. **Wyatt,** Nicolas. "David's Census and the Tripartite Theory," *VT* 40 (1990): 352–60.

On Solomon

Ahlström, Gösta W. *The History of Ancient Palestine from the Palaeolithic Period to Alexander's Conquest* (JSOTSup 146; Sheffield: JSOT Press, 1993), 501–42. **Alt,** Albrecht. "Israels Gaue unter Salomo," in idem, *Kleine Schriften zur Geschichte des Volkes Israel* (3 vols.; Munich: Beck, 1953–59), 2:276–88. **Alt.** "Menschen ohne Namen," in idem, *Kleine Schriften,* 3:198–213. **Ball,** E. "The Co-Regency of David and Solomon (1 Kings I)," *VT* 27 (1977): 268–79. **Bartlett,** John R. "An Adversary against Solomon, Hadad the Edomite," *ZAW* 88 (1976): 205–66. **Bloch-Smith,** Elizabeth M. "'Who Is the King of Glory?' Solomon's Temple and Its Symbolism," in *Scripture and Other Artifacts: Essays on the Bible and Archaeology in Honor of Philip J. King* (ed. Michael D. Coogan, J. Cheryl Exum, and Lawrence E. Stager; Louisville: Westminster John Knox, 1994), 18–31. **Dietrich,** Walter. "Das harte Joch (1 Kön 12,4): Fronarbeit in der Salomo-Überlieferung," *BN* 34 (1986): 7–16, repr. in idem, *Von David zu den Deuteronomisten: Studien zu den Geschichtsüberlieferungen des Alten Testaments* (Stuttgart: Kohlhammer, 2002), 157–163. **Donner,** Herbert. "Israel und Tyrus im Zeitalter Davids und Salomos," *JNSL* 10 (1982): 43–52. **Dreher,** Carlos A. "Das tributäre Königtum in Israel unter Salomo," *EvT* 51 (1991): 49–60. **Friedman,** Richard Elliot. "Solomon and the Great Histories," in *Jerusalem in Bible and Archaeology: The First Temple Period* (ed. Andrew G. Vaughn and Ann E. Killebrew; SBLSymS 18; Atlanta: Society of Biblical Literature, 2003), 171–80. **Fritz,** Volkmar. "Salomo," *MDOG* 117 (1985): 47–67. **Fritz.** "Die Verwaltungsgebiete Salomos nach 1.Kön. 4,7–19," in *Meilenstein: Festgabe für Herbert Donner zum 16. Februar 1995* (ed. Manfred Weippert and Stefan Timm; Wiesbaden: Harrassowitz, 1995), 19–26. **Handy,** Lowell K., ed. *The Age of Solomon: Scholarship at the Turn of the Millennium* (SHANE 11; Leiden: Brill, 1997). **Hurowitz,** Victor. *I Have Built You an Exalted House: Temple Building in the Bible in the Light of*

Mesopotamian and North-West Semitic Writings (JSOTSup 115; Sheffield: JSOT Press, 1992). **Jamieson-Drake,** David W. *Scribes and Schools in Monarchic Judah: A Socio-Archaeological Approach* (JSOTSup 109; Sheffield: Almond, 1991). **Keel,** Othmar, and Christoph **Uehlinger.** "Jahwe und die Sonnengottheit von Jerusalem," in *Ein Gott allein? JHWH-Verehrung und biblischer Monotheismus im Kontext der israelitischen und altorientalischen Religionsgeschichte* (ed. Walter Dietrich and Martin A. Klopfenstein; OBO 139; Fribourg: Universitätsverlag; Göttingen: Vandenhoeck & Ruprecht, 1994), 269–306. **Knauf,** Ernst Axel. "King Solomon's Copper Supply," in *Phoenicia and the Bible: Proceedings of the Conference Held at the University of Leuven on the 15th and 16th of March 1990* (ed. Edward Lipiński; OLA 44; Studia Phoenicia 11; Leuven: Peeters, 1991), 167–86. **Kuan,** Jeffrey K. "Third Kingdoms 5,1 and Israelite-Tyrian Relations during the Reign of Solomon," *JSOT* 46 (1990): 31–46. **Lemaire,** André. *Les Écoles et la formation de la Bible dans l'ancien Israel* (OBO 39; Fribourg: Editions universitaires; Göttingen: Vandenhoeck & Ruprecht, 1981). **Mettinger,** Tryggve N. D. *Solomonic State Officials: A Study of the Civil Government Officials of the Israelite Monarchy* (ConBOT 5; Lund: Gleerup, 1971). **Millard,** Alan R. "King Solomon's Shields," in *Scripture and Other Artifacts: Essays in Honor of Philip J. King* (ed. Michael D. Coogan, J. Cheryl Exum, and Lawrence E. Stager; Louisville: Westminster John Knox, 1994), 286–95. **Millard.** "Texts and Archaeology: Weighing the Evidence, the Case for King Solomon," *PEQ* 123 (1991): 19–27. **Miller,** J. Maxwell. "Solomon—International Potentate or Local King?" *PEQ* 123 (1991): 28–31. **Muhly,** James D. "Timna and King Solomon," *BO* 41 (1984): 275–92. **Na'aman,** Nadav. *Borders and Districts in Biblical Historiography: Seven Studies in Biblical Geographic Lists* (JBS 4; Jerusalem: Simor, 1986). **Niemann,** Hermann Michael. *Herrschaft, Königtum und Staat: Skizzen zur soziokulturellen Entwicklung im monarchischen Israel* (FAT 6; Tübingen: Mohr Siebeck, 1993). **Pritchard,** James B. "The Age of Solomon," in *Solomon and Sheba* (London: Phaidon, 1974), 17–39. **Rupprecht,** Konrad. *Der Tempel von Jerusalem: Gründung Salomos oder jebusitisches Erbe?* (BZAW 144; Berlin: de Gruyter, 1977). **Särkiö,** Pekka. *Die Weisheit und Macht Salomos in der israelitischen Historiographie: Eine traditions- und redaktionskritische Untersuchung über 1 Kön 3–5 und 9–11* (SESJ 60; Helsinki: Finnische Exegetische Gesellschaft; Göttingen: Vandenhoeck & Ruprecht, 1994). **Thiel,** Winfried. "Soziale Auswirkungen der Herrschaft Salomos," in *Charisma und Institution* (ed. Trutz Rendtorff; Gütersloh: Mohn, 1985), 297–314. **Wälchli,** Stefan. *Der weise König Salomo: Eine Studie zu den Erzählungen von der Weisheit Salomos in ihrem alttestamentlichen und altorientalischen Kontext* (BWANT 141; Stuttgart: Kohlhammer, 1999). **Zwickel,** Wolfgang. "Die Kesselwagen im Salomonischen Tempel," *UF* 18 (1986): 459–61.

II.2.1. SAUL—DAVID—SOLOMON: THREE RULERS IN PROFILE

If Saul had not existed, no one would have invented him. Old Testament historiography expends too much effort, first in raising doubts about his election, then in justifying his rejection; it labors too hard to wipe away all suspicions that David may have illegitimately usurped the throne that we could imagine Israel's first king to be a fictive character, created to expound a paradigm of monarchy in Israel.

It is true that Saul's name does not appear in any extrabiblical text. It is also true that many of the narratives contain several legendary features as well as elements of devotional literature. But these narratives also contain many unpretentious and thus credible clues to his persona and his actions. There are also very prosaic texts that go against the later pro-Davidic trend, providing us with an image of Israel's first king that lacks sharp contours but paints a recognizable picture nonetheless.

Saul originated in a town called Gibeah located in the Benjaminite hills. It was no city but a village that was probably as inconspicuous as its name: "hill." A closer identification was probably provided by a surname: "Gibeah in Benjamin," also "Gibeah of God" in relation to a nearby sanctuary, and later—after Saul had become important—"Gibeah of Saul."

Saul came from a farming village, and he himself is described as a farmer, which in itself is unusual. The "spirit of God" overcame him and moved him to action in the act of plowing the fields when he heard that an enemy force had come upon an Israelite village (1 Sam 11). A different narrative describes him as a young farmboy sent on an errand to find his father's lost donkeys (1 Sam 9). This does indicate, however, that Saul was not just anyone but the member of a highly regarded and wealthy family. Donkeys are valuable, even at times royal animals; a servant or slave accompanied Saul in his search, and right from the beginning Saul is given a genealogy covering five generations: he was the son of Kish ben Abiel ben Zeror ben Becorath ben Aphiah—an unusually long genealogy granting Saul a certain sense of aristocracy. Kish (and Saul as his son) is referred to as a גבור חיל: labels that signal high economic, social, and military status.

Saul's family belonged to the tribe of Benjamin. In the legendary but not necessarily completely fictional scene where the sacred lot determines the future king (1 Sam 10:19–21), the text mentions the organizational units of tribal society: Saul and his family belonged to the clan Matri (a name not mentioned in 9:1 and hardly invented), and this clan belonged to the tribe of Benjamin. The place of an individual or a group in society is not determined by membership in a certain caste or a certain occupation, nor is it determined by an economic or political hierarchy; instead, it is determined by kinship— even if often more ideal than real. It is quite remarkable that an individual could rise to the throne in a system that divides power and influence into such clearly segmented areas.

Saul's tribe Benjamin belonged to the tribes of central Palestine that were responsible for most of the dynamic that led to the settlement of the mountains. In a biblical context, Benjamin belonged to the Rachel tribes (Gen 30), who were allotted a leadership role among the tribes. Unlike Ephraim, Benjamin was a relatively small tribe. This fact may have encouraged the tribes to accept a king from Benjamin, if they were going to accept a king at all.

Regardless of where he came from, Saul seems to have been a man who was certainly capable of rousing hope. It may well be the product of court literary conventions when 1 Sam 9:3 says that he was a "choice and fine" young man, even the best man in all of Israel. (It is remarkable, however, that this style is applied to Saul and not to David.) He definitely seems to have been a large man, one who "was taller than all the people from his shoulders upward" (9:2; 10:23). Time and again the Bible describes him as strong, ready for battle, even dangerous. The Philistines apparently hated—and feared!—him more than any other Israelite (1 Sam 31).

According to the biblical depiction, an evil spirit increasingly plagued Saul; that is, he suffered from abnormal moods and seizures brought on by his suspicions and later his knowledge that David was his divinely designated successor. Interpreters have diagnosed several different medical conditions: meningitis, depression, or schizophrenia. Whether any of these come close to the truth or whether we are facing the product of Davidic propaganda (Ahlström) can no longer be determined. In any case, we can state that the biblical texts describe Saul in very different contexts as hesitant, choleric, shifting, fearful, then again wild and unflinching—the portrait presents us with a very difficult character. The massacre of an entire priestly family (1 Sam 21–22) is indeed an action that we would only believe a psychologically deficient ruler to be capable of. The Bible does not, however, portray Saul as evil to the core but rather as a tragic figure unable to escape a confusing and unrelenting fate. There is no reason why this portrait could not be true in general terms. It is also quite credible that the incessant rise of a David ben Jesse was one of the problems with which Saul was unable to deal. Other problems worsened the situation, as we will see below.

Saul had a family. He had four sons with his main wife Ahinoam—Jonathan, Ishio or Eshbaal,[9] Malchishua, and Abinadab (1 Sam 14:49; 31:2)—as well as two daughters, Merab and Michal (1 Sam 14:49). The elder daughter

---

9. Both names, which could have belonged to the same person, are perverted in the Hebrew text: Ish-io ("Yнwн exists") became Ish-vi (1 Sam 14:49), and Esh-baal ("Baal exists"; see 1 Chr 8:33; 9:39) resp. Ish-baal ("Man of Baal") became Ish-bosheth ("Man of shame," 2 Sam 2:8, etc.).

was married to a certain Adriel of Meholah, a village in northern Ephraim, the younger with the ambitious David from Bethlehem in Judah (1 Sam 18). When discord later separated David and Saul, Michal was given to a man from Gallin (1 Sam 25:44, a town close to Jerusalem; see Isa 10:30)—until David demanded her back (2 Sam 3). Saul also seems to have had two sons with a concubine named Rizpah (2 Sam 21:8). An uncle of his father had a son, Abner, the cousin of Saul, who became his general (1 Sam 14:51).

Saul and almost his entire family lost their lives at the same time. The king and three of his sons fell in the decisive battle against the Philistines (1 Sam 31:2). The last surviving son and brief successor, Eshbaal, was murdered, as was Abner (2 Sam 3–4). The sons of Rizpah and some of Saul's nephews were executed in a somewhat obscure incident (2 Sam 21). Michal returned to David's side but did not have any children with him (6:20–23). One remaining son of Jonathan was handicapped; David made sure that he remained closely tied to his house (2 Sam 9; 16:1ff.; 19:25ff.). Saul's line thus vanished completely in a short time.

The biblical writers claim (the textual evidence is very precarious at this point) that Saul reigned for only two years; according to the calendars of the ancient Near East this would imply fourteen months. It seems that later Deuteronomistic redactors intended to add the typical set phrase for royal dates without having access to exact numbers. Thus they wrote, Saul was this many years old when he became king, and he was king for this many years in Israel (1 Sam 13:1); later scribes filled the second gap with "two"—what would we give if we could fill both gaps with firm numbers! We can state in general that Saul probably reigned for a longer period and accomplished greater deeds than the later perspective of David and his followers want us to believe.

David and his son and successor Solomon are both allotted a reign of forty years (1 Kgs 2:11; 11:42). Their deeds and characters are portrayed in a much better light than in the case of Saul. Just as we may suspect the colors of Saul's portrait to be too dark, the colors of David and Solomon's portraits are most likely too bright. In the Bible, "forty years" is a round number symbolizing fullness and also the passing of one full generation. In the case of David, the forty years are divided into a seven-year rule over Hebron and thirty-three years in Jerusalem. In 2 Sam 2:11 we encounter a not so round and thus historically credible number of seven and a half years. There are some indications that both these kings did rule for an extended period of time. The tradition describes David as a young man (1 Sam 16–17) and as an old man who can no longer be warmed by a young woman (1 Kgs 1). We witness how he met several different women and won them over (e.g., Michal, Abigail, or Bathsheba: 1 Sam 18; 25; 2 Sam 11), we read that they give him seventeen sons and several daughters (listed in order of birth and grouped by their birthplaces Hebron and Jerusalem in 2 Sam 3:2–5; 5:13–16), and we watch how the sons grew up, fell into conflict among themselves and with their father, and in part lost their lives—until, finally, the tenth son, Solomon, ascended to the throne (2 Sam 13–19; 1 Kgs 1–2). The combination of all these events does result in the long life of a king.

With Solomon, the situation is different and yet similar. At least according to the biblical text, Solomon describes himself to God as a "young boy" who does not know what to do when faced with the many tasks that lie ahead of him (1 Kgs 3:7–8). Then we observe as he organizes his kingdom and gains wisdom and wealth; we observe how he initiates and completes the construction of his palace and the Jerusalem temple (according to an internal chronology, this took thirteen and seven years, respectively, together twenty years, 1 Kgs 6:1; 7:1; 9:10); we observe how he initiates many other large construction projects and government actions; and we see him gather many foreign women into his harem (supposedly seven hundred main wives and three hundred concubines, 1 Kgs 11:1, 3)—in short, such a full kingship may well have lasted forty years. With Solomon, however, the fairytale elements are even more noticeable than with David.

The texts describe David's character in much greater detail than Solomon's. He came from Bethlehem, a village barely 20 km south of Jerusalem. For the biblical authors, it clearly was a Judahite village, yet it was very close to the sphere of influence of the city-state Jerusalem. He is said to have been the youngest of eight sons of his father Jesse; the three oldest are mentioned by name (1 Sam 16:1–13; 17:13–14). In adventure narratives and narratives justifying the rise of an individual, the youngest brother is quite often destined for greatness. He will be the last to inherit anything, if anything is left over, and he is the most likely to risk following an alternate path of life (see also Luke 15:11ff.). David's path led the young man to Saul's court, where he launched an amazing career as the king's musician, warrior, and finally weapons bearer. It did not take him long to become an officer and leader of Saul's mercenary troops. As such he grew more successful and popular than the king himself (1 Sam 16–18). There is no way to prove whether this description matches historical reality; it is not impossible. A brief, inconspicuous scene describes him as the king's son-in-law and thus as one of the members of his table (noticeable, in this case, by his absence, 1 Sam 20:25). The fact that Saul was suspicious of David as a possible rival for himself and his son Jonathan may be viewed as a phantasm of the king or the pro-Davidic narrator—had it not actually occurred that David became the rival of Saul and his successor Eshbaal and eventually the successor of both.

Be that as it may, hiding in the Judahite south as a vassal of the Philistine king of Gath (whatever the reasons for this may have been), David built a private army and wove a tight web of loyalties. The city of Ziklag (perhaps the Tell es-Seba' close to contemporary Beersheba), the villages and hamlets in the mountains of southern Palestine (see 1 Sam 30:26–31), and a loyal band of mercenaries, numbering between four hundred and six hundred men, constituted the power base that carried him to the throne.

Unlike Saul, David's rise did not take its starting point from the collective will of the mountain settlers. The members of the tribes did not lift him onto a shield (David thus also had no cause to hide, as Saul did); instead, David organized his own career—guided by fate or his own determination—first in relation to the Israelite king, then in the context of the Philistines, and finally in his own country. If Saul appears to us as the leader of the people as well as of the people's army, David appears as a mercenary, the leader of a militia, a warlord. As such, he became king first over Judah and then over Israel, once the young Israelite state and the Philistine confederation weakened and torn each other apart. He then defeated the Philistines among a number of other neighboring states and turned his state into the most important power center in Syria-Palestine (2 Sam 1–8). Again, not everything necessarily happened as the biblical narratives tell it, but the basic picture drawn by the Bible seems coherent and plausible—and it allows us to reconstruct a headstrong and idiosyncratic portrait of Israel's second king. David was a brilliant tactician and strategist; he adroitly juggled various political balls, played off his enemies against each other, waited patiently for the right time to make his move, and knew when to take decisive action. His path led continually upward, even if it took a roundabout route. He was a man of good fortune, not a tragic figure.

All this does not imply that David did not experience any political or military turbulence. He seems to have faced life-threatening situations already as a young man, but he was saved in each case by individuals loyal to him or by his own cunning (1 Sam 19; 21:11–16; 2 Sam 21:15–17; 23:9–10). The Bible makes Saul out to be his most dangerous enemy, and David escaped his repeated angry persecution only with great effort (1 Sam 18–26). As long as he was on his way to the throne, dangers seemed to bounce off him without causing him noticeable harm. In his years of maturity, however, at the zenith of his own power, he was shaken by severe political setbacks: deadly strife within his own family and rebellions that uprooted the foundations of his empire (2 Sam 13–20). It is tempting to view these two aspects as the fiction of the biblical narrators, but there are historical analogies. For revolutionaries and conquerors such as Alexander, Caesar, Genghis Khan, Napoleon, or Lenin, the sky seemed to be the limit before they were brought back to earth by the persistence of circumstances and individuals around them. The same seems to have happened to David. A ruler forced to flee from his capital in haste and who is obliged to subdue his own people by his mercenary troops can no longer shine as a supernatural hero.

Toward the end of his rule, David appeared to be an old man hardly capable of action. Others had taken matters into their own hands. Yet even now he remained the final decision maker. Solomon owed to David the fact that he, not his older brother Adonijah, ascended to the throne. Once more David threw his political weight (and the military weight of his mercenaries) into the arena, guiding events at the last moment along his chosen pathways (1 Kgs 1–2). These last images of David, when he took leave of power and of life yet still shaped the future, are an impressive contribution to David's characterization.

Solomon presents us with an entirely different situation, both in regards to the biblical portrait and to the historical reality that shines through in general contours. As much as he seems the creature of others upon ascending to the throne—David, Nathan, Bathsheba, and Benaiah all operated in the background—he knew how to use the coup d'etat to his advantage and acted against his opponents with determination. He immediately suspended the leading oppositional figures and had them liquidated (1 Kgs 1–2). Once this brutal job has been accomplished, we start to observe other aspects of Solomon's character. The text praises his wisdom (1 Kgs 3), appreciates his state building (1 Kgs 4), and describes his wealth (1 Kgs 5; 10) and his large construction activities (1 Kgs 5–9). We will see that this depiction is an inflation of historical reality but not entirely the result of creative speculation. Solomon seems to have been a ruler who intended to and was able to consolidate what he had received from David; he stabilized the state on the inside, strengthened its structures, and created symbols of state power.

The further historical development shows that Solomon was indeed successful in realizing his goals but that his vision of the state had to be curtailed. Solomon seems to have held on to power until the end of his life. We do hear of rebellions in the center and on the fringes of his empires—information placed deliberately at the end of the Solomon narratives by the redactors (1 Kgs 11)—but the first major upset of the state established by him and David did not occur until after his death: his son and successor Rehoboam was unable to prevent the secession of the Israelite north from the Judahite south (1 Kgs 12). Concerning the south, however, no one after Solomon could change the fact that Jerusalem was the political, economic, and religious center of this state and that, like him, every king after him would be a member of the Davidic dynasty.

The kingdom of David and Solomon remained as an ideal for the entire history of the kingdoms of Israel and Judah—even though (or perhaps exactly because) it was as much a dream projected into the past as it was historical reality. Annalists dated the kings in one kingdom in connection with the kings in the other (from 1 Kgs 15:1 on at regular intervals); prophets moved from one state to the other, or at least spoke beyond their particular borders, because they assumed responsibility for the people of God also on the other side of the border (e.g., Amos 7:10ff.; Hos 5:8ff.; Isa 28:1ff.); idiomatic sayings ("from Dan to Beer-sheba") and fixed ideas ("from the Euphrates to the streams of Egypt") were determined by the image of a Davidic-Solomonic empire. Following the collapse of the Assyrian Empire, King Josiah did not have any reservations against acting also on former Israelite soil (2 Kgs 23:15–19, 29). The Deuteronomistic Historians during the exile held fast to the idea of a unified people of God joined from north to south, and even though the Chronicler is fixated on Judah and Jerusalem, he too paints a picture of a Solomonic empire including all of Israel when he writes his large genealogy in 1 Chr 1–9; last but not least, the expectation that a messiah would arise from David's house always included all of Israel both north and south, at home and in the Diaspora (e.g., Hos 3:5; Ezek 34:23–30).

Solomon's state thus decisively influenced Israel's self-image regardless of any and all political strife and ideological deviation. It is no surprise, therefore, that biblical traditions expanded his figure to legendary proportions. Whereas the literary tribute to Solomon in 1 Kings covers his character with gold and silver, a different aspect of his characterization influenced other traditions of the Old Testament: his proverbial wisdom. According to tradition, the "wise Solomon" wrote not only Proverbs but also Ecclesiastes and the Song of Songs as well as the deuterocanonical Wisdom of Solomon. He is, however, credited with writing only two psalms (72; 127)—almost nothing compared to the seventy-three psalms of David. The idea that David was a poet is supported by the oldest songs of the books of Samuel (2 Sam 1:19–27; 3:33–34; see also 1 Sam 16:14ff.) and is thus historically credible at its core. Should the idea of a wise King Solomon be so different?

II.2.2. Enthronement and the Order of State

According to biblical tradition, Saul rose to the throne by a process legitimized by the will of the people. Strictly speaking, he ascended to the throne in different ways: it was either a special group of delegates, a band of prophets, the conscripted army, or a public gathering that recognized him as the right man for the job. It is probably futile to try to determine the historically correct version. There is little more hope in attempting to describe Saul's kingdom in successive stages of structural and geographical expansion (Edelman; Ahlström). It is much more plausible to assume that various legends have already influenced the oldest material available to us. This material, however, does communicate general information on Saul's rise to the throne: Saul did not rise to power on his own initiative, much less by force; rather, he was placed in this position by his contemporaries—even against his will, if we are to believe certain traditions. It seems that various circles were free to voice their doubts about and opposition to the monarchy (1 Sam 10:27; 11:12–13). Thus Israel's first king was not viewed as a power-hungry tyrant but as a *primus inter pares*. The majority was in favor of his rule and agreed on mutual rights and privileges (10:25). If this had not been the case, the pro-Davidic tendencies of biblical historiography would not have been able to invent it.

What kingdom belonged to Saul? The tradition is quite clear on this point: the kingdom of Israel. Israel of that time, however, was not the entire territory of middle, northern, and southern Palestine with its inhabitants—even if later authors believed this to be the case. It is quite noticeable that all the place names mentioned in the Samuel and Saul narratives are limited to a very small area: Mizpah, Gilgal, Gibeah, Ramah, Geba, Michmash. These are all villages within the territory of Benjamin, perhaps within southern Ephraim. It is possible that the members of the tribes of Benjamin and Ephraim referred to themselves as "Israelites" once they decided to create a polity that transcended tribal boundaries. This ethnically charged designation is much older than Saul's kingdom. About 1220 b.c.e., Pharaoh Merneptah boasted: "Plundered is Canaan with every evil; Carried off is Ashkelon; seized upon is Gezer; Yanoam is made as that which does not exist; Israel is laid waste, his seed is not … All lands together, they are pacified" (*ANET,* 378). Perhaps a century later the Song of Deborah celebrated a victory of "Israel" over "Canaan" (Judg 5, esp. 5:2, 13, 19). This song of praise (see the detailed analysis in vol. 2 of this series) distinguishes between "Israel," situated in the mountain regions of Palestine, and "Canaan," which controlled the plains. Once these two groups actually engage in battle, "Israel" does not even appear in full. The Song of Deborah rebukes the Galilean and Transjordanian tribes that refused their support. This victory did not conquer "Canaan" and incorporate it into "Israel." It seems that the settlers were able only to shake off the oppression of the city kings. Soon after the Philistines rose to power in the Canaanite cities and plains. This led to increased pressure, to which several "Israelite" regions succumbed. Again, probably only a few parts of virtual Israel came together to gather in opposition and establish a state. It is no coincidence that we read how some circles in "Israel" asked, "How shall he help us?" (1 Sam 10:27). This statement probably reflected not only hesitation in the face of external risk factors but also resistance against a new central power. Elements opposed to the state (בני בליעל, "sons of Belial"!) thus refused to honor the new king or present him with gifts, that is, with tributary payments. At a later point the text states that Saul generously forgave these groups (1 Sam 11:13), but it does not state that they had changed their attitude toward the state.

It is thus not only possible but likely that Saul, as king of "Israel," did not rule over the entire territory of Palestine and its inhabitants. The plains of "Canaan" were outside of his sphere of influence, in any case; even the mountain settlers were not unified as a whole in support of the king. When, following Saul's death, his general Abner placed Saul's son on the throne as king over *all of Israel,* the text lists what belonged to "Israel" at that point: Gilead, Ashur,[10] Jezreel, Ephraim, and Benjamin—that is, only the central Palestinian mountain region with a slight extension in the northeast toward Gilead and Jezreel[11] (see fig. 13). There is no reason not to suppose that Saul's own territory was located within much of the same borders.

A series of rather incidental and thus more credible textual comments supports this suggestion. When Saul first engaged the Philistines, there were Philistine outposts and Philistine marauders and troops right in the middle of Benjaminite territory (1 Sam 13–14). We could imagine that Saul changed this fact through his military actions. This may be true, but the Philistine presence was not eradicated so thoroughly that the Philistines were unable to force a decisive battle in the northern foothills of the Ephraimite mountains and display Saul's corpse on the wall of Beth-shean, south of the Chinnereth. They, not Saul, controlled the string of Canaanite cities along the Jezreel Valley up to the Carmel. The Galilean tribes were probably not even able to assist the king of Israel in his ultimate affliction, even if they had wanted to.

A different conflict between Saul and a Canaanite enclave in the Benjaminite-Judahite mountains, described only cryptically in the texts, cost the lives of eight of Saul's offspring, including his official successor. Joshua 9 contains a legendary tradition according to which the Canaanite city Gibeon in western Benjamin successfully employed a ruse to attain a privileged status from the new ruling power while other Canaanites were killed or driven away. According to Josh 9:17, the villages of Chephirah, Beeroth, and Kiriath-jearim all belonged to Gibeon. The narrative clearly expresses

---

10. It is not clear what "the Ashurite" refers to. The Peshitta and Vulgate have emended the text to read "Geshur," a southern Aramaic fiefdom (see 2 Sam 13:37) that can hardly have been part of Saul's kingdom. The frequent emendation to "Asher," a Galilean tribe (see Judg 5:17), is just as unlikely. Diana Edelman ("The 'Ashurites' of Eshbaal's State," *PEQ* 117 [1985]: 85–91) suggests an Asherite clan that settled in the hills of Ephraim; this would result in a coherent background for our text.

11. Unlike most scholars, Gösta W. Ahlström locates Jezreel not in the Jezreel Valley but much farther south in the northern hills of Ephraim or Manasseh.

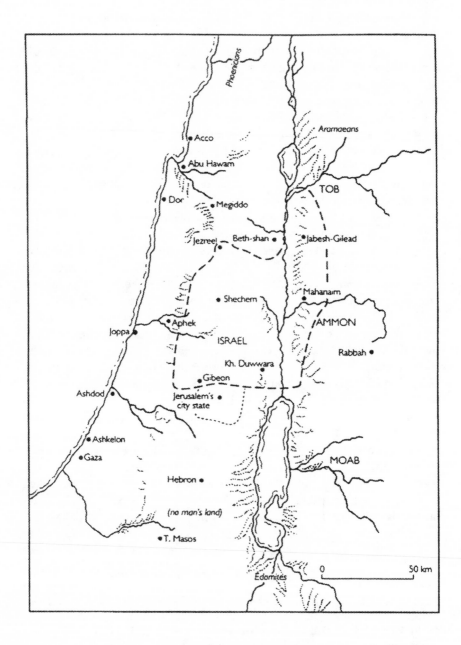

Figure 13: Saul's kingdom

a sense of alienation between "Israel" and the ethnic groups living in these locations. In 2 Sam 4 we read that Saul's son and successor Eshbaal was killed by two men from Beeroth. The text explicitly states that Beeroth was considered part of Benjamin but that the inhabitants of Beeroth were forced to flee and relocate elsewhere (2 Sam 4:2–3). This may allude to an attempt by Saul to incorporate the Canaanite enclave of Gibeon into his territory by force. His successor suffered the revenge for this encroachment. These events are also likely the background for 2 Sam 21, where we read that a famine once weighed heavily upon the land. At David's request, Yhwh provided the reason for this famine: "There is blood guilt on Saul and on his house, because he put the Gibeonites to death" (21:2). David turned to the inhabitants of Gibeon (some apparently survived!), who demanded the extradition and execution of seven members of the house of Saul as compensation (21:3–6). David accepted this demand, the men were executed, and soon after the rain started to fall (according to the narrative, however, the rain started only after Rizpah, mother of two of the executed men, successfully pleaded for their honorable burial!). All this points to the fact that Saul expanded his kingdom to include the territory of the Gibeonites and that this expansion cost his family dearly in the end.

We do not know whether Saul also attacked other Canaanite regions and attempted to incorporate them into his kingdom. The Philistines were probably capable of preventing large successes in this area. We know of at least one city that remained Canaanite until David succeeded in conquering it, even though it was located only 10 km southeast of Gibeon and even closer to Gibeah of Saul: Jerusalem (see 2 Sam 5). It seems that not only the string of cities in the Jezreel Valley but also those in the Philistine heartland up to Jerusalem, including Upper and Lower Beth-horon, Beth-shemesh, Kiriath-jearim, and Aijalon, resisted Saul's expansion. From this point of view, it becomes highly unlikely that the Judean Mountains were part of Saul's kingdom, since it lies south of this string of cities. This territory, specifically Bethlehem, was the home of one of Saul's better-known soldiers: David. But many men served as mercenaries outside of their country—just as David later served the Philistines. Nevertheless, the Judahite south was not hermetically sealed off from Saul. Several traditions tell how Saul led military campaigns into that area (1 Sam 15; 23ff.). It is unlikely, however, that he ever established a permanent rule over this territory.

Saul thus became and remained king due to the voluntary assent of the tribes of central Palestine. This determined the strength and the weakness of his reign. Should his followers deny his authority, should this power base disappear, then he would have no way of enforcing his authority to remain in power.

The situation was different for David. He did originate in Bethlehem of Judah, and he did gather a troop of desperados and seasoned warriors from the Judahite south; however, he did not rely on the full support of the settlers of the Judean Mountains. On the contrary, it seems that members of these very settlers repeatedly betrayed him to Saul when the latter was trying to apprehend him (1 Sam 23:19; 24:1; 26:1). David had to flee in a hurry from the small city of Keilah because he feared that the inhabitants would betray him (1 Sam 23:1–13; see Veijola for the oldest layer of this narrative). We also hear of the—probably exemplary—case where a wealthy and influential individual of the village of Carmel refused David's claim to authority (a refusal that cost him his life and his wife, 1 Sam 25). In short, David did not succeed in gaining much ground in Judah and was forced to withdraw to the Philistines.

It is not certain whether "Judah" even existed as a unified tribe such as "Benjamin." The wave of settlements did not reach southern Palestine until relatively late. Whereas central Palestine had long-established fixed structures, the southern area most likely had not yet achieved such internal unity. The Song of Deborah does not even mention Judah. The narratives and lists of "liberators" and "judges" contain the names of all sorts of Israelite tribes but never the name of Judah.[12] The original Saul traditions do not mention Judah; the name first appears in 1 Sam 15 and then following 1 Sam 22, where we are already in the sphere of influence of Davidic-Judahite historiography.

It does not seem as if David's kingship emerged out of the communal will of a tribal unity called "Judah." On the contrary, it seems that David's activities and finally his arrival in Hebron first established the foundations for the political entity later referred to as "Judah." The political power that had carried David up to this point was the will—of the Philistines. And the means by which David was able to realize his and their intentions was—his private army. It is hard to deny that the formation of the state under David grew from a very different starting point than that with Saul.

The first step on David's path to the monarchy was as peripheral as it was unusual: he accepted a city as feud from the national enemies of his lord Saul, from the Philistines (1 Sam 27). Thus he became city king by the grace of the Philistines, or, more moderately, a lesser king or vassal, actually not much more than a major of a town within the Philistine sphere of influence. We should hardly assume that the inhabitants of Ziklag were asked their opinion when David entered the city with his six hundred mercenaries. King

---

12. Othniel (Judg 3:7–11), as a figure a pale artificial construct of Deuteronomistic authors, is connected only to "Caleb," not to "Judah," and Ibzan (12:8–10) is only referred to as a Bethlehemite, not as a Judahite. The reference to "Judah" in Judg 10:9 as well as 15:9, 10, 11 is Deuteronomistic and of uncertain age.

Achish of Gath gave Ziklag to David in order to establish a stronghold in the southeast of Philistine territory, to protect this territory, and to provide a starting point for raids against the settlers in the Judean Mountains and against nomadic groups of the southern Negev and northern Sinai. These intentions were a source of disagreement between David and his Philistine lord. David was apparently able to seize enough loot from the groups in the far south to support his troops and to provide taxes to Gath without attacking his own fellow tribesmen; he even seems to have provided them with spoils from his forays—a tactical stroke of genius that (together with the necessary unscrupulousness) fits well with the image of the historical David. A probably authentic list mentions the recipients that most benefited from David's spoils: a series of towns and villages (such as Carmel and Hormah), as well as tribal groups (Jerahmeelites, Kenites) that later would belong to the kingdom of Judah (1 Sam 30:26–30). Thus David skillfully and intentionally prepared his continued rise to the throne.

His next goal was the city of Hebron, the geographic center of the southern mountain area of Palestine, an ancient Canaanite city that was then the center of the region settled by the Calebites (Josh 14:13–14). It is no coincidence that Hebron was also named, even emphasized, in the list mentioned above (1 Sam 30:31). An oracle is said to have led David to Hebron (2 Sam 2:1), but this oracle was definitely in accord with David's own plans. Once again nothing is said of what the inhabitants of Hebron thought: "David brought up the men who were with him, every one with his household, and they settled in the towns of Hebron" (2:3). The Calebites either embraced his arrival or were powerless to prevent it. David could not have made this move without Philistine knowledge and approval; otherwise, we would have heard at least something of Philistine opposition. This opposition did not occur probably because the Philistines believed that they would gain control over the southern part of the mountain region through their vassal. The area of Benjamin and Ephraim farther north was ruled either by Eshbaal (thus the biblical account) or still by Saul, a situation that would have made the relationship between these two men even more precarious. The Israelite kingdom was also seemingly powerless to prevent David's move into the heartland of the Judean Mountains.

The Bible reports without commentary what then happened in Judah: "The people of Judah came, and there [in Hebron] they anointed David king over the house of Judah." The subject of the action is "the men," that is, the heads of the families of "Judah." It seems that they constituted themselves as the "house of Judah" in the act of anointing David king. The text conveys that they did this voluntarily, without force. We hear nothing of their motives. Perhaps they were frightened, just as the Calebites of Hebron; or they were bowing to Philistine dominance, embodied by David; or they saw in him the only source of order and security in turbulent times of war (regardless of whether Saul had already been killed or whether he was still engaged in his final battle with the Philistines); or they were ready for this step due to internal developments, just as the tribes of central Palestine before them; or David's diplomacy had made them ready.

"Judah" is obviously the summary term for the settlers of the Judean Mountains south of Jerusalem and in the Negev north of Beer-sheba (most likely identical to Ziklag). The tribal groups who lived here, including the towns and cities located in this area, gathered to constitute a "house" and appointed David to be the head of this "house." The initiative was carried by the "men," thus by the people. This process does have a quasi-democratic ring to it. It is noticeable, however, that the text fails to mention any contribution that David made to this process. There is no word of a royal covenant defining the rights and privileges of both sides. The Judahites anointed David without any conditions; if there were any conditions at all, they were set by David. The birth of the Judahite kingship thus contained an element of absolutistic reign. This element would surface again in David's story, but also in the later history of this kingship.

The relationship between David and the Israelites in the north was different. Once he succeeded in destabilizing the reign of the house of Saul (which, according to the biblical account in 2 Sam 2–4, had already started to corrode from the inside), "all the elders of Israel came to the king at Hebron, and King David made a covenant with them at Hebron before Yhwh, and they anointed him king over Israel."[13] The anointing was preceded by a contractual agreement; the king had not only rights but also duties. This is how the tribes of the north were accustomed to doing things. When Saul had been elected, they had "put down a law of the king before Yhwh" (1 Sam 10:25). All this points to a certain understanding of what the monarchy should be. The tribal delegates—the "elders," perhaps a kind of constitutional body—worked out a contractual agreement with an appropriate candidate. Both they and the king were bound by this agreement. Should the king not meet the conditions of this agreement, the Israelites considered themselves free from his rule. This is likely what happened in the rebellions of Absalom and Sheba. We do not

---

13. The other version of this story in 2 Sam 5:1–2 is clearly a redactional addition and thus younger. In this version "all the tribes of Israel" came to David—it seems that the text is referring to a large public gathering—and assured him that he was of their "bone and flesh," that he had proven himself as leader, and that the promises of Yhwh were with him. The redactor intended to change the contract into a relation of sympathy and adoration (one-sided!).

know whether these contracts included regulations on the formation of a dynasty. We know only that the dynastic principle was never securely embedded in Israelite history, as can be seen by the division of the kingdom (1 Kgs 12) and the frequent uprisings, especially in the north.

It is a testimony to David's political flexibility that he was able to meet such different expectations for kingship. He also established a third type of kingship over Jerusalem. This city and its surroundings had remained an independent city-state. Because it was located exactly between the territories of Israel and Judah, David could not tolerate this independence. According to the Bible, once he was appointed king he took control of Jerusalem. Scholarship does not agree on whether he used force or gained control by peaceful means. The text in 2 Sam 5:6–9 is very short and quite enigmatic. Should we take the word ṣinnôr to mean "aqueduct," and does David allow or forbid the "striking of the Jebusites"? According to the parallel text in 1 Chr 11:4–6, the city was taken when Joab entered it by means of the water supply tunnels (he was later rewarded by being appointed general). This seems possible, especially as 2 Sam 5:6 also mentions that the "king with his men" went against the city, a fixed expression for a private army. It makes sense that David would have made use of this army (or at least threatened to employ it). If he had drafted an army from Judah (or even Israel) and led it against Jerusalem, this city would have been incorporated into the territory of Judah (or Israel). This way it became the private possession of the king. It is no coincidence that Jerusalem (or a part thereof) has often been called the "City of David"—as an expression of possession.

The city with its inhabitants and institutions (such as the temple) belonged to the king. This status does not seem very free, especially compared to the covenant made by Israel in the north, but it did carry its own privileges. The royal residence was naturally favored when it came to investments and construction projects, not to mention the fact that many of the elite also resided here. The communal wealth of the land flowed to a large degree into the capital. In the history of the monarchy, Jerusalem maintained this special status. The standing phrase "Judah and Jerusalem" (following the exile, "Jerusalem and Judah") is witness to this fact. The separate mention of Jerusalem would be unnecessary if Jerusalem had been fully incorporated.

When David united the kingdoms of Judah and Israel and became also the city king of Jerusalem (and probably still of Ziklag as well), he thus ruled over the southern and central mountains of Palestine. This was not all. We read in 2 Sam 24:1–9 that David had his general Joab undertake a public census. The result of this census, reported in the last verse (800,000 warriors in Israel, 500,000 in Judah), is much too high, of course, as is the case in many ancient listings. The remaining information in the text, however, is quite credible, for the text does not view the census as a worthy accomplishment of David but rather as a sacrilege: the people of YHWH should not be counted! David, however, did just that. According to the text, Joab and his officers traversed the boundaries of the Davidic kingdom in order to register all the men fit for military service:

> They crossed the Jordan and began from Aroer and from the city in the middle of the valley,[14] [then to] Gad and on to Jazer.[15] Then they came to Gilead and to the area below Hodshi,[16] and they came to Dan and went around to Sidon and came to the fortress of Tyre and to all the cities of the Hivites and Canaanites; and they went out to the Negev of Judah at Beersheba. (2 Sam 24:5–7)

Even if this description is not clear on every point, it does result in a coherent picture (see fig. 14). (1) In the east, David's kingdom included certain areas of the Transjordan: not just the Israelite settlements of Gilead (which already belonged to the territories of Saul and Eshbaal), but also Ammonite land down to the Arnon Valley, center of the Moabite homelands. This fits with the notice in 2 Sam 12:30 that David had acquired the crown of the king of Ammon. It seems that David annexed large parts of Ammonite territory.[17] According to 2 Sam 8:2, 13–14, David did defeat Moab and Edom and demand tribute from them, but these areas were never a part of the Davidic kingdom.

(2) In the north, all of Galilee belonged to the Davidic kingdom (it was not part of the territory controlled by Saul and Eshbaal). This included the upper Jordan Valley up to Dan at the foot of Mount Hermon as well as the upper Galilean mountains all the way to the Phoenician coast; the text does not mention whether the Phoenician cities of Sidon and Tyre were also included, but this would have been extremely unlikely.

(3) In the west, the Mediterranean coast seems to have been the border; the cities of the "Hivites and Canaanites" probably refer to the area formerly controlled by the city-states in the Jezreel Valley and the coastal plains, such as Taanach, Megiddo, and Dor. The cities of the Jordan Valley, such as Hazor and Beth-shean, were included in any case. If Saul was satisfied with the

---

14. This information is cryptic and has never been fully explained. It probably refers to a location at the Arnon.

15. See Num 21:32; 32:1–3.

16. Otherwise unknown. Perhaps we can change the text with the Septuagint to read Kadesh and connect this location to the town of the same name in Naphtali; see Josh 12:22; 19:37; 21:32; Judg 4:6, 11.

17. The territory of "Gad," probably at the north end of the Dead Sea, was later a source of conflict between Israel and Moab (compare the stela of King Mesha!).

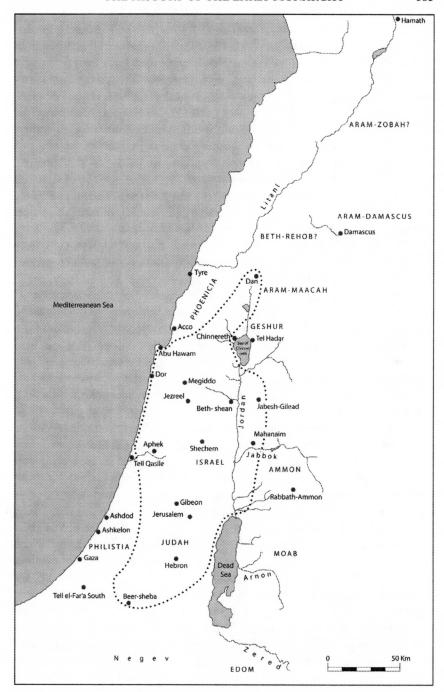

Figure 14: The heartland of David's kingdom

Canaanite enclave of Gibeon, then David did not rest with winning Jerusalem and continued to integrate all the ancient city-states in the Palestinian plains. There are even less indications here of the use of force than in the case of Jerusalem (and definitely less than with Ammon). Perhaps the Canaanites were not unwilling to join this new state with its promising economic prospects—especially since the old power of the Philistines had been put in its place (see §II.2.9 below). Perhaps David's politics (like Solomon's a generation later) were so appealing that his expansion did not seem like a conquest.

(4) The expansion stops—correctly!—at the boundaries of Philistine territory as well as at the Sinai, but it does include the Judean Negev down to Beer-sheba. Just as Dan marks the borderline in the north, Beer-sheba marks the borderline in the south, thus explaining the standing phrase "from Dan to Beer-sheba" as a synonym for the entire territory of Israel. The imaginary line connecting these two borders runs pretty much straight through the northern, southern, and central Palestinian mountain regions—the actual homeland of the Davidic kingdom.

The Davidic kingdom that emerges from this description was a remarkably disparate entity. The various kingdoms, the former city-states, the territorial states, as well as the core and fringe areas—only the person of the king held all this together. Even if political and economic interests may also have surfaced, the cohesion of David's kingdom was based on the ruler himself. The various segments of the kingdom were bound to him by different degrees of loyalty; David had to maintain a balance between them, which was most likely a difficult juggling act requiring much political skill and also at times a severe hand, if not unscrupulousness. When the northern tribes attempted to secede, David squashed this rebellion without mercy (see 2 Sam 20 and §II.2.10 below). It seems that he was successful in preventing any major disruptions to the unity and extent of his kingdom. It is almost surprising that David's successor, Solomon, was able to maintain and keep alive this conglomerate that was so focused on the person of his father.

Solomon's rise was very different from that of Saul and even of David. In contrast to the first two kings of Israel, Solomon was the son of a king. He did not have to earn this office; he inherited it. According to the biblical depiction, he made hardly any public appearances before ascending to the throne. We hear nothing of possible negotiations with political bodies or representatives of various regions. According to 1 Kgs 1, Solomon rose to the throne based on his father's decision (possibly influenced by his mother and the prophet Nathan). This process, so important for the entire kingdom, occurred hidden from public view in the depths of the royal palace. The center of power in Jerusalem seems to have become so dominant that the decisions made there were valid for the entire kingdom.

True, the transfer of power from David to Solomon did not occur without tension and conflict. It seems that only Jerusalem and Judah were unanimous in their acceptance that David's successor had to come from the house of David. The dynastic principle, dominant in the entire ancient Near East, came to bear on this issue, even though David himself did not owe his rise to power to this principle. The creation of a Saulide dynasty in the north had failed, but the creation of a Davidic dynasty in the south was successful. It is no coincidence that even a century later the northern state was referred to as "Israel" but the southern state as the "house of David" (see §II.1.4.1 above, the stela of Tel Dan). In short, there was no conflict over *whether* a son of David should become king, only *which* son should inherit this office. After the oldest princes Amnon and Absalom had both lost their lives (or better, were killed), the possible candidate was the next-in-line Adonijah. According to the biblical narratives, he saw himself—as his rival Solomon also saw him—as the natural contender for the throne (1 Kgs 1:5; 2:14). His claim was supported by forces of strategic importance: by his brothers, that is, the royal household (with the exception of Solomon, David, and Bathsheba); by Judahite court officials; and by Judah in general, represented by the head of the army, Joab, and the priest Abiathar (1 Kgs 1:7–9). Yet there was also a rival party in support of the much younger Solomon: the priest Zadok and the prophet Nathan, two members of the clergy (these clergy members appear only in traditions written following the Jerusalem period); Benaiah, the commander of the royal guard stationed in Jerusalem; and, of course, Bathsheba, who was wed by David as the widow of Uriah only after he took up residence in Jerusalem. In short, a Jerusalem party opposed a Judahite party. What had been combined in the person of David now drifted apart: Adonijah embodied the territorial state of Judah; Solomon embodied the city-state of Jerusalem. The one would have given the settlers, farmers, and ranchers on the mountain priority; the other favored the economy and culture of the city as well as the old city aristocracy. It seems that both sides had become so closely interconnected and dependent on each other that a separate existence was no longer possible. Both had to exist together, and one side had to become dominant over the other. Solomon won this struggle for power—not least due to the determined involvement of the Cherethites and Pelethites, David's elite mercenary troop—and settled all opposition on the Judahite front by means of a few well-placed assassinations.

The sources provide only indirect clues as to why and how Solomon was also able to assume David's authority in the Israelite north as well as east of the Jordan. The so-called list of provinces in 1 Kgs 4:7–19 could be of importance in this context. This list mentions the names and residences of leading officials who were appointed by Solomon to govern central and northern Palestine. It is not easy in each case to determine the exact location of these residences or regions, but we can clearly see the intent of integrating the entire territory of the former Canaanite city-states as well as the Israelite tribes while organizing them into twelve provinces. Following Alt's theories, still relevant today, we can distinguish between provinces that were clearly determined by rural Israelite elements and those determined by urban Canaanite elements (see fig. 15). It seems that Solomon attempted to create a kind of balance between these two population groups by separating them and giving them separate regions and tasks. At the same time, he wanted to bind them together by incorporating them into an overarching system of provinces and subordinating both to the central administration in Jerusalem by means of the officials he appointed.

We find a remarkable analogy about a millennium earlier in Egypt. Following the first so-called interim, a period of political turbulence, the powerful ruler and founder of the Twelfth Dynasty, Amenemhet I, integrated Upper and Lower Egypt while dividing his kingdom into clearly defined areas: "He made that a city knew its boundaries with another city, that these boundaries were established as firm as the heavens."[18] This clear division created judicial security and peace—as well as dependence on the one who had created and supervised the division. Perhaps we can stretch the analogy so far as to say that the era before the establishment of the state, with its alternation of dependency and strife between rivaling settlers and city dwellers, between Philistines and Israelites, was a kind of "Palestinian interim" that was ended by (David and) Solomon.

David and Solomon created an order of state that was characterized by a decisive concentration of power in Jerusalem and a simultaneous disintegration and distribution of all other power centers among the various regions with different loyalties toward the central ruler. The grand order of state erected by David from various loosely connected territories as well as the division into substructures instituted by Solomon in at least one of these territories both followed the eternal truth of *divide et impera*.

As under David, there was an attempt at secession in the north under Solomon—more precisely, among the Israelite tribes in the north. It seems that the mountain settlers noticed this web of dependence cleverly and decisively cast upon them by Jerusalem and attempted to escape from the net. As before, the secession was put down by force (1 Kgs 11:26–28, 40). Even

---

18. A text from Beni-Hasan, quoted according to Elena Cassin, Jean Bottéro, and Jean Vercoutter, eds., *Vom Paläolithikum bis zur Mitte des 2. Jahrtausends* (vol. 1 of *Die Altorientalischen Reiche*; Fischer Weltgeschichte 2; Frankfurt am Main: Fischer Bücherei, 1965), 319.

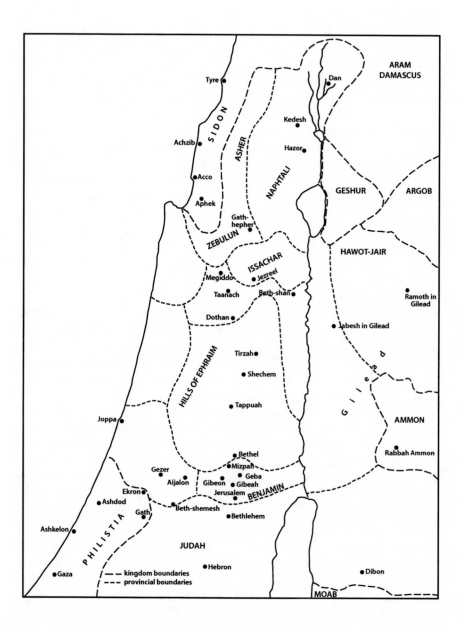

Figure 15: The provinces of Solomon

though the entire kingdom remained intact, Solomon was forced to accept a loss of territory in the Israelite north. According to an unsuspicious biblical comment, he presented the king of Tyre with twenty cities in the region of Galilee as compensation for material assistance and artisans for his construction projects. The biblical writer tries hard to soften this embarrassing episode by portraying the Phoenicians as highly unsatisfied with their end of the bargain (9:11). On the other hand, Solomon received the city of Gezer as an endowment on the occasion of his marriage to the pharaoh's daughter—a considerable increase in power against the Philistines (9:16). The entire list of cities (9:15–17), including Gezer, in combination with archaeological findings (see §II.1.3 above), allow us to assume that Solomon initiated considerable construction activity in the Israelite far north as well as to the far reaches of the Judahite south. It remains debatable whether these fortifications were intended mainly as a protection against the outside or as a means of securing a stable order on the inside; in either case, they demonstrated the presence of the state "from Dan to Beer-sheba."

Older scholarship tended to speak of a "Davidic-Solomonic empire" and thus created associations with ancient and modern empires that were not appropriate. The rule of these two kings was probably much less glamorous and powerful than as portrayed by the biblical authors and many historians in the past. On the other hand, it is also inappropriate to follow the recent tendency of certain scholars to diminish and marginalize the early Israelite state that David founded—building on the preparatory work accomplished by Saul—and that Solomon consolidated, which was quite an impressive power structure. The basic feat of these kings was the combination of Judah (with Jerusalem) and Israel into a united monarchy. These separate territories, unified under the rule of one king, thus achieved enough political, economic, and military importance to secure respect and independence in the southern Levant of the time. In regard to its internal structures—under David but also still under Solomon—it was not a centralized, monolithic "empire" but a so-called clientele state that bound various different regions, classes, cities, tribes, military units, and so forth into a matrix of different loyalties primarily to the king even though they were connected only loosely with each other (see Master 2001; Dietrich 2006). This state was held together primarily by the person of the king and depended on his ability to keep in balance the various, partially contrary interests. If the king was unable to perform this balancing act, these interests could quickly lead to imbalances or even to a collapse of this artful construction—as happened immediately following Solomon's death (1 Kgs 12).

II.2.3. ADMINISTRATION AND TAXES

It seems that Saul's rule over Israel matched what we think of today as a functioning state only to a small degree. We can even ask whether the terms "kingdom" and "state" are really appropriate in this context. In more recent research, especially in the United States, the term "chiefdom" has become the preferred choice of terms, since several important elements of statehood are missing in Saul's reign. Nowhere in the Saul traditions do we find clear indications of a developed state organization, namely, an effective administration governing the economics and society of the entire territory. One particular scene, a description of Saul's royal table, is symptomatic: "The king sat upon his seat, as at other times, upon the seat by the wall; Jonathan sat opposite, and Abner sat by Saul's side, but David's place was empty" (1 Sam 20:25). The king, the crown prince, the leader of the army (and cousin of the king), and the commander of the mercenary troops (and son-in-law, who had recently defected)—this was the entire leadership in Saul's state. We hear nothing of ministers, diplomats, or scribes.

At one point in the narrative a further "servant of Saul" steps into view: an Edomite named Doeg, "the leader [literally: the strong one, the commander] of the shepherds who worked for Saul" (1 Sam 21:8). This attribute is interesting. It seems that Saul owned large herds for which he appointed an overseer. It may not be coincidental that this overseer was an Edomite, since the Bible reports of a king of Moab who paid his tributes to the king of Israel with the wool of lambs and sheep (2 Kgs 3:4). It seems that sheep herds formed the economic backbone east of the Jordan; these were the areas with the greatest expertise in that particular line of business. In the regions west of the Jordan, agriculture was dominant. Saul himself is portrayed as standing behind the plow (1 Sam 11), and he came from a high-bred, wealthy family (1 Sam 9). It seems that he maintained his family's possessions during his reign, even expanding them. We also discover on the side that David gave Meribaal, the descendant of Saul, "all the land of Saul," literally, his entire "field," and ordered his estate manager to work this land together with his fifteen sons and twenty servants (2 Sam 9:7, 9). All this points to a decent-sized territory that belonged to Saul.

Saul needed his lands and herds primarily to feed his family. Since his court was limited to his family, as we have seen, this probably included the entire leadership of the state! Israel's first king came at no cost to his subjects, except perhaps an especially large portion of the tribal lands of Benjamin. There is, however, a further cost factor that comes into view in the context of the David-Saul narratives: Saul's soldiers. Once, after David had again escaped, Saul berated "his servants who stood about him, 'Hear now, you Benjaminites, will the son of Jesse give every one of you fields and vineyards? Will

he make you all commanders of thousands and commanders of hundreds?'"
(1 Sam 22:7). Saul's words are very revealing, even if they are not a direct historical report but rather were placed into Saul's mouth by the narrators. The
"servants" of Saul (עבדים) who stood around him were of the house of Benjamin (although we have heard of at least one Edomite). The king rewarded
them for their services on two levels: with land and with posts as officers.
The text does not say from where he took these lands. It stands to reason
that it was not his own or that of his family; these lands would not have been
large enough, and the Benjaminites—according to the words used—were not
stewards of royal lands but rather owners of their own lands and vineyards.
It seems that Saul provided them with land—or allowed them to provide
themselves with land that either was without owner or that was taken from its
previous owners. We could think of the conflict with the Gibeonites and the
flight of the Beerothites (2 Sam 4; 21). On such occasions, and perhaps also
when the Philistines were successfully pushed back, land became available
and was given to Saul's servants. This also implies that Saul did not have to
levy a general tax in order to pay his followers. There is no indication in the
text that he ever erected the necessary administration.

This situation changed already under David and even more so under
Solomon. The clearest indications for this fact are the "cabinet" lists of David
(2 Sam 8:16–18; 20:23–26) and of Solomon (1 Kgs 4:1–6). These lists mention the leading court officials and refer to their particular departments. The
following chart provides an overview that highlights the relative order of the
various individuals and departments.

	2 Sam 8	2 Sam 20	1 Kgs 4
of the army	1. Joab	1. Joab	4. Benaiah
of the Cherethites and Pelethites	5. Benaiah	2. Benaiah	– – –
of conscripted labor	– – –	3. Adoram	8. Adoniram
secretary	2. Jehoshaphat	4. Jehoshaphat	3. Jehoshaphat
scribes	4. Seraiah	5. Sheva	2. Elihoreph, Ahijah
priests	3. Zadok, "Abia-thar"	6. Zadok, Abiathar, Ira	1. Azariah ben Zadok[19]
	6. David's sons	– – –	– – –

---

19. This text mentions in the fifth place "Zadok and Abiathar" as "priests," just as
in 2 Sam 23. Because the post of general had already been passed from Joab to Benaiah,
Abiathar was probably already relegated out of office (1 Kgs 2:26–27). If Azariah as son of
Zadok had already taken over the office from his father, then the list as a whole was composed quite late, possibly even in the temple.

of the governors	- - -	- - -	5. Azariah ben Nathan
friend of the king	- - -	- - -	6. Zabud ben Nathan
of the house/palace	- - -	- - -	7. Ahishar

We can probably assume that this does not represent the entire administration, only the leading ministers and officials during the Davidic–Solomonic era. Each of the individuals listed here commanded a number of lesser officials who were organized according to their own hierarchies.

This is especially clear in the case of the head of the army, who was primarily in charge of the militia but also commanded the mercenaries in case of war. The militia itself was divided into groups of one thousand and one hundred, commanded by a שׂר (most often translated "high official" or "officer"); these numbers are better understood regionally than numerically as units that had to be put up by individual regions or settlements. The mercenary troop consisted of several different units with their own commanders (such as the "heroes," the "Cherethites and the Pelethites," the "Thirty" [2 Sam 23:8ff.]); prior to the battle against Absalom, we see how David instructed the various units and leaders of the army (18:2).

Other traditions inform us that "the one in charge of conscripted labor" commanded not only the laborers but also a score of overseers arranged in their own hierarchy (see 1 Kgs 5:27–30 [the numbers are exaggerated]; 11:28). We can assume a similar situation for the one "in charge of the house," that is, the person responsible for purchasing for and provisioning of the royal court. The large number of institutions and persons—agricultural estates, herds, construction troops, storage management, purchasing, cooking, washing, manufacturing, servants, the harem, and so forth—allows us a brief glimpse into the differentiated system of responsibilities and individuals that had to be managed by this person.

The three lists, read in parallel, show a certain degree of continuity.[20] David seems to have reorganized his cabinet once. The most important innovation was the introduction of a minister for conscripted labor; it seems that David already instituted what is explicitly said of Solomon: conscripted labor used for the execution of large construction projects important for the state as a whole (e.g., fortifications and streets). In this, as well as in other things,

---

20. Two assumptions underlie this statement: (1) the lists in their present context are not dependent on a literary level but independent in origin and handed down in their original form and order; (2) the version in 2 Sam 8 is older than the text in 2 Sam 23.

Solomon followed in his father's footsteps. He not only kept the minister for conscripted labor but also held on to about half of David's ministers. To be sure, certain individuals were eliminated (Joab, Abiathar); others may have stepped down due to age and were replaced (e.g., David's scribe, whose name is somewhat uncertain, as well as the priests Zadok and Ira).

On the other hand, the lists show distinctive progress when compared to the situation under Saul. Only two men had any kind of official role under Saul: Abner and David—both military men and both relatives of the king. Under David, Joab and Benaiah took on their roles. Joab likewise was a relative, more precisely a nephew of the king. The priests of Nob had been the religious leaders in Saul's state, but Saul ended their leadership with a massacre, whereas David took one of their number, Abiathar, as well as Zadok, probably a Jerusalemite, and made them "ministers of religion." David added further officials: the "secretary" (literally, the "reminder") and the "scribe." The former, referred to by Herbert Donner as the "head of chambers" (1982), was probably the chief of political staff in the palace, responsible for everything not covered by "war" and "religion," such as foreign affairs and domestic policies. He was most likely in charge of important people such as the political advisors of the king (see 2 Sam 17: Ahithophel and Hushai). The "scribe" was not merely the head of the writing staff. Egyptian and Ugaritic analogies point to an individual responsible for the royal accounts and administration, for the training of not only scribes but also of the entire elite of the state, and for the state archive (production and storage of important royal documents, such as contracts, letters, lists, annals, and including epic texts, at least in the Ugaritic analogy). The office of "scribe" only makes sense if this official as well as his colleagues, including the vassals and their officers, also had access to scribes who were ultimately responsible to the chief scribe. We thus can assume that David's court and Solomon's even more so gave much occasion to produce and manage written documents.

This assumption is supported by several basic facts: David had to provide for a large number of people (his extended family, his ministers and other high officials, his mercenaries, all with their families and servants), and all this required a logistical superstructure. David had organized a huge and elaborate feast on the occasion of bringing the ark of the covenant to Jerusalem (2 Sam 6), and this feast had to be managed and subsidized. He led many wars, conscripted soldiers, and equipped and fed them at least in part; it is no coincidence that he initiated a public census. He composed songs that were handed down word for word to later generations. In general, there are so many memories of the Davidic era that it is hard to believe that they are due merely to oral traditions.

Solomon's list of ministers is a development of David's list. A few positions have been added, such as the person in charge of "the house," that is, the head of palace management. As "secretary," Jehoshaphat most likely covered this area under David; now the palace administration was more complex and elaborate. Under Solomon there was no longer a chief of the mercenaries. This may indicate that the military sector had lost importance in the cabinet, but it is more likely that it indicates an increase in Benaiah's importance, who now held all military groups in his hands. Solomon rewarded his supporters in the struggle with Adonijah: the general Benaiah as well as Nathan the prophet and Zadok the priest rose in importance. These three were likely held in honor and remained in office until the end of their lives; three of their sons (if the coincidence of names indicates a coincidence of individuals) were appointed to high office: a son of Zadok to the post of his father and two of Nathan's sons to entirely new positions. One became the "friend of the king," perhaps the highest and most trusted advisor (according to Donner, a special minister without a specific department). The other became "head of the governors" (על־הנצבים).

At this point, it is necessary to take a brief look at the list of provinces in 1 Kgs 4:7–19. This list contains these very "governors" (נצבים) who were appointed to the twelve northern Israelite provinces and who had to report to Azariah ben Nathan as minister.

Name	Residence	Territory
son of Hur		hills of Ephraim
son of Deker	Makaz	Shaalbim, Beth-shemesh ...
son of Hesed	Arubboth	Socoh, Hepher
son of Abinadab		region of Dor
Baana ben Ahilud	..	Taanach, Megiddo, Beth-shean ...
son of Geber	Ramoth in Gilead	Gilead, Bashan ...
Abinadab ben Iddo	Mahanaim	
Ahimaaz		Naphtali
Baana ben Hushai		Asher
Jehoshaphat ben Paruah		Issachar
Shimei ben Ela		Benjamin
Geber ben Uri		Gad

Among the provincial governors was Ahimaaz (4:15), probably the son of Zadok and trusted follower of David (see 2 Sam 15:25ff.; 18:19ff.), as well as a son of Ahilud (1 Kgs 4:12) and one son of Hushai (4:16). The former may have been a brother to the minister Jehoshaphat ben Ahilud, the latter a son of David's advisor Hushai (see 2 Sam 15; 17). Two other governors were Solomon's sons-in-law (1 Kgs 4:11, 15), which provides an interesting glimpse into the political function of the harem and the royal sons born from it. It is especially interesting that the list contains no less than five "individuals without a name" who are not referred to by their own names but only as "son of X." Albrecht Alt has convincingly interpreted this phenomenon as a remnant of Canaanite cultural heritage.[21] In Ugarit, a royal retainer often was referred to not by his own name but rather by the name of the ancestor who formed the special relationship with the king. This fits with the fact that these governors of Solomon all served in predominantly Canaanite provinces. By granting them these high offices, the Israelite king likely intended to make use of the experience and connection of proven families of the Canaanite administration. At the same time, the feeling of being dominated by a foreign power was lessened for the Canaanite population.

What was the task of these governors? If we are to believe the preamble to the list of provinces in 1 Kgs 4:7, they were appointed to supply the palace with food on a monthly rotation, which according to 1 Kgs 5:2–3 was no small task: "118 hectoliters flour, 236 hectoliters fine flour, also 10 fatted oxen, 20 pasture-fed cattle, a hundred sheep, besides harts, gazelles, roebucks and fatted fowl" a day![22] Even if the amounts were smaller, the governors would have had to take from the surplus of the provinces, that is, raise taxes in monetary or material form.[23] Somewhat more hidden, but thus more credible, is a statement found in 1 Kgs 9:23 that tells of a different task given to the governors. The text speaks of 550 chief officers in service of the governors (שָׂרֵי־הַנִּצָּבִים) who were placed in charge "of (conscripted) labor" (עַל־הַמְּלָאכָה). These labor officers of the provincial governors (the number may once again be exaggerated) were probably not directly in charge of overseeing the labor itself; this was the task of the minister of labor, Adoniram, and his people. These officers were rather in charge of gathering necessary contingents of the laborers from the provinces and delivering them to the overseers. One of these officers was Jeroboam, the subsequent king of the northern kingdom of Israel. According to 1 Kgs 12, conscripted labor was the (historically plausible) reason for the secession of northern Israel from the united monarchy. It seems that the burden placed by Solomon on his subjects

---

21. *Kleine Schriften zur Geschichte des Volkes Israel* (3rd ed.; 3 vols.; Munich: Beck, 1964), 3:206.

22. The figures are taken from Martin Noth, *1. Könige 1–16* (BK 9/1; Neukirchen-Vluyn: Neukirchener, 1964); Noth comments that these figures, implying several thousand residents at court, must be highly exaggerated and also a relatively late addition to the text

23. The context of 1 Kgs 5:2 indicates that these tributes were given by foreign vassals, not by Israelite provinces. In analogy to the comments on conscripted labor in 1 Kgs 9:20–22 (see §III.2.4 below), this could be a dogmatic reworking of historical reality.

was too heavy and their desire for freedom too great. Both aspects, however, are true only for northern Israel.

Hermann Michael Niemann rejects the idea that the lists in 1 Kgs 4:7ff. refer to provinces and their governors at all. He argues that Solomon's kingdom was not yet this well organized, his rule over the north not yet this strong, for such an interpretation to be justified. He instead proposes that the so-called governors were merely Solomon's "trusted allies," perhaps something like commissioned representatives of the king's interests in the north, which was only loosely associated with Jerusalem. The so-called provinces do not cover the entire territory of northern Israel and merely focus on specific towns and regions. They are no more than vaguely defined spheres of influence to which Solomon sent his representatives. It is unlikely that these men would have had the power or the order to raise taxes (Niemann does not address the responsibilities of the נצבים in terms of conscripted labor). Such well-developed state organization did not exist until the Omride dynasty in the ninth century, not until the eighth century in the south. Niemann is to be credited with questioning hypotheses on Solomon's kingdom that are too colorful and imaginative, as well as too modern; instead, he cautiously paints a much more modest picture of this era. (With Ernst Axel Knauf, we can observe a similar intention that is developed much more radically.) On the other hand, there is no need to confront biblical witnesses that are characterized by such a high degree of inner plausibility and historical contingency as the list in 1 Kgs 4:7 with too much skepticism.

II.2.4. Economics and Social Issues

Economics is not one of the more important topics in biblical texts; this is also true for the texts on the early monarchy. We have already discussed that the archaeological sources for this time period are not very abundant. It is still logical to assume that the formation of a centrally administered territorial state in an area that was formerly structured along tribal lines and by city-states brought about decisive economic and thus also social changes. This is also true if the entire state administration was not as structured and not as influential for societal developments as earlier research had indicated. A new social stratum developed in any case, however large and important it may have been: the royal court with its members, servants, and officers; and the rural-agricultural regions of Israelite settlers joined together with the urban Canaanite cities and their agricultural lands under the roof of the state. Large construction projects were initiated that served not local but state or royal interests (palaces, temples, city walls, fortifications, strongholds, residences for soldiers, storage buildings, streets); economic contact was made with regions close by and father away—in part through military force, in part through peaceful trade. This led to a flow of goods to a degree larger than Palestine had ever before seen.

The biblical traditions contain definite clues regarding the economic and social changes brought about by the newly established monarchy. As an aside to the description of crown prince Absalom as an especially handsome man, the text mentions that the hair of his head was cut once a year and weighed "two hundred shekels by the king's weight" (2 Sam 14:26). We thus find evidence for a royal measurement—possibly a projection from a later time but not necessarily so—that guaranteed equal and comparable prices and weights throughout the kingdom. Such an inconspicuous but effective procedure facilitated and strengthened trade and increased judicial reliability.[24]

It is plausible to assume that these "royal measurements" determined the tributes to be delivered to the royal court. According to the list of provinces in its current shape, these tributes came from at least the different regions of northern Israel (1 Kgs 4:7; see also 5:7). Perhaps fixed amounts of tributary payments were demanded from the inhabitants of these regions. In the so-called "rights of the king" that Samuel presents as a warning to the people following their demand for a king—this list may originate from the early monarchy, but this is not certain—we read: "The king will take the tenth of your grain and of your vineyards and give it to his officers and to his servants; he will take the tenth of your flocks" (1 Sam 8:15, 17). This text also refers to a further source of income for the king: the land claimed by the crown. "He will have your sons plow his grounds and reap his harvest. He will take the best of your fields and vineyards and olive orchards and give them to his servants" (8:12, 14). We thus hear of Israelites who worked on royal lands and servants (עבדים) who managed land given to them by the king.

Other narratives contain similar indications. We have already mentioned Saul's lands and the lands he gave to his retainers (§II.2.3 above). These lands were cultivated primarily according to the substitution principle: from them, the manager derived the provisions necessary for himself and his house. It is likely that managers also sold the surplus from their agricultural activities;

---

24. In "The Enigma of the Shekel Weights of the Judean Kingdom" (*BA* 59 [1996]: 122–25), Yigal Ronen refers to measurement stones found in Judah that are inscribed with the hieratic symbols for 1, 2, 5, 10, 15, 20, 30, and 50 but that actually represent weights in the series 1, 2, 4, 8, 12, 16, 24, and 40. This latter system is Assyrian and displaced the former Egyptian system from about 700 B.C.E. on. These stones are evidence of official measurements from the earlier monarchy. Why should such a system not have existed in the earliest monarchy?

this surplus could then be exchanged for luxury items or precious metals. One could certainly have become rich in the service of the king. The royal house itself would definitely have accumulated great wealth, not necessarily because of greed but due to reasons of state policy. A king must represent wealth not only his people but also to other nations abroad; this is one of the functions of a monumental palace with representative pillars (1 Kgs 7:1–12) and a throne covered with decorations in ivory (10:18–19). This is also one of the reasons for fortified cities and an impressive army. A king must be able to be generous. This is shown especially with Solomon in great detail, yet we find the basic idea already with David. The king organizes great festive banquets that prove his gratitude toward the deity and show the people how fortunate it is to be subject to this king (2 Sam 6:13, 19; 1 Kgs 3:4; 8:62–63 [the numbers are most likely exaggerated]). The king donates sanctuaries (2 Sam 24:24; 1 Kgs *5–8; 11:7) and endows them with great wealth (1 Kgs 7:51). The king gives gifts to entire regions where it is politically prudent to do so (1 Sam 30:26–31), even to foreign potentates (1 Kgs 10:13; see also the payment and counterpayment exchanged by Hiram of Tyre and Solomon, diplomatically surely intended as reciprocal gifts, 1 Kgs 5).

The king's wealth did not primarily serve his indulgence and consumption but placed on him the responsibility to use it well and even to distribute it. His sources of income seemed to come not only from his own kingdom but also from the outside. King David amassed riches through his wars (we can no longer, however, estimate what these wars cost him or, better, his people): he took spoils not only from the Amalekites (1 Sam 30:26–31; see also Saul in 15:9) but apparently also from the Arameans (2 Sam 8:7–8) and the Ammonites (12:30). He is said to have received tributary payments (8:10–11) and forced subjected nations into compulsory labor (12:31). According to tradition, Solomon took money from abroad mainly by peaceful means. A flourishing trade with chariots and horses between Egypt and Asia Minor (1 Kgs 10:28–29) yielded a profit for Solomon's state due to the customs and taxes collected (10:15). A trade fleet, created and managed together with the Phoenicians, is said to have brought gold and luxury items into the country (9:26–28; 10:22).

As mentioned above, even if the portrait of the early monarchy and especially the Solomonic era is painted with exaggerated gold colors and the result of the wishful thinking of a later era, the texts do principally show us the possibilities that kings were able to utilize to gain wealth (and this would then also be true at least in part for Israel's early kings). There is no doubt that the new state developed a new center of economics and wealth surrounding the royal court. This center profited the king and his family as well as his loyal followers. This led to the development of an elite that had not previously existed like this.

The changes in the social structure produced not only winners but also losers. At the very least we can say that in certain areas not everyone participated equally in the increasing political and economic wealth created by the kingdom. This assumption is supported by historical probability as well as by indications in the texts. In general, we can assume that the rulers particularly cared for their own power base by granting their supporters a series of privileges: Saul favored the Benjaminites, David and Solomon favored the Judahites and the Jerusalemites. In David and Solomon's kingdom, it seems that only the northern Israelites paid taxes and were called to compulsory labor (1 Kgs 4; 12). Benjamin, Saul's tribe, also belonged to northern Israel; they had been favored by Saul with high-ranking posts (1 Sam 22:7), but these posts were occupied mainly by Judahites (or foreign mercenaries) under David and Solomon (2 Sam 23). For lesser posts, David seems to have used individuals from the north and the south in equal numbers (24:1–9). When Solomon developed a chariot force (1 Kgs 5:6; 10:26), he probably relied on the nobility of the Canaanite cities. These cities—above all Jerusalem—were the true beneficiaries of the large royal construction projects, yet the territories of the Israelite tribes had to finance and execute these projects in equal measure. Thus the newly developed state led to an unequal distribution of wealth and resources.

This does not imply that these resources were distributed equally before the state was established. We might assume such a situation in the territories of the tribal settlements. *Between* the tribes, however, there were vast differences in terms of wealth (it is no coincidence that the provinces in Solomon's list in 1 Kgs 4:7–19 start with several names that are grouped around Ephraim as a center of power), and *within* the tribes the wealth was also distributed unequally. We are informed in 1 Sam 22 that David drew to him a militia consisting of "the distressed, the indebted, and the discontented." With these men behind him, David extorted a protection fee from the cattle-breeder Nabal (1 Sam 25). The so-called "law of the king" in 1 Sam 8:11–17 threatens the people that the ruler will conscript young men to be bodyguards, officers of the royal militia, or manufacturers of weapons, young women to be mixers of salves or cooks in the palace—a warning that apparently is addressed not to the lower but to the upper classes. These texts may indicate that wealthy farmers perceived the monarchy as a burden and a threat, whereas the lower classes on the fringes of society hoped for protection and possible social improvement from the king. These attitudes may also be behind the episode described in the argument between David and Michal on the occasion of the ark's return (2 Sam 6:20–23): Michal accused her husband that he had forgotten all codes of conduct and had not met the expectation of the higher classes. David retorted that he did not aim to please Michal and her circles but rather "the female slaves of his followers." A king thus had the right and the freedom to stand in solidarity with the lower against the higher classes.

Regardless of this, the sources of income newly acquired by the kings would not have flowed into the pockets of the little people but would have benefited primarily the royal power centers in the cities, including the royal servants, traders, and artisans living there. It is no coincidence that the call to secede twice gathers Israel "to the tents" (2 Sam 20:1; 1 Kgs 12:16). It was not the case that all Israelites were nomads or desired to return to a nomadic past; the tents were rather the symbol opposite to the royal intention of establishing fortified structures of stone. A state requires stability as well as a certain amount of urbanity; the Davidic-Solomonic state needed the (Canaanite) cities, but the Israelites, originally mainly farmers and cattle breeders, wanted a greater degree of mobility, more influence, more freedom. It is only consequential that, according to the traditions, the secessionist movement was incited over the issue of conscripted labor, perhaps also taxes (1 Kgs 12:4), the burdens of which also had to be carried in full by the mountain regions, whereas the cities in the plains enjoyed its main benefits.

If we are to trust the narrative in 2 Sam 15:1–6, Absalom's uprising was already set off by the fact that the "men of Israel" felt that King David was treating them unjustly. Absalom was able to foster this feeling and use it for his own ends. The text is not clear about what exactly the dissatisfaction of the Israelites was; it also does not mention how David could have rectified this injustice. Who were the people who came to the king? Is "Israel" in this case a sociological or an ethnic entity? Did these people come as petitioners to an audience or as a party to a court case? Did the king execute the office of judge, or was this institution restricted entirely to the communal court "at the gate"? In "cases" brought before the king by Nathan or the wise woman of Tekoa (2 Sam 12:1–5; 14:4–10) or by the figure of Meribaal (19:27–30), David could apparently pronounce judgment immediately, at least according to the narrators. Solomon also was a judge de facto (1 Kgs 2) and de jure (3:16–28) immediately following his ascent to the throne, again according to the narrators. Perhaps these were especially grave and pressing cases that specifically concerned issues of the monarchy in which the king was allowed to make a decision. In any case, we can certainly agree with the narrator's assumption in 2 Sam 15 that a rebellion of the scope and consequence of Absalom's rebellion was also occasioned by severe shortcomings on the part of the king.

A few individual situations highlight some appalling aspects of the early monarchy. The focus is understandably, if somewhat unjustly, on the king and his immediate surroundings. Still, what happened on these occasions is so horrific that the warnings in the "law of the king" (1 Sam 8:11–17) seem harmless by comparison. Saul was capable of massacring an entire family of priests (1 Sam 22). David was willing to exterminate a citizen along with everyone who could "piss against a wall" (the vulgar language befits the brutality of David's intention), all because this person refused to pay tribute to him (1 Sam 25). The texts generally seem to expect that individuals who became a problem for the king would be exterminated without hesitation (1 Sam 11:12; 18:11; 2 Sam 16:9; 19:22; 1 Kgs 2). David "took" the wife of a serving officer as soon as the occasion arose and had the officer maliciously killed once the scandal threatened to become public (2 Sam 11–12). One of David's sons raped his half-sister and was murdered by his brother (2 Sam 13).

This leads us to the role of the various women. There were several strong and politically influential personalities among them, but even they were used in the end. Bathsheba was at first nothing more than the object of David's desire; eventually, however, she played an important role in the battle for the throne, even if she had to remain in the background while manipulating the power wielded by men (2 Sam 11; 1 Kgs 1–2). Abigail was able to soothe David's lust for murder, but she had to bring along great cleverness as well as many gifts and willing submissiveness to do so (1 Sam 25). Michal did save David's life, but she was torn up in the battle for prestige and power that was waged between two dynasties (1 Sam 19:11–17; 2 Sam 3:14–16; 6:20–23; 21:8–9, in the Hebrew text). There is no reason to suppose that the events occurred exactly as narrated in the texts; still, these stories do highlight the power of the king over the life and well-being of his subjects, especially of his female subjects.

II.2.5. CULTURAL AND SPIRITUAL LIFE

The innerbiblical and postbiblical reception history portrays particularly King Solomon as the embodiment of education and high spiritual and intellectual prowess. He is seen as the prototypical wise king. It was impossible not to imagine that the great collections of Hebrew wisdom as we encounter it in the book of Proverbs were "proverbs of Solomon, the son of David, the king of Israel" (Prov 1:1). Likewise, when a title within this book mentions "Hezekiah's men" as the collectors, it had to be the "proverbs of Solomon" that they collected (25:1). The Song of Songs and, somewhat more indirectly, Ecclesiastes were also attributed to Solomon (Song 1:1; Eccl 1:1, 12ff.); this probably did no disservice to these books, as this attribution was a decisive factor in their acceptance into the canon.

The root of the theme of "wise king Solomon" is found already in the Solomon traditions in the books of Kings (in truth, these roots go even further into the royal ideology of the ancient Near East; see Wälchli 1999). Repeatedly

Solomon is portrayed as being incredibly wise. At the beginning of his reign, he asks for wisdom in a revelatory dream and is granted his request (1 Kgs 3:4–15). Immediately afterward, he proves this wisdom in the famous "Solomonic judgment" (3:16–25). He is said to have written 3,000 proverbs and 1,005 songs, thus rising to the top of all the wise men of the Orient (5:9–14). He is supposed to have competed in wisdom with the legendary Queen of Sheba, impressing her greatly (10:1–13). The entire depiction basically aims to portray Solomon's successful rule as the fruit of his extraordinary wisdom.

In the twentieth century, Old Testament scholarship tended to depersonalize this image of the wise king by describing the Solomonic era as a time period in which advanced and enlightened intellectualism flourished. In his *Theology of the Old Testament*, Gerhard von Rad described the early monarchy as one of the eras of special vitality and productivity in the intellectual history of Israel. The three large histories that, according to von Rad, originated during this time period—the histories of David's rise and the succession to his throne as well as the Yahwist history (which spans from creation to the conquest of the land)—are characterized by a particular distance between the narrators and their subject matters, by the ability to deal with broad historical developments and interconnections, the setting of the characters in a completely demythologized secular world, as well as by a strong desire for artistic achievement, a dramatizing of events, and the art of rhetoric. As a whole, a picture emerges of an era of intensive "enlightenment" and general intellectual progress.

This frequently described "Solomonic enlightenment" seems to be less a historical fact and more a phenomenon of the history of reception and scholarship. The early dating of the histories mentioned above into the early monarchy now seems to be too optimistic, and the biblical portrait of the wise Solomon is considered highly idealistic and perhaps even ideological. It remains a fact, however, that the list of Solomon's officials includes a pair of brothers as "scribes" (ספרים, 1 Kgs 4:3). Such scribes also existed in David's cabinet (2 Sam 8:17; 20:25), although their position does not seem to have been as prominent as with Solomon. Those under the supervision of these high officials may have been primarily responsible for rather mundane tasks—writing contracts, archiving documents, and so forth—but perhaps they were also involved in the educational process or in the production of literature. This does not yet answer who the audience might have been for such literature and how large this audience was. Scholars do not agree on whether the presence of *scribes* indicates the existence of *schools*. André Lemaire is quite optimistic on this issue; he even dares to imagine a public education of at least the higher social classes. In contrast, David W. Jamieson-Drake argues from the basis of archaeological evidence that a culture of writing existed in

Judah only after the eighth century, outside of Jerusalem only in locations that were directly involved in the royal administration. We can thus disregard the possible existence of writing schools during the early monarchy. This issue is of utmost importance for evaluating the possibilities not only of the production of literature but also of its reception in ancient Israel. It is true that it would be overconfident to assume a public school system during the monarchy. We can probably work with the assumption that the art of writing (and reading) was basically handed down within a master-student relationship. There is no reason, however, not to assume that scribal training took place in a royal court that employed a head writer along with several other writers. In addition, the Amarna Tablets inform us that the Canaanite cities had long known individuals who could write; this tradition with its representatives was certainly assumed by the new Israelite state and used in service of the Israelite king. Within these scribal circles, we can assume the existence not only of administrative documents but also of literary works. These works may have played a role in scribal education as well as served to entertain and to refine the higher classes of society.

It has often been claimed that Solomon or his scribes already established a kind of natural science: the creation of lists containing natural phenomena for the purpose of classification and interpretation (see Alt on 1 Kgs 5:13). The analogous texts used to support this argument, however, are all quite late (Gen 1; Job 38–39); the same could be true of the texts relating to Solomon. We cannot exclude the possibility that these texts are later additions attempting to glorify Solomon by raising him to then-current standards of natural science.

As Solomon became the embodiment of wisdom, so later redactors and readers saw David as the embodiment of poetry and song. The Jewish painter Marc Chagall always portrayed David with a harp in his hand. David is connected with seventy-three psalms in the biblical Psalter. The book of Chronicles shortens the narratives surrounding his rise to no small degree and completely omits the succession narrative. However, it has David break out into an extended song of praise once he has brought the ark back to Jerusalem (1 Chr 16, a text constructed from parts of Pss 96; 105; 106). In the following chapters his highest concern is the creation of various orders for service in the temple, especially the guilds of singers employed there (1 Chr 22–29).

As in other instances mentioned above, we are dealing here with idealistic and typological interpretation of topics that are embellishments of a historically true core. Three narratives describe how David stepped out of his provincial surroundings in Bethlehem: the story of his anointing by Samuel (1 Sam 16:1–13); the story of his employment as a musician and weapon bearer in Saul's service (16:14–23); and the story of his victory over Goliath (1 Sam 17). If any of these stories can claim historical credibility, then the narrative in the middle can, especially as it seems to be the oldest. In this story David's musical talents are connected to Saul's sickness—David's music has a palliative effect on Saul's suffering—and could be the invention of a pro-Davidic narrator. This narrator, however, had no doubt that David was highly talented in this area.

Another even more reliable source is present in two songs that are explicitly connected to David and that still seem to be present in their original poetic form: the laments over Saul and Jonathan, on the one hand (2 Sam 1:19–27), and over Abner, on the other hand (3:33–34). David's personality emerges so strongly, especially from the first of these laments, a gripping first-person lament over his friend Jonathan, that we can hardly doubt its authenticity, as is generally agreed among scholars. Any speculative setting that introduces a royal poet who had assumed the voice of the king is much more arbitrary and unlikely than the simple assumption that David himself was a poetically (and musically) talented individual. The lament over Saul and Jonathan shows such an artful chiastic structure and deliberate succession of motifs that it can serve as a prototype for the poetic genre "lament over a deceased." We should thus refer to David as a remarkable poet—not a self-evident attribute of a king, especially a conqueror.

Standing on this foundation (and on other works that David may have composed or that were attributed to him), it is not hard to explain the development of the tradition of David as singer and harpist, as psalmist, poet, and man of prayer.

II.2.6. Cult and Religion

In the ancient Near East, the king played a central role for the cultic life of the nation. In Egypt he was considered to be of divine descent, and even though he was denied this apotheosis in Syria and Mesopotamia, he was here also a kind of connecting link between heaven and earth. Near Eastern depictions often portray kings as worshipers of the gods: they stand with arms raised before the deity, and although they are much smaller than their object of veneration, they are much larger and more important than other human worshipers who also stand before the gods in similar poses. More than any other mortal, including religious officials, the king bore the responsibility for maintaining an intact relationship between heaven and earth, between gods and human beings. The king was commissioned by the gods to uphold the very order on earth that was suited to the gods and beneficial for humans.

In this sense, Saul was a true Near Eastern king only in the most remote sense—that is, if those who handed down the traditions did not suppress a great deal of material. We observe how he made use of oracles, as everyone did in those days (1 Sam 9; 28[25]). For this purpose, he actually took a priest with a special oracle instrument, the ephod, with him when waging battle against the Philistines (1 Sam 14:18–19[26]). The very same narrative also contains a quite mysterious and possibly secondary episode in which Saul dedicated an altar on the battlefield, insisting that animals be slaughtered according to Torah prescriptions even during battle (14:32–35). In all of these contexts, the king basically stands on a par with all other religious individuals of his time. It seems that the narrators considered him to be someone who participated in the religious life of his tribe and his people without having a special cultic function.

The Bible paints a very different picture of David and then especially of Solomon. It is true that David starts as a simple pious man and king who is afraid of allowing even small distances between himself and God (1 Sam 26:19), who prayerfully seeks God's presence in times of trial (2 Sam 15:31), and who seeks clarity about God's will when facing a decision, whether by oracle (1 Sam 23:2, 4, 9–12; 2 Sam 2:1; 5:19, 23) or through prophetic decree (1 Sam 22:5; 2 Sam 7:2). In all of this David appears no different from Saul. He does, however, take on additional roles that move him closer to the ancient Near Eastern ideal of a king who mediates between heaven and earth. We read in 2 Sam 24 that he brought great travesty upon his kingdom by deciding to perform a public census and that he was also able to remove this travesty from his people. As if by a miracle, he came to perceive a sacred place close to Jerusalem; a sacrifice performed at this location reconciled the deity with the land (24:25). David subsequently bought this particular piece of land from the Jebusite Araunah and paid for the animals sacrificed there, thus coming into possession of this sacred piece of earth. This text most certainly provides

---

25. Redactors loyal to the Torah held it against Saul that he turned to a necromancer in one particular case (1 Sam 28:3, 9–10). It is thus especially important to emphasize that two of Saul's sons bore YHWH-phoric names: Jonathan and Ishvoh. In this, the anachronism may be excused: David was no more "orthodox" than Saul.

26. It is quite strange that, according to the Hebrew text, Saul did inquire (or better, failed to inquire) of the oracle not by means of this instrument (as the Greek text has it) but rather by means of the ark. Is this a textual error? Or had Saul already returned the ark, or was the ark never lost? We should be careful not to put too much emphasis on a single deviating text. It has not yet been fully determined what the "ephod" was. It most likely was a piece of clothing attached to a divine image that contained a kind of lot and that was later, due to the rise of monotheism, worn by the priest.

us with an etiology for the claim of the house of David to Mount Zion and the temple subsequently constructed here. Thus David joins the long list of royal Near Eastern founders of temples and cultic proceedings.

The fact that prophets appear in this narrative as well as in others—Gad and Nathan are mentioned by name—fits well with a religious characterization of David that was open to influences from ancient Near Eastern thought. The letters from Mari from the eighteenth century B.C.E. and later Neo-Assyrian texts mention prophetic figures (including female figures!) who admonish and warn, seeking to gain influence within the royal court. Ugaritic texts are completely silent on this issue, but the coincidental discovery of an Ammonite (?) Balaam text and, of course, the biblical texts show extensively that the prophets were a reality in the religious world of Palestine.[27] We have already been told that Saul found his father's donkeys and subsequently the kingship through the mediation of a "seer" and a band of prophets (1 Sam 9:1–10:16). David even had a prophet as his constant companion, thus allowing him to clarify God's will if the need arose.

Apart from the prophets, the king was constantly surrounded by priests who were experts on the conditions required for a reconciled relationship between God and humans. Abiathar is said to have accompanied David ever since David's days as a fugitive; Zadok joined him in Jerusalem. The priests were responsible for orderly sacrificial proceedings, probably also for inquiries by oracle. The great importance accorded to them by David can be seen by the fact that they were included in his cabinet list: aside from Abiathar and Zadok we also encounter a certain Ira (2 Sam 20:25–26) as well as the "sons of David" (2 Sam 8:17–18). This odd fact is an especially clear indication of the influence of Near Eastern royal ideology on David's thought and action. Royal sons and, of course, the king himself were so close to the realm of the divine that priestly dignities were bestowed upon them almost as a matter of course. It is no coincidence that the Araunah narrative portrays David as the one who, as priest, performed the necessary sacrifices that led to the reconciliation with the deity (2 Sam 24:25).

This priestly function is seen with even greater clarity in David's behavior when returning the ark to Jerusalem (2 Sam 6). This narrative describes a great feast that David initiated to honor the God YHWH who was entering the city. We are told how David himself wore a short priestly apron, performed ritual sacrifices, and was carried away by ecstatic dancing before the ark (6:13–14). The ark, however, takes center stage. It is led with all honors

---

27. On this issue, see Manfried Dietrich et al., *Deutungen der Zukunft in Briefen, Orakeln und Omina* (TUAT 2/1; ed. Otto Kaiser et al.; Gütersloh: Mohn, 1986).

through the city and is placed in a *tent* (6:17), a clear indication of the basic mobility of this cultic artifact as well as the deity present upon it. It is also a sign of the nonurban attitude toward life held by the Israelites. The presentation of a sacred tent in the middle of the City of David symbolizes the political and religious balancing act that David performed in this context. The ark had been sacred to the middle Palestinian tribes during the time period before the establishment of the state; it had then fallen into the hands of the Philistines and had subsequently become not only unreachable but also unimportant to the Israelites (see 1 Sam 4–6). David remembered the ark and used it in a clever political and religious move: a Judahite by descent, he resided in a formerly Canaanite city; the Israelite element was in danger of being neglected. By taking ownership of the genuinely (northern) Israelite ark, moving it to his place of residence, and granting it proper cultic attention, he was able to present himself as an Israelite to the Israelites.

The deity worshiped as the one enthroned above the ark was clearly YHWH, apparently carrying the epitaph "of hosts" (probably referring to heavenly hosts, not Israelite troops); sometimes he also bears the title "one who sits enthroned upon the cherubim" (2 Sam 6:2), a title that was probably added only in Jerusalem. The previous leading deity of Jerusalem had not been YHWH but rather perhaps Shalem or Zedeq or even the sun-god.[28] By identifying the Canaanite with the Israelite God, David unified not only the religions but also the regions of his kingdom. This, at least, was probably David's intention—and it was a complete success for the duration of his reign. As the deity worshiped in Jerusalem, YHWH received various attributes formerly attached to deities at home in Canaan (such as the King of the Gods); still, there was no doubt that it was YHWH, the God of Israel, who was enthroned on Zion. Thus the Israelites and the Canaanites were united in religious matters. The Judahites to whom YHWH had been no stranger—the Bible portrays groups such as the Calebites and the Kenites as having a trusting relationship with this God from the dawn of time—were able to recognize YHWH first as the family deity of this dynasty and finally as their national deity. This process of integration, initiated by David, was so successful that Judah had no difficulty seeing itself as "Israel" in the sense of "the people of YHWH" once the northern kingdom of Israel had collapsed.

---

28. See Othmar Keel and Christoph Uehlinger, "Jahwe und die Sonnengottheit von Jerusalem," in *Ein Gott allein? JHWH-Verehrung und biblischer Monotheismus im Kontext der israelitischen und altorientalischen Religionsgeschichte* (ed. Walter Dietrich and Martin A. Klopfenstein; OBO 139; Fribourg: Universitätsverlag; Göttingen: Vandenhoeck & Ruprecht, 1994), 269–306.

Solomon continued the religious policies of his father. He likewise sought to become an Israelite to the Israelites, but even more a Canaanite to the Canaanites. A spiritual leader headed his cabinet: Azariah the son of Zadok (1 Kgs 4:2).[29] Under David's rule there still had been a historically based and explicable duality between the rural priest Abiathar and the urban Jerusalem priest Zadok. In the events surrounding Solomon's succession to the throne, however, these two had sided with different parties. So, following his victory, Solomon deposed Abiathar (1 Kgs 2:26–27) and left all religious matters to Zadok and his son and successor. This shift entailed an increase in the importance of the Canaanite element in Israel's official religion.

It is certainly no coincidence that the first major religious festival took place at the "high place" of Gibeon, a sanctuary that was most likely of Canaanite origin and character. Solomon is said to have sacrificed a hecatomb of animals (1 Kgs 3:4), although the text does not say to which deity. The Deuteronomistic redactors feel compelled to excuse Solomon's actions by stating explicitly that the temple, for them the only true sanctuary of Yhwh, had not yet been built.

This would soon change. According to the biblical text, the construction of a temple on Mount Zion was at the center of Solomon's thought and action. The Hebrew verb בנה, however, can mean "to enlarge, alter" as well as "to build (new)." If we pull the mysterious story in 2 Sam 24 into this context, we could arrive at the conclusion that Solomon did not build a completely new sanctuary from scratch but rather enlarged an already-existing and much smaller Jebusite sanctuary and turned it into a large temple. The high place located north of the old Jebusite city as well as the City of David, the tip of which can still be seen in the rock that stands at the center of the Dome of the Rock, may have been the site of an age-old pilgrim sanctuary. Solomon had this location raised (the "Millo") and thus established a larger plateau for construction. This subsequently became the site of a larger temple. The inner sanctuary, which was a separate construction from the rest of the building (see 1 Kgs 6:2–3, 16–20), may have incorporated the basic building fabric of the ancient sanctuary and thus participated in its religious dignity—just as on countless occasions new religions did not eliminate older sanctuaries but rather integrated them into newly constructed places of worship.[30] There are also many close analogies to the shape of Solomon's temple in the

---

29. Abiathar and Zadok still appear side by side in 1 Kgs 4:4; this is most likely a secondary adaptation to the Davidic lists.

30. Here are only two examples that shall stand for countless others: the church Santa Maria sopra Minerva in Rome and the Umayyad mosque in Damascus that seems to have incorporated a Christian basilica.

sanctuaries of Syria and Palestine. In regard to the two pillars that stood at the entrance to the temple, "Jachin" and "Boaz" (1 Kgs 7:15–22), there are minor examples outside of Israel, but only on a literary level: in connection with the Melqart temple in Tyre (Herodotus) and with the Ashtarte temple in Heliopolis (Lucian). The stands of bronze were decorated with lions and bulls (7:29, 35); the text frequently mentions plantlike decorations, pomegranates and palm trees—images that are all well-known in the religious iconography of the ancient Near East.[31]

Although major Canaanite or generally Oriental aspects thus doubtlessly characterized Solomon's temple, we also should not overlook the specifically Israelite elements. The first noticeable feature is a major effort to remain aniconic, that is, to abstain from figurative displays in general and specifically of the deity. The one strong exception seems to be the cherubim, yet these fairy creatures—half animal, half human—were the embodied refusal of any "rational" figuration. They also served as the throne upon which—highly exalted but invisible (Isa 6:1–2)—YHWH was seated! The ark was also placed beneath the wings of the cherubim—another symbol of the invisible God on the throne. We have seen that this ark was a decidedly Israelite cultic artifact; by placing it in the holy of holies, Solomon paid respect to his Israelite subjects and their religious traditions and convictions. The ark no longer stood in a tent but in a walled room without windows (1 Kgs 8:12). Even if the carrying poles were still attached (in such a way that they were still barely visible from the holy place in front of the inner sanctuary, 8:8), no one thought of ever again carrying the ark into battle as a palladium of war. The God above the ark had become sedentary; he had focused his presence on Mount Zion and the holy city of Jerusalem. According to the theology of Zion, whoever dared to take on Zion also had to take him on; this faith turned virulent in situations of crisis (2 Kgs 19:32–34; Jer 7:3; Ps 46). This faith also had to survive the destruction of the temple by the Babylonians in 586 B.C.E.—yet subsequently also witness the fall of Babylon and the reconstruction of the temple under Persian rule. The fact that the victorious general Titus displayed the ark on his triumphal arch when the Romans destroyed the Second Temple shows that this sacred "box" (whether it was the original, returned by the Persians, or a later reproduction) played an important role right up to the final destruction of the temple and the cessation of any kind of temple cult.

---

31. See Othmar Keel and Christoph Uehlinger, *Göttinnen, Götter und Gottessymbole: Neue Erkenntnisse zur Religionsgeschichte Kanaans und Israels aufgrund bislang unerschlossener ikonographischer Quellen* (QD 134; Freiburg: Herder, 1992), 189–96.

Solomon not only "built" the temple on Mount Zion, equipping it (according to the biblical account) with lavish decorations. He and his successors on the throne of David were doubtlessly also committed to guaranteeing ordered and functioning cultic procedures. Visible proof of this is the fact that Solomon, as David before him, took on a priestly role—at least during the dedication of the temple. The ark was moved from the City of David to Mount Zion by priests and set up at its new location, but the king participated in the sacrifices, spoke the ritual phrases when the ark was set down, blessed the people, and prayed to YHWH on their behalf (1 Kgs 8:1–14). He is also said to have amassed treasure in the temple that was used to finance the temple service (7:51). Thus Solomon operated completely within the parameters of ancient Near Eastern royal ideology in which the king was responsible for establishing, equipping, protecting, and cultivating a national sanctuary as the symbol of an ordered and harmonious relationship between God and the state.

The Deuteronomists tell us with all expressions of horror that Solomon promoted not only the temple of YHWH in Jerusalem but also several other sanctuaries dedicated to the worship of other deities (1 Kgs 11:7–8). This is quite credible. As important as the royal sanctuary on Mount Zion was for religious policy, it was only later generations who came up with the idea that Zion had to be the one and only legitimate cultic site for all of Israel.

II.2.7. FOREIGN AFFAIRS AND TRADE POLICIES

We hear nothing of any kind of foreign policy under the rule of Saul. Either the tradition suppressed such information or the geographical parameters and the sphere of influence of Israel's first king were limited to those parts of northern Israel that belonged to his kingdom. From this point of view, we easily gain the impression that Saul did not really establish a state but rather a *chiefdom*. Any contact with neighboring peoples was limited to military conflict. Even Saul's mercenary troops, if they included any foreigners at all, were more an instrument of military strategy than of foreign policy.

Once again, it was David who drastically changed this picture. Already the fact that he resided abroad for some time (even if involuntarily!) reveals a much wider horizon. He later defeated the Philistines, but he neither eradicated them completely nor integrated them into his kingdom; he thus seems to have intended some kind of tension-laden co-existence. After all, his elite military unit, the Cherethites and the Pelethites, bore a partially Philistine name. The text explicitly mentions another military unit of six hundred men that was commanded by the Philistine Ittai (2 Sam 15:18–22). In various ways

David bound the states (or perhaps rather the chiefdoms) of the Edomites, the Moabites, the Ammonites, and supposedly even the Arameans to his state, thus creating a buffer zone surrounding his home territories. Even if this situation was created by force and could be upheld only temporarily, it shows us David's intention to establish a stable foreign policy that encompassed the entire region. The text tells us that David entertained friendly relations with the Phoenicians, specifically with their most important city Tyre and its king Hiram, using cedar wood from the Lebanon and Phoenician artisans when constructing his palace (5:11). This could well be a retroactive projection from the Solomon traditions, but if David built a palace in Jerusalem at all—and there is no reason to doubt this fact[32]—then it is quite plausible that he made use of Phoenician materials and experts; even Mesopotamian rulers desired the wealth of lumber in the Lebanon.

With monarchies, marriage is often a special variety of foreign policy. This was also the case for David (and for Solomon—but not for Saul!). David married, so it seems, women of high standing from various parts of his kingdom: Abigail, the widow of a rich landowner; Ahinoam from the Judahite south; Michal, a daughter of Saul, the king of Israel.[33] It is especially interesting to note that a certain Maacah, daughter of King Talmai of Geshur, was one of David's wives. Geshur was a small Aramean principality that bordered Israel to the north and was probably to be found in the area of the Golan (see Josh 13:11). When David engaged in battle with the Arameans, he fought against all sorts of states or tribes, but not against Geshur (2 Sam 10:6). Was this the result of his marriage politics? The Geshurite princess Maacah bore David a son and a daughter, Absalom and Tamar. When Absalom fled after killing his half-brother Amnon in revenge for the rape of his sister, he fled to "Talmai ben Ammihud, king of Geshur," and thus to his grandfather. This king then offered him protection for three years until Absalom was able to return to Jerusalem unpunished. All this describes a quite close relationship between the royal houses of Geshur and Judah.

---

32. Recently claims have even been made that archaeological evidence for this palace has been found; see Eilat Mazar, "Did I Find King David's Palace?" *BAR* 32/1 (2006): 17–27, 70.

33. According to tradition, David did not choose Bathsheba intentionally; at the very least, according to 2 Sam 11:3 and 23:34 (if can read these passages in this manner!), she was the daughter of one of the "thirty heroes of David," granddaughter of the famous royal advisor Ahithophel from the Judahite Gilo, and the wife of a foreign officer. We can say nothing of the origin of the wives Haggith, Abital, and Eglah (2 Sam 3:4–5). To include the beautiful Abishag: she came from the northern Israelite town of Shunem.

David does not seem to have made contact with more distant countries. If we classify Saul's sphere of influence as local, then David's would be
regional—and Solomon's international. This can already be seen in the origin
of the women who made up Solomon's harem. The text emphasizes on more
than one occasion that no less a person than the pharaoh of Egypt wanted to
have Solomon as his son-in-law. He even put up a substantial dowry: the city
of Gezer, which had been conquered for this very purpose (until this point it
had remained Canaanite, perhaps under Philistine protection; see 1 Kgs 3:1;
9:16). A different marriage connection pointed eastward: one of Solomon's
wives and the mother of the crown prince Rehoboam was the Ammonite
Naamah (1 Kgs 14:21). It should be mentioned in this context that the role
of the king's mother, גבירה, was of great political importance,[34] so it is quite
astonishing (and testimony to the international climate of Judah during that
time) that a foreigner could attain this position. In a sweeping summary 1 Kgs
11:1 states in exaggeration: "King Solomon loved many foreign women along
with the daughter of Pharaoh: Moabite, Ammonite, Edomite, Sidonian, and
Hittite women"—in total (and almost certainly including local women!) seven
hundred main wives and three hundred concubines (11:3). If only a fraction
of this can be seen as historical reality, it would be sufficiently strong evidence
for a foreign policy on the basis of marriage politics during Solomon's reign.

There are, however, also other indications. Solomon's wisdom is compared to the wisdom traditions of Mesopotamia and Egypt and with famous
wise men of the Orient (1 Kgs 5:10–11; see also 10:1–13). Even if Solomon
himself was not this "wise" and the intellectual climate in his court was not
quite as cosmopolitan as reported here, we cannot doubt that education, science, and the arts—including the art of reading and writing—was not limited
nationally but was an international endeavor with many international connections. The use of letters in writing had become commonplace in all of
Syro-Palestine; the genres and the topics of wisdom literature are comparable
everywhere. Even if only very little was written in Solomon's court and the
intellectual standard was quite low, this writing and standard would have had
an international horizon.

Solomon's trade relations, or rather those of his traders, were also international (see above §II.2.4.). Horses and chariots were traded between Asia
Minor, Syria, and Egypt (1 Kgs 10:28–29); a trade fleet sailed the Mediter-

---

34. See Herbert Donner, "Art und Herkunft des Amtes der Königinmutter im Alten
Testament," in *Festschrift Johannes Friedrich zum 65. Geburtstag am 27. August 1958 gewidmet* (ed. R. von Kienle et al.; Heidelberg: Winter, 1959), 105–45; on the possible religious
influence, see Susan Ackerman, "The Queen Mother and the Cult in Ancient Israel," *JBL*
112 (1993): 385–401.

ranean (with the western goal "Tarshish," probably identical with the Spanish Tartessos) as well as the Red Sea (with the goal "Ophir," located either in Yemen or in East Africa). This is what the tradition relates, and it also includes the realistic information that Israelite sailors would not have been capable of such voyages, that they were dependent on joint ventures with the Phoenicians (9:26–28; 10:11, 22). However large the participation of the Israelites may have been in these business ventures, there is no need to doubt the existence of lively trade relations between Israel and Phoenicia.

One name occurs quite often: Hiram, king of the large Phoenician harbor city of Tyre. Hiram is said to have equipped the ships sailing to Ophir (1 Kgs 9:27), which is not impossible considering that the adventurous and trade-experienced Phoenicians could gain access to the Red Sea only through Israel, or better Judah.[35] Hiram is also reported to be the one who actively supported Solomon in constructing the palace and the temple. The Phoenician king supplied cedar and cypress timber as well as gold (as a kind of credit, 5:20; 9:11); Solomon paid him with all an agricultural society could offer: grain and olive oil and, when necessary, villages with all their inhabitants (9:11). "There was peace between Hiram and Solomon, and the two of them made a treaty" (5:26b). Included in this treaty were not only shipments of material goods but also the transfer of know-how. Phoenician artisans, sailors, and masons were active in Israel (5:23, 32). One individual, who apparently did all the metalwork on the inside of the temple, is mentioned by name: once again a certain Hiram, the son of a metalworker from Tyre and a woman from the northern Israelite tribe of Naphtali (7:13–14).

We are thus given a quite extensive and detailed picture of cosmopolitan foreign affairs and international trade relations under Solomon's rule. It is astonishing, how much had changed over the period of less than three generations.

II.2.8. Army and Military Equipment

When Saul first opposed the Philistines, the biblical tradition paints his initial position in bleak colors. Not only was the enemy present in Saul's own

---

35. In 1 Kgs 22:48 we read of an attempt of the Judahite king Jehoshaphat (867–850) to build a "Tarshish ship to sail to Ophir" that failed miserably already at Ezion-geber. On this occasion, northern Israel, itself closely allied to Phoenicia, especially to the city of Sidon, is said to have offered nautical assistance (22:49). Even if Jehoshaphat rejected this joint venture, it at least seemed to be a possibility. Why should it not have already been realized once before, ca. 150 years earlier during the reign of Solomon?

territories, but this adversary was also vastly superior in terms of military strength and especially weaponry: "Now there was no smith to be found throughout all the land of Israel, for the Philistines said, 'The Hebrews must not make swords or spears for themselves'; so all the Israelites went down to the Philistines to sharpen their plowshare, mattocks, axes, or sickles" (1 Sam 13:19–20; the following text speaks of the—no doubt quite high—prices for these services). This information does not point to a complete monopoly in iron, but certainly to a monopoly in the processing of iron, especially for the manufacturing of weaponry or of tools that could be used as weapons: "So on the day of the battle neither sword nor spear was to be found in the possession of any of the people with Saul and Jonathan, although Saul and his son Jonathan had them" (13:22). Only the noblest of the Hebrews, the (future?) king and his son possessed such weaponry.

It seems that Saul was successful in reducing Philistine pressure to a certain degree while building a relatively effective Israelite army. "Whenever Saul saw any strong or valiant warrior, he took him into his service" (1 Sam 14:52). Saul, according to this brief statement, created an elite troop of professional soldiers. According to 2 Sam 2:15, this troop consisted (primarily?) of Benjaminites; however, the Judahite David also rose up through these ranks (1 Sam 18). Apparently this troop was not very big; 1 Sam 13:15 and 14:2 speak of six hundred men. At the very least, they would have had to be fed and paid. Apart from the fact that they were certainly allowed to raid the enemy at will, the king would have had to provide them with a basic income. The king's own lands and especially "gifts" would have served this purpose—gifts that his subjects had to or wanted (not) to give him (1 Sam 10:27). These gifts were most likely a kind of payment for the service of keeping law and order.

Larger forces supplemented the mercenaries on special occasions. The texts frequently mention a body of three thousand men; this is said to have been a selection from all men able to go to war (1 Sam 13:2; 24:3; 26:2). According to tradition, Saul actually mobilized all the able men for certain military ventures: for the blitz against the Ammonites (1 Sam 11) and the decisive battle against the Philistines (29:1; 31). Both of these were battles of quasi-national importance. For smaller skirmishes, Saul would have limited himself to the use of his mercenaries.

We should not assume that a general draft existed under Saul's rule. David was the first to have his general perform a public census (2 Sam 24:1–9), thus inciting much unrest (hardly just with God!). Saul would have been able to fall back on groups of volunteers from the various regions and tribes of "Israel" who would then follow him—or not follow him. In 1 Sam 13 we read how Saul engaged in battle with the Philistines by staging a coup against a Philistine governor—and then expected the men of Israel to follow him. These men realized that "Israel had become odious to the Philistines" (13:4) and actually responded to Saul's summons. Once the Philistines approached in full force, however, they quickly ran off. These are very difficult parameters for a military leader to work with!

These parameters were made even more difficult by the miserable weaponry available to Saul's troops, at least at the beginning. It seems that only Saul and his son Jonathan possessed a sword and a spear (1 Sam 13:22); since the Israelites were not allowed to manufacture iron tools, it would be going too far to even speak of an "armed mob."

All this would radically change under David's rule. True, his military career started in a more humble setting than that of Saul, since he was a mercenary in the service of the king, but he quickly rose through the ranks and was thus familiar with the life of a mercenary from the inside. After leaving Saul's court, he gathered mercenaries around himself, once again about four hundred to six hundred men. He provided for these men through raids and by collecting protection money.

Unlike earlier with Saul, we now gain insight into the internal hierarchy of David's elite warriors. Apart from the "Three," a unit of highly decorated heroes of whom incredible stories were told (2 Sam 23:8–17), there also were the "Thirty." This unit came into existence during David's time in Hebron, perhaps even earlier, and continued to exist when David relocated his residence to Jerusalem. A list found in 23:24–39 informs us of the names of the Thirty and their places of origin. At the top of the list we encounter only individuals from southern Palestine who probably were already with David during his time as a fugitive rebel. The following ranks also contain Aramean, Ammonite, Canaanite, and even Hittite mercenaries, probably as a replacement for fallen comrades.

The unit of the Cherethites and the Pelethites consisted only of foreign mercenaries, at least according to the unit's name. Their leader was Benaiah, himself apparently a member of the Thirty (2 Sam 23:20–23). For the rest, David, like Saul, trusted the positions of leadership to members of his own clan: Abishai, the commander of the Thirty (23:18), and Joab, the general, were brothers ("sons of Zeruiah," a sister of Jesse) and David's cousins.

Joab held the leading position in David's cabinet (2 Sam 8:16; 20:23), which is a telling piece of information about the importance of the army in David's state. It seems that Joab rose to the top rank during the conquest of Jerusalem (1 Chr 11:6). Under David's orders, Joab conducted a public census in the core areas of Israel and Judah and was thus able to gather information on the military resources of the land (2 Sam 24:1–9). Acting pretty much on his own, Joab led various military campaigns against the Ammonites and the

Arameans (2 Sam 10). Joab also interfered in the political machinations of the royal family (2 Sam 14). He was primarily responsible for crushing Absalom's rebellion and beat down the rebellion of Sheba completely on his own (2 Sam 18–20). Joab was able to openly oppose the king (19:6–8), and Joab almost played the decisive role in determining David's successor (1 Kgs 1–2). In times of war, Joab commanded both the mercenaries and the general militia. In certain special cases, David himself assumed command (2 Sam 12:26–31), but it seems that he increasingly stopped leading the troops into battle himself, trusting them instead to proven military leaders (18:1–5).

Chariots were one branch of military service not present in David's army: light chariots drawn by two or four horses with a charioteer and a warrior. When David happened to lay hands on a large number of chariots with horses following a battle with the Arameans, he had almost all of the horses hamstrung; it seems that he did not know what to do with them (2 Sam 8:4).[36] The traditions also do not speak anywhere of larger military edifices such as barracks, stables, or storage houses, and it seems that David only expanded and fortified Jerusalem (see 2 Sam 5:9 as well as the archaeological findings on the City of David; see above §II.1.3.1.).

As much as we can speak of David as a soldier-king and conqueror, as important as the army was in his rise and in the construction, expansion, and stabilization of his kingdom, the military sector was quite limited when compared to the society as a whole. The main military burden was shouldered by a limited number of professional soldiers who were located either on the field in battle or in the residence of the king. They were probably not very visible in general. The king—and following successful campaigns the mercenaries themselves—provided the income and equipment. Larger military engagements necessitated gathering the general militia; these men appear not to have lived in barracks, were not trained on a constant basis, and were not elaborately equipped with weapons. Members of the militia who went into battle were probably equipped and provided for by their families (see 1 Sam 17:17–18). This type of military system is not very cost-intensive.

All this changed under Solomon. Even though we are not told that he engaged in any military campaign (with the exception of the internal uprising reported in 1 Kgs 11:26–27, 40), we read that he greatly expanded the military apparatus. First, Solomon entrusted the entire military apparatus to his general Benaiah (1 Kgs 4:4). David never allowed a single general to accumulate

---

36. We do not have clear information either on the numbers or on the technical terms. We are probably not dealing with cavalry (as is assumed by a few translations) but with work horses. Even the lowest number recorded in the textual traditions (1,700 in the MT) is most likely an exaggeration.

this much power (see 2 Sam 8:16, 18; 20:23). It is true that Benaiah's rise did start under David's rule. In comparison to 2 Sam 8, the list in 2 Sam 20 shows that Benaiah had risen from the fifth to ..1e second position directly behind Joab, a quiet but significant confirmation of the diminishing relation between David and Joab that is reflected in the narrative texts (compare the execution of Absalom and David's attempt to replace Joab by Amasa in 2 Sam 18–20). On the other hand, we should note that the army no longer takes first place among the officials recorded on Solomon's lists; this may be a confirmation of the other traditions that the civil sector became much more important than the military sector under Solomon's rule.

The militia, which still operated on an ad hoc basis under Saul and was organized under David and used in important military decisions, no longer seemed to be of any importance under Solomon. We read nothing of its existence and nothing at all about its possible use. The fact that David's mercenary leader Benaiah now led the military on his own seems to indicate a shift of military importance: away from the people who could be called to arms (and might or might not follow) and toward a professional army that was responsible solely to the king. The general draft was most likely regulated in the treaties that existed between Saul or David and the people. Solomon did not make such a covenant and thus had no claim to a general draft. Perhaps he, being opposed by Joab (and thus also the Judahite militia), was not even unhappy about this development. Perhaps he did not want the people armed, trusting instead in his mercenaries. Solomon thus did much to establish and equip a professional army. He fortified cities and built chariot cities (1 Kgs 9:19) that provided protection against external enemies as well as control over possible internal unrest. He did not station only infantry in these cities: "Solomon gathered together chariots and horses; he had fourteen hundred chariots and twelve thousand horses, which he stationed in the chariot cities" (1 Kgs 10:26; according to 5:6 there were four thousand stalls of horses and twelve thousand horses). These numbers are quite high but not completely unbelievable. According to Assyrian sources, the—admittedly powerful—Omride dynasty sent two thousand chariots into the battle of Qarqar, again a generous estimate.

II.2.9. External Enemies and Wars

The main enemy who troubled Saul and still David were the Philistines. It seems that they played an important, even if involuntary, role in Saul's rise. Their superiority in Palestine was so overwhelming that Israel grew willing actively to oppose them. With a coup against the Philistine governor, who apparently resided in Gibeah, Saul incited a widespread uprising and thus the conditions for his own rise. "All of Israel heard: Saul had defeated the garrison of the Philistines, and also that Israel had become odious to the Philistines" (1 Sam 13:4). Many "Hebrews" thus decided to follow Saul's call to arms, and a major battle ensued against the Philistines, who surprisingly were not able to keep the upper hand (1 Sam 13–14).

The summary in 1 Sam 14:47ff. mentions several external enemies whom Saul is said to have dealt with: the Moabites, the Ammonites, the Edomites—thus the neighbors east of the Jordan; the Arameans of Zoba, a southern Syrian principality; the Philistines; and, finally, the Amalekites. This information matches the Saul narratives only to a certain degree, in the case of the Amalekites, the Ammonites, and the Philistines. We thus cannot say that this summary is a later distillation of the narrative traditions. Who would have been interested in crediting Saul with further battles, culminating in the final sentence: "Wherever he turned he found help" (1 Sam 14:47 LXX),[37] especially after Saul had fallen into disfavor apparently with God but clearly with the pro-Davidic Judahite authors?

In the case of verse 48 alone, where the war against the Amalekites is mentioned, the situation is more difficult. This could be a later addition to the larger and (in its final form late) narrative in 1 Sam 15, especially since the text seems somewhat tacked on. On the other hand, the narrative could also be a midrash to an old notice in 14:48, or, as a third possibility, both texts may witness to an actual war between Saul and the Amalekites. This third assumption is not refuted by the fact that this tribe generally lived as nomads in the far south, in the Negev and Sinai. The Edomites (14:47!) also lived far to the south, and David also had to deal with the Amalekites—this is undoubtedly historical. Even the subsidiary argument that David was a Judahite and thus closer to southern Palestine proves nothing: Benjamin is located only slightly farther north than Judah, and Saul is reported to have spent some time in this area (1 Sam 22ff.).

Saul's wars in general seem not to have been wars of expansion but rather of defense and border protection. We at least do not hear that he ever attempted to annex southern Palestinian territories. It remains unclear what his reasons were for sometimes initiating military forays into these regions.

---

37. Thus the Greek tradition and similarly the Syriac and Latin traditions. In contrast, the Hebrew text changed the expression for somewhat dogmatic reasons—Saul was not allowed to be successful!—from יוֹשַׁע or יַשְׂבִּיל to יַרְשִׁיעַ "he did evil." If this text is original, then the entire list in 14:47 might be considered nonhistorical because its tendency was anti-Saul. Scholarship, however, has reached a rare consensus on this issue: a scribe could not bear the pro-Saulide intention of the text he was copying.

As nomads, the Amalekites may have wandered far into the north; the Edomites and especially the Moabites may have allied themselves with the Ammonites. The Ammonites in any case encroached on Gilead, a traditional dwelling place of the central Palestinian tribes. It is stated on several occasions that Saul felt responsible for and acted on behalf of these tribes: The town of Jabesh in Gilead is connected to Saul not only through the admittedly legendary narrative in 1 Sam 11 but also through the description of the kingdom of Eshbaal in 2 Sam 2:9 and especially in 2:4–7 and 21:12, two very different texts not from the Saul traditions but from the David traditions. In other words, Davidic politics knew of and respected the special bond between Jabesh and Saul and his house. The fact that Israelite settlers in Gilead had to suffer from Ammonite attacks did not occur for the first or the last time under Saul (see Judg 10–11; Amos 1:13).

Finally, the Philistines had long been Israel's arch-enemy (e.g., Judg 13ff.; 1 Sam 4). Starting from their home country in the southwestern Palestinian coastal plain, they entered the mountain regions inhabited by (Judahite and) Israelite settlers. Saul's aim was to push them back to the coast. It seems that he was quite successful in this, at least in the beginning. This is expressed not only by the summary in 1 Sam 14:47 but also in the large narrative in 1 Sam 13–14, even if the final text seeks to ascribe credit for this exploit to Jonathan and not to Saul. This is already indication of a pro-Davidic tendency, as is the narrative of David's victory over Goliath and of David's subsequent rise in Saul's army: Saul is always depicted in a negative light when compared to David, the young and glorious hero. If there were victories over the Philistines at this point in time, however, they must be credited to King Saul; it would have hardly been important to historians that a certain David ben Jesse was part of Saul's army if this David had not himself become king later on.

It was this David who succeeded in putting a final end to the Philistines' expansionist tendencies. It seems that he already started this process while still a mercenary and officer in Saul's army. Indeed, if he served there at all, he would have battled the Philistines. The next stage that follows in his career, however, places him in the service of the Philistines. Under the cover of their claim to supremacy, David continued to approach his goal of becoming leader of Judah and Israel. Sooner or later, this goal would have to collide with Philistine interests. The old traditions in 2 Sam 21:15–22 and 23:8–23 are full of anecdotes about encounters, duels, and guerilla attacks in which David and his men measured themselves primarily against the Philistines. These reports probably originated during David's time in Hebron. Yet even as the leader of the united monarchy, David had to deal with Philistine attacks (or the Philistines believed that they had to deal with the threat of the state established under David), and he finally succeeded in delivering the final blow. As strange and legendary as the narratives in 2 Sam 5:17–25 may be, they reflect a two-fold victory west of Jerusalem; in the end, the Philistines were thrown back behind Gezer and thus back to their original territory.

David was even more successful in the east. Surveying from south to north, we read that the Edomites suffered a major defeat and high casualties in the Wadi Arabah; according to 1 Kgs 11:15, the massacre approached geno-cide. David "set garrisons [נצבים] in Edom…, and all the Edomites became David's servants" (2 Sam 8:14). The Moabites were also defeated: two-thirds of all the warriors captured were liquidated without mercy, "and the Moabites became servants to David and brought tribute" (8:2). The war against the Ammonites is not summarized in 2 Sam 8 but is narrated in detail in 2 Sam 10–12: Joab attacked these neighbors with the mercenary troops, stormed the capital Rabbah, and, once the city's collapse was imminent, summoned the king, who had remained behind in Jerusalem, to lead the final charge. "So David gathered all the people together and went to Rabbah and fought against it and took it. He took the crown from their king's head…, and it was placed on David's head. He also brought forth the spoil of the city, a very great amount. He brought out the people who were in it and set them to work with saws and iron picks and iron axes.[38] … Thus he did to all the cities of the Ammonites" (12:30–31). If we read the text literally and do not assume that it is merely somewhat more imaginative than other texts, then David made himself king of Ammon, thus incorporating this land into his united mon-archy. The situation was different with Edom (and probably also Moab): here he forced provincial governors upon these territories, allocating to them an inferior status. Whether the fate of the Ammonites was any happier than that of their southern neighbors (in as much as they survived) may be doubted.

These traditions on David's encroachment into Transjordanian territo-ries are credible for several reasons. It seems that the Philistines, previously the dominant force in Palestine, did not extend their expansion beyond the Jordan; their forces were possibly too limited for such endeavors, and Isra-elite and proto-Judahite settlers in the mountains also stood in their way. When the mountain regions consolidated and grew stronger, they created an equal and opposing force to the Philistines—certainly a favorable situation for those who lived east of the Jordan. We can also assume that the conflict between the Israelites and Philistines threatened the stability of the age-old trade route along the Via Maris, which would have heightened the attrac-

---

38. What follows are several unclear words that seem to indicate work in brickyards. Some versions and exegetes hear in this context and in the previous mention of the "king" (whose name we know from 2 Sam 10:1!) an allusion to the Ammonite god Milcom (see 1 Kgs 11:7).

tion of the Road of Kings east of the Jordan. This again may have been the reason for David's attack toward the east once he had pacified the west: his kingdom was to participate in international trade, even control this trade as much as possible. The welfare of the land (and, of course, of the royal house) was highly dependent on this control. We can see this negatively with Saul and positively with Solomon.

It is thus easy to explain why the battles with the Ammonites were immediately followed by the battle with the Arameans. The trade routes heading north through Palestine led inevitably into Aramean territory. The Arameans were the direct neighbors to the north of Israel and Ammon; Arameans lived north of the Gennesaret, in the Beka Plain, in Damascus, along the Orontes and the Euphrates. They were, however, not organized as a large state. This made it all the more important that they prevent a single opposing power in Palestine that controlled both the Via Maris and the Road of Kings and thus all trade routes to Egypt and into southern Arabia. For this reason the Arameans frequently interfered with Palestinian affairs, often exploiting the animosity between Ammon and Israel (e.g., to put pressure on Israel and especially on the region of Gilead; see 2 Kgs 8:12, 28; Amos 1:3, 13).

It is thus quite plausible that several different Aramean principalities (Zobah, Rehob, Tob, and Maacah) took action following David's, or better Joab's, attack on Ammon (2 Sam 10:6; in 8:3–6 Damascus is mentioned alongside Zobah). It seems that Joab was able to thwart their advance, otherwise Rabbah could never have been conquered. Whether "Aram became subject to David and paid tribute," as the well-known phrase in 8:6 states, is quite doubtful. David may have held his own against the Arameans, winning the occasional battle and capturing a certain amount of material goods from them. Permanent subjugation, however, would have entailed major military campaigns into the Aramean homeland and constant control of the Syrian territories; we do not find any mention of this in the texts.

This much can be stated: David succeeded in protecting his kingdom against external forces while substantially increasing his sphere of influence. He was able to keep the Philistines and the Arameans, the two most powerful opponents in the struggle for political power in the region, at bay. He did not have to fear interference from the north or from the west once he consolidated Judah, Israel, and Canaan in the Palestinian heartlands and subordinated the entire area east of the Jordan to this consolidated kingdom.

David's successor Solomon strengthened the army but, following biblical silence on this issue, did not use it even once. Perhaps we should praise him for this. The biblical authors definitely want to portray him as a king of peace: "During Solomon's lifetime Judah and Israel lived in safety, from Dan to Beer-sheba, all of them under their vines and fig trees" (1 Kgs 5:5).

The Bible does not hide from us, however, that the kingdom established by David already began to crumble under Solomon. An Aramean from the principality of Zobah secured power in Damascus by military force, establishing serious opposition to Israel (11:23–25), and an Edomite prince is said to have returned from Egyptian exile and liberated his country from dependence on Israel (11:14–22). We do not hear that Solomon took any military action against these developments. One specific military event, the incursion of Pharaoh Sheshonq into Palestine, which according to extrabiblical chronology must have occurred during Solomon's rule, is dated by the biblical texts decidedly *after* Solomon's reign: in the fifth year of Rehoboam, Solomon's son and successor (14:25). This redating goes along with information that signals a peaceful relationship between Israel and Egypt under Solomon: his marriage to a daughter of Pharaoh (3:1; 7:8; 9:16; 11:1); and his trade in horses and chariots with Egypt (10:28). On the other hand, we do read that the royal Egyptian court granted asylum to at least two enemies of (David and) Solomon, the Edomite Hadad mentioned above as well as the Israelite Jeroboam, thus more or less directly supporting their eventually successful struggles for independence (11:18–19, 40). This is augmented by the fact that Sheshonq's military campaign was much more directed against northern Israelite than against Judahite cities (see above §II.1.4.1.); this would be quite hard to explain once a protégé of Pharaoh, Jeroboam, had risen to power in Israel. Was Solomon thus involved *at least once* in military conflict and had to suffer defeat? According to 1 Kgs 14:26–28, a passage probably taken from the temple registers, the temple and palace treasure gathered by Solomon was lost and replaced by inferior substitutes: it was impossible to imagine (and would have had severe consequences for the biblical image of this immeasurably wealthy king) that Solomon himself would have been witness to this!

As a last topic, we should look at a strange and offensive variant of ancient military strategy: enacting a ban,[39] that is, utterly exterminating the enemy. The uniqueness of this phenomenon consists in the fact that this military action was not performed for the sake of any secular goal but for the sake of the deity alone. There were of course no wars at the time that were led without any religious implications: each group, each nation, each general, each king was convinced that their deities went into battle with them, as did the deities of the opposing side. Without the help of one's own deity, all was lost and subject to the whim of the foreign deities (see, e.g., 1 Sam 4:7–8; 14:12;

---

39. See Walter Dietrich, "The 'Ban' in the Age of the Early Kings," in *The Origins of the Ancient Israelite States* (ed. Volkmar Fritz and Philip R. Davies; JSOTSup 228; Sheffield: Sheffield Academic Press, 1996), 196–210.

17:37; 28:19; 2 Sam 8:6, 14; 10:12). In many cases, however, this religious element was not the main reason for a war, at least not the main concern of
the narratives. The armies performed their work in a technical, almost pro-
fane manner: the military goals were defined, and strategies and tactics were
chosen. Military engagements were certainly motivated by military, political,
and concrete material gain that leaders and armies hoped to achieve. This was
not the case when enacting a ban. This type of military engagement occurred
rarely and only when the very existence of one's own group was threatened,
leaving the group with nothing to lose and making victory itself the only military goal. In this case, the enemy was placed under a ban (חרם): the enemy
was segregated (this is probably the basic meaning, which can still found in
the Arabic word *harem*) from the secular sphere and handed over completely
to the deity (one's own deity, of course). Nothing could be gained from an
enemy placed under a ban in this manner: no slaves, no women, sometimes
not even spoils. Everyone and sometimes everything had been dedicated to
the deity and had to be handed over to the deity through extermination (the
most radical form of making something useless). David and perhaps already
Saul enacted such a ban against the Amalekites (1 Sam 15; 30). Perhaps the
traditions of the horrendous actions against military adversaries (e.g., the
massacre of Moabite prisoners in 2 Sam 8:2 or the extermination of all the
males in Edom in 1 Kgs 11:16) should also be subsumed under the category
of enacting a ban. We know from the inscription of the Moabite king Mesha
from the second half of the ninth century that these passages are not just
flights of fancy—whether traumatic or utopian—invented by biblical storytellers. The inscription proudly describes a successful enactment of the ban
against Israel, or better against Israelite settlers east of the Jordan (actually
using the biblical term חרם!).

II.2.10. INTERNAL STRIFE AND CIVIL WARS

The establishment of a state in Israel and the resulting development of a
new power center in Palestine occurred in separation from and defense
against other smaller and larger powers in the region. All of Syro-Palestine
was involved in a restructuring of political power; this led in many cases to
the establishment of new states and to the creation of borders and spheres
of influence. The new Israelite state was intent on securing a most favorable
position within this array of various powers. This intention, however, only
describes half of the potential violence inherent in establishing the state.
These external factors were augmented by the grim internal strife that originated from the inner structure of the young Israelite state itself.

From the beginning, Israel was not an ethnically unified national state. The various groups of settlers from the mountain regions already belonged to different ethnic groups and were never a homogenous unit. Immigrants and emigrants, farmers, shepherds, and mercenaries, allies of the Phoenicians, the Canaanites, or the Philistines, northern, central, and southern Palestinian tribes, wealthy and poor, militant and peace-loving individuals—the new state gathered a very colorful group of various different people.

The Israelite and the Judahite "tribes" lived in fundamental tension with the Canaanite cities (especially since these were controlled by the Philistines). The territories of these city-states not only included geographically and ecologically favorable areas but also intruded into the territories between the various tribes that saw themselves more and more as a unit. Since these tribes, following their basic worldview, did not intend to establish city-states but a territorial state, it was only logical that already Israel's first king was faced with the issue of incorporating "Canaan" into the newly established state. The various kings approached this problem along different lines. Saul forcefully attacked the Canaanite city of Gibeon, whose territory reached far into the Benjaminite mountain region (see Josh 9). Even if this venture was initially successful, the seed of this violence bore deadly fruit later on (2 Sam 4; 21). David acted on a much wider scale and, in the end, was also more successful. He defeated the Philistines in battle and thus eliminated the force that protected the Canaanite cities. Even if he possibly had to conquer Jerusalem, he did not destroy it but established it instead as his place of residence (2 Sam 5). He flattered the Gibeonites (2 Sam 21). He was thus able to integrate all the cities into his kingdom, and we read nothing of any force used in the process. Solomon finally placed everything on the Canaanite card: the Jerusalem party secured his rise to the throne (1 Kgs 1), he acknowledged Gibeon as a sacred site (3:4), and he combined the Canaanite cities in his kingdom to separate provinces, thus giving them equal status to the Israelites (4:7–19). From this point on, "Israel" and "Canaan" were one unified state. The old fundamental tension between them, however, had only been covered, not eliminated. The opposition between the urban-hierarchical and the rural-nonhierarchical principles seems to have been one of the driving forces of the history of the states of Israel and Judah right up to their demise; indications for this opposition include several dethroned kings both in the north and in the south as well as the prophetic social criticism that seems to be based on an egalitarian vision for "Israel" and its God YHWH.

The opposition between the Israelite north and Judahite south was another severe source of tension. It grew during the early monarchy and discharged itself again and again, constantly leading to new disruptions—far beyond the end of the monarchy!

Saul's kingdom was oriented toward northern Israel. His adversary and successor David was a Judahite. The Bible narrates how David rose through the ranks in Saul's court and how these two were separated by irreconcilable differences. This is not historically impossible, even if the tendency unilaterally to blame Saul definitely has the taste of propaganda. The incredibly power-sensitive and cunning David soon saw his chance to dethrone Saul from the vantage point of his Judahite home county; the Philistines functioned as a wonderful tool for this task. David was able to act and plan from the south against the north underneath the umbrella of Philistine protection and thus beyond the reach of Saul. If Saul did not reign for a mere two years (as the textually corrupt passage in 1 Sam 13:1 suggests) but perhaps for much longer, then we are faced with the possibility that David already resided as a kind of a Judahite counterking in Hebron during Saul's lifetime. In this role, David caused much more trouble for Saul's son and successor Eshbaal than the Philistines. The Bible tells us in detail of the military encounters between David's and Eshbaal's troops (2 Sam 9). The same camps that would soon be united in one monarchy here face each other as enemies! "There was a long war between the house of Saul and the house of David; David grew stronger and stronger, while the house of Saul became weaker and weaker" (2 Sam 3:1). David pursued his goal of destabilizing the northern Israelite kingdom by military means augmented by diplomacy: with transparent intention, he flattered the inhabitants of Jabesh in Gilead, the most loyal of Saul's supporters besides the Benjaminites (2:4–7); he wed a princess of the Aramean principality Geshur (3:3), thus putting pressure on Eshbaal's kingdom from two sides; he humiliated and weakened the house of Saul by forcing the extradition of princess Michal and by provoking the betrayal—and perhaps even the death—of general Abner (2 Sam 3). Once Eshbaal himself was murdered (2 Sam 4), the northern kingdom fell into David's lap like a ripe apple. It was only a late pro-Judean redactor, however, who inserted the statement that all the Israelites were happy about this fate (5:2). According to an older tradition, Israelite delegates worked out a contract with David, probably with equal measures of tenacity and reluctance, before anointing him king. The foundation of this unified monarchy thus promised anything but harmony for the future.

It seems that Absalom's uprising originated in this duality between Israel and Judah, but it is impossible to determine this for certain, due to the narrator's vague use of language in this context. The term "(all of) Israel" is mentioned frequently, perhaps most strikingly in the summaries that describe the beginning and the end of the uprising: "Absalom sent secret messengers throughout all the tribes of Israel, saying, 'As soon as you hear the sound of the trumpet, then shout: "Absalom has become king at Hebron!" ' " (2 Sam

15:10). After the battle in the hills of Ephraim we read: "The men of Israel were defeated there by the servants of David.... And the troops came back from pursuing Israel..., and all of Israel fled, each man to his tent" (2 Sam 18:7, *16–17). This last comment is clearly related to the secession call of the northern Israelites that was sounded whenever Israel turned their backs on the Davidic dynasty: "Each man to his tent, Israel!" (2 Sam 20:1; see 1 Kgs 12:16). Perhaps Absalom's uprising was supported primarily by northern Israel, even if it took its starting point in Hebron in the southern regions of Judah (2 Sam 15:7–12); this starting point may be a deliberate allusion to the anointing of David by the northern Israelites (5:3). In this reading, Absalom would have promised a kingdom to the Israelites that would have met the contractual terms of the royal covenant better than David's kingdom. The text thus speaks again and again of *Israel* or of the *men of Israel* when it describes Absalom's recruiting methods (2 Sam 15:2–13). All this does not mean that Judahites were not involved in the uprising. Absalom's general Amasa and his advisor Ahithophel were definitely Judahites—and obviously not these two alone. When David made his way back to Jerusalem following his victory in battle, a seemingly bizarre competition arose between Israelites and Judahites over who would have the privilege of bringing the king home, a competition that David skillfully fostered and escalated (19:10–16). If we can trust the narrative, the Israelites—who had just fled!—would have been even more willing to accept any condition than the Judahites. Thus the Judahites had also turned their backs on David and had to be won back once again through clear concessions.

This led immediately to the next conflict between the north and the south. Whether the Israelites were incensed over the repeated favoritism shown the Judahites or disappointed over Absalom's failed uprising, the Benjaminite Sheba had only to blow the horn and spread the secession call so that "all the people of Israel withdrew from David and followed Sheba son of Bichri, but the people of Judah followed their king steadfastly" (2 Sam 20:2). It does not appear that Sheba intended to establish a separate Israelite state, perhaps in continuation of Saul's kingdom, or attack Judah, which had remained Davidic; he simply attempted to remove northern Israel from David's rule—perhaps with the goal of returning Israel to the prestate existence that had been its way of life not so long ago (see Crüsemann). David did not allow this to happen, was not able to allow this to happen, since it contradicted his vision of a state that combined Judah, Israel, and Canaan. His mercenary troops immediately set out after the secessionists; it quickly became clear that the group of hard-core secessionists was quite small and had failed to gather substantial support from anywhere in the land. Sheba was cornered and liquidated in the far north of Israel. Even if northern Israel was not ravaged by major battles during this campaign, we can hardly assume that the Israelites were enthusiastic about this kind of reunification with, or better, prevented separation from, the Judahite south.

We mentioned earlier that the twelve provinces listed in 1 Kgs 4 that were responsible for the upkeep of the royal court and probably also for the supply of conscripted labor were limited to northern Israelite (and Canaanite) territories. If a comparable organization did not exist in Judah—and we have no indication that this was the case—then we must recognize a clear discrimination against the north in relation to the south. All the costs created by the monarchy had to be shouldered by the north on its own, whereas most of the benefits flowed into the south. It is no wonder that the only uprising that the text mentions during the reign of Solomon was instigated by the north and that it was led by a leading figure within the system of conscripted labor that existed in northern Israel, more precisely in Ephraim (1 Kgs 11:28). Jeroboam was unsuccessful at first, being forced to flee into Egyptian exile, but his second attempt achieved its goal. He did, however, first have to wait for Solomon's death and observe how his fellow countrymen started contractual negotiations with the successor Rehoboam. Once the new ruler proved himself completely inflexible in his demands, Israelite frustration broke the dam of Judahite supremacy (they stoned the minister of labor conscription!) and carried the rebel who was waiting in exile to power. It was now no longer possible to restore a nonhierarchical tribal society; the north was faced with the only option of establishing a kingdom of its own. This state, even if unstable, was capable of survival. Attempts at destabilization, following David's example, proved unsuccessful (14:30; 15:5–6, 16, 17–22). It would not take very long before the larger Israel attained greater importance than the smaller Judah. Under the rule of the Omride dynasty, the relation between these two kingdoms had basically reversed the situation under David and Solomon: Judah moved into the role of a junior partner, if not vassal, of Israel. The Davidic Jehoshaphat is said to have exclaimed, "I am as you are; my people are your people, my horses are your horses" (1 Kgs 22:4), when the Omride Ahab called him to participate in a war against the Arameans. Over the course of time, however, Judah seemed to be more fortunate: hidden away in the mountains of southern Palestine, it survived the Assyrian onslaught that destroyed their more important and more exposed brothers—but not without having done their part to facilitate this destruction (2 Kgs 16:7–9). In the end, the Judahite kingdom was destroyed as well, yet the foundation for its spiritual and intellectual survival had already been laid.

III. The Literature of the Time Period

III.1. Hypotheses on the Literature from the Early Monarchy

Dietrich, Walter, and Thomas **Naumann**. *Die Samuelbücher* (EdF 287; Darmstadt: Wissenschaftliche Buchgesellschaft, 1995), partially translated in *Reconsidering Israel and Judah: Recent Studies on the Deuteronomistic History* (ed. Gary N. Knoppers and J. Gordon McConville; SBTS 8; Winona Lake, Ind.: Eisenbrauns, 2000), 276–318.

Biblical research has dealt intensively with the biblical portrait of the early monarchy, its origin and growth. What parts make up the whole, what sources were used, who reworked these sources and when, and what were their intentions? The results of this research include a few large and numerous small hypotheses, almost as many as there are scholars working on these issues. The following discussion can address only some of the more important theories. It will highlight persuasive observations and plausible theories but also pay attention to their inconsistencies and discontinuities. Scholars have postulated several smaller and larger works of historiography: the succession narrative, the narrative of David's rise, the Solomon narrative, the ark narrative, and, finally, the narrative of Samuel's youth. All these histories, including their own sources and layers of redaction, are no more than hypothetical entities. We can hardly prove their once-independent existence, no more than we can prove that they actually originated during the early monarchy and are thus credible as eyewitness accounts.

It is thus not surprising that the most recent research, perhaps with the exception of German-language research, has emphasized synchronic approaches to the final text over against diachronic approaches aimed at the growth process of the text. This change in perspective is justified, as the first chapter of this book has shown. Already in this first chapter, however, we distinguished between the final text produced primarily by a Deuteronomist redaction and a pre-Deuteronomist precursor. Even this older text cannot be seen as a unified body but itself shows traces of diachronic growth.

The refusal to perceive and acknowledge the undeniable signals of textual growth leads to an abandonment of the historical, political, and societal contexts of the text in favor of a literary, aesthetic, and theological profiling of the biblical account of the early monarchy. Such reading threatens to become more two-dimensional and shallow than necessary or appropriate. The books of Samuel and Kings confront us not with novels but with literature containing many traditions. The authors were not free and did not consider themselves to be free and independent in their narrative composition; instead, they incorporated traditions handed down to them. They even distanced themselves from their own work far enough that their own personalities as writers are hard to grasp. We know nothing of their names or their lives. Only their texts may inform us of their intentions and influences—their own texts as well as the manner in which they interacted with earlier texts or information. On the one hand, we need to respect their desire not to step out into the limelight by reading the texts synchronically as a final product. On the other hand, if we understand their redactional activities, their lives and times, our understanding of their texts and stories will gain depth and transparency, and our interpretation will avoid some of the subjectivity and arbitrariness that otherwise threatens.

III.1.1. The So-Called Succession Narrative

Ackerman, James S. "Knowing Good and Evil: A Literary Analysis of the Court History in 2 Samuel 9–20 and 1 Kings 1–2," *JBL* 109 (1990): 41–60. **Bietenhard,** Sophia K. *Des Königs General: Die Heerführertraditionen in der vorstaatlichen und frühen staatlichen Zeit und die Joabgestalt in 2 Sam 2–20; 1 Kön 1–2* (OBO 163; Fribourg: Universitätsverlag; Göttingen: Vandenhoeck & Ruprecht, 1998). **Blenkinsopp,** Joseph. "Theme and Motif in the Succession History (2 Sam XI,2ff.) and the Yahwist Corpus," in *Volume du Congrès: Genève, 1965* (VTSup 15; Leiden: Brill, 1966) 44–57. **Blum,** Erhard. "Ein Anfang der Geschichtsschreibung? Anmerkungen zur sog. Thronfolgegeschichte und zum Umgang mit Geschichte im alten Israel," *Trumah* 5 (1996): 9–46. **Brueggemann,** Walter. "On Trust and Freedom: A Study of Faith in the Succession Narrative," *Int* 26 (1972): 3–19. **Carlson,** R. A. *David the Chosen King: A Traditio-Historical Approach to the Second Book of Samuel* (Stockholm : Almqvist & Wiksell, 1964). **Conrad,** Joachim. "Der Gegenstand und die Intention der Geschichte von der Thronfolge Davids," *TLZ* 108 (1983): 161–76. **Delekat,** Lienhard. "Tendenz und Theologie der David-Salomo-Erzählung," in *Das Ferne und nahe Wort: Festschrift Leonhard Rost zur Vollendung seines 70. Lebensjahres am 30. November 1966 gewidmet* (ed. Fritz Maass; BZAW 105; Berlin: Töpelmann, 1967), 26–36. **Dietrich,** Walter. *Prophetie und Geschichte: Eine redaktions-*

geschichtliche Untersuchung zum deuteronomistischen Geschichtswerk (FRLANT 108; Göttingen: Vandenhoeck & Ruprecht, 1972). **Dietrich.** *David, Saul und die Propheten: Das Verhältnis von Religion und Politik nach den prophetischen Überlieferungen vom frühesten Königtum in Israel* (2nd ed.; BWANT 122; Stuttgart: Kohlhammer, 1992). **Dietrich.** "Das Ende der Thronfolgegeschichte (2000)," in *Von David zu den Deuteronomisten: Studien zu den Geschichtsüberlieferungen des Alten Testaments* (Stuttgart: Kohlhammer, 2002), 32–57. **Flanagan,** James W. "Court History or Succession Document? A Study of 2 Samuel 9–20 and 1 Kings 1–2," *JBL* 91 (1972): 172–81. **Hübner,** Ulrich. *Die Ammoniter: Untersuchungen zur Geschichte, Kultur und Religion eines transjordanischen Volkes im 1. Jahrtausend v.Chr.* (ADPV 16; Wiesbaden: Harrassowitz, 1992). **Kaiser,** Otto. "Beobachtungen zur sogenannten Thronnachfolgeerzählung Davids," *ETL* 64 (1988): 5–20. **Langlamet,** François. "Pour ou contre Salomon? La rédaction prosalomonienne de I Rois I–II," *RB* 83 (1976): 321–79, 481–528. **Langlamet.** "David et la maison de Saül: Les épisodes 'benjaminites' des II Sam. IX; XVI,1–14; XIX,17–31; I Rois, II,36–46," *RB* 86 (1979): 194–213, 385–436, 481–513; 87 (1980): 161–210; 88 (1981): 321–32. **McCarter,** P. Kyle. "'Plots, True or False': The Succession Narrative as Court Apologetic," *Int* 35 (1981): 355–67. **Otto,** Eckart. "Die 'synthetische Lebensauffassung' in der frühköniglichen Novellistik Israels," *ZTK* 74 (1977): 371–400. **Pury,** Albert de, and Thomas **Römer,** eds. *Die sogenannte Thronfolgegeschichte Davids: Neue Einsichten und Anfragen* (OBO 176; Fribourg: Universitätsverlag; Göttingen: Vandenhoeck & Ruprecht, 2000). **Rad,** Gerhard von. "Der Anfang der Geschichtsschreibung im alten Israel," in idem, *Gesammelte Studien zum Alten Testament* (3rd ed.; TB 8; Munich: Kaiser, 1965), 148–88. **Rost,** Leonhard. *Die Überlieferung von der Thronnachfolge Davids* (BWANT 42; Stuttgart: Kohlhammer, 1926), repr. in *Das kleine Credo und andere Studien zum Alten Testament* (Heidelberg: Quelle & Meyer, 1965), 119–253, trans. as *The Succession to the Throne of David* (trans. Michael D. Rutter and David M. Gunn; Sheffield: Almond, 1982). **Seiler,** Stefan. *Die Geschichte von der Thronfolge Davids (2 Sam 9–20; 1 Kön 1–2): Untersuchungen zur Literarkritik und Tendenz* (BZAW 267; Berlin: de Gruyter, 1998). **Veijola,** Timo. *Die ewige Dynastie: David und die Entstehung seiner Dynastie nach der deuteronomistischen Darstellung* (AASF B/198; Helsinki: Suomalainen Tiedeakatemia, 1975). **Veijola.** "Salomo—der Erstgeborene Bathsebas," in *Studies in the Historical Books of the Old Testament* (ed. J.A. Emerton; VTSup 30; Leiden: Brill, 1979), 230–50, repr. in idem, *David: Gesammelte Studien zu den Davidüberlieferungen des Alten Testaments* (Helsinki: Finnische Exegetische Gesellschaft, 1990), 84–105. **Veijola.** "David und Meribaal," in idem, *David*, 58–83. **Whybray,** R. N. *The Succession Narrative: A Study of II Samuel 9–20; I Kings 1 and 2* (SBT 2/9; Naperville, Ill.: Allenson, 1968). **Würthwein,** Ernst. *Die Erzählung von der Thronfolge Davids—Theologische oder politische Geschichtsschreibung?* 1974 (ThSt 115; Zürich: Theologischer Verlag, 1974), repr. in idem, *Studien zum Deuteronomistischen Geschichtswerk* (BZAW 227; Berlin: de Gruyter, 1994), 29–79.

In 1926 Leonhard Rost threw a stone into the waters of biblical research that continues to cause waves. He discovered the history of the succession to David's throne, the so-called "succession narrative," as an independent source; today scholars are no longer certain that this source ever existed. According to Rost, the succession narrative included 1 Sam 4–6; 2 Sam 6–7; 9–20; and 1 Kgs 1–2. In terms of the quantity and range of genres, these texts cover a wide area and are connected only by the fact that they all deal with the subject matter of the succession to David's throne.

Rost's claim is most surprising with respect to the ark narratives in 1 Sam 4–6 and 2 Sam 6, since these texts do not seem to deal with the succession but rather—as indicated by the title—with the ark, an important cultic object in the Jerusalem temple. The text clearly states that it was David who brought the ark to Jerusalem and his successor Solomon who placed it in the temple. More important, however, is the fact that the ark narrative ends with a conflict between David and Michal, the daughter of Saul and one of David's wives (2 Sam 6:16, 20–23). This conflict ends with the statement that Michal did not bear any of David's children—for Rost, this statement is directly relevant to the succession to David's throne.

We encounter a similar situation in 2 Sam 7. The chapter contains many themes—the issue of the delayed construction of the temple (7:1–11a) or David's piety expressed in a long prayer (7:18–29)—that are not directly related to the succession. The issue of succession does appear, however, in 7:11b and 16, which led Rost to conclude that the narrator of the succession narrative incorporated both of these texts and the ark narrative as prior sources; according to Rost, this narrator shows his skill particularly in the fact that he leads his readers slowly to the issue most important to him.

This main issue is fully present in 2 Sam 9. The text deals with the question whether Jonathan's son Meribaal, a member of the former royal family, might be eligible for succession to the throne; 2 Sam 9 indicates that this possibility will not be an option, and the continuing narrative confirms this fact. In 2 Sam 10 the issue of succession is once again absent: the text narrates the conflict with the Ammonites and their allies, the Arameans. In 2 Sam 11, however, we discover why all this—according to Rost, another prior source— had to be inserted at this point. During this conflict, David became involved with Bathsheba and fathered Solomon, who would ultimately sit on David's throne. At the end of the chapter, the reader does not yet know that this will be the case. Several older sons of David were the first candidates for the throne: Amnon, Absalom, Adonijah. However, none of them would win the race to the throne; they all lost their lives in the process.

Amnon was David's firstborn. We do not hear whether he aspired to the throne, yet he was first in line to succeed his father. He lost everything, however, on account of his heinous behavior toward his half-sister Tamar, the sister of David's second-born, Absalom. Absalom murdered Amnon and was thus first in line for the throne. After leaving the country so that the dust could settle over his fratricide, he returned—and immediately worked toward replacing David. This goal was premature, since David was not yet willing to step down. Absalom paid for the conflict between father and son with his life. These tumultuous events gave rise to Sheba's rebellion. Although with Sheba David did not eliminate a direct rival, he was successful with Joab's help in preventing a loss of power in the north of his kingdom.

A gap in the narrative follows these events. The issue of succession has come to a halt. We reencounter David as a weak old man close to death, as is indicated by the short narrative of Abishag of Shunem (who will become the very reason for the death of the next candidate for the throne, Adonijah). Adonijah presented himself publicly as the future king, only to be overwhelmed by the well-known events that led to Solomon's surprising claim to the throne: Adonijah's celebration at En-rogel; the secret conversations in David's bedroom; and the anointing of Solomon at Gihon. The outcome was cruel but in a sense unavoidable: Adonijah and his most important supporters were eliminated, and in the end "the kingdom was established in the hand of Solomon" (1 Kgs 2:46).

This, according to Rost, is the culmination of the entire narrative: the report of how Solomon, not a member of the house of Saul and not one of Solomon's older brothers, rose to the throne. The narrative was concerned with explaining and legitimizing this somewhat surprising outcome. According to Rost, the succession narrative was not simple propaganda—it is too complex and abysmal to be that blatant—but was written "in majorem gloriam Salomonis" (1965, 128). This conclusion is supported by the few instances where the narrator reports how God himself evaluated the events. According to 2 Sam 11:27, David's behavior in the Bathsheba-Uriah affair was "evil in the eye of YHWH"; this led to the death of Bathsheba's first son and to the birth of her second son, Solomon. Of Solomon, the text reports very explicitly that YHWH *loved* him (12:24). Later, at the turning point of Absalom's rebellion, the rebel decided to follow Hushai's (poisoned) advice and turned against Ahithophel's (fully correct) advice. The narrator comments that YHWH had ordained this to happen; thus judgment was pronounced on the person who was the most serious candidate for the throne besides Solomon.

For the rest, Rost believed that God's views were not conveyed by the narrator but placed in the mouths of other characters. (He did not yet entertain the heretical thought that the narrator is capable of irony and fully aware that humans speak erroneously of God). The narrator had God intervene in earthly affairs on very few occasions. Once Uriah had been murdered, YHWH sent Nathan to David and "struck" Bathsheba's first child. In all other instances, human beings carry the plot—perhaps with God acting through them. YHWH is recognized indirectly in the course of events (132). The situation is entirely different in the ark narrative, which the narrator used as a prior source!

Rost examined the succession narrative not only according to its external features (scope, composition, use of sources) and its subject matter (succession to David's throne) but also in terms of its artistic merit. With great care he showed the various stylistic devices used by the narrator: the use of vocabulary and images, the characterization of the figures, the interconnection of scenes and plot lines (110–25). He concluded that his discussion showed that the succession narrative was a cohesive whole unified by stylistic and formal features (132).

Regarding the time of the narrative's composition, Rost explicitly supported the idea that it was written during Solomon's reign in the tenth century B.C.E. (127); the author could have been Abiathar or Zadok's son Ahimaaz or any other person not directly mentioned but connected to the court. After all, Rost concluded, a mere debate over names cannot hide the fact that this author was one of the greatest narrators in the Hebrew language (128).

To this day Rost's careful and impressive reasoning has granted his thesis almost canonical standing, at least within German Old Testament scholarship. Nevertheless, there are several gaps and difficulties that we must examine more closely.

The *theme* of the large narrative unit postulated by Rost (succession to David's throne) is not as clear as Rost would like to believe. This is most obvious with regard to the so-called prior sources. To include the ark narrative in the succession narrative merely because of the few verses in 2 Sam 6:16, 20–23 is like wagging the dog by the tail. His statement that the large chapter 2 Sam 7 centers exclusively on verses 11b and 16 is hardly more convincing. Scholars now believe that these verses, which speak about David's "eternal house," are quite late additions by a Deuteronomistic redaction (Veijola 1975, 72ff.; Dietrich 1992, 116ff.). Rost believed that verses 13b, 22–24 were Deuteronomistic, whereas verses 8–11a, 12, 13a, 14–15, 17 were pre-Deuteronomistic additions; the remaining text belonged to the original succession narrative. This suggestion is not tenable. It also remains unclear who would have inserted 2 Sam 8 into the supposedly coherent narrative of 2 Sam 7 and 9ff., since 2 Sam 9 itself is much more focused on David replacing Saul than Solomon replacing David. The chapter tries to show David's generosity toward the house of Saul; it does not address the question of who will succeed him. The reports of the wars with the Ammonites and the Arameans in 2 Sam 10 are much more closely connected to the war chapter 2 Sam 8 than to the topic of succession. In contrast, the war narrative 2 Sam 11:1 and 12:26–31 clearly functions as the frame for the Bathsheba-Uriah affair, which itself only reports the birth of the future successor at the very end. Although the large narrative complex of Amnon, Tamar, and Absalom in 2 Sam 13–20—including Absalom's rebellion and Sheba's apostasy—artfully combines many different individual narratives into a cohesive whole, this whole is concerned with many different topics (events in the house of David, relations between the father and his sons and his sons with each other, men and women, political strife and civil war during David's reign, tensions between Judah and Israel and a war of secession). The question of succession to the throne is at most only part of the general context. The issue of succession appears, one might say for the first time, in 1 Kgs 1–2.

These observations have led many scholars—especially where Rost was not as influential as in German-language exegesis—to suggest a different theme for the narratives of 2 Samuel. R. A. Carlson believes that, whereas the Deuteronomistic depiction (he does not even assume earlier sources!) portrays David as blessed in 1 Samuel, 2 Samuel portrays David as cursed. Joseph Blenkinsopp emphasizes that the text deals not only with David's "succession" but also with his "legitimization" (1966, 47). James W. Flanagan superscribes the David narratives with the deliberately open title "Court History." David M. Gunn self-consciously titles his book not "Succession Story," but *The Story of King David,* a story that starts not with 2 Sam 9 (or earlier sources) but rather with 2 Sam 2. The story is concerned with David's rise to the throne, his reign, and the establishment of his dynasty; Solomon and his claim to power are but a secondary issue. Joachim Conrad mentions David's use and preservation of power as a central theme of the succession narrative (a title that he oddly retains). This use of power is described paradigmatically in the way in which David deals with the people around him. It remains to be asked whether the above-mentioned issues can be solved by new emphases and titles.

The next problem centers on the *intention* of the succession narrative. Based on such pro-Solomonic passages as 2 Sam 12:24–25 and 1 Kgs 1–2, it is understandable how Rost could claim that the narrative displayed a strongly positive attitude toward Solomon (128). Rost never questioned that the text displayed a pro-*Davidic* attitude. In many instances, however, we encounter quite a different attitude to David and definitely to Solomon. We can exclude the so-called prior sources, since the narrator—if Rost's theory is correct—merely allowed other voices to be heard by including them. The Bathsheba-Uriah narrative in 2 Sam 11 undoubtedly portrays David in the darkest colors. With great care and cleverness, Nathan succeeds in manipulating David into confessing his sin (2 Sam 12). This confession deflects the deserved death penalty from him to the son conceived in adultery and allows the next son, Solomon, to be the child of a legitimate encounter, but no one can believe this birth story to be honorable—the scandal leaves an indelible blemish. The negative aspects continue when Solomon's mother Bathsheba, inspired by Nathan, conspires on behalf of her son and appeals to an oath that had never been mentioned before, leaving the reader with decidedly mixed feelings about the whole thing. The reader shudders even more in the face of the list of targets designated for liquidation that Solomon accepts following his ascent to the throne. The fact that David himself created this list (1 Kgs 2:5–10) is no real comfort; we find ourselves asking why David did not take action in these cases himself and why he commands Solomon to do so now. As a matter of fact, David's portrait in the so-called succession narrative is a mixture of light and shadow. He is not only an adulterer and murderer but also the one who sends Tamar to Amnon, thus sharing in the responsibility for her rape; he is the one who allows the rapist to go unpunished but sends him in the end to his murderer; he is the one who eventually forgives Absalom his fratricide, who fails to resist his preparations for rebellion, and thus also who contributes to the events that lead to his son's death; he is the one who is unable to control the violent Joab and Abishai, who does not restrain Adonijah (with his promoter Joab!)—not to forget the portrait of a feeble, shivering, impotent old man that 1 Kgs 1:1–4 dares to paint! David is the one who, in the end, is at the mercy of Bathsheba's and Nathan's intrigues and causes—willingly or not—the death of another son, Adonijah. Pro-Solomonic? Pro-Davidic?

Critical scholarship has reacted to these narrative features (known also to Rost but not considered very important) in various ways. In his commentary on Jeremiah, Bernhard Duhm suggested already in 1901 that this prophet was a member of the family of Abiathar, who had been exiled by Solomon to Anathoth. Because Abiathar was the author of the succession narrative, Jeremiah's writing skills could be seen as a family trait. This theory would explain a certain animosity against Solomon combined with the great loyalty and admiration for David that accompanied Abiathar throughout his life. Rost commented on this quaint theory, that if Abiathar were to be seen as an author at all, he would more likely be the author of the narratives on David's rise in which he plays a much more prominent role (128). We, of course, can say nothing about Abiathar's writing skills. There are also several exegetes who do not see an attitude critical of Solomon and pro-Davidic, but the other way around (and much more radically than Rost!), a tendency toward pro-Solomonic and criticism of David. Eckart Otto suggests that upon his rise to power Solomon acted with wisdom, strictness, and decisiveness; he thus avoided the mistakes made by the hesitant, wavering, mistaken David (1977, 386). Stefan Seiler pursues this line of thought even further (1998, 184–86), suggesting that David's mourning over Absalom was completely without reason and that the narrator fully agreed with Joab's critique of the weepy king (2 Sam 19). These interpretations are questionable, to say the least! According to R. N. Whybray, the succession narrative is a propagandistic body of wisdom teaching that portrays both David and Solomon as exemplary figures. P. Kyle McCarter simply refers to the narratives as "court apologetic" written in the form of Hittite royal propaganda. The fact that the kings are not displayed throughout in golden colors of adoration is due to the fact that the truth was known and could not be completely hidden. In contrast, Lienhard Delekat follows a very different and highly critical interpretation when he suggests that the entire succession narrative aimed to portray David and Solomon, and, as a matter of fact, the entire monarchy as such, in a negative light. Würthwein, Langlament, Veijola, and Bietenhard attempt to reconcile these opposite tendencies by resorting to diachronic analysis and distinguishing between an older, almost contemporary, critical version and a milder, younger version that was added over the course of the monarchic era or even during the time of the exile.

All this presents us with a new problem that must be addressed: the question of the *unity* or *disunity* of the succession narrative. Rost already identified certain passages as secondary additions, but these passages are minor compared to the radical cuts made into Rost's carefully described body of texts by more recent historical-critical scholarship.

Rost believed that 2 Sam 12:7b–12 (Nathan's very expansive threat that follows his brief but harsh "You are the man" in 7a); 14:25–27 (the description of Absalom that interrupts the narrative flow); 18:18 (the insertion of the notice on the memorial for Absalom); 20:23–26 (the list of David's officials); and 1 Kgs 2:3–4, 11 (a typically Deuteronomistic royal phrase) were secondary additions. More recent historical-critical scholars such as Würthwein, Langlamet, Veijola, and Bietenhard attribute much larger passages to later additions and redactional activity:

> ➤ the so-called Benjaminite episodes (esp. in 2 Sam 9; 16; 19), which are intended to show that David did not usurp the throne but always acted with mercy and generosity toward members of Saul's house;
> ➤ the report on the first military conflicts with the Ammonites and the Arameans, which portray David as an innocent victim of Ammonite aggression but also as a wise and skilled military leader;
> ➤ the stories on Nathan's first appearance and the death of Bathsheba's first son in 2 Sam 12, which show that David was not an unrepentant tyrant and that Solomon was not the result of the adultery with Uriah's wife;
> ➤ the exoneration of David and simultaneous incrimination of Joab connected to the return of the future rebel Absalom to Jerusalem in 2 Sam 14 and to his subsequent liquidation in 2 Sam 18;
> ➤ the introduction of David's loyal advisor Hushai and the defamation of his David-critical opponent Ahithophel in 2 Sam 17;
> ➤ the very pro-Solomonic speeches as well as David's last will, which excuses Solomon's murders in 1 Kgs 1–2.

The diachronic separation of an original text decisively critical of David and Solomon and later pro-Solomonic, pro-Davidic redaction(s) has the benefit of leaving us with an original text that has clear outlines and unambiguous intentions. On the one side, we have the old succession narrative, of which the beginning no longer exists, but that included the Bathsheba-Uriah scandal and the birth of the crown prince as its first complete narrative; on the other side, we have the cynical statement, "Thus the kingdom was established in the hand of Solomon" (1 Kgs 3:1). In between these two boundaries we encounter a collection of depressing stories in which members of the royal household play the leading roles: David as an adulterer and murderer, obsessed with power and his sons, all without exception frightening individuals, rampant, vain, mischievous, vengeful, murderous, and power-hungry; Solomon as one who gained the throne by intrigue and a coup d'etat and whose first actions proved him to be a bloody tyrant. This narrative was written soon after the events themselves. The author was well informed of the activities of the royal court, but he also often claimed to know what he could not have known. He hardly belonged to the inner royal circle, including the circle around the defeated candidate Adonijah, but was rather from among democratically minded Israelite citizens where basic norms of human behavior were still important and where the behavior of the royal family was met with a mixture of anger and disgust, especially since the entire people of Israel had to suffer the consequences (see further Würthwein).

This extremely cynical original succession narrative was dulled and mitigated by later redactors who placed these narratives in the service of quite different intentions. The stories were no longer meant to uncover the misdoings of the royal family, of the monarchy in general; instead, they were to portray David and Solomon as capable and successful rulers who may not have been free from temptation but who were ultimately leaders blessed with divine favor (see Langlamet and Bietenhard on the pro-Solomonic redaction during the time of the monarchy). These rulers would prove God's faithfulness to his promises to David despite all the malpractice and confusion (see Veijola on the Deuteronomistic redaction of the exile). The precise relation of these added redactional layers, including the texts that belonged to each, has not been fully clarified.

One interesting aspect of the historical-critical dissection of Rost's succession narrative deserves to be highlighted. Rost, and subsequently Gerhard von Rad with even greater emphasis, focused on the three passages in 2 Sam 11:27b; 12:24–25; 17:14b, in which God's judgment on individual actions is reported to the reader. Von Rad contrasts these texts with the reticence otherwise practiced by the narrator, who merely creates psychological and politically plausible causal connections between different events. In these three cases, however, the author reveals his basic conviction that God ultimately does guide history—not by interrupting the chain of events with miraculous interventions but by silently working behind events that seem initiated by human beings alone. Von Rad could not praise this combination of educational concern and simple, deep-seated piety too highly. In light of recent scholarship, however, all three of these passages should be seen as secondary additions to the text and thus cannot be used to describe the worldview of the author of the succession narrative!

As tempting as it may be to separate the tensions in the text according to different textual layers, we cannot neglect the problems that accompany this approach. In a Jewish understanding of tradition, it is not at all normal for those passing on the tradition to turn the work of their predecessors completely on its head. Such radical changes as proposed above, where a text critical of David, Solomon, and the monarchy became a text highly in favor of David, Solomon, and the monarchy, can hardly be found anywhere else in the Hebrew Bible, starting from the prehistory to the legal codices and the prophetic texts to Job and the books of Chronicles—not to mention later rabbinic interaction with traditional material. The rule does not disprove the possibility of the exception, but the various tendencies and textual layers cannot even be clearly separated in our case (see Dietrich 2000 = 2002).

➤ The transition from the Bathsheba-Uriah narrative to the Nathan narrative in 2 Sam 11:27b—one of the three "theological" passages—is said to be a secondary addition because the phrasing that "the thing that David had done was evil in the eyes of YHWH" is reminiscent of Deuteronomistic language (Dietrich 1972). This is correct, but we must not neglect the fact that David himself exhorts Joab through a messenger two verses earlier—in an unquestionably original context— that "the thing should not be evil your eyes" (12:25).

➤ One of the Benjaminite episodes is the narrative on Shimei the Benjaminite, who severely curses David during his flight from Jerusalem. This Shimei throws himself at David's mercy upon his return and is eventually liquidated by Solomon, as David had commanded (2 Sam 16:5–13; 19:17–24; 1 Kgs 2:8–9, 36–46). This outcome does not match the supposed tendency of all Benjaminite episodes to portray David as merciful and generous. (Or is it another Shimei in 1 Kgs 1–2 than in 2 Samuel?)

➤ The individual characters of the succession narrative are often so ambiguous that it is impossible to locate them within one or another textual layer. Is David's indulgence of his sons only a weakness, his grief over his escape from Jerusalem mere play-acting, his cleverness in infiltrating Absalom's inner circle only negative, his pain over the loss of his son not real and moving, his helplessness in old age not touching? What is the narrator's attitude toward Bathsheba, Nathan, Jonadab, Zadok, and Abiathar, and to which textual layer do they and their actions belong? Why are figures such as Ahithophel and Joab only partially incriminated, retaining characteristics that are admirable and profound?

➤ Certain clearly pro-David and pro-Solomonic passages cannot be excised from the original succession narrative without severely damaging the careful narrative web of interacting events and dialogues. If a redactor had first introduced Joab as the person who brought Absalom back from exile (2 Sam 14), then the motive for the execution of the rebel prince, initiated personally by Joab, would disappear (2 Sam 18). It is also impossible to separate the measures taken by David to prevent the death of his son—also in the presence of Joab!—out of their narrative context; the refusal of the soldiers to follow Joab's order because of David's prior command and the race between two messengers to David in Mahanaim would be incomprehensible. As a whole, the repeated messenger scenes with Jonathan and/or Ahimaaz either show pro-Davidic (2 Sam 15; 17), pro-Davidic and Joab-critical (2 Sam 18), or pro-Solomonic (1 Kgs 1) tendencies; to excise them from the narrative would mean destroying its structure.

The succession narrative as defined by Rost is not a unified narrative work of a single author. Nevertheless, we should treat any attempt to reduce this narrative to a completely coherent original form, without tension and with a clear narrative intention, with great caution.

A final problem with Rost's hypothesis and certainly its current historical-critical variants remains: we cannot ignore the fact that the succession narrative *has no real beginning*. It is impossible for such a piece of narrative art, even in its original form as described by Würthwein, to begin with the sentence, "In the spring of the year, the time when kings go out to battle" (2 Sam 11:1). Even if this first sentence were to be explained as a reference to 2 Sam 10 (but why connect these texts in the first place?), the following text would use the characters of David and Joab without properly introducing them. The original beginning must thus either be reworked or lost. It was not without reason that Rost went all the way back to the ark narrative, not only because these narratives seemed connected thematically, but also because he did not find a convincing beginning anywhere else. If we include his so-called prior sources, then all main characters (except for David!) and even secondary characters are fully introduced (so Rost 1965, 124). But where are Joab and his brother Abishai introduced, or Abiathar (and Zadok)?[1] Further, why do the very short "introductions" of Amnon and Absalom (as "sons of David" in 2 Sam 13:1) as well as Adonijah (as "son of Haggith" in 1 Kgs 1:5) not mention that they are respectively the *oldest* sons of David—a fact of utmost interest to the question of succession? In the case of Adonijah, this information is given at a later point; it is presented in such a casual fashion that the text seems to assume that readers are already aware of this fact (1 Kgs 2:15). On the other hand, we cannot determine from 2 Sam 11 what rank Solomon had among the royal sons (probably a very low rank, which would explain why Adonijah had so many prominent supporters and why Solomon's rise to the throne had to be initiated by an intrigue that came as a complete surprise to his rivals).

From this point of view, the succession narrative would become much easier to understand if the two lists of David's sons in 2 Sam 3:2–5 and 5:14–16 were a part of it. There we encounter the order Amnon–Chileab[2]–Absalom–Adonijah, followed by five other sons and, finally, in the tenth position, Solomon. We also discover in the narrative of David's rise what is otherwise lacking: the previous history of Joab and Abiathar, both so very important for the succession narrative (2 Sam 2–3; 1 Sam 22:20–23). These are very noticeable connections that bridge the apparent gap between the two narrative works on King David (one on his rise to power and the other on his succession), but they are not the only ones.

➤ The "Benjaminite episodes" also find their prehistory in the narratives on David's rise, especially the Meribaal scenes (2 Sam 9; 16:1–4; 19:25–31) that are connected to the stories of David's friendship with Jonathan (1 Sam 18:1, 3; 20:12–17, 24b; 23:16–18), to the redactional notices 2 Sam 4:2b–4, and to David's lament over Jonathan and Saul (2:19–27).

➤ David justifies the execution of Joab to Solomon by referring to his murders of Amasa and Abner (1 Kgs 2:5); the first of these murders is narrated in 2 Sam 3:27. The motif of the "sons of Zeruiah," whom David views with great suspicion (19:23), is prepared in 1 Sam 26:6–8; 2 Sam 2:18–23; 3:27, 39, among others.

---

1. 2 Sam 10:7ff. already assumes that the reader is familiar with these two officers; 2 Sam 8 is not part of the succession narrative; the two do not appear in the ark narrative or in Nathan's promise. The two priests also appear in 2 Sam 15:24 without introduction.

2. A son of Abigail who is otherwise completely absent from the Davidic traditions. This fact warns us against simply assuming the same *author* for these lists and the succession narrative.

➤ The sudden appearance of the ark (2 Sam 11:11; 15:24–25) and the tent in which it is located (1 Kgs 2:28–30) seems to assume a previous tradition such as 2 Sam 6. Rost's theory of a "previous source" is not the only possible explanation.

➤ The motif of "shedding innocent blood" ties together the narratives of David's rise and the succession narrative (1 Sam 25:26, 31, 33; 2 Sam 1:16; 4:11; 16:7–8; 1 Kgs 2:5–6, 32–33, 37).

It might be possible to explain these bridges between the succession narrative and the narratives of David's rise as secondary connections—by the hand of the pro-Solomonic (Langlamet) or Deuteronomistic redactor (Veijola). However, not all the connections can be explained convincingly in this manner. Exegetes using a more synchronic approach have taken an opposite route and attempted to extend the succession narrative—which then can hardly retain this title—beyond its beginning, at least back to 2 Sam 1–5 (Flanagan, Gunn), if not further back into 1 Samuel. In this case, we would not be dealing with two separate narratives, a succession narrative and a narrative of David's rise, but with one unified Davidic narrative. This prompts the question: Who wrote this narrative, and what sources did he use? This question will continue to occupy us.

III.1.2. The So-Called Narrative of David's Rise

Alt, Albrecht. "Die Staatenbildung der Israeliten in Palästina," in idem, *Kleine Schriften zur Geschichte des Volkes Israel* (3rd ed.; 3 vols.; Munich: Beck, 1964), 2:1–65, trans. as "The Formation of the Israelite State in Palestine," in idem, *Essays on Old Testament History and Religion* (trans. R. A. Wilson; Garden City, N.Y.: Doubleday, 1968), 223–309. **Brueggemann**, Walter. *David's Truth in Israel's Imagination and Memory* (2nd ed.; Minneapolis: Fortress, 2002). **Conrad**, Joachim. "Zum geschichtlichen Hintergrund der Darstellung von Davids Aufstieg," *TLZ* 97 (1972): 321–32. **Dick**, Michael B. "The 'History of David's Rise to Power' and the Neo-Babylonian Succession Apologies," in *David and Zion: Biblical Studies in Honor of J. J. M. Roberts* (ed. Bernard F. Batto and Kathryn L. Roberts; Winona Lake, Ind.: Eisenbrauns, 2004), 3–20. **Dietrich**, Walter. *David, Saul und die Propheten: Das Verhältnis von Religion und Politik nach den prophetischen Überlieferungen vom frühesten Königtum in Israel* (2nd ed.; BWANT 122; Stuttgart: Kohlhammer, 1992). **Dietrich**, ed. *David und Saul im Widerstreit: Diachronie und Synchronie im Wettstreit: Beiträge zur Auslegung des ersten Samuelbuches* (OBO 206; Fribourg: Academic; Göttingen: Vandenhoeck & Ruprecht, 2004). **Ficker**, R. "Komposition und Erzählung: Untersuchungen zur Ladeerzählung (1 S 4–6; 2 S 6) und zur Geschichte vom Aufstieg Davids (1 S 15–2 S 5)" (diss. theol., Heidelberg, 1977). **Fischer**, Alexander A. *Von*

Hebron nach Jerusalem: Eine redaktionsgeschichtliche Studie zur Erzählung von König David in II Sam 1–5 (BZAW 335; Berlin: de Gruyter, 2004). **Grønbæk,** Jakob H. *Die Geschichte vom Aufstieg Davids (1.Sam.15 – 2.Sam.5): Tradition und Komposition* (AThD 10; Copenhagen: Munksgaard, 1971). **Gunn,** David M. *The Fate of King Saul: An Interpretation of a Biblical Story* (JSOTSup 14; Sheffield: JSOT Press,1980). **Kaiser,** Otto. "David und Jonathan: Tradition, Redaktion und Geschichte in I Sam 16–20: Ein Versuch," *ETL* 66 (1990): 281–96. **Klein,** Johannes. *David versus Saul: Ein Beitrag zum Erzählsystem der Samuelbücher* (BWANT 158; Stuttgart: Kohlhammer, 2002). **Lemche,** Niels Peter. "David's Rise," *JSOT* 10 (1978): 2–25. **Lingen,** Anton van der. *David en Saul in I Samuel 16–II Samuel 5: Verhalen in politiek en religie* ('s-Gravenhage: Boekencentrum, 1983). **McCarter,** P. Kyle. "The Apology of David," *JBL* 99 (1980): 489–504. **Mettinger,** Tryggve N. D. *King and Messiah: The Civil and Sacral Legitimation of the Israelite Kings* (ConBOT 8; Lund: Gleerup, 1976). **Mildenberger,** Friedrich. "Die vordeuteronomistische Saul-Davidüberlieferung" (diss. theol., Tübingen, 1962). **Nübel,** Hans Ulrich. "Davids Aufstieg in der Frühe israelitischer Geschichtsschreibung" (diss. ev. theol., Bonn, 1959). **Rendtorff,** Rolf. "Beobachtungen zur altisraelitischen Geschichtsschreibung anhand der Geschichte vom Aufstieg Davids," in *Probleme biblischer Theologie: Gerhard von Rad zum 70. Geburtstag* (ed. Hans Walter Wolff; Munich: Kaiser, 1971), 428–39. **Rost,** Leonhard. *Die Überlieferung von der Thronnachfolge Davids* (BWANT 42; Stuttgart: Kohlhammer, 1926), repr. in *Das kleine Credo und andere Studien zum Alten Testament* (Heidelberg: Quelle & Meyer, 1965), 119–253, trans. as *The Succession to the Throne of David* (trans. Michael D. Rutter and David M. Gunn; Sheffield: Almond, 1982). **VanderKam,** James C. "Davidic Complicity in the Deaths of Abner and Eshbaal: A Historical and Redactional Study," *JBL* 99 (1980): 521–39. **Veijola,** Timo. *Die ewige Dynastie: David und die Entstehung seiner Dynastie nach der deuteronomistischen Darstellung* (AASF B/193; Helsinki: Suomalainen Tiedeakatemia, 1975). **Weiser,** Artur. "Die Legitimation des Königs David: Zur Eigenart und Entstehung der sogen. Geschichte von Davids Aufstieg," *VT* 16 (1966): 325–54. **Whitelam,** Keith W. "The Defence of David," *JSOT* 29 (1984): 61–87.

Already in 1926 Leonhard Rost had considered whether the succession narrative as he defined it was a not particularly unified part of a larger whole or whether this narrative had not been preceded by reports on David's earlier deeds and experiences. There is indeed such material in 1 Sam 23; 27; 29–30; and 2 Sam 3–5, but an analysis of these passages shows, as he stated, that they form a coherent depiction of David's flight from Saul as well as the events that led to his rule over Judah and Israel and his conquest of Jerusalem, and that the style and the composition of this narrative, as well as the narrator's attitude toward cultic practices, are quite different from what can be observed in the succession narrative (Rost 1965, 132–33).

These observations laid the groundwork for the suggestion of an independent narrative of David's rise. Although Albrecht Alt used this theory for his presentation of the history of the early monarchy (1964, 15, 36), (German-language) scholarship did not develop it in detail until thirty years later. Two dissertations (Nübel and Mildenberger) attempted such a reconstruction, but it was not until a 1966 essay by Artur Weiser and a book by Jakob Grønbæk five years later that the "narrative of David's rise" appeared as a clearly defined narrative work. It seemed that its scope, its influences, its location, and its intention had been analyzed convincingly.

The narrative work thus postulated stretched from 1 Sam 15 (or 16) to 2 Sam 5 (or 8) and narrated the fate of David beginning with his appearance at Saul's court and including his adventures following his escape from Saul (first in the Judean desert, then among the Philistines), his actions following the death of Saul, his inauguration as king first of Judah, then of Israel, and, finally, his location to Jerusalem, perhaps including the initial stages of building his kingdom—thus the rise of David from a shepherd boy to the most glorious ruler of Israel.

Unlike the succession narrative, the narrative of David's rise has a "mosaic character" (Weiser). There are hardly any continuous narrative strands that hold the entire work together, as is the case with the succession narrative (we have to think only of the quartet David–Bathsheba–Nathan–Solomon that shapes the plot in 2 Sam 11 and 1 Kgs 1–2). In contrast to the general Joab and the messengers Ahimaaz and Jonathan in the succession narrative, the characters are described in much less detail, with the possible exception of the main characters David and Saul. We are hard-pressed to find plot development to the degree present in 2 Sam 13–20, where all events are a direct consequence of Amnon's rape of Tamar, and we cannot find large-scale chiastic structures of the kind present in 2 Sam 15–19, where David's departure from and return to Jerusalem are narrated in mirror fashion.

This leads to the conclusion that the narrator of the story of David's rise could not or did not want to compose his narrative with the same degree of freedom as the narrator of the succession narrative; he was more likely the collector of preexisting material—probably in oral, not written, form—than the creative author of a narrative history. Researchers have consequently suggested that these texts are closer to the actual events than the succession narrative, as the narrator of the former felt more bound by what he had heard. The only exception may be the narrative block in 2 Sam 2–5, where the text describes the formation of the state and the plot develops sequentially, almost in the style of the succession narrative. Here the author seems to show his full artistic talent. (Alexander A. Fischer has identified an extended redactional activity in just these chapters which he dates into the seventh century B.C.E.) This does not mean that the remaining text was put together merely as a conglomerate of disparate materials. Several narrative features and stylistic devices can be explained only if we assume an intentional composition of the whole.

For example, the statement that YHWH was *with* David, which explains David's good fortune, connects all the various texts. On the other hand, David seems to seek out interaction with YWHW much more than in the succession narrative. Several scenes describe divine inquiry by oracle, prophetic assistance, and so forth, which portray David's actions as guided by God (see 1 Sam 23:2, 4, 9–12). Even the text in 1 Sam 18ff., which comprises several separate scenes, is knit together by various narrative strategies: the rival opposition between Saul and David; the formal regular alternation between short notes and detailed narratives (Rendtorff); or the motif of David's *flight* from Saul. The narrator also enjoys combining parallel but also apparently opposing narratives, resulting in narrative sequences and clear narrative sections (e.g., the double narration of David's sparing of Saul in 1 Sam 24; 26; the repeated victory song by the women in 1 Sam 18:7; 21:12; 29:12). The first impression that these texts are a conglomerate of unconnected individual traditions thus turns out to be false.

The intention of such a history of David's rise seems obvious. The texts describe with great sympathy and admiration how David inexorably and single-mindedly moved toward his final goal, despite adversaries, obstacles, and several detours forced upon him. It is almost as if God's elected possessed an inner compass that never allowed him to stray too far from his path and that always brought him back to his goal. It is most admirable (and most emphasized by the narrator!) that David always kept his hands clean and his conscience pure despite danger and temptation, more to the point, that God enabled him to keep them clean. David was relentless only toward external enemies such as the Philistines or the Amalekites. Toward his own enemies he showed almost immeasurable patience and generosity; he was truly aware that God was "with him" and that he did not have to defend his own cause. From beginning to end the history of David's rise shows "the tendencies to legitimate David by YHWH" (Weiser). This endeavor is easily understood once we consider that David was not the son of his predecessor and that almost all of the family of his predecessor had died prematurely. The suspicion must have been great that David's rise to the throne was too good to be true, that David may have usurped the throne. Once scholars discovered parallels to the apology of the Hittite king Hattušiliš III—a usurper who also claimed to be the youngest among his brothers, persecuted and driven into exile, who returned to "liberate" his own people and assume power with divine approval—this line of thinking exploded: the history of David's rise was an "apology of David" (McCarter, Whitelam). It became the consensus among scholars that all the crimes of which the texts absolve David were indeed committed by him (Lemche, VanderKam). For if we take out all the passages that are clearly pro-Davidic, then we are left with facts that must scare any nonprejudiced reader. The fact that such an "apology" would be located in Jerusalem, with the circles of the Davidic court and historically in close proximity to David himself, is an obvious conclusion.

It is quite interesting to follow how these ideas were anticipated outside of exegetical circles by modern creative writers. In his *König David Bericht* (1972), the novelist Stefan Heym presents an imaginative, ironic-critical portrayal of the creation of the history of David's rise and the succession narrative in the Jerusalem of Solomon. With varying approaches, other more recent David novels attempt an empathic view of the early Israelite monarchy and its characters (Joseph Heller, *God Knows*, 1984; Torgny Lindgren, *Bathsheba*, 1984; Grete Weil, *Der Brautpreis*, 1988; Allan Massie, *Ich, König David*, 1996). It is quite entertaining and insightful to follow the intuition of these authors.[3]

We should keep in mind, however, that the existence of a separate, self-contained historical work about David's rise, very old and with its own clear intention, is not as certain as the description above may have indicated, even if this is the consensus among many scholars in this area.

The first problem arises with the observation that this self-contained historical work has no clear *narrative beginning or ending*. David first appears in 1 Sam 16, but he has already been announced earlier, even though his name is not explicitly mentioned (1 Sam 13:13–14; 15:28). In addition, Jonathan already begins to surpass his father Saul in 1 Sam 14: he is the crown price who will not strive for kingship himself but will pass it over to David. Is this not the first instance of a general theme that will determine all of David's rise, even before David appears on the scene? There are also several parallels between narratives of David's rise and the Saul narratives, and it is hardly possible to read one without the other (Samuel anoints both Saul and David [1 Sam 10; 16:13]; Saul is "among the prophets," once at the beginning of his career and once in the presence of David [10:11–12; 19:23–24]).

Just as we encounter an open beginning, we also find no clear ending separating the history of David's rise from the so-called succession narrative. Such an ending is most often seen in 2 Sam 5. However, the notice that David had defeated "the Philistines from Gibeon to Gezer" (5:25) is hardly a convincing final sentence. Such a sentence might be found in 5:10 or 5:12, two comments praising David's accomplishments, but it would be difficult to

---

3. See Walter Dietrich, "Von einem, der zuviel wußte," "Gott, Macht und Liebe," and "Der Fall des Riesen Goliat," in idem, *Von David zu den Deuteronomisten: Studien zu den Geschichtsüberlieferungen des Alten Testaments* (Stuttgart: Kohlhammer, 2002), 100–112, 113–19, 120–33.

separate these comments from the previously reported conquest of Jerusalem (5:6–9), the list of the sons who were born in Jerusalem (5:13–16), and the ark narrative (2 Sam 6); these texts clearly presume the victory over the Philistines (5:17–25). Once the ark arrives in Jerusalem, the issue of temple construction (7:1ff.) is a logical next step, which itself leads directly to the promise of a dynasty (7:11ff.). Rost claimed that 2 Sam 6 and 7 introduced the succession narrative, and we noted that the succession narrative presumes much of what is narrated in the history of David's rise (e.g., the list of sons in 2 Sam 3; 5; the introduction of the characters of Abiathar, Joab, and Abishai). Thus these two narrative works can be separated only with a certain degree of violence.

We could, of course, resort to the theory that all these links connecting the history of David's rise with its immediate and extended contexts are secondary additions by a redactor. The question as to who might have combined such varying narrative works or sources as the history of David's rise, the succession, and the ark narrative, as well as the Saul narratives, is perhaps best answered by referring to Deuteronomistic redactors. Timo Veijola has proposed this supposition most stringently. He starts with 1 Kgs 1–2 (as did Rost!) and separates a secondary, pro-Davidic and pro-Solomonic layer, which he classifies as Deuteronomistic. He then examines, working backwards, all the material not merely from the succession narrative but from all Davidic narratives, searching for texts that are related to the redactional layer in 1 Kgs 1–2. In the narratives of David's rise these include primarily statements by David himself in which he professes his innocence toward the family of Saul (2 Sam 3:28–29, 38–39; 4:2b–4), as well as statements by other parties that declare his kingship to be God's will (Jonathan: 1 Sam 20:12–17; 23:16–18; Saul: 24:18–23a; Abigail: 25:*21–34; Abner: 2 Sam 3:9–10, 17–19; the tribes of Israel: 5:1–2).

Despite their obvious strengths, these suggestions contain a twofold weakness. The language used in most of the passages referred to as Deuteronomistic differs from what is usually referred to as Deuteronomistic language, as influenced by Deuteronomy. Regarding the subject matter, there are several other passages in the narratives of David's rise and the succession narrative that are closely related to those chosen by Veijola, passages for which he with good reason does not dare to postulate Deuteronomistic authorship. For example, David also insists on his innocence in 1 Sam 24:7, 11–15; 26:18–20; 27:1; 2 Sam 1:13–16. Saul's words in 1 Sam 24:18–23 are hardly different from those in 26:21–25, and Abigail's speech in 1 Sam 25 is closely connected to the speech of the wise woman of Tekoa in 2 Sam 14 (a passage that, if secondary, is usually seen as a pre-Deuteronomistic prodynastic addition to the text).

The Deuteronomistic redactors were not the first to hold a pro-Davidic, prodynastic position; in fact, such a position is somewhat surprising for a group of redactors working soon after the collapse of the Davidic state. A pro-Davidic and prodynastic attitude was most likely present among individuals, writers, or redactors commenting on e· ·nts during the monarchy. In any case, these deliberations lead us to the question of the *unity* or *disparity* of the narratives in 1 Sam 15 (or 16)–2 Sam 5 (or 8). If this material does not owe its composition primarily to the Deuteronomistic redaction, then we are faced with a pre-Deuteronomistic, prodynastic redaction of the text. It is true that the nature of the narratives on David's rise as seen with a critical eye have repeatedly fostered the suspicion that these narratives were not written as a unified whole (perhaps even during the early monarchy). The material is too disparate, even contradictory, and without a clear intentional goal. As long as scholars still assumed that the pentateuchal sources reached into the books of Samuel, these observations made for rewarding work along simple lines of explanation. The various reports of David's appointment to Saul's court (1 Sam 16–17), the repeated marriage (or cancelled marriage) with one of Saul's daughters (18:17–27), Saul's repeated sparing of David (1 Sam 24; 26), the repeated defection to the Philistines (21:11–16; 27:1–7), the repeated portrayal of Saul's death (1 Sam 31; 2 Sam 1)—What could be more obvious than explaining these phenomena with a source hypothesis, by suggesting that two formerly independent narratives had been combined into a whole? As much as recent scholarship follows a diachronic paradigm, it tends toward a kind of supplementary hypothesis, according to which an older original layer was expanded by a later supplementary layer. The vast disparity, however, of the suggested models of diachronic growth gives little reason to hope for a consensus on this issue. The isolation and reordering of the texts that supposedly belonged to the original layer presents the greatest challenge and seems to be an almost hopeless hypothetical enterprise. Thus the *original layer*, most often dated to the early monarchy, is regarded as pro-Saul and pro-Davidic (Nübel) or only pro-Davidic (Mildenberger, Kaiser) or pro-Saul (Humphreys, van der Lingen). The *supplementary layer*, most often dated after 722 B.C.E., is viewed as critical of the monarchy (Nübel) or decidedly pro-Davidic (Mildenberger, Humphreys, van der Lingen, Kaiser). It seems that some consensus has been found at least on this last issue—which is not surprising, considering the basic attitude of the so-called narrative of David's rise.

A composition-critical approach seems more promising than the above-mentioned theories. Tensions and inconsistencies in a narrative work may point not merely to the joining of two older sources or to the supplementation of an older narrative by a later author. A *single* author may also have composed *his* work from prior existing material that was not or only partially combined previously. In the case of the author of the narrative on David's rise, this would mean that he took the (separate) materials passed on to him, brought them into a plausible chronological sequence, connected them as well as possible, added a few comments here and there, and thus created for the first time a narrative opus describing the rise of King David. This theory could do without any need for unity in style and intention. The author as described above may not have seen it as a burden but rather as an advantage that David was introduced in several different ways, that Saul was repeatedly spared, that there were two versions of Saul's death. Even more, he seems to have repeated certain passages and statements himself. He did not intend to compose a smooth one-dimensional portrait of David and his rise; rather, he emphasized its many facets and the depth of meaning behind them. He also did not dare to use his own imagination but passed on information that he had received previously—perhaps even from oral sources.

This leads us to the question regarding the context of *location and time* in which this historical work was composed. Even if we do not deny but rather accept as a likely hypothesis that this narrative opus was still expanded and redacted following its composition, then the scope of sources used in this narrative was quite large. We have not succeeded in isolating a large later redactional layer, with the exception of single traces of Deuteronomistic redaction. This has serious consequences for our attempts to date the text. If even those stories that scholars often classify as secondary are part of the narrative of David's rise, then we lose the possibility of maintaining a very early date for the narration. This includes the very legendary story of David's anointing in 1 Sam 16:1–13, the almost baroque story of David's victory over Goliath in 1 Sam 17, or Abigail's courtly speech in 1 Sam 25. None of these texts is a possible product of the early monarchy. The situation may be different in regard to the narratives of David as a weapon carrier and musician in 1 Sam 16:14–23, the narratives of the conflict between David and the landowner Nabal in 1 Sam 25, or the narrative of David's sparing of Saul in the cave at En-gedi in 1 Sam 24. This material may have been transmitted to the narrator of the history of David's rise as an oral tradition and may contain very old material at its core. The very interconnected narrative in 2 Sam 2–4 may have itself been an old narrative collection before it was incorporated into its present context. Finally, on several occasions we find a direct source reference, indicating a written source (2 Sam 1:17).

Although some doubts remain, we may be able to date the so-called history of David's rise (or better, the textual layer in the books of Samuel connected to this history) to the time of Hezekiah (see Conrad). This would imply dating the text to the time assumed for the supplementary redactional layer by historical-critical exegesis. Following the collapse of the northern kingdom in 722 B.C.E., which brought many fugitives bearing their own traditions to the south, there may have been a perceived need to deal with the subject matter contained in these texts: the transfer of power from the Benjaminites (i.e., the northern Israelite Saul) to the Bethlehemites (the Judahite David). The many controversies and conflicts between Israel and Judah following the division of the kingdom handed down to us in the books of Kings allow us to suppose that the north never forgot certain irregularities that were part of this transfer of power. Israel's first king had not been forgotten, including the fact that he had been a northern Israelite. His memory was held in honor in the north, even though this memory was not worth much in the south. This is indicated by the narrative of Saul's death in 1 Sam 31, which was included in the history of David's rise, as well as by many Saul traditions in the first half of 1 Samuel that paint quite a positive picture of Israel's first king.[4]

This leads us to conclude that the textual layer examined here was created in Judah, more precisely in Jerusalem, and that its author, or those who transmitted the material, were open to the perspective of the (recently destroyed) northern kingdom. This explains their openness for including material on Saul. It seems as if a Judahite author incorporated northern Israelite material in order to compare and contrast the first two kings as representatives of north and south. (Johannes Klein demonstrates precisely this in intrinsic analyses of those texts that compare Saul and David in a direct or indirect manner.)

Finally, we should comment on the *tendency* of the narratives contained in this textual layer. The suggestion that the texts represent Jerusalem court propaganda is closely tied to the supposed early date of this material. We could indeed imagine an apologetic-polemic literary opus during the time of David or Solomon, even shortly after the division of the kingdom, that painted David in glorious colors while creating a very dark picture of Saul. Over the course of time, however, especially following the collapse of the northern kingdom, this need for excessive black-and-white imaging would have decreased. Only a very vengeful spirit indeed would have presented the depressed and decimated northerners with the summary evaluation: "It had to happen like this because it was God's will!" The David and Saul narratives, however, do not display such a vengeful spirit. King Saul is not just the villain, and David is not the perfect hero (cf. once more Klein). After all, the main role is played by God. He is the one who carries David throughout

---

4. Against W. Boyd Barrick ("Saul's Demise, David's Lament, and Custer's Last Stand," *JSOT* 73 [1997]: 25–41), who argues that these narratives are pro-Davidic and critical of Saul.

his life, almost like a child who discovers that his fortune occurs without his own doing, without his own understanding, and without confronting any real dangers that might throw him into the abyss. Saul also initially experiences God as incredibly present and generous, but this experience changes as God becomes stern and withdrawn and Saul's own fate more and more obscure and unmanageable. Saul is thus faced with a situation in which every event is an occasion for mistake and tragedy.

Apart from this theological level, the characters Saul and David are also not portrayed as psychological antitypes. Saul is a winning character, at least in the beginning, and toward the end we feel sorry for him instead of being disgusted by him. His speeches to David, after he has been spared, are full of insight and sadness (1 Sam 24:18–22; 26:21–25). As much as we (following Near Eastern custom) can associate a man's family with him, we encounter noble characters among Saul's relatives: Jonathan, Michal, Eshbaal, and Abner. The narrator does not confront his readers with a one-sided Saul-critical point of view. The same is true for the character of David, whose actions following the death of members of Saul's family are determined by respect and loyalty (which, in truth, also works in David's favor, yet we should not suspect David of opportunism; such suspicion would of course have been far from the narrator's mind). Concerning David, on the one hand, he is the heroic figure; on the other hand, he is not above human weakness. He is the one whose actions lead to the massacre of the priests of Nob (which he clearly confesses, 1 Sam 22:22); he is guilty of attacking the physical integrity of Saul (which leaves him with a guilty conscience, 1 Sam 24:5–6); he immediately resorts to a bloody vendetta because Nabal does not submit to his demands (a vendetta that Abigail barely prevents, as David himself admits, 1 Sam 25:34); he defects to the national enemy, the Philistines (1 Sam 27); he allows himself to be used in the war against Saul's kingdom (even if not as an aggressor, 2 Sam 2). He consistently operates with great cleverness, strategic wit, and success. The portrayal certainly commands respect but not necessarily sympathy.

We may thus describe the intention of the Saul-David narratives as pro-Davidic but not as propagandistic. We are not dealing with a political pamphlet but with great narrative art that is addressed to its historical readers and that also provides us today with much reason for our own careful, thoughtful, and critical reading of the text. These narratives paradigmatically provide us with the portrayal of a certain time period in Israel's history, to confront us with the discussion of not only historical but also important theological and ethical issues: the dialectic between election and rejection; the relation between human and divine wills; the interrelatedness of fate and sin; the need for and the limits of state power; the tension between politically advantageous and ethically responsible action; the relation between politics and religion; the double existence of Israel as an independent polity and as the people of God; and the contrast and comparison of different political interest groups in Israel. All exegesis of these texts must take this intention into account.

III.1.3. The Ark Narrative

Brueggemann, Walter. *Ichabod toward Home: The Journey of God's Glory* (Grand Rapids: Eerdmans, 2002). **Campbell,** Antony F. *The Ark Narrative (1 Sam 4–6; 2 Sam 6): A Form-Critical and Traditio-Historical Study* (SBLDS 16; Missoula, Mont.: Scholars Press, 1975). **Davies,** Philip R. "The History of the Ark in the Books of Samuel," *JNSL* 5 (1977): 9–18. **Dietrich,** Walter. *Samuel* (BKAT 8/1.3, 4; Neukirchen-Vluyn: Neukirchener, 2006, 2007). **Dus,** Jan. "Der Brauch der Ladewanderung im alten Israel," *TZ* 17 (1961): 1–16. **Ficker,** R. "Komposition und Erzählung: Untersuchungen zur Ladeerzählung (1 S 4–6; 2 S 6) und zur Geschichte vom Aufstieg Davids (1 S 15–2 S 5)" (diss. theol., Heidelberg, 1977). **Flanagan,** James W. "Social Transformation and Ritual in 2 Samuel 6," in *The Word of the Lord Shall Go Forth: Essays in Honor of David Noel Freedman in Celebration of His Sixtieth Birthday* (ed. Carol L. Meyers and Michael O'Connor; Winona Lake, Ind.: Eisenbrauns, 1983), 361–72. **Fohrer,** Georg. "Die alttestamentliche Ladeerzählung," *JNSL* 1 (1971): 23–31, repr. in idem, *Studien zu alttestamentlichen Texten und Themen (1966–1972)* (BZAW 155; Berlin: de Gruyter, 1981), 3–10. **Gutmann,** Joseph. "The History of the Ark," *ZAW* 83 (1971): 22–30. **Janowski,** Bernd. "Keruben und Zion: Thesen zur Entstehung der Zionstradition," in *Ernten, was man sät: Festschrift für Klaus Koch zu seinem 65. Geburtstag* (ed. Dwight R. Daniels, Uwe Glessmer, and Martin Rösel; Neukirchen-Vluyn: Neukirchener, 1991), 231–64. **Maier,** Johann. *Das altisraelitische Ladeheiligtum* (BZAW 93; Berlin: Töpelmann, 1965). **Miller,** Patrick D., Jr., and J. J. M. **Roberts.** *The Hand of the Lord: A Reassessment of the "Ark Narrative" of 1 Samuel* (Baltimore: Johns Hopkins University Press, 1977). **Rost,** Leonhard. *Die Überlieferung von der Thronnachfolge Davids* (BWANT 42; Stuttgart: Kohlhammer, 1926), repr. in *Das kleine Credo und andere Studien zum Alten Testament* (Heidelberg: Quelle & Meyer, 1965), 119–253, trans. as *The Succession to the Throne of David* (trans. Michael D. Rutter and David M. Gunn; Sheffield: Almond, 1982). **Schäfer-Lichtenberger,** Christa. "Beobachtungen zur Ladegeschichte und zur Komposition der Samuelbücher," in *Freiheit und Recht: Festschrift für Frank Crüsemann zum 65. Geburtstag* (ed. Christof Hardmeier, Rainer Kessler, and Andreas Ruwe; Gütersloh: Gütersloher, 2003), 323–38. **Schicklberger,** Franz. *Die Ladeerzählungen des ersten Samuel-Buches. Eine literaturwissenschaftliche und theologiegeschichtliche Untersuchung* (FB 7; Würzburg: Echter, 1973). **Seow,** Choon Leong. *Myth, Drama, and the Politics of David's Dance* (HSM 44; Atlanta: Scholars Press, 1989). **Smelik,** Klaas A. D. "The Ark Narrative Reconsidered," in *New Avenues in the Study of the Old Testament: A Collection of Old Testament Studies, Published on the Occasion of the Fiftieth Anniversary of the Oudtestamentisch*

Werkgezelschap and the Retirement of Prof. Dr. M. J. Mulder (ed. A. S. van der Woude; OTS 25; Leiden: Brill, 1989) 128–44. **Smelik.** "Hidden Messages in the Ark Narrative," in idem, *Converting the Past: Studies in Ancient Israelite and Moabite Historiography* (OTS 28; Leiden: Brill, 1992) 35–58. **Willis,** John T. "An Anti-Elide Narrative Tradition from a Prophetic Circle at the Ramah Sanctuary," *JBL* 90 (1971): 288–308.

The so-called ark narrative tells of events that occurred during the time of David (2 Sam 6) as well as before the time of Saul (1 Sam 4–6). Thus this narrative could have been composed during the early monarchy, with even older sources. According to Rost, as described above (§III.1.1.3), the ark narrative was one of the sources handed down to the succession narrative, which itself was thought to have been written during the time of Solomon. Standing at the other extreme in terms of dating is the hypothesis that the entire ark narrative was written only during the time of the exile (Smelik).

Smelik believes that the narrative is a parable on the time of the exile. Just as Judah is now (partially) in exile, the ark "then" went into exile, and just as the ark "then" found its way back home, the Diaspora will also find their way back home. God himself will bring this about, just as he did "then." The ark narrative also specifically reacts to the fact that the Babylonians had stolen the sacred artifacts from the temple, just as the Philistine had done "back then." Even if the respective texts no longer mention the ark (it probably fell victim to the flames when the temple burned; see 2 Kgs 25:13–17; 2 Chr 36:18; Ezra 1:9–11), the ark may have been the symbol for the whole temple inventory. In my view, it would be nothing short of heroic to tell a story of a sacred artifact only once it had been destroyed or robbed. It seems much more likely that such stories were told (still) while the ark existed and was venerated: during the monarchy. There is no need to dispute that the ark narrative would have been given a new and sad relevance during the time of the exile, but this is hardly the context in which it was first told. This hypothesis is already contradicted by the fact that we can easily separate truly exilic, that is, Deuteronomistic, passages from the rest of the text: 1 Sam 2:27–36*; 4:8; 6:6). We can also clearly recognize that only the ark is exiled in the ark narrative, with Israel remaining in its own country, whereas the Babylonian exile was all about the inhabitants being taken from their home country.

According to the old and still convincing theory presented by Rost, the ark narrative is an etiological tale explaining what the ark was and how it came to be in Jerusalem. Its *Sitz im Leben* was the Jerusalem temple cult, and its addressees were pilgrims and worshipers who took part in the activities of this temple. This presumes that both parts of the narrative, 1 Sam 4–6 (probably with an introduction in 2:12–17, 22–25, *27–36) and 2 Sam 6, originally belonged together, which has recently been disputed by several scholars (see

Schicklberger; Miller and Roberts). They argue that David's introduction in 2 Sam 6 is too abrupt, that the terminology used in both parts is too divergent, and that it can hardly be supposed that someone would have split an original narrative into two sections so far apart. These objections are outweighed by arguments that, in my view, carry much more weight. In both parts the narrative tells not of persons but of a cultic artifact; both sections connect the ark to the cherubim and to YHWH who is enthroned above the cherubim (1 Sam 4:4; 2 Sam 6:2); both narrate how the ark, because YHWH is enthroned above it, develops its own forceful and even threatening activity; both narrate how the ark goes on a journey, with Jerusalem as its final goal (even the itinerary in 1 Sam 5–6 seems to point to Jerusalem, not Kiriath-jearim [1 Sam 7:1] as its destiny); and in both cases the "house of Abinadab on the (cultic) hill" is the starting point for the last leg of the journey (1 Sam 7:1; 2 Sam 6:3–4). We can thus hardly avoid the conclusion that 1 Sam 4–6 and 2 Sam 6 belong together, at least within the context of tradition history. This is also a strong argument against using 1 Sam 4(–6) as the supposed original beginning of the Samuel narratives while denying the existence of an ark narrative (Willis, Gitay, see §III.1.4 below).

Even assuming that chapters 1 Sam 4–6 and 2 Sam 6 belong together, some scholars doubt that this material is a literary unit. For example, Georg Fohrer uncovers four to five separate textual layers, of which at least the oldest goes back to the early monarchy. However, the arguments presented in this case can hardly be called convincing. Tensions in the final text do not necessarily presuppose different sources; they are also—and better—explained in the context of tradition or redaction history.

There have been several remarkable observations especially in the context of the possible tradition background of these texts. Originally the ark was probably a kind of palladium of war for the northern Israelite tribes. By rescuing this artifact from oblivion and bringing it into his new capital, David was able to foster Israelite loyalty to him and simultaneously to endow the new capital of the entire kingdom with a religious sanctity (Flanagan, Gutmann). Solomon then placed this portable and formerly mobile cultic artifact into the holy of holies of the new (or rededicated) sanctuary on Mount Zion (1 Kgs 8:1–13). Important beliefs connected to this artifact had to disappear in light of this development. On the other hand, however, the ark now became a central, perhaps even the central, part of the developing faith in YHWH's mighty presence on Mount Zion (Janowski). Since this belief gained supreme importance in the eighth century, especially following the failed siege of Jerusalem in 701 B.C.E., Schicklberger assumes that the ark narrative was created during this time.

III.1.4. THE SO-CALLED NARRATIVE OF SAMUEL'S YOUTH

Birch, Bruce C. *The Rise of the Israelite Monarchy: The Growth and Development of 1 Samuel 7–15* (SBLDS 27; Missoula, Mont.: Scholars Press, 1976). **Brueggemann,** Walter. "I Sam 1: A Sense of Beginning," *ZAW* 102 (1990): 33–48. **Dietrich,** Walter. *David, Saul und die Propheten: Das Verhältnis von Religion und Politik nach den prophetischen Überlieferungen vom frühesten Königtum in Israel* (2nd ed.; BWANT 122; Stuttgart: Kohlhammer, 1992). **Dus,** Jan. "Die Geburtslegende Samuels I.Sam 1. (Eine traditionsgeschichtliche Untersuchung von I.Sam 1–3)," *RSO* 43 (1968): 163–94. **Gitay,** Yehoshua. "Reflections on the Poetics of the Samuel Narrative: The Question of the Ark Narrative," *CBQ* 54 (1992): 221–30. **Gordon,** R. P. "Who Made the Kingmaker? Reflections on Samuel and the Institution of Monarchy," in *Faith, Tradition, and History: Old Testament Historiography in Its Near Eastern Context* (ed. Alan R. Millard, James K. Hoffmeier, and David W. Baker; Winona Lake, Ind.: Eisenbrauns, 1994), 255–69. **Hylander,** Ivar. *Der literarische Samuel-Saul-Komplex (1 Sam 1–15): Traditionsgeschichtlich untersucht* (Uppsala: Almquist & Wiksell, 1932). **Lehnart,** Bernhard. *Prophet und König im Nordreich Israel: Studien zur sogenannten vorklassischen Prophetie im Nordreich Israel anhand der Samuel-, Elija- und Elischa-Überlieferungen* (VTSup 96; Leiden: Brill, 2003). **Mommer,** Peter. *Samuel: Geschichte und Überlieferung* (WMANT 65; Neukirchen-Vluyn: Neukirchener, 1991). **Noth,** Martin. "Samuel und Silo," *VT* 13 (1963): 390–400. **Polzin,** Robert M. "The Speaking Person and His Voice in 1 Samuel," in *Congress Volume: Salamanca, 1985* (VTSup 36; Leiden, Brill, 1986), 218–229. **Rendtorff,** Rolf. "Die Geburt des Retters: Beobachtungen zur Jugendgeschichte Samuels im Rahmen der literarischen Komposition," in idem, *Kanon und Theologie: Vorarbeiten zu einer Theologie des Alten Testaments* (Neukirchen-Vluyn: Neukirchener, 1991), 132–40, trans. as "The Birth of the Deliverer: 'The Childhood of Samuel' Story in Its Literary Framework, in idem, *Canon and Theology: Overtures to an Old Testament Theology* (trans. Margaret Kohl; Minneapolis: Fortress, 1993), 135–45. **Schley,** Donald G. *Shiloh: A Biblical City in Tradition and History* (JSOTSup 63; Sheffield: JSOT Press, 1989). **Tsevat,** Matitiahu. "Die Namensgebung Samuels und die Substitutionstheorie," *ZAW* 99 (1987): 250–54. **Weiser,** Artur. *Samuel: Seine geschichtliche Aufgabe und religiose Bedeutung: Traditionsgeschichtliche Untersuchungen zu 1 Samuel 7–12* (FRLANT 81; Göttingen, Vandenhoeck & Ruprecht, 1962). **White,** Marsha. "'The History of Saul's Rise': Saulide State Propaganda in 1 Samuel. 1–14," in *"A Wise and Discerning Mind": Essays in Honor of Burke O. Long* (ed. Saul M. Olyan and Robert C. Culley; BJS 325; Providence, R.I.: Brown Judaic Studies, 2000), 271–92. **Wicke,** Donald W. "The Structure of 1 Sam 3: Another View," *BZ* 30 (1986): 256–58. **Willis,** John T. "Cultic Elements in the Story of Samuel's Birth and Dedication," *ST* 26 (1972): 33–61.

Scholars have often seen 1 Sam 1–3 as a separate composition with its own tradition history. This narrative is concerned with Samuel, the miraculous events surrounding his birth, his dedication by his mother to temple service under Eli in Shiloh, and the divine revelation foretelling Eli's end. Two scenes are inserted into this narrative progression: the description of Eli's evil sons (1 Sam 2:12–17, 22–25); and a story of a nameless man of god who presented Eli with a lengthy oracle of woe (2:27–36). These latter texts have nothing to do with Samuel, but only with the future fate of the house of Eli.

This topic warrants a few additional comments. First, the speech by the man of God reaches into a distant future. It foretells not only the catastrophes of 1 Sam 4 (the defeat of the Israelites by the Philistines, the loss of the ark, and the eradication of the house of Eli) but also the massacre of the priests of Nob by Saul (1 Sam 22) and even the cult centralization under Josiah that removes the cultic privileges of the rural priests (2 Kgs 23). We can hardly avoid the conclusion that this prophecy is a *vaticinium ex eventu* and, at least in its final form, a Deuteronomistic creation (see Mommer). It may contain an older strand belonging to the ark narrative (see III.1.3). Second, the scenes describing the evil performed by the house of Eli directly prepare for the catastrophic events in 1 Sam 4. Because the priests of the ark were priests of this kind, the ark could not aid Israel in war! There are many reasons to understand both scenes together with the introduction of Eli's sons and the ark in 1 Sam 1:3 as integral parts of the ark narrative, which was placed by a later redaction in its present context (Dietrich). If we assume that the narratives of Samuel and of the house of Eli were connected before the Deuteronomistic redaction, we are forced to include also 1 Sam 4(–6) with 1 Sam 1–3; otherwise, the former scenes would have no ending. Third, this combination of 1 Sam 1–3 with 1 Sam 4–6 and perhaps even 1 Sam 7—we should only think of the appearance of the place name Ebenezer in 4:1 and 7:12—led to strong objections to separating the Samuel narratives from the ark narratives (Gitay; Willis). On the other hand, these materials are divergent enough that the assumption of separate origins remains probable. Thanks to redactional skill, however, which created a unified text despite these differences, it is appropriate and fruitful to perform a synchronic analysis apart from diachronic questions.

The actual narrative of Samuel's youth describes the fate given to Samuel at birth: he was to be leader of Israel. At first, however, it almost seemed as if there would be no birth; the story of the barren Hannah, who did receive a son in the end, thanks to an oracle given by Eli almost by accident (1 Sam 1), is one example of the fact that famous men are often provided with a miraculous birth story.[5]

---

5. The motif is a standard element of many legends and fairytales. In this context it should suffice to refer to the birth narratives of Moses and Jesus. The closest formal connection to Samuel's birth narrative in 1 Sam 1 is Samson's birth narrative in Judg 13.

The oscillation of the central motif שאל in 1 Sam 1 between the names שמואל and שאול, only the first of which is explained etiologically, led older research to propose a radical hypothesis regarding the tradition history of this text: originally 1 Sam 1 did not tell the story of Samuel's birth but rather of Saul's birth (Hylander; Dus; more recently Gordon). Such proposals lead to suppositions that no longer can be verified and should be avoided, especially since the present etiology would have been fully acceptable to ancient Hebrew ears (Tsevat) and because the possible reference to the name *Saul* may have been known and intended by the original narrators.

The origin of this narrative may be found in the fact that the mother gratefully dedicated her son to the deity (1 Sam 2), eventually leading to the consecration of the child as a Nazirite, a kind of monastic existence. Samuel thus became Eli's servant—and very soon the deity no longer addressed the master but rather his apprentice (1 Sam 3); in other words, Samuel quickly rose above Eli. According to the present text, God announced the end of Eli and his sons to Samuel (3:11–14), which presupposes a connection to the ark narrative. The original text may have instead spoken of Eli's replacement by Samuel or other momentous events (Dietrich; Mommer). In any case, the narrative ends with the comment that Samuel became the leading man (of God) in Israel (3:19–21).

Normally we would not regard the youth stories of famous men as particularly bestowed with historical credibility, especially if they contain miraculous elements. The story of Samuel's youth has often been referred to as "idyllic" and regarded as a creation of a much later time, full of colorful imagination and pious legend. As Martin Noth pointed out, one aspect that does not fit this assumption is the motif of Samuel's service in the temple of Shiloh. For later generations, Samuel was a prophet, not a priest, and Shiloh (according to 1 Sam 4; Jer 7:12) was a place beset with horrible memories that would not have been arbitrarily connected to one of Israel's honored leaders. Can we thus assume that there is some historical memory that shines through the narrative of Samuel's youth, memories of the important sanctuary at Shiloh and of the real origin of Samuel from within the sphere of this sanctuary? This question is closely connected to the issue of whether and how the Samuel narratives continued and were developed (see §III.2.3.1 below).

III.1.5. The Book of the History of Solomon

Brettler, Marc. "The Structure of 1 Kings 1–11," *JSOT* 49 (1991): 87–97. **Dietrich,** Walter. "History and Law: Deuteronomistic Historiography and Deuteronomic Law Exemplified in the Passage from the Period of the Judges to the Monarchical Period," in *Israel Constructs Its History: Deuteronomistic Historiography in Recent Research* (ed. A. de Pury, T. Römer, and J.-D. Macchi; JSOTSup 306; Sheffield: Sheffield Academic Press, 2000), 315–42. **Frisch**, Amos. "Structure and Its Significance: The Narrative of Solomon's Reign," *JSOT* 51 (1991): 3–14. **Jepsen**, Alfred. *Die Quellen des Königsbuches* (2nd ed.; Halle: Niemeyer, 1956). **Parker**, Kim Ian. "Repetition as a Structuring Device in 1.Kings 1–11," *JSOT* 42 (1988): 19–27. **Särkiö**, Pekka. *Die Weisheit und Macht Salomos in der israelitischen Historiographie: Eine traditions- und redaktionskritische Untersuchung über 1 Kön 3–5 und 9–11* (SESJ 60; Helsinki: Finnische Exegetische Gesellscahft; Göttingen: Vandenhoeck & Ruprecht, 1994). **Wälchli**, Stefan. *Der weise König Salomo: Eine Studie zu den Erzählungen von der Weisheit Salomos in ihrem alttestamentlichen und altorientalischen Kontext* (BWANT 141; Stuttgart: Kohlhammer, 1999). **Würthwein**, Ernst. *Das Erste Buch der Könige, Kapitel 1–16* (2nd ed.; ATD 11.1; Göttingen: Vandenhoeck & Ruprecht, 1985).

A further literary source on the early monarchy is actually cited in 1 Kgs 11:41 at the end of the narratives on Solomon: "And the remaining words/actions of Solomon [דברי שלמה, the *res gestae Salomonis*] and everything that he did and his wisdom, are they not written in the book of the acts of Solomon?" The question is rhetorical, the original reader being referred to a source that describes the Solomonic era in greater detail than the Bible. Unfortunately, this work has not survived the passage of time. Skeptics (e.g., Würthwein) believe that it never existed, that the biblical author merely wanted to substantiate his description by means of a blind reference.

The original author of the Deuteronomistic history of Solomon, however, makes similar comments after almost every section on a particular king, such as: "The rest of the acts of Rehoboam and all that he did, is it not written in the book of the acts of the days of the kings of Judah?" (1 Kgs 14:29). For Israelite kings, he refers to a book of the "days of the kings of Israel." Hardly anyone now assumes that these references are fictional. It does seem that one or two annals were kept in Jerusalem that included (in analogy to Babylonian court annals) important dates and events from the reign of that king and that correlated (this is without analogy) the dates of the Judahite and the Israelite kings. The latter fact could not have been the case for Solomon, since he ruled Judah and Israel as a unit. It could very well be true that the division of the kingdom was the motivation for starting the creation of such a "synchronic chronicle" (Jepsen).

It is possible that an analogous work already existed for Solomon. This assumption, however, does not provide us with arguments for the age and source value of such a "book of the history of Solomon." This much, however, would be clear: it would have to be older than the author who refers to it in 1 Kgs 11:41 (perhaps the author of the Deuteronomistic History, perhaps also the author of a previous work that was used by Deuteronomistic Historians).

Determining the scope and content of such a source is difficult, since we cannot know how often it would have been redacted, shortened, or expanded. When 1 Kgs 11:41 speaks of "deeds" and of the "wisdom" of Solomon described in such a source, we see from 1 Kgs 3–11 that this could have included anything and everything. Following a *via negationis,* we of course would have to subtract anything that was added in the Deuteronomistic redaction or even after this redaction. The Deuteronomistic redaction organized the material in such a fashion that Solomon became a model of perfection until he completed the construction and dedication of the temple. The pericope on the construction of the temple contains many references to the Deuteronomistic additions in 2 Sam 7. The promise of a dynasty given there has been fulfilled (1 Kgs 5:19; 8:15–16, 20), so the house of God that David had already intended (but was not permitted) to build could now be built (1 Kgs 5:17–18; 8:17–19). Solomon's blessing and prayer on the occasion of the temple dedication (1 Kgs 8:15–61) clearly reflects the language of exilic and postexilic piety (the actual context of this prayer is the Second Temple that stood on Mount Zion from 515 B.C.E. on). Following this pious climax of Solomon's rule, the text begins to include dark aspects of Solomon's character (this is clearly a result of the redactional composition). A Deuteronomistic redactor (it can be questioned whether he was the first) has God address a long warning and exhortation to Solomon: everything depends on his loyalty to the Torah; if this loyalty wavers, the entire kingdom will be shaken (9:1–9). What follows is a comment on the extradition of Galilean settlements to Hiram, king of Tyre, for his assistance in the construction of the temple (9:10–14) and then a text dealing with the fact that Solomon fortified many cities with the aid of conscripted labor (9:15–23). This was still reported in 5:27–32 with a great deal of pride; now this fact appears as a problem, and the conscription of labor is explicitly revised to include only the non-Israelite population. The fact that the temple and the palace were covered with gold (10:10–22), that the king initiated flourishing trade relations with—of all nations!—Egypt and purchased—of all things!—chariots of war (10:26–29), that he surrounded himself with all kinds of foreign, that is, pagan women (10:1–9; 11:1–8) may not have been evaluated favorably by the Deuteronomistic redaction. The respective laws in the Deuteronomistic law of the kings (Deut 17:15–17) lead us rather to conclude that the Deuteronomistic redaction was highly critical of these facts (see Dietrich; Würthwein's assumption that the postexilic era was the first to coat Solomon's image in gold as a means of praising his memory is thus not necessary). According to the biblical description, punishment quickly followed Solomon's actions: God allowed Edomites and Arameans to gain independence and the northern Israelites to start a revolution (not for the first and not for the last time, 1 Kgs 11:14–40).

It is quite likely that the redaction composed this portrait of the initially infallible, then fallible king Solomon with the aid of older materials taken from the "book of the history of Solomon." But what was contained in it? Did it contain only lists and enumerations as we find them predominantly in 1 Kgs 4 and 9–10, or did it include also narratives such as the dream revelation and Solomon's prowess as judge in 1 Kgs 3 or the visit by the Queen of Sheba in 1 Kgs 10 and of early separation tendencies in the kingdom (1 Kgs 11; Würthwein would like to classify 3:16–28; 10:1–10, 13; 11:14–25 as *post*-Deuteronomistic!)? Was the construction of the temple (1 Kgs 5–8) already contained in this source, and if so, with how much detail? Was this source almost contemporary to the events contained in it (thus the majority opinion) or a product of the late monarchy (Wälchli)?

III.1.6. The So-Called Yahwist History

Blenkinsopp, Joseph. *The Pentateuch: An Introduction to the First Five Books of the Bible* (ABRL; New York: Doubleday, 1992). **Blum,** Erhard. *Die Komposition der Vätergeschichte* (WMANT 57; Neukirchen-Vluyn: Neukirchener, 1984). **Blum.** *Studien zur Komposition des Pentateuch* (BZAW189; Berlin: de Gruyter, 1990). **Carr,** David M. *Reading the Fractures of Genesis: Historical and Literary Approaches* (Louisville: Westminster John Knox, 1996. **Crüsemann,** Frank. *Der Widerstand gegen das Königtum: Die antiköniglichen Texte des Alten Testamentes und der Kampf um den frühen israelitischen Staat* (WMANT 49; Neukirchen-Vluyn: Neukirchener, 1978). **Eißfeldt,** Otto. *Hexateuchsynopse: Die Erzählung der fünf Bücher Mose und des Buches Josua mit dem Anfange des Richterbuches* (Leipzig: Hinrich, 1922). **Fohrer,** Georg. *Introduction to the Old Testament* (10th ed.; initiated by Ernst Sellin; trans. David E. Green; Nashville, Abingdon, 1968). **Gertz,** Jan Christian, Konrad **Schmid,** and Markus **Witte,** eds. *Abschied vom Jahwisten: Die Komposition des Hexateuch in der jüngsten Diskussion* (BZAW 316; Berlin: de Gruyter, 2002). **Henry,** Marie-Louise. "Jahwist und Priesterschrift: Zwei Glaubenszeugnisse des Alten Testaments," in idem, *Hüte dein Denken und Wollen: Alttestamentliche Studien, mit einem Beitrag zur feministischen Theologie* (ed. Bernd Janowski and Edward Noort; BThSt 16; Neukirchen-Vluyn: Neukirchener, 1992), 11–40. **Houtman,** Cees. *Der Pentateuch: Die Geschichte seiner Erforschung neben einer Auswertung* (CBET 9; Kampen: Kok Pharos, 1994). **Köckert,** Matthias. *Vätergott und Väterverheissungen: Eine Auseinandersetzung mit Albrecht Alt und seinen Erben* (FRLANT 142; Göttingen: Vandenhoeck & Ruprecht, 1988). **Levin,** Christoph. *Der Jahwist* (FRLANT 157; Göttingen: Vandenhoeck & Ruprecht, 1993). **Noth,** Martin. *Überlieferungsgeschichte des Pentateuch* (Stuttgart: Kohlhammer, 1948), trans. as *A History of Pentateuchal Traditions* (trans. Bernhard W. Anderson; Chico, Calif.: Scholars Press, 1981). **Pury,** Albert de, and Thomas **Römer,** eds. *Le Pentateuque en question: Les origines et la composition des cinq premiers livres de la Bible à la lumière des recherches récentes*

(3rd ed.; Le Monde de la Bible 19; Geneva: Labor et Fides, 2002 (BoMi 19). **Rad,** Gerhard von. "Beobachtungen an der Moseerzählung Exodus 1–14," *EvT* 31 (1971): 579–88. **Rendtorff,** Rolf. *Das überlieferungsgeschichtliche Problem des Pentateuch* (BZAW 147; Berlin: de Gruyter, 1976). **Römer,** Thomas. "Hauptprobleme der gegenwärtigen Pentateuchforschung," *TZ* 60 (2004): 289–307. **Rudolph,** Wilhelm. *Der "Elohist" von Exodus bis Josua* (BZAW 68; Berlin: Töpelmann, 1938). **Schmidt,** Werner H. "Ein Theologe in salomonischer Zeit? Ein Plädoyer für den Jahwisten," *BZ* 25 (1981): 82–103. **Schmidt.** "Plädoyer für die Quellenscheidung," *BZ* 32 (1988): 1–14. **Seebaß,** Horst. "Vor einer neuen Pentateuchkritik?" *TRev* 88 (1992): 177–86. **Soden,** Wolfram von. "Verschlüsselte Kritik an Salomo in der Urgeschichte des Jahwisten," *WO* 7 (1974): 228–40. **Van Seters,** John. *Abraham in History and Tradition* (New Haven: Yale University Press, 1975).

Some scholars still support the old theory that the oldest version of the history of Israel's pre- and early history in the books of Genesis to Numbers (perhaps including Joshua) is an excellent witness to the Solomonic "enlightenment." It is impossible to describe the scope of the discussion on the Pentateuch in this context. A few brief sketches must suffice:

➤ The so-called source hypothesis presumes different parallel accounts with independent origin that were later combined by various redactors (compare the creation of a Gospel harmony from the New Testament Gospels).

➤ We can isolate a D (Deuteronomy) source with a high degree of certainty.

➤ We can also determine a P (Priestly) stratum, even though there is debate on whether this stratum is the oldest source for the Pentateuch (older source hypothesis as well as some contemporary scholars, dating the non-P material after the P strand), the youngest source for the Pentateuch (newer source hypothesis), or a late redactional addition to the text (most recent discussions).

➤ We are thus left with material prior to P (or, more neutrally, the non-P material). The newer source hypothesis is certain it has found a Yahwist (J) stratum, not so sure about a Elohistic stratum (E). Rudolph assumed that E consisted of ad hoc additions to J. In the most recent discussions, a few scholars have proposed that E was the oldest stratum that was later expanded by J texts. Others believe J to be its own source but assume a much later date for this text (Van Seters: exilic); others again see J as an exilic redactional layer (Levin).

➤ Among those who assume that J is old, there are those who divide this layer into a (Solomonic) final version and a literary precursor dating before the time of the Israelite monarchy (Eißfeldt, Fohrer).

Enough hypotheses. Let us deal with the supposition that the "Yahwist" wrote a large literary work on Israel's early history during the time of Solomon. Scholars have identified the following characteristics of such a work:

➤ It begins with creation (whereas E begins with Abraham), with a primal history that focuses not on Israel's special relation to God but on "God and the world." It deals with basic aspects of human existence as a created existence in relation to God. From this primal human and world history grows the history of Israel as exemplified by Abraham, Isaac, Jacob, Jacob's sons, Israel in Egypt, and so forth. God uses this people to establish a special relationship to all human beings, even to his creation as a whole. Already here his name is YHWH: Israel's God is the Creator and God of all the world. (It should be obvious how daring it was to assume that all this was conceived and written down during the early monarchy, at the beginning of history writing in Israel and before all prophetic activity.)

➤ Israel establishes an identity under the eyes and guidance of its God; it experiences slavery and liberation, threats and preservation in the desert, instruction about and commitment to the Torah, and probably also the conquest and division of the promised land. (Why the story already ends here, or perhaps even with the death of Moses, and does not reach up to the early monarchy—as was sometimes supposed—is very difficult to explain.)

➤ Scholars have often searched for information on the time of Solomon in the J stratum. The sons of Jacob and their descendents were seen as the embodiment of tribal existence prior to the monarchy; Abraham and Moses were defined as leaders who preceded the king; Israel's experiences in Egypt became a mirror of life during the time of Solomon (von Soden, Crüsemann). During a time of external glory and success, the Yahwist warned against hubris and arrogance and created, in directly anticyclical fashion, a pessimistic anthropology (Henry).

These interesting discoveries and time-honored convictions are, however, severely called into question by the following:

➤ Many texts from the J stratum can hardly be the result of the intellectual and spiritual milieu of the early monarchy. They show clear traces of later (exilic) creation (e.g., strong Deuteronomistic language, including such important texts as Gen 12:1–4; 15; Exod *3–5; 32; already Noth believed that the J source, as defined by him, was saturated with many secondary additions). Regardless of this fact, it would be an overreaction to turn the source hypothesis on its head and place the entire J stratum into an exilic context: Judahite-Hebrew thoughts on God, the world, and Israel always included reflection on history and tradition, including in preexilic times!

➤ Thus the pre-P material is divided not so much horizontally (Eißfeldt, Fohrer, the division between J and E) as vertically along thematic lines (Noth's "topics of the Pentateuch," which he sought and found in the oral traditions that preceded the J stratum): primeval history, patriarchal history, the Joseph story, the Moses story, the revelation at Mount Sinai, the wilderness narratives. Each of these sections most likely experienced its own growth process before it was combined with one or the other section and incorporated into the growing matrix of the Pentateuch.

➤ How far back do the individual literary precursors go? Do they reach back to the early monarchy or perhaps even earlier? We can make such an assumption for parts of the patriarchal narratives, at least for the Moses narratives; in the case of the primeval history and the Sinai material, however, this early date can hardly be defended).

Erhard Blum has examined the patriarchal narratives in great detail and has placed the final version of the patriarchal narratives into the late seventh century during the time of Josiah. The earliest large narrative collection dealt with Jacob and was created shortly after the divided kingdom. Yet we can certainly reckon with earlier versions of these traditions, that is, from the early monarchy or even before. It remains an interesting fact that the totality of all the neighboring peoples mentioned in the contexts of *all* the patriarchs *together*[6] matches the peoples mentioned in 2 Sam 5; 8; and 10 precisely; in both contexts these peoples are forced to maintain a respectful distance from Israel. Perhaps we should be less convinced than Blum that the Abraham and Isaac material do not contain early material as well.

The Moses narratives show enough similarity to the Solomonic era that we could imagine these texts to be a parable about or against Pharaoh/Solomon (who were even related!). We have to think only of such motifs as conscripted labor and chariots of war. These parallels are augmented by ancient memories of nomadic rituals (Passover, circumcision), desert wanderings, and encounters with God at the mountain of God, none of which need be much later than the early monarchy itself; it is not necessary to suppose the time of Josiah and the exile as the context for their creation.

---

6. We can exclude the strange chapter Gen 14 from this discussion.

The Pentateuch thus may not present us with a glorious witness to a wide-reaching Solomonic enlightenment, but we do encounter lively and intensive intellectual and spiritual creativity in dealing with subjects from the most recent era, the time of the early monarchy, as well as from older and oldest "Israelite" history.[7] This should not be immediately discounted as impossible. The plausibility of this assumption rises once we consider how much of a historical incision the development of the state was (even if the state itself was relatively modest) and how great the need must have been to process this innovation on an intellectual and spiritual level.

III.2. The History of the Early Monarchy and Its Literary Precursors

Bietenhard, Sophia K. *Des Königs General: Die Heerführertraditionen in der vorstaatlichen und frühen staatlichen Zeit und die Joabgestalt in 2 Sam 2–20; 1 Kön 1–2* (OBO 163; Fribourg: Universitätsverlag; Göttingen: Vandenhoeck & Ruprecht, 1998). **Campbell,** Antony F. *Of Prophets and Kings: A Late Ninth-Century Document (1Samuel 1– 2Kings 10)* (CBQMS 17; Washington, D.C.: Catholic Biblical Association of America, 1986). **Dietrich,** Walter. "Die zweifache Verschonung Sauls durch David (I Sam 24 und I Sam 26)," in *David und Saul im Widerstreit: Diachronie und Synchronie im Wettstreit: Beiträge zur Auslegung des ersten Samuelbuches* (ed. Walter Dietrich; OBO 206; Fribourg: Academic; Göttingen: Vandenhoeck & Ruprecht, 2004), 232–53. **Dietrich.** *David: Der Herrscher mit der Harfe* (Biblische Gestalten 14; Leipzig: Evangelische Verlagsanstalt, 2006). **Fischer,** Alexander A. *Von Hebron nach Jerusalem: Eine redaktionsgeschichtliche Studie zur Erzählung von König David in II Sam 1–5* (BZAW 335; Berlin: de Gruyter, 2004). **Humphreys,** W. Lee. "From Tragic Hero to Villain: A Study of the Figure of Saul and the Development of 1 Samuel," *JSOT* 22 (1982): 95–117. **Klein,** Johannes. *David versus Saul: Ein Beitrag zum Erzählsystem der Samuelbücher* (BWANT 158; Stuttgart: Kohlhammer, 2002). **Langlamet,** François. "David et la maison de Saül: Les épisodes 'benjaminites' des II Sam. IX; XVI,1–14; XIX,17–31; I Rois, II,36–46," *RB* 86 (1979): 194–213, 385–436, 481–513; 87 (1980): 161–210; 88 (1981): 321–32. **Nitsche,** Stefan Ark. *David gegen Goliath: Die Geschichte der Geschichten einer Geschichte: Zur fächerübergreifenden Rezeption einer biblischen Story* (Altes Testament und Moderne 4; Münster: LIT, 1998). **Veijola.** Timo. "Salomo—der Erstgeborene Bathsebas," in *Studies in the Historical Books of the Old Testament* (ed.

---

7. It should be briefly mentioned that material from Joshua and Judges may also go back to the early monarchy, such as the "Benjaminite conquest legends" in Josh *1–9 or the list of "minor judges" in Judg 10:1–5 and 12:7–15 and perhaps some of the "hero narratives" in Judg *4–16. We will not discuss this further, as there are hardly any criteria for a somewhat plausible dating of these texts to the early monarchy.

J. A. Emerton; VTSup 30; Leiden: Brill, 1979), 230–50, repr. in idem, *David: Gesammelte Studien zu den Davidüberlieferungen des Alten Testaments* (Helsinki: Finnische Exegetische Gesellschaft, 1990), 84–105. **Willi-Plein, Ina.** "ISam 18–19 und die Davidshausgeschichte," in *David und Saul im Widerstreit: Diachronie und Synchronie im Wettstreit* (ed. Walter Dietrich; OBO 206; Fribourg: Academic; Göttingen: Vandenhoeck & Ruprecht, 2004), 138–71.

Despite the difficulties connected to diachronic analysis (difficulties also present with synchronic interpretation!), some of which have been mentioned previously, we will now attempt a diachronic analysis of the literature dealing with the early monarchy. We will focus on the time period between the early monarchy itself and the exile, the time during which the traditions collected prior to that point were incorporated into the Deuteronomistic History and reshaped for that purpose (see §I.3 above).

The observations made about previous hypotheses warn us against assuming too close a connection between the actual historical events and the earliest production of texts. It seems that the events were recorded only considerably after the events themselves occurred. The tenth and the ninth centuries were not yet time periods in which we can assume large-scale literary production and intellectual activity.[8] Then as now, there certainly were individuals capable of such activity, but the external circumstances and the educational possibilities simply did not yet exist for most. There was also no audience for such literature; there were but a few people capable of reading and writing. A market for literature did not exist even in rudimentary form. The first literary documents were not highly intellectual books but rather contracts and bills, perhaps also a simple form of accounting for certain circles and their possessions, some diplomatic correspondence, a few reports on politically important activities at court—at most, various collections of short texts.

The more we move away from the early monarchy, the more the possibility increases for a literary production that truly deserves this name. Not until the book of Chronicles in the late Persian (or perhaps even Hellenistic) period do we encounter the characteristics of free creative writing (including historiography)—and even this writing was bound to a certain degree by

---

8. See the disillusioning remarks of David W. Jamieson-Drake (*Scribes and Schools in Monarchic Judah: A Socio-Archaeological Approach* [JSOTSup 109; Sheffield: Almond, 1991]) and Hermann Michael Niemann (*Herrschaft, Königtum und Staat: Skizzen zur soziokulturellen Entwicklung im monarchischen Israel* [FAT 6; Tübingen: Mohr Siebeck, 1993]). Even if these two scholars are too skeptical, their basic insights and the data supporting them are beyond doubt.

the older texts contained in the books of Samuel and Kings. The Deuteronomistic History shows clearly that it used various older traditions that existed to a large degree in written form. It engages this material by selecting from it, expanding it, and commenting on it. Earlier stages of these writings were probably highly influenced by oral traditions that had been collected and joined to larger narrative units.

In the following we will thus begin with the smallest literary units and even with purely oral traditions that may reach back all the way to the early monarchy (it must be emphasized that this in itself does not imply anything about the historical credibility of these traditions). As a next step, we will observe the growth of these traditions until they became available to the Deuteronomistic Historians (on their work, see §I.3). The presentation of this growth process follows a model of crystallization: larger, thematically unified narratives grow, starting individual traditions, which are then combined to form a large narrative opus with multifaceted intentions.

III.2.1. INDIVIDUAL TRADITIONS

Several *songs and proverbs* contained in the books of Samuel and Kings lead us far back in time. We find explicit references to the origin of two poetic texts. In 2 Sam 1:19–27 we encounter a "lament over Saul and his son Jonathan" that is explicitly credited to David. He is said to have given the order to "teach" this song to the sons of Judah (perhaps even combined with instruction in archery), and it was written in "the Book of the Upright" (1:17–18). The Davidic authorship of this text is accepted by the vast majority of scholars.[9] It seems that this song was recited again and again, keeping its memory alive until it was included in a larger song collection. The title "Book of the Upright" is probably a reference to the real or assumed authors of the songs gathered in this collection. Aside from the lament over Saul and Jonathan credited to David, it also included the ark sayings in 1 Kgs 8:12–13 credited to Solomon and the saying on the temporary halting of the sun and moon in Josh 10:12–13 credited to Joshua: all of these poems are referenced: "from the Book of the Upright."[10] Other songs in the Davidic traditions do not

---

9. Hans Joachim Stoebe (*Das zweite Buch Samuelis* [KAT 8/2; Gütersloh: Gütersloher Verlagshaus, 1994], 96), however, refers only to the highly personalized verses 25–27 as a "Davidic composition"; he classifies the rest as a national song of lament. Yet even in the compiled form, he assumes that this song is old.

10. In order to substantiate this book by means of 1 Kgs 8, we must refer to the Greek text (which does not contain the source reference in Josh 10) in slightly modified form.

have this reference, but their carefully composed poetic structure allows us to assume that they were passed on without modification. David is also said to have composed a lament over Abner, who was murdered by Joab (2 Sam 3:33–34); this poem does not have the same aesthetic quality as the lament over Saul and Jonathan, but it remains a side witness to David's poetic ambitions (unless we assume a poetically talented ghostwriter).

A short victory song sung for Saul and David by the Israelite women is quoted three times: "Saul vanquished his thousands, David his tens of thousands" (1 Sam 18:7; 21:12; 29:5). With its pro-Davidic and anti-Saulide subtexts, this simple song, reminiscent of contemporary demonstration slogans, is witness to a virulent polemic between the two royal houses. The same is true for the secession call: "We have no part in David, and we have no heritage in the son of Jesse! Everyone to his tent, Israel!" It is quoted not only in 2 Sam 20:1 but also in 1 Kgs 12:16 in a somewhat extended version. This version also includes the derisive taunt that David should look after things in his own house, which probably refers to the impending division of the kingdom. We can explain the twofold occurrence of this phrase in one of two ways. It may have been part of the collective memory of the people, in which case it was uttered repeatedly and thus found its way into biblical writing, or a biblical narrator used this slogan intentionally in two different contexts in order to characterize the divided kingdom as a long-standing development and not a sudden surprise.

It should be obvious that the lengthy psalms in 1 Sam 2:1–10 (the song of Hannah) and 2 Sam 22–23 (two psalms of "David") are not to be read in connection with the old songs mentioned above. These psalms are later compositions that react not only to the early but the entire monarchy, perhaps even the following time periods, reflecting on this time with profound theological insight.

The lists, on the other hand, are very old texts that never fell out of use. Our texts contain a number of examples:

> the list of towns in which Samuel operated (1 Sam 7:16)
> the list of countries with which Saul waged war (1 Sam 14:47)

The Septuagint reports the ark sayings at a different point and ends the report with the following statement: ουκ ιδου αυτη γεγραπται εν βιβλιω ωδης. This would indicate the Hebrew הלא היא כתובה על־ספר השיר—with the exception of the last word (and the introductory particle) the same phrase as in 2 Sam 1:18 and Josh 10:13. In order to avoid having to deal with an otherwise unknown "Book of the Song," it may be prudent to assume that the LXX switched the consonants י and ש when reading הישר. See Martin Noth, *1. Könige 1–16* (BK 9/1; Neukirchen-Vluyn: Neukirchener, 1964), 172–73.

- ➤ the list of Saul's relatives (1 Sam 14:49–51)
- ➤ the list of cities and villages that received gifts from David while he was in Ziklag (1 Sam 30:27–30)
- ➤ the list of regions and towns belonging to the kingdom of Eshbaal (2 Sam 2:9)
- ➤ the list of David's sons (2 Sam 3:2–5; 5:13–16)
- ➤ the list of David's high officials (2 Sam 8:16–18; 20:23–26)
- ➤ the list of the so-called Thirty, David's elite military unit (2 Sam 23:24–39)
- ➤ the list of the boundary points of David's kingdom (2 Sam 24:5–8)
- ➤ the list of Solomon's high officials (1 Kgs 4:1–6)
- ➤ the list of Solomon's representatives (1 Kgs 4:7–19)
- ➤ the list of cities fortified by Solomon (1 Kgs 9:17–18)

These texts contain no narrative material whatsoever. They are determined by a nominal style; verbs are rare. The text primarily lists personal and place names with great sobriety. In contrast to the description of the various parts of Goliath's armor (1 Sam 17:5–7) or the gifts given to David by Abigail (25:18), these "true" lists are not incorporated into the narrative at all. They present us with blocks of information loosely associated with the narrative context. In all the cases mentioned above, we should assume that we are dealing with documents that were known to the respective authors and that were included by them into their text as best as they could. It is particularly noticeable that all of the lists, perhaps with the exception of the first, seem to have been written and passed on within the context of the royal court.[11]

This is also true for the next group of texts, the enumerations that incorporate some narrative material. These include David's wars reported in 2 Sam 8. Only a few sentences refer to each conquered nation, reporting the key aspects of the particular campaign: the execution of prisoners; the hobbling of horses; and the enslavement of the population. In 2 Sam 21:15–22 and 23:8–17, 18–23 we read anecdotes of noteworthy heroic acts performed by David's men. We are briefly told something of the threat posed by the respective enemy and the courage or unconditional loyalty of David's men. Further, 1 Kgs 5:11 lists proverbial wise men—only to mention that Solomon was even wiser. The description of the construction and decoration of the temple in 1 Kgs 6–7 indicates that the author used lists with great care but without great

---

11. For old list material within the biblical history of the early monarchy, see Nadav Na'aman, "Sources and Composition in the History of David," in *The Origins of the Ancient Israelite States* (ed. Volkmar Fritz and Philip R. Davies; JSOTSup 228; Sheffield: Sheffield Academic Press, 1996), 170–86.

narrative esprit. Even those enumerations that contain some narrative material suggest that their literary precursors were lists written down to ensure the precise communication of information.

On several occasions we also encounter short notes in the text that may have also existed independently in written form. Their original context can no longer be determined. The note that Samuel's two sons—referred to by name!—were judges in Beer-sheba (1 Sam 8:2) seems to have no purpose, and we would have to admire anyone who invented this information. Several short notes are offered in 1 Sam 22:1–5: David's retreat into the cave of Adullam and his assembly of four hundred mercenaries gathered from the fringes of society and representing David's source of power; the precautionary relocation of David's parents to neighboring Moab; an oracle by the prophet Gad that caused David to go to Yaar-hereth. This compilation of separate short notes supports the assumption of prior written sources. It would not be too audacious to assume that David himself had annals written already from the beginning of his career. We encounter the note on Samuel's death, lament, and burial twice, in 1 Sam 25:1 and 28:3. The notes in 2 Sam 14:26–27 (on Absalom's hair and on his children) and in 18:18 (on the Absalom monument in the King's Valley) stand completely isolated from the rest of the succession narrative. The note that Solomon married a daughter of Pharaoh (1 Kgs 3:1) is connected neither to the previous Davidic and succession narratives nor to the subsequent story about Solomon's dream in Gibeon. The number of such notes increases in the Solomon traditions, especially in 1 Kgs 5 and 9–10; they seem to be combined in a kind of mosaic without narrative development.

The subsequent material in the books of Kings contains many such notes. The great majority of scholars assume that they were taken from the annals of the kings of Israel (or Judah). These annals seem to have been royal annals that listed and reported important facts, dates, and names of the respective kings. This listing is given synchronically, that is, by relating contemporary events in Judah and Israel to each other. If we observe a similar style in the examples mentioned above, then we are led to the possibility that such royal annals already existed for the early monarchy. Prior to the divided kingdom, these annals could not have been synchronic in the above-mentioned sense; it is not impossible, however, that important events at court were recorded in this manner. We do know that David instituted a "scribe" among his high officials; Solomon even employed two of them (2 Sam 8:17; 20:25; 1 Kgs 4:3). Like other high officials, these scribes probably commanded a score of underlings. If we assume such royal annals for the early monarchy, then the lists and short notes mentioned above were probably taken from this source.

III.2.2. Extended Narratives

We can easily assume that information on the early monarchy was also transmitted orally instead of merely being codified in annals. These oral transmissions were probably more expansive than the material in the annals; they would have continued to grow in length with continual retellings through modification and expansion of the material. We can trace such a case in the books of Samuel. In the context of several anecdotes on David's heroes (2 Sam 21:19), we read how a certain Elhanan of Bethlehem vanquished the giant Philistine warrior Goliath of Gath. In 1 Sam 17 we encounter a story, or more likely two interwoven narratives, about how David himself accomplished this heroic act. We can recognize a long and complex history of transmission that incorporated many beliefs, insights, and experiences, thus transforming a short military anecdote into a lengthy heroic story and moral tale.[12]

Many individual narratives contained in the texts under discussion will have similarly resulted from short memories or anecdotes. These short notes may reach back far into history (as in the case of the victory over Goliath), or they may have been added over the course of time. It is one of the defining characteristics of the historiography of the books of Samuel and Kings, especially in regard to the early monarchy, that it is heavily dependent on short individual narratives that underwent a long history of transmission in oral and in written form. The authors of the narrative whole combined narratives that were handed down to them to a more (2 Sam 13–20) or less (1 Sam 16–31) coherent narrative sequence. We should classify these later authors more as novelists and less as historians, even though neither role excludes the other.

We can still recognize how many narratives developed from a narrative core that was expanded and developed in a long history of transmission before it was put into writing. How long this history of transmission was must be decided separately for each individual case and will often remain unanswered. Yet even if we assume that the first processes of writing occurred in the later eighth century, we still move quite close to the time of the early monarchy.

> ➤ At the core of the narrative in 1 Sam 9:1–10:16 and 13–14 stands the story of a nameless seer who appointed Saul ben Kish, who had set

---

12. See Walter Dietrich, "Der Fall des Riesen Goliat: Biblische und nachbiblische Erzählversuche," in *Bibel und Literatur* (ed. Jürgen Ebach and Richard Faber; Munich: Fink, 1995), 241–58; idem, "Die Erzählungen von David und Goliat in I Sam 17," *ZAW* 108 (1996): 172–91; both reprinted in idem, *Von David zu den Deuteronomisten*, 120–33, 58–73.

out only to find his father's donkeys, in a secret gathering of Israelite leaders to lead the tribes in battle against the Philistines. This battle was to be the first in a series of victories over this dangerous enemy. This early narrative was expanded by several additions that reinterpreted this initial material: the nameless seer was none other than the prophet Samuel; the place of the anointing was near Samuel's residence in Ramah; the anointing was followed by an encounter with a band of prophets; Saul engaged in a battle for authority with Samuel; Saul really had no military strength with which to oppose the Philistine enemy; Saul enforced the ritual slaughter of looted animals during the battle; Saul entered into conflict with Jonathan over an oath of abstinence; and his son Jonathan was actually the one who defeated the Philistines.

➤ In 1 Sam 10:10–12 and 19:18–24 we see how two narratives developed from a proverbial saying: "Is Saul also among the prophets?" These two narratives explain a saying that even then was obscure. Both narratives combine prophecy with the phenomenon of ecstasy and postulate that *even Saul,* after all a king and no prophet, was affected by this phenomenon. One version shows a certain degree of sympathy for Saul; the other portrays him quite negatively. The second version also contains a seemingly common motif that occurs again in 2 Kgs 1: a king may attempt to arrest a prophet three times, but he will not be successful. This motif points to the fact that the power of the state is not suited to deal with prophecy. In the current literary context of the second version, David, not the prophet (Samuel), is the real object of the futile attempt to enforce royal power.

➤ Many adventure stories about Saul's pursuit of David were probably told in Judah. One story centered around the "Rock of Escape" (1 Sam 23:24–28), another on the village of Keilah (23:1–13), one on the spring in En-gedi and the caves found there (1 Sam 24), and one on the hill of Hachilah (1 Sam 26). Each story has retained its specific local color, but all have been set into the sequence of David's flight from Saul, and all were expanded by later additions. Thus it is repeatedly stated that the Ziphites betrayed David's hiding place to Saul, that David was able to use the priest Abiathar and the ephod to inquire of the oracle, that David had the opportunity to murder Saul but resisted this temptation, and that David and Saul spoke to each other on several occasions without truly achieving reconciliation.

➤ The story of David, Nabal, and Abigail in 1 Sam 25 contains a readily recognizable narrative core (David's actions as an outlaw; his attempts to extort "protection money"; Nabal's resistance; the diplomatic activity of Nabal's wife Abigail; the death of Nabal and the marriage of Abigail to David); this narrative core was later extended through extensive speeches by the characters.

➤ The core of the narratives about David's sojourn with the Philistines was probably the knowledge that David had lived among the national enemy for a certain period of time and had attained the city-kingship over Ziklag during this time period before moving his residence to Hebron. Perhaps the large narrative about the Amalekites in 1 Sam 30 also has an old origin, but it was not necessarily connected to the idea that David was a vassal of the Philistines.

➤ The narrative of Saul's journey to the necromancer was probably shortened and originally contained a more detailed description of the woman who used the magical practices. It was also expanded by several pieces of information (the religious critique of necromancy, perhaps the figure of Samuel, definitely the reference to Samuel's earlier statements to Saul).

➤ Of the two narratives on Saul's death in 1 Sam 31 and 2 Sam 1, the first seems to be earlier. It breathes the spirit of northern Israel, as the narrator accompanies Saul to his death with great sympathy. The other narrative places David at its center and attempts to distance him from Saul's death as much as possible. In comparison with 1 Sam 31, it contains no new information outside of the "evidence" manufactured by the Amalekite. It is interesting, however, that the text reports how David received the royal insignia from the Amalekite; it seems that these were displayed in Jerusalem, giving rise to the suspicion that they had been stolen from Saul on the night of his death.

➤ Two narratives about Solomon are not developed from an older narrative but are rather examples of a widely known traditional sujét. In the narrative of Yhwh's appearance to Solomon in a dream in Gibeon (1 Kgs 3:4–15) we find remnants of an incubation ritual (the initiation of a theophany through a certain type of cultic behavior) and the genre-typical element of a single wish granted to the hero. It is not necessary to assume that Yhwh was the deity in question from the beginning; even "Solomon" is but the quasi-historical personification of a fairytale prototype. The subsequent narrative tells of an encounter between Solomon and two women fighting over who is the true mother of a child. Solomon succeeds in deciding the case (3:16–27). This basic motif is also quite common; the specific narrative use of the motif, however, is shaped by ancient Near Eastern or Israelite beliefs (such as the idea that the two women are prostitutes so that they have no *paterfamilias* to represent them at court). Both narratives show clear signs of literary growth and redaction.

➤ The text in 1 Kgs 12:3–20 confronts us with a very different narrative genre. It is a historical-political morality tale, originating most likely in the context of the Jerusalem court during the monarchy. Groups connected in critical loyalty to the house of David reflect upon the fact that northern Israel separated from the united kingdom. They disapprove of the secession of the northern tribes, referring to it as downright *criminal* (12:19). At the same time, they place some of the blame at the feet of the Jerusalem court. The royal advisors and the young king Rehoboam contributed to igniting the revolutionary embers by means of their insensitive, cocky, and radically asocial behavior (12:8–14). This narrative perhaps served as a case study in the royal education of princes and advisors at the Jerusalem court. Isaiah, a Jerusalem prophet of the eighth century, seems to have understood the division of the kingdom as a national tragedy (Isa 7:17), perhaps through the influence of this narrative.

The second book of Samuel shows several elements of continuous literary composition and deliberate historical description. Even here, however, we are dealing not with the writers of novels nor with historians, but with narrators of short stories. Individual narratives are also the starting point in this case, providing the foundation for the narrative whole, but they are combined into a narrative whole with greater intensity and deliberation than in any other textual corpus discussed thus far. Individual episodes such as the death of Asahel or Absalom (2 Sam 2:18–24; 18:9–15), David's adultery and the rape of Tamar (11:1–5; 13:1–22), or Sheba's secession (2 Sam 20) are the basis for the large narrative opus. On the other hand, all these episodes are a part of a single plot. They are prepared for by other episodes and lead in turn to subsequent events.

We thus reach the next level in the transmission history of these traditions, the narrative collections and novellas.

III.2.3. Narrative Collections and Novellas

We can recognize several shorter and longer textual units within 1 Sam 1 and 1 Kgs 12. These units clearly exceed the limits of a short note or an individual narrative, but they are still a prior stage to the final text. They appear as separate units on a thematic and stylistic level, and we can even postulate a *Sitz im Leben* with a certain degree of plausibility. They have their own transmission history and were most likely codified in written form before they were incorporated into the large history of the early monarchy. The texts belonging to these units do not necessarily have to stand together in their present context; they also do not have to be included in their entirety. On the contrary, when they were incorporated into a larger narrative whole, they were pulled apart, reorganized, shortened, or extended. They are a kind of precursor to the large works of narration or historiography that stand at the end of the transmission history of the material on the early monarchy. These large works were thus not freely composed but were compiled of disparate material handed down to the redactors, often already in preorganized fashion. We recognize a basic principle of the creation of biblical traditions—at least in regard to the texts discussed in this volume. The later textual levels depend on older, partially oral traditions. Biblical historiography is thus strongly influenced by traditional material. When examining narrative collections and novellas concerning the characters of the early monarchy, we are looking at an intermediate level between the individual narrative and the final text. This intermediate level is not flat, neither in regard to time nor to subject matter. On the contrary, the various narrative works that will be discussed below were created by different circles or authors at different times who worked with various methods and differing intentions.

In the subsequent presentation we will not follow the sequence given in literary history but rather the "canonical" order in which the postulated novellas appear in the biblical text. There will be the occasional overlap and displacement due to the work of the later redactors. The comments on these individual "sources" will be longer or shorter, depending on whether the particular hypothesis is already familiar to exegetical discussion or has to be developed as a new hypothesis (see especially §III.1).

III.2.3.1. The Samuel–Saul Narrative

Scholars have long regarded the so-called youth narrative of Samuel (see §III.1.4 above) as a self-contained literary entity *sui generis*. Perhaps this narrative is the beginning of a longer story that continues beyond the ark narratives in 1 Sam 4–6.

Exegetes have long noted that Samuel's birth narrative centers on the *Leitwort* שאל ("to request, ask for") and that the consonants of this word seem to connect much more closely to the name "Saul" than to the name "Samuel." This led to the thesis that we are faced with a text that originally was not part of the Samuel narrative but rather of the Saul narrative. The one "asked for" was none other than Saul, who was then anointed by a seer (1 Sam *9–10) and who started to do battle with the Philistines and completed this endeavor successfully (1 Sam 13–14; 1 Sam *7).[13] Even if such constructions are wildly adventuresome, they point to a basic truth: there are narrative connections that go way beyond 1 Sam 1, even beyond 1 Sam 1–3. The figure of Saul is closely connected to the figure of Samuel, starting not only with Samuel's anointing of Saul. Stated negatively, it is likely that there never was a youth narrative of Samuel that only communicated something about Samuel alone. In fact, the story of Samuel's rise was probably told only with respect to his role in the foundation of the Israelite state and the enthronement of the first king.

If we examine the narratives beyond 1 Sam 1–3 in 1 Sam 7–12 from this point of view, we might locate the continuation of the Samuel narrative either in 1 Sam 9:1–10:16 or in 1 Sam 7–8; 10:17–27 (and 1 Sam 11). The latter texts have long been classified as part of the sequence of narratives that speak negatively of the monarchy; thus they are seen as late texts, ever since Martin Noth as Deuteronomistic texts. This sweeping late dating of the texts has repeatedly given rise to several well-argued objections. It seems that we can identify a pre-Deuteronomistic textual layer that is concerned with Samuel's role first as a leader in the battle against the Philistines and the establishment of order in Israel (1 Sam *7) and then as midwife in the establishment of the monarchy (8:1–5; 10:*17–27; 11). Interestingly enough, Samuel acts in 1 Sam 7 initially as a priest, which corresponds to his "training" in 1 Sam 1–3 (whereas later traditions see him as a prophet). In 1 Sam 10:20–21 he initiates—as priest?—the drawing of lots that focuses the narrative intention: from the tribe (Benjamin) to the clan (Matri[14]) to the family (ben Kish) to Saul (שָׁאוּל), the one "requested." This narrative focusing is analogous to the genealogy that introduces Saul in 1 Sam 9:1–2, with the difference that the genealogy in 9:1 constitutes the beginning of a narrative and thus a different narrative level, whereas 10:17ff. introduces a new character into an already-established narrative. Saul's inauguration as king in 10:22–24 is connected on a redactional level to the story of Saul's victory in the battle against the Ammonites in 1 Sam 11 by the motif of the resistance of certain circles against a new king (10:26–27; 11:12–13) as well as the figure of Samuel. This connection, however, is a secondary connection on the level of a small novella on Samuel and Saul. The thus-emerging historical novella may have found its conclusion in the summary of Saul's deeds in 14:47–52.

---

13. Ivar Hylander, *Der literarische Samuel-Saul-Komplex [1 Sam 1–15]: Traditionsgeschichtlich untersucht* (Uppsala: Almquist & Wiksell, 1932).

14. The name of this clan occurs nowhere else in the tradition. This is a strong argument for the early dating of this passage. The claim that this passage was composed after the example in Josh 7:16–18 turns the actual dependency of these texts on its head.

It should be obvious that all the texts discussed above, including the material incorporated into them, originated within the horizon of a northern Israelite narration; Judah, Jerusalem, and the house of David are completely absent from this material. The subject matter of this novella is a highly important turn in the history of Israel: the transition from the tribal organization of Israel, still represented by (Eli and) Samuel, to the establishment of a state connected to the name of Saul. Under Samuel's leadership, the leader confirmed by God, Israel dared to take the bold step from the old world into the new. The reasons for this development were found not in foreign affairs—the previous Philistine danger had (seemingly) been averted, the Ammonites were not yet on the move—but rather on the domestic front. The stability of the polity did not seem secure under the leadership of (spiritual) tribal leaders. The people desired continual leadership that would unite all of Israel with a strong hand. Not everyone in Israel was pleased with this development, but the new leader proved himself gloriously in the subsequent conflict with the Ammonites. Saul was the successful founder of the first functioning Israelite state.

We should search for the historical location of this Israelite founding myth in the northern kingdom before 722 B.C.E. (but not much earlier!). The geographical location may have been the sanctuary at Mizpah, which plays an important role in the narratives as a kind of successor to the sanctuary of Shiloh, which was probably destroyed early on (see 1 Sam 7:5, 7, 11, 16; 10:17).

III.2.3.2. The Narratives on the Fate of the Ark

As we have seen earlier (see §III.1.3 above), there seems to have been a narrative that told of the journey of the ark from the Ephraimite Shiloh though various Philistine cities and the border region between Philistine and Israelite-Judahite settlements to Jerusalem. This account is found primarily in 1 Sam 4–6 and 2 Sam 6. This ark narrative seems to contain traditions that are obviously Israelite—such as the remembrance of Shiloh as the earlier location of the ark as well as its function as a palladium of war for the northern tribes—but its geographic and ideological *Sitz im Leben* is Jerusalem, where the ark ended up, according to 2 Sam 6. It seems that Jerusalemites told the story of how this peculiar cultic artifact came to the Judahite capital from the Israelite north via Philistine territory.

We read in 2 Sam 6:17 that David placed the ark in a tent sanctuary. Perhaps this was the place deemed appropriate for its storage from of old, perhaps already in Shiloh. One of the most characteristic features of the ark was the fact that it could be *carried*, and thus also taken into battle (see 1 Sam

4; 2 Sam 11:11; 15:24–25). The God YHWH who was enthroned above the ark was mobile and could be transported to the location where his followers needed him. This was clearly communicated by the fact that not only the ark itself but also its place of storage could be transported. The tent of the ark, or rather the ark in the tent, was a symbol of YHWH's readiness to depart from his present location. In quiet times, the ark and the tent seemed to have stood still at the spot designated for it in Jerusalem. Thus it became possible that priests and oil for anointing could be taken from there in order to anoint Solomon (1 Kgs 1:39).

It is, however, not very likely that the ark narrative was composed during the years in which the ark stood in or close by Jerusalem in its tent. This was only the case for a few short decades. Solomon soon placed the ark into the holy of holies of the temple he erected. The holy *box* was positioned in such a way that a large curtain that separated the holy of holies from the adjacent holy area concealed it. Only the ends of the carrying sticks were visible and reminded those who saw it of the ark's former mobility and thus of the mobility of the God enthroned above it (see 1 Kgs 8:6–8). From this point on, that is, from the mid-tenth century on, the ark was bound to one location; it was no longer taken from the temple for the purpose of battle. Together with the cherubim it now constituted the figurative but imageless ensemble that embodied YHWH's permanent presence on Mount Zion. This constellation inspired Isaiah's vision of YHWH on the throne in the eighth century; the Babylonians also encountered it in the sixth century when they conquered Jerusalem. During these long centuries, the sagas and legends that we now read in the ark narratives developed.

Unless we are very mistaken, the collection of ark narratives is not limited to 1 Sam 4–6 and 2 Sam 6. It is quite possible that an early version of the traditions of the ark and the tent during the desert wanderings (Exod 25; 37; Deut 10) were connected to the Jerusalem cult. We can assume this with greater certainty for the narrative on the transferal of the ark from the City of David to the temple (1 Kgs *8:1–9).

This narrative is connected on many levels to 1 Sam 4–6 and 2 Sam 6. In every case the ark goes on a journey. The picture is not one of an annual procession but of a one-time journey with a set itinerary (from the temple of Dagon in Ashdod [1 Sam 5:1ff.] to the various Philistine cities to the house of Abinadab in Kiriath-jearim [1 Sam 6:21; 7:1]; from the house of Abinadab in Baale-judah [! 2 Sam 6:2] to the house of the Gittite Obed-Edom [6:10–11] to the City of David [6:12]; from the City of David to Solomon's temple [1 Kgs 8:1, 6]). In every case the leaders of the people initiate the transfer of the ark (the Philistine city kings in 1 Sam 5–6, David in 2 Sam 6, Solomon in 1 Kgs 8), but the general population is very involved in the events (in the case of the

Philistine cities in 1 Sam 5–6, with great suffering; in the case of the *house of Israel* in 2 Sam 6 and the *elders* and *men of Israel* in 1 Kgs 8:1–3, with great joy); specific priests of the ark are responsible for the ark's proper transfer (1 Sam 4:4; 7:1; 2 Sam 6:3; 1 Kgs 8:3b, 6 [the Levites of 1 Sam 6:15; 1 Kgs 8:4 are secondary additions]). The holiness of the ark must be respected, and punishment threatens any denial of this respect (1 Sam 5–6 *passim*; 2 Sam 6:6–7). For this reason also, the transfer of the ark is accompanied by a multitude of sacrifices (1 Sam 6:14; 2 Sam 6:13; 1 Kgs 8:5). The individual stages are important not merely as a record of the past but also for the present—this is indicated by the recurring phrase "until this day" (1 Sam 5:5; 6:18; 2 Sam 6:8; 1 Kgs 8:8; the comment in 9:9 that the ark contained nothing but the Decalogue is a clear Deuteronomistic addition).

We can recognize that the ark narratives in 1 Sam 4–6; 2 Sam 6; and 1 Kgs 8 were not written as a literary unit. This collection of texts is clearly composed of various different episodes that are not completely coherent. We are faced instead with a collection of narratives of a unified work of historiography. The collection includes a battle narrative as well as pious legends, etiologies, and historical anecdotes. The place names, however, do join each other to provide us with a continual journey that, despite several interruptions, finds its way from the temple in Shiloh to the temple in Jerusalem. Without this goal in 1 Kgs 8, the narrative would remain a mere torso.

We could certainly ask whether the narrative continues beyond 1 Kgs 8:8 to perhaps include the solemn dedication of the ark in 8:12–13 and the blessings and sacrifices in 8:14, 62–63. It seems, however, that we are dealing here with an additional redactional layer, whether a separate temple source or a book of the history of Solomon or a history of the early monarchy (see §III.2.4 below). The dedication of the ark is provided with its own source reference in the Septuagint: "Is this not written in the book of the song" (or, with reference to 2 Sam 1:18 "…in the book of the Upright"). These texts would thus have been taken from such sources and not from the ark narrative. The reports on the dedication of the temple—aside from 8:14, 62–63, as well as 8:10–11—are an integral part of the report on the construction of the temple. Thus the ark narratives would have included only 1 Kgs 8:*1–8.

These observations present a plausible case that a separate ark narrative was stored and transmitted within the Jerusalem temple. This narrative was anything but fully coherent and was composed of various traditions. We must therefore assume a lengthy process of transmission and redaction and abandon the idea of an early date for the ark narrative as a whole, not to mention the time of the early monarchy itself. The situation is similar to that of the David narratives: the combination of various divergent narrative materials into a structured whole requires time, especially if some sections of the narrative contain legendary elements and an advanced narrative style. This is especially the case for 1 Sam 5–6, where individual episodes were combined to create the picture of a journey that spread terror throughout the land of the Philistines. In contrast, 1 Sam 4 (the report of the loss of the ark to the Philistines); 2 Sam 6; and 1 Kgs 8 (the reports of the transfer of the ark to Jerusalem and then to the holy of holies of Solomon's temple) may contain historically accurate information about the early monarchy and even earlier time periods.

According to this information, the Philistines succeeded in capturing Israel's palladium of war, a feat that would indicate their temporary oppressive dominance in Palestine. At some point the Philistines lost interest in this trophy and deposited it on the border to Benjamin and Judah. But Israel also seemed to have no more interest in this cultic artifact: faith in the ark and the warlord YHWH had been greatly shattered. The political and military situation did not contribute to reviving this faith. In the face of Philistine oppression, the people had chosen an earthly warlord, the king. Saul did fight against the Philistines until he fell in battle against them. David actually defeated the Philistines—and remembered the ark. The ark's triumphal entrance into Jerusalem was once again a symbol, this time for Israelite dominance in Palestine. Solomon placed the portable and mobile cultic artifact into the holy of holies of the new sanctuary on Mount Zion (1 Kgs 8; possibly a non-YHWHistic sanctuary was replaced by a temple dedicated to YHWH). Important aspects of the belief associated with the ark now had to be abandoned; it became an important part, perhaps even the central part, of a belief in YHWH's powerful presence on Mount Zion. It seems logical that many stories and legends started to appear surrounding the mysterious "box" contained in the holy of holies. When the Assyrians did not conquer Jerusalem in 701 B.C.E., unlike Samaria, this faith in Zion rose to new heights. On this occasion the ancient military context of the ark and the God of the ark was revitalized. We can readily assume that the ark narrative was created during this period, even though several of its individual traditions are much older.

This political-religious context moves us to understand the ark narrative not as a monolithic ideological narrative but rather as an etiological tale explaining the origin of the ark. The narrative presents us with a reason for the special status of the ark, the uniqueness of this odd cultic artifact, by referring to its history. The narrative, however, provides no justification for a possible political or even military (mis)use of the ark. Perhaps Solomon's decision to place the ark in the holy of holies was motivated by the wise insight that the ark would thus be best protected from such misuse. His decision to put the ark in the temple, as well as David's decision to bring it to Jerusalem, can also be understood as their attempt to ensure God's permanent presence and assistance. The faith in Zion did develop in this direction as we can see from the harsh prophetic critique of later times (Mic 3:11; Jer 7). The ark narrative seems to have more in common with such oppositional voices than with the official and probably popular belief in the invulnerability of Zion. The fact that Yhwh is enthroned in Zion does not mean that Zion cannot be conquered. The narrative on the loss of the ark in 1 Sam 4 teaches that Yhwh is very capable of withdrawing from the people's attempt to control him. Yhwh remains free and autonomous, even free to humble the arrogance of his people (1 Sam 4; 2 Sam 6:6ff.), free to restrain Israel's enemy (1 Sam 5–6), and free again to turn back to his people (2 Sam 6:12ff.) and guarantee his presence among them (1 Kgs 8). In classic dogmatic terms, the ark narrative propagates *certitudo* but not *securitas*, certainty, but not security.

III.2.3.3. Narratives on the Rise and Fall of the House of Saul

If our analysis is correct (see §III.2.3.1 above), the Samuel-Saul narratives form the narrative structure for the first half of 1 Samuel. These narratives include, at least in their original form, the chapters 1 Sam 1–3; 7–8; 10:17–27; 11:1–15; and 14:47–52. In this context, the author of the history of the early monarchy incorporated the beginning of the ark narrative (1 Sam 4–6; see §III.2.3.2 above) and a further narrative on the rise (and, as we will see below, the fall) of Saul.

The two lengthy narratives in 1 Sam 9:1–10:16 and 1 Sam 13–14 focus on Saul: the former on how he went forth to find his father's donkeys and found the royal crown, the latter on how, with his son Jonathan, he defeated the Philistines. There are two passages that link these narratives: 1 Sam 10:5–8 and 13:3–4. When explaining the anointing to Saul, Samuel tells Saul that he should go to Gibeah (probably Saul's hometown, here referred to as "Gibeah of God"), "where the captain of the Philistines [textual emendation] resides." There "the spirit of God will come upon him," and he will be "turned into another person." Once this occurs, Samuel says to Saul, "then do what your hand finds for Yhwh is with you. Then you shall go before me to Gilgal and, behold, I will come down to you … and I will let you know what you shall do" (10:5–8). In 1 Sam 13:3–4 we read, "And Jonathan struck down the captain of the Philistines who was in Gibeah. And the Philistines heard. And Saul blew the horn in all of the land: 'Hear, you Hebrews!' And all of Israel heard that Saul had struck down the Philistine captain and that Israel had become odious to the Philistines. And the people were called out and followed Saul to Gilgal." Both passages work as prediction and fulfillment.

The narrative sheds much light on the severe and unchallenged Philistine oppression of Israel prior to the founding of the state. The *Hebrews* flee in panic when Philistine troops approach (1 Sam 13:5); Philistine marauders can move through Benjamin without encountering any opposition; the Philistines have established a tightly controlled weapons monopoly (13:17–22). It is quite intentional that the Israelites are referred to as *Hebrews* in this context, a term otherwise only used in the exodus narratives. In both cases the leaders must deal with several unruly elements in the population—as is the case with the *Habiru*, who made much trouble for the Palestine city kings and their Egyptian overlords according to the Amarna correspondence of the late Bronze Age (see the first volume of this series).

We certainly cannot use the entire composition in 1 Sam 9:1–10:16 and 1 Sam 13–14 as a source for the historical situation in Palestine in the tenth century. The text clearly shows traces of earlier versions and later redactions. The *seer* who approaches the donkey-seeking Saul with great honors and duties was not always *Samuel*; this name and this character are a secondary addition to the story. According to the present text, Samuel anoints Saul to be the *nagid*, a title that seems to indicate the "designated king" in the David narratives (see 1 Sam 13:14; 25:30; 2 Sam 6:21; 1 Kgs 1:35). The use of this term in this context might have been introduced to balance the narratives on Saul's enthronement in 10:17ff. and 11:15. Saul himself was most likely anointed *king*. Further, 1 Sam 10:*5–6, 10–12 added a secondary prophetic tradition that included the proverbial saying, "Is Saul also among the prophets?" (in addition to 10:12, see 19:24). Another secondary scene is the conflict between Samuel and Saul in 1 Sam 13:7ff. anticipated in the strange command in 10:8 that Saul should wait for Samuel for a week in Gilgal. Samuel (or the "seer") most likely actually met Saul on harmonious terms in order to tell him *what he should do*. As the final text destroys this harmony, it also has Jonathan, not Saul, enact the role of the victor over the Philistine captain. The Saul of 1 Sam 9 does not strike the reader as a mature individual who has a son with military experience. Instead, he appears as a young man who, led by the "seer," becomes a hero in 1 Sam 13. According to the current text, Saul seems old and indecisive, even a security risk for his troops. He almost killed the young hero Jonathan! Jonathan, however, is a pro-Davidic figure in the Saul-David narratives; he embodies the legitimate transfer of power from Saul to David. In the original text, Saul probably defeated the Philistines gloriously and was then presented to the people as king by the "seer"; perhaps the narrator transferred this plot sequence to the events in 1 Sam 11, where the motif of the renewal of the king seems out of place.

The original pro-Saul, now pro-Davidic narrative collection in 1 Sam 9:1–10:16 and 1 Sam 13–14 is the prequel to a much longer narrative. David determines the plot from 1 Sam 16 on, but Saul and his house continue to appear on the scene. In a substantial number of narratives the Saulides remain the sole or at least the determining characters. It is noticeable that none of these Saulide or Benjaminite episodes demeans Saul. Even where David appears, the narrative does not resort to a black-and-white evaluation of events and characters and avoids creating David as a figure of light and Saul as a figure of darkness. Saul and his house are continually portrayed with respect; nevertheless, we get the impression that this house is not the recipient of divine blessing. As much as the narrative begins with hope for Saul (1 Sam 9:1–10:16), dark shadows soon appear on the horizon (1 Sam 13). The house of Saul leads a tragic existence. Most of the members of this house lose their life before their time, and those who survive are entirely dependent on David's generosity. We thus encounter a narrative on Saul and his house, but it is told from a Davidic perspective. This narrative collection may have contained the following texts:

1 Sam 9:1–10:16	Saul goes forth to find the donkeys of his father and is anointed king of Israel.
13–14	Saul and/or his son Jonathan attack the Philistine captain at Gibeah and win a decisive battle against the Philistines at Michmash.
17:1–18:4	In another war against the Philistines, David of Bethlehem defeats the warrior Goliath and wins the affection of Jonathan.
20:1–21:1	Saul chases David away; Jonathan defends him but remains with his father.
26: 1–25*	Saul pursues David, who in turn pursues Saul and spares him.
28:4–25	The Philistines move toward a final battle; a necromancer foretells Saul's imminent death.
31:1–7	Saul and his sons Jonathan, Abinadab, and Malchishua die in the final battle against the Philistines.
31:8–13	The men of Jabesh pay final homage to Saul and his sons.
2 Sam 2:8–10	General Abner, Saul's uncle, appoints Saul's son Eshbaal king over the north.
2:12–17	The men of Judah win a (substitute) battle against the Benjaminites.
2:18–32	Abner kills Asael, the brother of David's military leaders Joab and Abishai, in self-defense.
3:6–11	Following a conflict with Eshbaal, Abner makes contact with David.
3:12–16	David demands and enforces the release of Saul's daughter Michal.

3:20–21	Abner negotiates with David in Hebron.
3:22–37	Joab murders Abner; David mourns over him.
4:1–8a, 12	Eshbaal is murdered; David has the murderers executed.
5:3	The elders of Israel come to Hebron and anoint David king.
21:1–14	Seven members of the house of Saul are executed and buried in honor next to the remains of Saul and his sons.
9:2–13	David is told by Saul's estate manager Ziba of the existence of Jonathan's son Meribaal; he takes care of him (and of his son Mica).
16:1–4	Ziba denounces Meribaal to David and is rewarded.
16:5–7	The Saulide Shimei heavily insults David.
19:20–24	Shimei is pardoned by David.
19:25–31	Meribaal is rehabilitated by David (to the detriment of Ziba).
20:1–2, 14–22	The Benjaminite Sheba calls the north to secede and fails.

Even a cursory glance over this collection shows us that the texts gathered here are quite divergent. Some of them are isolated single narratives (e.g., the story of David and Goliath in 1 Sam 17 or the narrative of Saul's encounter with the necromancer in 1 Sam 28 or of the execution of seven members of the house of Saul in 2 Sam 21). Other texts are connected to each other in a narrative sequence (e.g., 2 Sam 2–3, where Abner's fate is described in several interconnected episodes). Again, other texts seem to have been torn from their original context and placed into their current context (such as the Benjaminite episodes in 2 Sam 16 and 19). Despite these differences, all the texts share the fact that they emphasize the fate of Saul and his house in the midst of narratives about David. Many of these episodes reveal detailed knowledge about the processes within the house of Saul or about the fate of individual members of the house of Saul. We gain the impression that we are dealing with traditions of Benjaminite origin. On the other hand, we cannot deny the overall Judahite perspective of these texts. The narratives do not focus on Saul and his house per se but on their relation to David. David always appears fair in his treatment of the house of Saul, whether as adversary, partner, aid, or friend. When members of the house of Saul die one after the other, sometimes even in groups, these events are never connected to any fault of David but are explained as tragic fate or unfortunate circumstance. Readers are supposed to understand that the house of Saul had no future but had to make room for David and his reign. The pro-Davidic tendency is part of the earliest stages of the text (see the depiction of David's mourning over Abner in 2 Sam

2–3) and cannot be regarded as a secondary addition. This pro-Davidic tendency, however, was continually increased as the original history of the early monarchy was redacted and expanded as follows.

1 Sam 17: The narrative on David and Goliath displays a Davidic ideology particularly in the lengthy speeches (17:32–37, 44–48), including the repeated phrase that "God was with David" (17:37), the descriptions of David at court (17:42), or the explicitly theological comments in 17:45–46 (17:47 seems to be an even later addition). The negative evaluation of Saul in 17:8, 11, together with an old separate tradition about the victory of the young sling-bearing soldier David over Goliath (17:4–11, *48–50), was probably also added by the final redactor. The narrative "From Shepherd Boy to Israel's Hero" may have been part of a Benjaminite narrative collection that told of how a formerly unknown David (17:12–14) received the love of prince Jonathan (18:1, 3–4) and the daughter of the king as his wife (17:25! 18:17?) due to a surprising victory over a Philistine elite soldier.

1 Sam 20: This narrative was expanded from a pro-Davidic point of view, especially in the speeches. According to the original narrative, Saul was primarily incensed over the close (and homosexual? see 20:30) friendship between his son Jonathan and David. Saul feared that this upstart would turn out to be a rival for the crown prince. Jonathan had to discover that his father intended to kill his friend and thus aided him in escaping (see the same motif in 1 Sam 19:11–17 in relation to Jonathan's sister Michal; see §III.2.3.4 below).

1 Sam 26: The narrative of the sparing of Saul by David—which interestingly features Saul's uncle and general Abner—is expanded from a pro-Davidic perspective especially in the dialogues 26:8–11, 15–25a that bring this narrative more in line with the parallel story in 1 Sam 24.[15]

1 Sam 28: The original narrative describes King Saul with great compassion. Saul moves toward his death with much uncertainty but with great courage. This portrait was later expanded with anti-Saulide colors: Deuteronomistic authors accused Saul of a severe religious faux pas because of his inquiry of the necromancer (28:3b, 9–10). They described how Samuel repeated his devastating judgment from 1 Sam 15 once he was conjured up from the dead (28:17). The comments that Yhwh had turned away from Saul (cf. 28:16 with 1 Sam 16:14) and that Saul did not have any contact with Yhwh (cf. 28:6 with the many reports on David's use of an oracle, e.g., 1 Sam 23:4, 12; 30:8; 2 Sam 2:1) may originate from the narrator of the history of the early monarchy.

---

15. See Dietrich, "Die zweifache Verschonung Sauls," 232–53.

2 Sam 2–3: The narrative sequence on Abner seems to have been expanded especially in 2 Sam 3. In 3:9–10 Abner legitimates the transfer of power from Saul and Eshbaal to David. In 3:14–15 Eshbaal is the one who delivers Michal to David, even though this does not seem very plausible and creates tension with 3:12–13; the original narrative may have stated between 3:12 and 3:16 that Abner had brought Michal. This tradition does not speak of the fact that Michal had formerly been David's wife. The passages in 3:17–19 are additions of the final redactor that serve to legitimize David's reign. The material in 3:28–29 (30) and perhaps the entire passage in 3:31–39 serve apologetic functions. In this text, in which perhaps the lament over Abner may be an old tradition (3:33), David is clearly separated from Abner's murder. This is a characteristic feature of the entire narrative: David is never to blame for the demise of an adversary—with the clear exception of the case of Uriah.

2 Sam 4: The passage in 4:8a–11 pursues purely apologetic interests and connects this chapter closely to 2 Sam 3 and also to the freely composed narrative in 2 Sam 1. This does not mean that David did not have Eshbaal's murderers executed in the original narrative (4:12).

2 Sam 21: The narrative on the ritual execution and burial of seven members of the house of Saul that served to end a famine belongs to an appendix in 2 Sam 21–24 added probably by a Deuteronomistic redactor. It has often been suggested that this gruesome chapter originally belonged before 2 Sam 9. If this is true, did the author of the history of the early monarchy omit this material (because it was too compromising?), and did a later redactor add it on at the end (out of a fundamentally critical attitude toward the monarchy?), thus giving it a new place within the collection of David traditions?

2 Sam 16:1–7 and 19:20–31: The author of the final narrative connected the scenes in 2 Sam 16 and 19 closely to the sequence of events surrounding Absalom's uprising. It is impossible to show whether these passages originally belonged to a larger source before entering their present context. It is at least notable that the Benjaminite episodes are somewhat isolated from their immediate context. We would only need short introductory sentences (e.g., "During the time when David fled from Absalom out of Jerusalem" or "When David returned after his victory over Absalom") in order to transform these episodes into parts of a separate collection.

2 Sam 20: This chapter is not really a narrative on the house of Saul, but Sheba is a Benjaminite, just like Shimei and Meribaal. Sheba's attempted secession could have signaled the transformation of a Saulide claim to power into a general demand for northern independence. The narrative is not completely isolated from its surroundings, but it does follow somewhat surprisingly after the Absalom episode. It seems that this material was passed on to the final author and motivated him to make the north-south issue into the general background for Absalom's uprising and into the central theme of 2 Sam 19.

When the narratives discussed above were created and collected, the fate of Saul and his house, of the Benjaminites and the northern Israelites, during the time of David was well known in Judah. Perhaps it would have been desirable to forget many of the details, but the subject matter was too virulent to be suppressed. Judah had to deal with the fact that there had been a dynasty *prior* to David that had claimed the kingship. The narrators indeed show a certain degree of sympathy, respect at minimum, toward the Israelites and especially toward the house of Saul. If we consider the fact that later traditions increasingly eradicated the memory of the house of Saul, then we gain the impression that we are dealing with a relatively early stage in the history of these traditions. These narratives, at least in part and in their original form, may have their historical origin relatively close to the early monarchy. In the books of Kings, more precisely in the passages concerning the division of the kingdom, we encounter several notes on severe tensions between Judah and northern Israel (e.g., 1 Kgs 14:30; 15:7, 32). The territory of Benjamin (!) seems to have been a special bone of contention that was fought over with great fervor. This is no surprise, as this territory was only a few kilometers away from the Judahite capital of Jerusalem. In 1 Kgs 11:29–39, a late layer of the text, Benjamin is simply mentioned in conjunction with Judah as the territory that remained in the hands of the house of David following the secession of the north. We read in 15:16–22 of an actual war fought between the kingdoms of Israel and Judah over fortified cities in the border region between Judah and Benjamin. Such political events may have constituted the background for the narratives about Saul and his house in the books of Samuel. These texts would thus express the conviction that the Davidic south was superior to the north but that the northern Israelites, especially the Benjaminites, had no reason to bring any ancient claims to bear on the house of David. On the contrary, the fall of the Benjaminite dynasty and the transfer of power to David were completely justified as well as unavoidable. If the Benjaminites were to have a chance for the future, then it was only in close connection to and under the protection of the Davidic reign in Judah. Whether the inhabitants north of the Judahite homelands heard this message and accepted it is something we will never know.

III.2.3.4. The Narrative Collection on "David the Outlaw"

There are several traditions recorded in 1 Sam 19–2 Sam 2 that are quite divergent but that all center on one topic: David's fate as a fugitive from Saul that led him through Judah and the Negev to the Philistines, where he became a city-king of Ziklag before returning to Judah and becoming king in Hebron.

Everything that goes beyond the basic topic "flight and return of David" can be readily seen as a later addition to the early narrative by the author of the whole history of the early monarchy (see §III.2.4 below).

1 Sam 16:1–13: The anointing of David is a pro-Davidic counterpart to the narrative of the anointing of Saul in 1 Sam 9:1–10:16. As is well known, this narrative conflicts with the two other traditions that introduce David to the readers, 1 Sam 16:14–23 and 1 Sam 17. This text is a programmatic and secondary prequel to the David story. The author derived the names in 16:6ff. from 17:12ff. Further, 1 Sam 16:12 is written in a typical courtly style. The motif of David's anointing (and the anointing of his rival Saul!) is taken up only in other young texts such as 1 Sam 24:7; 26:9; 2 Sam 1:14; 3:39; 19:22.

1 Sam 17: This lengthy and magnificent chapter has a multilayered history of transmission and redaction.[16] In large parts it most likely was part of the history of the early monarchy. It does conflict somewhat with 16:1–13 and especially with 16:14–23: David appears in 17:12–14 as a completely unknown character, and Saul does not seem able to recognize his own weapons carrier after he has defeated the Philistine warrior (17:55–58)! The final author may have actually enjoyed the image of a somewhat confused Saul, but he was mostly interested in creating a multifaceted and many-colored image of David.

1 Sam 18:1–19: In contrast to the narrative collection of David as outlaw, this passage is full of explicitly pro-Davidic comments: David is successful, everybody loves him, and Yhwh is *with him*. This statement is a theological *Leitmotif* present in the entire narrative. Regarding the communication of information, the language is very standard and could well be redactional (David is given several offices and is successful whatever he does). Other passages anticipate material that will return later (regarding the victory song of the women in 18:7, see 21:12 and 29:5; regarding Saul's spear in 18:10–11, see 19:10). Jonathan's love for David (18:1, 3–4) belongs to a further motif present in the entire narrative (see 1 Sam 20; 23:14ff.; 2 Sam 9; 16:1ff.; 19:25ff.). The failed marriage with Merab, Saul's oldest daughter, probably belongs to the tradition of the Goliath narrative (1 Sam 17:25!).

1 Sam 19:18–24: This anecdote, which has David flee unexpectedly to the northern hills of Ephraim, is probably a correction of the pro-Saul tradition

---

16. See Walter Dietrich, "Die Erzählungen von David und Goliat in I Sam 17," *ZAW* 108 (1996): 172–91.

in 1 Sam 10:10–12 and served to connect David with Samuel, who otherwise is so concerned with Saul (see also 16:1–13).

1 Sam 20; 23:14b–18: The scenes centering on Jonathan serve to slow down the plot development. According to 1 Sam 19:9–17, David is already a fugitive and knows exactly that his life is threatened; 1 Sam 20 broaches this topic once again. Both meetings between David and Jonathan appear to float freely in terms of the immediate context but also in regards to setting. The close friendship between David and the crown prince plays an important role for the narrative, which surpasses any need for historical plasticity. It would, however, be a mistake to view this material as purely fictional, as a comparison with 2 Sam 1:26 shows. In short, 1 Sam 20 could also make use of an older tradition (see §III.2.3.4 below), although 1 Sam 23:14b–18 is probably only the product of the narrator's imagination.

1 Sam 21:12b: The courtiers of Achish state two reasons for their unease with David's presence when he seeks asylum in Gath: "Is this not the king of the land?" they ask in verse 12a. In verse 12b they quote the aforementioned victory song that is also quoted in 1 Sam 18:7 and 29:5 and that seems to function as a bridge between the various narrative units. The use of the quote in this context works wonderfully to push any suspicions aside that David would have cooperated with the Philistines against Saul and Israel. The first reason is enough to force David to leave the Philistines as quickly as possible. It is known in Gath that it is said in Judah (hardly in Israel!) that he is "the king of the land"—of the Judahite mountain regions. In the center of this region, in Hebron, David will eventually be proclaimed king (2 Sam 2:4).

1 Sam 25:1a: The note of Samuel's death belongs to other large narrative contexts.

1 Sam 25:43–44: This and other reports on David's family are part of the large history of the early monarchy. The reference to the fate of Michal in this context anticipates the following Michal episodes: 2 Sam 3:12–16; 6:16, 20–23.

1 Sam 27:1, 3b, 4: David's soliloquy in verse 1 is redactional, as are many speeches. The final narrator has David justify why he can no longer avoid deserting to the Philistines. Verse 4 confirms his thoughts. Verse 3b is to be read in context of the family notes in 1 Sam 25:43–44; 2 Sam 2:2aβb; 3:2–5; and 5:13–15 that anticipate the question of succession.

1 Sam 28 and 31: These narratives deal with Saul and his fate. David does not appear in these texts, especially not as an outlaw and fugitive.

1 Sam 29; 2 Sam 1: These narratives seem to be late compositions, not old traditions already belonging to the narrative collection of David's escape. Both episodes consist primarily of direct speech that deals mainly with removing David as far away as possible from Saul's tragic end during the battle of

Gilboa. This distance aims at separating Saul's end and David's developing career. The Philistines let David go from his military obligations because they do not trust him. The following narrative deliberately places David far south in the Negev during an Amalekite raid. Further, 2 Sam 1 interprets 1 Sam 31 from a Davidic point of view. David was not present at the battle of Gilboa; he received news of its outcome in *Hebron* through an Amalekite (!) messenger. The parallels and modifications to the report in 1 Sam 31 show that the man partially tells the truth, partially falsifies the event. He especially omits the fact that during the night he must have stolen Saul's symbols of power, which he brings David (!). David orders a general period of mourning—and subsequently has this unpleasant individual executed.

2 Sam 1:17–27: The final narrator inserted this old traditional lament into its present appropriate context; it seems that this text was handed down in its own collection of songs.

2 Sam 2:8–5:5: This text is the centerpiece for its own narrative collection (see §III.2.3.3 above).

What remains of the postulated narrative collection is still a large body of texts:

1 Sam 16:14–23	David comes from Bethlehem to Saul (to Gibeah).[17]
18:*20–27[18]	David wins Michal's love and becomes her husband.
19:9–10	David escapes an assassination attempt by the raging Saul.
19:11–17	David is aided in his escape by Michal.
21:1–10	David manipulates the help of the priests of Nob.
21:11–12a, 13–16	David tries unsuccessfully for the first time to desert to Achish, the Philistine king of Gath.
22:1–2	David gathers an independent militia in a cave at Adullam.
22:3–4	David brings his parents to Mizpeh in Moab.
22:5	David follows the advice of the prophet Gad and goes to Yaar-hereth.

---

17. The narrative shows clear signs of redactional activity: the final two words of verse 19 ("he who was by the sheep") connect to 16:1–3. The descriptions of the court in verse 18 and the phrase that YHWH was with David in 18b were inserted by the final narrator.

18. The verses 18:21, 22ab, 25b are probably additions by the final narrator, who accuses Saul of malicious intent and expands on the motif of David's popularity. We can observe a similar situation in the narrative addition in 18:28–30.

[22:6–23	David finds a companion in the priest Abiathar, who has fled to him from Nob].[19]
23:*1–13[20]	David settles temporarily in Keilah, which is threatened by the Philistines.
23:14a, 19–28	David moves around in the desert of Ziph, more precisely, at Horesh on the hill of Hachilah, as well as the desert of Maon in the Arabah, more precisely, at the Rock of Escape; he escapes Saul thanks to a Philistine raid.
24:*1–23[21]	David spares Saul in a cave at En-gedi.
25:*1b–42	David demands protection money in the area of Maon, more precisely, in the town of Carmel.
27:2–7	David receives the city of Ziklag as fiefdom from Achish of Gat.
27:8–12	David organizes raids and plunderings against nomadic groups in the Negev.
30:1–31	David defeats the Amalekites from his stronghold in Ziklag and distributes his portion of the loot to various townships in Judah, including Hebron.
2 Sam 2:1–4a	David resides in Hebron and becomes king of Judah.
5:6–12	David makes Jerusalem his residence.
5:17–25	David twice defeats the Philistines when they invade the plain of Rephaim.

---

19. It is also possible that this narrative was added later to the narrative collection of David the fugitive, even though there are several close connections to 1 Sam 21:1–10; this narrative is connected only indirectly with David (but through Abiathar!), perhaps foreshadowing the important role that Abiathar will play at a later point; see 2 Sam 15, 17, 1 Kgs 1–2.

20. Timo Veijola ("David in Keila," in idem, *David: Gesammelte Studien zu den Davidüberlieferungen des Alten Testaments* [Helsinki: Helsinki: Finnische Exegetische Gesellschaft, 1990], 5–42) postulates that the oldest tradition contained in this text is found in verses *1–5, the report on "David's daring raid against a troop of Philistines who threatened Keilah" (41); this old tradition was expanded by the "author of the history of David's rise" (perhaps better: the redactor of the narrative collection on David as outlaw) in verses *2, 4, *9–13 and subsequently by the Deuteronomistic redaction in verses 6, 10, 11a.

21. As with 1 Sam 25 (and 26, see above §III.2.3.3), the final narrator is especially present in this text. The long speeches—between David and his followers, between David and Saul, between David and Abigail—carry the primary intention of the large narrative work: the legitimate transfer of power from Saul to David (and Solomon) and the complete blamelessness of David in this process.

If we observe the beginning and the ending of this narrative collection, we can see clearly that the aim of this collection is to describe how a *nobody* became the king of Judah. This is truly the story of an astounding career but not the history of David's rise, as was postulated so often by Old Testament scholars (see §III.1.2 above). Not only are we missing the further development to the king of Israel but also the decline and end of Saul and his house as a prerequisite for such a rise. The relationship between north and south, the question of the transfer of power from the north to the south, is not the subject matter of this early narrative collection. These texts instead intend to show how a third power developed in the Judahite hills aside from the two competitors Israel and the Philistines, a power that was able to hold its own in this competition. There is no indication that kingship existed in Judah before David or that Saul also ruled over the south. Saul did organize several military raids into the south, perhaps even supported by local groups (see 1 Sam 23:19; 26:1). If 1 Sam 15 contains a historic core, the target of these attacks was the nomadic Amalekites (see also 14:48). According to the biblical description, however, David and his small militia were the actual target as they gained more and more influence in the area, becoming a regional power centered in Hebron. This is exactly what Saul had attempted to prevent and what caused severe problems for his kingdom and that of his son once this attempt had failed. All of this seems historically plausible, and thus this source might lead us quite close to the time period described in it.

According to the narrative collection, David's amazing career started when an unknown young man from the unimportant Judahite village of Bethlehem came unexpectedly to Saul's court. Not long thereafter, however, a very ill and erratic king drove this promising young man from his presence. All of David's activities and movements are described with great geographic precision so that we are faced with an itinerary of David's escape: from Gibeah of Saul cross-country through southern Palestine to the Philistines, from there to Ziklag in the southern Negev (perhaps close to Beer-sheba) to Hebron in the heartland of the Judean Mountains, finally to Jerusalem, David's permanent residence. Not all places mentioned can be located with certainty. It seems, however, that all of these places were known and could have been retraced and visited. Whether all of the place names mentioned in the text are a result of individual traditions or were inserted by the person who collected these traditions (i.e., where place names occur more than once), whether the order of the episodes in the present text is the original order, or whether the order was disrupted by later redactional activity (such as in the heavily redacted chapters 1 Sam 24–26)—all of this can no longer be determined conclusively.

One conspicuous characteristic of this narrative collection is the absence of theological argumentation and reflection but the presence of relative frequent divine aid for David as the divine protégé. We frequently encounter oracles—either as prophetic or as priestly oracle, some without classification—that save David at the last minute from a threatening situation or suggest to him the proper course of action. It seems to be the collector's intent to show that David stood in very close contact to God. He could expect divine aid and guidance at any time. This is the only reason why David is finally able to decisively defeat the Philistines. This ending (if a different ending was not discarded and if the two anecdotes in 2 Sam 5:17ff., 22ff. were not originally located in a completely different context[22]) is surprising only at first sight. The Philistine threat is actually a permanent subtext of these narratives. David wants to escape to the Philistines and risks his life in doing so (1 Sam 21:11ff.); at a later point they attack Saul in his homelands and enable David to escape from a sticky situation (23:27); then David finds refuge among the Philistines but has to hide his true intentions and actions from them (for which he has to pay a horrendous price! See 27:8ff.).

This narrative collection is certainly comprised of very different separate traditions. We encounter etiologies of names (e.g., 1 Sam 23:28; 25:25), military anecdotes (e.g., 1 Sam *24), short local traditions (e.g., 23:1–13; 27:1–7; 2 Sam 5:6–11), and individual dramatic episodes (e.g., 1 Sam 19:11–17; 21:2–10; 22:6–19). All these traditions originated within close temporal proximity to the events narrated in them; each tradition kept its own local coloring. Nevertheless, we are able to discern the ordering and composing hand of the one who gathered these collections into a narrative whole. Most notable are standard phrases describing David's life as a fugitive. David repeatedly *flees, escapes, runs away,* or *hides* (the Hebrew verbs are ברח, מלט, קום and יצא, נוס, סתר, and others). The narrative moves quickly, almost breathless. It seems as if the listeners are to empathize with how much David is threatened by external dangers, how often his life stands at the edge, how relentlessly he is persecuted—and why he simply had to go to the Philistines. It seems as if the narrative collection is concerned with explaining and justifying this precarious changing of sides—while simultaneously portraying its hero as creative, clever, courageous, and shrewd despite all of these threats. He is vastly superior to the sick king Saul who persecuted him with all his might. He is also superior to his liege lord Achish: not in terms of power but definitely in terms of intelligence. He turns his pursuer into the pursued and uses the one who

---

22. In 2 Sam 5:17 it is precisely the establishment of David as king of *Israel* that provokes the Philistine attack against him. This may be a redactional bridge to the following narrative. As an interesting aside, David retreats to his *fortress* (מצודה; see also verse 17), his desert stronghold (1 Sam 22:4, 5; 24:23; see also 2 Sam 23:14) as a response to this attack.

thinks he is using David. The narrator and the listeners savor the triumph created by the familiar paradigm of the small underdog who succeeds against all odds over his mighty adversaries. The narratives are proud to tell of a king who was not given the kingdom at birth but who earned the kingdom by surmounting overwhelming obstacles. It seems that these narratives on the great king David who started very small were a source of strength and comfort to the various narrators and their listeners.

In our biblical context, this narrative collection contains additional layers of meaning. The legendary founder of a dynasty was not conceived in heaven nor born in a palace. Yet heaven had determined that he arrive in the palace. Whoever wanted to be important in Israel—and David was definitely important—did not have to begin as someone important. Even those (perhaps especially those) who were not granted an easy life could be rewarded greatly in the end. The spectators were told: even (especially?) those who are dismissed as hopeless can be the ultimate winners. The aspects of lowliness and humility, of gentleness and modesty (see 1 Sam 16:1–13; 2 Sam 12; Ps 51) that were later added to the portrait of King David and that contributed to a large degree to the expectation of a coming Messiah (see Mic 5:1–5; Zeph 3:12–13; Zech 9:9; Matt 21:5) had their origin most likely in this narrative collection of David the fugitive and outlaw.

III.2.3.5. The Bathsheba-Solomon Novella

Two texts that are separated at great distance are combined through a common constellation of characters: 2 Sam 11–12 and 1 Kgs 1–2. In both cases five characters carry the plot: David, his general Joab, his wife Bathsheba, the prophet Nathan, and Solomon, the son of David and Bathsheba. In all the texts that lie between these two passages (2 Sam 13–2 Sam 20 or 24), only David and Joab appear, whereas the others are not even mentioned. There is no other instance in the traditions on the early monarchy where David and Solomon are portrayed so negatively. In 2 Sam 11 David is an adulterer and murderer; in 1 Kgs 1 he appears as a senile old man, the victim of a palace intrigue. Solomon's birth story is surrounded by scandal, the story of his rise to the throne soaked in blood. The present text does include positive aspects among the negative elements, but these aspects turn out to be secondary additions to a highly negative original text.

According to 2 Sam 12, the adulterer and murderer was led to repentance by Nathan, who then shifted the punishment from the deeply fallen king to the son conceived in adultery. Thus Solomon appears as the second child of a now-legitimate liaison whom YHWH refers to as his "beloved." Solomon's brutal actions following his assumption of power are justified by arguments given in part by David himself: Joab and Shimei have caused David much trouble and receive their due punishment (1 Kgs 2:5–6, 8–9, 31–32, 44); Adonijah draws punishment upon himself; and Abiathar's deposition and exile is not an arbitrary act but a sign of grace (2:13–27). The assumption seems obvious—and has been repeatedly suggested in the past (see §III.1.1 above)—that these texts, which exonerate David and especially Solomon, are secondary additions added for understandable reasons. A diachronic dissection can make use of redactional and source-critical observations. Which passages fit only with great difficulty into their present context (e.g., 2 Sam 12:25b; 1 Kgs 2:12, 24, 44), which passages refer to a larger horizon than their present context and are thus likely redactional (e.g., 2 Sam 11:20b, 21a; 1 Kgs 1:6b, 42ff. [see below]; 2:5–9, 11, *26, 31b–33, 44–45)? We also can take recourse to the question of tendency: Where does the text display a pro-Solomonic or a pro-Davidic attitude (e.g., in 2 Sam 10, where, in contrast to 2 Sam 11–12, David is portrayed as a peaceful king who is forced into war against his will[23])? Where does the text contain explicitly theological elements (e.g., in 2 Sam 11:27b; 12:1–5, *24–25; 1 Kgs 1:36, 48; 2:15bβ, 24, 33)?

We are left with the oldest textual layer, which can be divided into three acts.

Act 1: How Solomon was born. David sends Joab and the Israelite army against the kingdom of Ammon east of the Jordan (2 Sam 11:1). David himself remains in Jerusalem and commits adultery with the wife of an officer who is fighting with the army. When he does not succeed in foisting parentage onto the officer for the child conceived in adultery, he has him killed with the help of Joab and marries Bathsheba (11:2–27a). The child conceived in adultery is born and is named Solomon by his mother, Jedidiah by his father (12:*24–25). Joab conquers Rabbah Ammon, and David places the Ammonite crown on his own head (12:26–31). This first act is clearly framed by a war story, into which the infamous story of David's adultery and murder is inserted.

Act 2: How Solomon ascended to David's throne. Once David has grown very old—so old that not even beautiful Abishag of Shunem can warm him (1 Kgs 1:1–4)—Adonijah, son of David and Haggith, makes a claim to

---

23. See Georg Hentschel, "Die Kriege des friedfertigen Königs David (2 Sam 10,1–11,1; 12,26–31)," in *Überlieferung und Geschichte: Gerhard Wallis zum 65. Geburtstag am 15. Januar 1990* (ed. Helmut Obst; Wissenschaftliche Beiträge d. Martin-Luther-Universität Halle-Wittenberg A/125; Halle: Martin-Luther-Universität Halle-Wittenberg, 1990), 49–58; Randall C. Bailey, *David in Love and War: The Pursuit of Power in 2 Samuel 10–12* (JSOTSup 75; Sheffield: JSOT Press, 1990); Ulrich Hübner, *Die Ammoniter: Untersuchungen zur Geschichte, Kultur und Religion eines transjordanischen Volkes im 1. Jahrtausend v.Chr.* (ADPV 16; Wiesbaden: Harrassowitz, 1992), 171–75.

David's throne, and David does not expressly stop him (1:5, 6a). Adonijah wins Joab and Abiathar as his allies, while Zadok, Benaiah, Nathan, and a certain Shimei and his companions, the "heroes," do not favor him (1:7–8). Adonijah initiates a great feast, and these two groups become clear once more, now with the added aspect that all the other royal sons and the Judahite officials side with Adonijah, whereas Shimei is now missing and Solomon appears to replace him (1:11–27). They succeed in leading David to speak out in favor of Solomon as his successor and subsequently move to inaugurate him as king (1:28–34). Zadok and Nathan anoint Solomon king under the protection of the royal guard and their leader Benaiah, and the "people" (i.e., the inhabitants of Jerusalem) proclaim the new king (1:38–40). In the face of this fait accompli, the Adonijah party gives up their cause (1:41a, 49b); Solomon spares his opponent Adonijah—for now (1:50–53)!

Act 3: How Solomon cleaned up among his opponents. David dies, and Adonijah approaches Bathsheba and Solomon asking to marry Abishag, the last (not quite) wife of David. This request is interpreted as a grab for power and costs him his life (1 Kgs 2:10, 13–15abα, 16–23, 25). Abiathar, also a likely death candidate, is "spared" when Solomon deposes him and exiles him to Anathoth (2:26a). Joab is murdered at the altar in the sacred tent on order of the king (2:28–31a, 34). Last, but not least, Shimei meets his fate when he breaks the house arrest imposed on him by Solomon to recapture an escaped slave; he too is liquidated (2:36–41, 46a). Now the kingdom is established in Solomon's hand (2:26b).

It is no verdict, but rather an advantage, that the above attempt at reconstructing the original text concurs in many aspects with the suggestions presented by other scholars.[24] It differs, however in its insistence to limit this reconstruction to the actual narratives on Solomon. I do not believe that similar strata can be convincingly reconstructed within the remaining corpus of the so-called succession narrative.

Two particular decisions pertaining to the reconstruction made above need further explanation. Determining the entire passage 1 Kgs 1:41b–48 as a redactional layer may be surprising, because it does not seem to breathe the same apologetic spirit as the other additions. This impression, however, is incorrect. The messenger scenes with Jonathan ben Abiathar in verses 42–48 cannot be separated on a linguistic and topical level from the earlier messenger scenes with Jonathan (and Ahimaaz ben Zadok) in 2 Sam 17:17ff. and 18:19ff., which convey a very positive image of David. The same is true

---

24. Of the literature mentioned above in §III.1.1, we should mention especially the contributions by Veijola and Langlamet.

for both messenger scenes. The loud proclamation of the new king by the people (1 Kgs 1:39–40) that is clearly heard by those gathered around Adonijah (1:41a) is in itself sufficient to explain why they were taken with fear and quickly disbanded, as we are told in 1:49. (When "resuming" the narrative thread, the narrator may have decided to repeat the phrase of "those invited" [הַקְּרֻאִים] by Adonijah from 1:41a).

It was also assumed above that the Shimei mentioned in 1 Kgs 2:36–45 who was liquidated by Solomon was a different Shimei than the Shimei ben Gera of the house of Saul mentioned in 2 Sam 16:5ff. and 19:17ff. It is true that both Shimeis are identified with each other in 1 Kgs 2:8–9, 44, but this identification is the work of the redactor, who either made a mistake or who deliberately made use of traditional material in this way. Shimei is a very frequent name in the Bible; seventeen or eighteen people have this name, so mistaken identities are quite possible. This is even more likely since 1 Kgs 1:8, a list containing the followers of Solomon, actually mentions a person named Shimei who plays no further role in the narrative. I believe that this is the very Shimei who was liquidated by Solomon: not as an ally, of course, but as an opponent. Shimei turned from one to the other, as we can see from a comparison between the two lists in 1:8 and 10. The first mentions Shimei together with *his comrades, the heroes of David*.[25] The second list mentions the heroes again, but not Shimei. This means that, whereas the royal guard sided with Solomon (see also 2 Sam 20:7; 23:8ff. and other passages), Shimei turned away from him—and this costs him his life.

The original stratum in 2 Sam 11–12 and 1 Kgs 1–2 is a narrative of high aesthetic quality. The characters are carefully introduced, and their actions are linked as a cohesive plot. Individual scenes are shaped by dialogue that allows the personalities of the characters to come alive. The narrative as a whole is critical of David and Solomon, but we do not encounter wholesale judgments.

The first act is full of ambiguities. Neither Bathsheba nor Uriah are simply "good people," nor are David and Joab simply "evil." To be sure, David commits heinous deeds, but at first he is simply lecherous and then constrained by the consequences of his action. Joab does not appear as a thoughtless adjunct to murder; he instead criticizes David's arbitrariness subtly but clearly. The

---

25. Following LXX[L] we should read רֵעָיו הַגִּבּוֹרִים. Without reason and consequence, MT has an individual by the name of Rei (רֵעִי) appear. The likely suggestion that Shimei and the "heroes" belong together should be compared with the list of the גִּבּוֹרִים in 2 Sam 23:24–39. We do not encounter a man of this name. Was Shimei thus not a member of this elite unit—or can we dare to suppose an identity or mix-up between שִׁמְעִי and שַׁמָּה/שִׁמְאָה (23:24, 33, compare 23:11)?

character of Bathsheba is completely opaque, and we cannot tell whether Uriah is an upright, courageous soldier or a proud, awkward individual, whether he is fighting for his rights or tired of life. We are faced with a similar situation in act 2: David may be old and weak, but this is not evil in itself. Adonijah wants to become king, but is this so bad? There are two parties, but which one is right? Is Adonijah really celebrating with a harmless feast, or does the prominent guest list indicate something like a coup? When Nathan and Bathsheba take initiative, they may be acting out of real concern. Did David swear the oath to give the kingdom to Solomon or not? In the end, he does swear this oath so that Nathan and Bathsheba do not appear as liars. It is also unclear how Solomon's enthronement relates to David's resignation: Are we dealing with an intentional transfer of power or a coup d'etat? When Solomon rids himself of his opponents, is this not an understandable, perhaps even necessary, political move? He does allow Abiathar to live, and both Adonijah and Shimei provide him with reasons for their own liquidation. Finally, when Joab is blasphemously stabbed to death at the altar, did he not choose to die there himself?

I admit that some of these thoughts may sound cynical, but the author has made sure that readers can at least ask these questions without being able to answer them unequivocally. An easy black-and-white description would allow the reader to take sides too quickly, to discern the "moral of the story" and then to put the story aside. Then the story could no longer be what it intends to be: a paradigm for never-ending and continually returning questions. What relation is there between power and temptation, between power and the misuse of power? How do individuals deal with power, and how are we to evaluate those in power?

This narrative was probably written in close temporal proximity to the events reported. We do not encounter any indication of a horizon reaching beyond the time of Solomon. The geographical horizon is small and closely limited to Jerusalem. The text mentions the springs Rogel and Gihon and speaks of "the city" as if there were no other cities. There is no mention of any location or institution outside of Jerusalem or from Israel's later history. We hear that the ark was carried into war—before it was placed in Solomon's temple. It seems that during times of peace it stood in a "tent" with an altar from which sacred oil for anointing could be taken; priests officiated here, and we can speak of a sanctuary in the full sense. The narrator knows also of elite military units that were stationed in Jerusalem in the service of King David and that were already dissolved by Solomon (at least we no longer hear of them after 1 Kgs 3): the Cherethites and the Pelethites as well as "David's heroes." This local and temporal coloring makes it plausible to situate the narrative within the context of the Jerusalem of Solomon.

This should not indicate that we are dealing with a completely reliable contemporary historical source. The many instances of direct speech show clearly that much of the text is the product of the narrator's creativity—especially when dealing with speeches that occur in the palace interior during closed meetings. We may, of course, assume that these events occurred as narrated; this is exactly the narrator's art: to lead the audience to believe that it did occur as narrated. His text, however, is also based on facts that we can confirm with the appropriate care and reticence: in 2 Sam 11–12, the fact that David married Bathsheba, the widow of Uriah "the Hittite," who had fallen in the battle against the Ammonites; in 1 Kgs 1–2, the details on the sacred tent and the military units, the presence of two different candidates for David's throne along with their supporters—a more rural-tribal Judahite party and a more aristocratic Jerusalemite party—and the victory of the Jerusalemite Solomon, his ascension to the throne during David's lifetime, and the liquidation of the heads of the opposition.

We should finally mention that the old original narrative did not contain any explicitly theological elements. God and faith in God is certainly present everywhere for the narrator: oaths are taken in his name; he goes with his people into battle; kings are anointed with oil from his tent; his altar is an asylum. But the narrator does not have God appear as a character in the action, comment on the events, speak directly to human characters, or listen to communication from them. The events occur as a causal chain of events without interruption from the outside. The narrator does not see any necessity to draw the transcendent into the immanent; perhaps he even shies away from it.

III.2.3.6. The Book of the Story of Solomon

This source is formally cited in 1 Kgs 11:41: "And the rest of the deeds of Solomon and everything that he performed and his wisdom, is this not written in the book of the acts of Solomon?" It is most often assumed that this source reference was added by the Deuteronomistic Historian, who later refers in quite similar fashion to the "books of the days" of the kings of Judah and Israel (regularly from 1 Kgs 14:19 onward). We can also imagine that this reference was written by the author of the narrative on the early monarchy (see §III.2.4 below) and that the Deuteronomistic redaction used this passage as the model for its source references. Be this as it may, there must have been a "book of the story of Solomon," unless we are to assume that this reference is purely fictional. It must have been written before the end of the monarchy and have served as a collection of material for the narrative in 1 Kgs 3–11. Scholars disagree on the genre, scope, intention, and historical setting of this work (see §III.1.5 above); this is not surprising, considering the fact that we no longer have access to this work but only to the material taken from it.

We cannot assume that the entire text of 1 Kgs 3–11 was the actual "book of the story of Solomon," as it contains several clearly Deuteronomistic passages (e.g., 1 Kgs 5; 8; 9:1–9; 11:1–13) as well as texts taken from other sources (e.g., 8:12–13 from the "book of songs" [cf. LXX 8:13]; 8:*1–8 from the ark narrative; see §III.2.3.2 above). If we subtract these texts, we are still left with a considerable body of texts that could well have been taken from the "book of the story of Solomon" (we can neglect short expansions and glosses at this point).

> the narrative on Solomon's inaugural vision in the sanctuary of Gibeon, 3:4–15
> the narrative of the Solomonic judgment, 3:16–28
> the list of officials in 4:1–6
> the list of provinces in 4:7–19
> the reports on the construction of the palace (!) and the temple in Jerusalem in *5:15–7:51
> the notes on Solomon's economic, trade, cultural, and foreign policy in 5:1–14; 9:10–14,[26] 24–28; 10:14–29; 11:1, 3a
> the narrative of the state visit by the Queen of Sheba in 10:1–13
> the narratives on Solomon's adversaries (in Hebrew, *satan*!) who cause Solomon much trouble in 11:14–40.

We cannot be sure whether the order of the text in the Bible corresponds with the order in the "book of the story of Solomon" (even if the first two narratives must logically stand at the beginning and the rest follows a certain internal logic). It is also very difficult to determine which parts of the text are traditional and which passages were added by a redactor. Where the language differs from the Deuteronomistic Historian, several short summary evaluations may be redactional. These summaries may be the work of the author of the "story of Solomon." These include 1 Kgs 3:28; 5:9, 14; 10:4–5, 23–24. The entire speech of the Queen of Sheba may also be the work of the original pre-Deuteronomistic author.

---

26. The list of Solomon's construction activities in 1 Kgs 9:15–19 is also probably old, but it seems that it was first added by a Deuteronomistic redactor—also taken from the book of the story of Solomon?—who wanted to exculpate Solomon from the odious attachment to mass enslavement of his people (compare also his comments in 9:20–23 in contrast to 5:27–32).

Especially in those instances where the author steps out from behind the scenes, we recognize that the "book of the story of Solomon" is quite enamored with its hero. Critical comments appear in very few passages, such as the narratives on Solomon's adversaries in 1 Kgs 11:1, 14ff. or the short note regarding Solomon's payment of Israelite villages to Hiram, king of Tyre, in 9:10–13. All other texts are characterized by two aspects: a tendency toward formal description, as seen in the many lists of numbers and names, displaying a desire for true historical recording; and a recognizable enthusiasm for Solomon's many strengths, especially his wisdom and his wealth. What good fortune to be the subjects of this king! If 5:5 is not a later addition—its eschatological counterpart in Mic 4:4 might warrant this assumption—then the author considered the reign of Solomon to be a golden era: "Judah and Israel lived in safety, all of them under their vines and their fig trees."

If such praise is truly contemporary, then it leaves us with a bad aftertaste: only tyrants are praised in this manner. The presence of several different genres in the text, however, indicates that this material underwent a long process of growth. This process, especially in regard to the lists, could have already started during Solomon's time and continued to the middle and late monarchy. As a whole, the "book of the history of Solomon" presents us with an imaginative and colorful portrait rather than an exact photo of David's first successor.

III.2.4. The Narrative History of the Early Monarchy

It seems as if the narrative collections and novellas sketched above were already gathered into a narrative opus prior to the creation of the Deuteronomistic History. It most likely included the pre-Deuteronomistic texts from 1 Sam 9 (or 1 Sam 1) to 1 Kgs 1 (or 1 Kgs 12). We are dealing with a narrative history on the early monarchy. Defined minimally, this narrative history places David at its center and frames this portrait with short narratives on Saul (1 Sam *9–14) and Solomon (1 Kgs 1–2). Defined maximally, this narrative history creates a triptychon of portraits of Saul (and Samuel!) and Solomon, with David in the middle.

The minimal solution is supported by the fact that the resulting narrative is more unified by its clear concentration on David as the major protagonist. The material on Saul/Samuel and especially on Solomon is so different from the Davidic narratives that we would have to consider the author of this early narrative history already a redactor as well as an author: the high literary quality of the Davidic narratives speak against such a consideration.

On the other hand, there are several—perhaps even more—arguments that speak for a maximal solution. The Davidic narratives were not freely composed by one author from beginning to end but already made use of prior traditions. For this very reason scholars have assumed the existence of originally separate narrative units such as the succession narrative, the narrative of David's rise, the ark narrative, and so forth. It is also impossible to separate completely the figures of Saul and Solomon from the portrait of David. Thus the reader is left with the desire to learn more about the predecessor and the successor of this central figure than the texts in 1 Sam 9ff. and 1 Kgs 1–2 provide. Other positive signals support this evaluation. The ark narrative goes back to 1 Sam 4–6 and extends up to 1 Kgs 8; the idea that the author of the Davidic narrative would have taken only one section from this ark narrative, the text in 2 Sam 6, and inserted it into his narrative seems quite odd. The secession call of the northern Israelites appears in almost the exact same wording in 2 Sam 20:1 and 1 Kgs 12:16—the author of the David narrative loves such repetitions. The motif of the fathers who fail in regard to their sons occurs throughout the narrative: from Eli to Samuel to Saul (who almost killed Jonathan!) to David. The subject matter activated by this motif is the question of a successful or failed dynasty and the matter of stability or instability in Israel. Only David, with the help of God, is successful in establishing both. There are other common themes present throughout: the office of the priest (from Eli to Ahimelech to Abiathar and Zadok); the office of prophet (from Samuel to Gad and Nathan); the Philistine problem (from Eli to David); and the more general issue of Israel's oppression from foreign nations and the competence or incompetence of its respective leaders in dealing with this oppression (examples everywhere from 1 Sam 4 to 1 Kgs 11). The entire early monarchy is determined by the dual issue of external and internal violence, the violence in personal relationships as well as in the structures of society, especially concerning the king's claim to power over his subjects. Other examples of unifying tendencies in the narrative (but not of a unified narrative!) will be discussed below.

The suggested narrative history is not the work of an ingenious narrator; it is also not the collection of a few large narratives (e.g., the succession narrative or the narrative of David's rise), each written by an ingenious narrator. This narrative history is the combination of many older and younger sources that differ in style and intention. This statement is of supreme importance for general methodological and specific source-critical issues. This statement prevents us from approaching these texts as a large literary unit, as if we were dealing only with the final canonical text, with a timeless work of art, or even a Hellenistic novel. If this were the case, then all questions of the literary growth of the text and of the historical credibility of its contents would be useless. On the other hand, we have no reason to assume the existence of large narrative works encompassing the succession narrative, the narrative of

David's rise, or perhaps even the entire books of Samuel that go back to the time of the early monarchy and were written as a "court history" or an "apology of David."

III.2.4.1. Style and Intention of the Narrative History

The narrative history suggested is not very old (it must be younger than the youngest source incorporated into it), and it is not very young (it must be older than the Deuteronomistic redaction). It is only an indirect—but not worthless!—witness to the events and circumstances of the early monarchy. Aesthetic and theological issues are, however, more important to the text than the historical question. We are dealing with an ambitious and artful narrative that describes the early Israelite state with great differentiation and ambivalence.

The procedures and the intentions of the author are most clearly seen when we are able to isolate texts written by him from the surrounding source material. This is especially possible in the above-mentioned Bathsheba-Solomon novella (§III.2.3.5), as the final narrator had to modify the very clear intention of the source. Observing how the final author achieved these modifications is quite enlightening, providing us with criteria for observing his work in other passages.

With the aid of previous scholarship, the following passages from within 2 Sam 10–12 and 1 Kgs 1–2 can be reasonably identified as secondary (and pre-Deuteronomistic![27]) additions: 2 Sam 10:1–19; 11:*4, 27b; 12:1–7a, *7b–10, 11–24abβ, 25aβb; 1 Kgs 1:6b, 35–37, 41b–48; 2:1, 5–10, 15, 24, 26b, 31b–33, 35, 44–45.

This redactional layer can be isolated from the original stratum for several reasons. It is not as theologically reticent as the old text. YHWH appears frequently, is outraged at what occurred with Bathsheba and Uriah (2 Sam 11:27b), and sends the prophet Nathan (12:1). Once David confesses his sin to Nathan and the punishment is shifted from David to the child conceived in adultery, YHWH strikes the child (12:15), and it becomes sick and eventually dies. When Solomon is born, YHWH loves him (12:24). Benaiah speaks of YHWH's presence with Solomon (1 Kgs 1:37); Jonathan ben Abiathar reports that the members of the court wished YHWH's blessings upon Solomon (1:46); and David praises YHWH because of what has occurred (1:48). Adonijah confesses that it must have been YHWH who gave the kingdom not to him but

---

27. If my analysis is correct, there are only a few Deuteronomistic passages: an expansion of the prophetic speech in 2 Sam 12:7–10 (see my discussion in *Prophetie und Geschichte*, 127–31), the references to Judg 9:50ff. and 1 Sam 2:27–36 in 2 Sam 11:20b, 21a; 1 Kgs 2:27, as well as the clearly identifiable Deuteronomistic verses 1 Kgs 2:2–4, 11–12.

to Solomon (2:15); Solomon refers to the promise of YHWH, given to David, when he issues his orders for execution (2:24; see also 2:44–45).

Even if Solomon's speech mentioned in the last passage is highly exaggerated ("Blessed be King Solomon!"), possibly indicating an ironic subtext, all the passages mentioned above seek to modify the very dark picture of what transpired at Solomon's birth and ascension to the throne by adding the positive elements of the evaluations and actions of God. During the David-Bathsheba affair, this is at first quite painful (due to the conviction of the king and the death of the child), but it works out for the best in the end. All the surrounding participants (Benaiah, David, Solomon, even his adversary Adonijah), perhaps even the narrator, and in the end we as readers understand and are supposed to understand Solomon's enthronement as the result of God's will and guidance. The promise of a dynasty first takes on concrete shape in this very person, in the fact of his enthronement, and the text even indicates that what is to follow will even surpass what has already happened under David. The definite unease that accompanies a reading of 1 Kgs 1–2 is not eliminated, but it is diminished. It is *also* possible to understand the events as a necessary and healthy process that is part of YHWH's plan for the history of his people.

David and Solomon are both equipped with new character traits. David appears as a penitent ruler. He could have crushed Nathan once the inconvenient prophet left the confines of his parable. It was not without reason, however, that the narrator introduced Nathan previously with an incredibly generous message: the promise of a successor who would "go forth from David's bowels" (2 Sam 7:12) and even of an enduring dynasty. Now that this very Nathan appears with a very uncomfortable message, David will not be able to accuse him of base motives or resentment. Perhaps it is even part of the narrative psychology that David's trust in Nathan is one of the deciding factors (along with his guilty conscience) that leads him into the trap set by the parable. Further, it is to David's credit that his first sentence following Nathan's verdict is a full confession. This king is someone who has clearly made a mistake, but he is not a completely evil person. David cannot undo the "material compensation" that he pronounced himself as a reaction to Nathan's case example—the fourfold restitution of the lamb, that is, the removal of many wives (perhaps even of four sons?)—but he can undo the death penalty that he pronounced upon himself. Once again we are taken with David, who dares to protest against the unavoidable punishment against the child. Even though he must know why his child has fallen ill and that this illness will not be cured, he wrestles with God for a change in the child's fate. He believes that God can be moved even after the verdict has been pronounced—just as he himself can be moved because he is not an uncaring tyrant. God, however, is not moved any more than David's repentance has already moved him to spare the king. Once David realizes this fact, he is capable of a radical and striking change of heart. Instead of falling into severe depression in mourning for the child and in anger over God's relentlessness, he accepts his loss. Just as he previously wrestled with God, he now wrestles with his own emotions that must have torn him apart and caused his servants to expect the worst.

Another character trait is added to David in his last orders to Solomon (1 Kgs 2:5–9). It is beside the point whether we today agree with these actions. The dying king still has control over things and acts accordingly when he presents his successor with clear orders regarding what to do. Brutal and mean individuals such as Joab and Shimei—at least the redactor refers to them as brutal and mean—should not be allowed to die peacefully and go down to Sheol unpunished. David does not get his hands dirty personally; he leaves this task to his son and again to the violent Benaiah. Even if David and Solomon do carry the responsibility for these executions, the narrator seems to believe that this burden is not all that heavy. As there was no belief in justice after death, justice had to happen in this life (or not); yet aside from this, even David (the literary David!), who was not a brutal and mean individual and who made only one major mistake, which he immediately regretted, did not escape God's justice in this life. Even if the punishment did not fall on David himself, it did affect him personally. Regarding God's justice, it is also shifted onto the next generation: God does not merely reward David but through David also Barsillai and his children. In his last orders to Solomon, David thus acts in accordance with God's will; at least the narrator seems to think so.

Solomon also received new character traits through the redactional modification. We immediately recognize how the redactor highlights that God loved Solomon unconditionally (2 Sam 12:24) or has one of the other characters praise him of this fact. In 1 Kgs 1:37, 47 he is praised even more highly than David. Once he initiates the liquidation of his enemies (1 Kgs 2), the old narrative still emerges with its biting quality, but the redactor never misses an opportunity to provide Solomon's harsh actions with detailed explanations. He at times uses the delinquents themselves (as in the case of Abiathar and Shimei), at times other characters (Bathsheba in the case of Adonijah, Benaiah in the case of Joab), to convey to the reader that each of these decisions was carefully deliberated and highly justified, that none of these decisions was the result of arbitrary vengeful behavior.

Thus we can clearly separate the redactional layer from the original text of the Bathsheba-Solomon novella. It follows a general apologetic tendency without taking recourse to propaganda: David and Solomon are not superhumans, but they are kept on the right track through the grace of God, which ensures God's plan of salvation for his people. From a formal literary point of view, the redactional layer is characterized by frequently referring to material outside of the Solomon narrative. These references include the entire scope of the David and Saul narratives as well as later material on Solomon.

Nathan mentions Yhwh's previous blessings to the convicted king (2 Sam 12:*7–10) and announces the fate that will fall on his concubines during Absalom's rebellion (cf. 12:11–12 to 2 Sam 16:21–22). When Adonijah attempts to succeed David, he is paralleled to Absalom (1 Kgs 1:6b). The title *nagid*, given to Solomon, was long before used in connection with David and even Saul (1 Kgs 1:35; see 1 Sam 10:1; 25:30; 2 Sam 6:21[28]). Joab had repeatedly used the shofar (2 Sam 2:28; 18:16; 20:22) and is the first to hear its sound in 1 Kgs 1:41b. The appearance of Jonathan, son of Abiathar, as messenger is reminiscent of similar scenes during Absalom's rebellion (cf. 1 Kgs 1:42ff. to 2 Sam 17:17ff.; 18:19ff.). The promise of Nathan in 2 Sam 7 is referred to with special emphasis (1 Kgs 1:48; 2:24, 33). The murders of Abner and Amasa that are blamed on Joab (1 Kgs 2:5, 32) are told in 2 Sam 3 and 20; the orders about Barsillai and Shimei (1 Kgs 2:7–9, 44) refer to events that took place during Absalom's rebellion (2 Sam 16:5–13; 17:27–29; 19:17–24, 32–40). The sparing of Abiathar is justified by the priest's loyal service to David (1 Kgs 2:26b), of which we were told from 1 Sam 22:23 onward.

Just as the redactor repeatedly refers to previous narrative material, he also makes reference to later material: David speaks of Solomon in 1 Kgs 2:9 as a "wise man" (איש חכם; cf. 2:6)—one of the central topics of the Solomon traditions. The note on the replacement of Joab by Benaiah and Abiathar by Zadok in 1 Kgs 2:35 is possibly connected to the list of Solomon's officials in 1 Kgs 4:4, which is again connected to the similar list of David's officials in 2 Sam 8:16–18 and 20:23–26. Finally, the redactor may have identified the Shimei of 1:8, who is *not* liquidated according to the present text, with Shimei ben Ela, Solomon's governor of the province of Benjamin (1 Kgs 4:18).

We probably will best understand the language, beliefs, and worldview of this large narrative and its author if we analyze some of its main topics more closely, starting with 2 Sam 11–12 and 1 Kgs 1–2.[29]

---

28. These are occurrences of this title that may be pre-Deuteronomistic. In these cases the individual is called to be *nagid* over "Israel (and Judah)." In contrast, the Deuteronomistic instances speak of a *nagid* over "Israel, the people of Yhwh" (1 Sam 9:16; 13:14; 2 Sam 5:2; 7:8; 1 Kgs 14:7; 16:2). In 2 Sam 6:21 we encounter a similar phrase, but here we read both expressions: על־עם יהוה and על־ישראל; the first could well have been added to the second.

29. Recently some exegetes became aware of the pre-Deuteronomistic and extended redactional layer described above: Johannes Klein, *David versus Saul: Ein Beitrag zum*

III.2.4.2. On the Duality between Israel and Judah in the Narrative

According to the present text, Solomon's rise to power was still influenced by the relation between the royal Davidic house to the Israelite north. With the figure of Shimei, a Benjaminite and relative of Saul appears in 1 Kgs 1–2. We have previously encountered this person as a vindictive enemy of David during his escape from Jerusalem (2 Sam 16:5–13) and as a humble petitioner during David's return to Jerusalem (19:17–24). The author of our narrative informs us that this dark character was not able to cast any shadows on David or on Solomon.

Shimei had cursed David and accused him: "Begone, begone, you man of blood, you worthless fellow [איש הבליעל; see the same expression in 1 Sam 10:25; 2 Sam 20:1]! YHWH has avenged upon you all the blood of the house of Saul, in whose place you have been king" (2 Sam 16:7–8). The transfer of power from Saul to David must have been connected with the suspicion of usurpation and murder, otherwise this accusation would not appear here, otherwise David would not be explicitly excused every time a member of Saul's house died.

After Joab murders Saul's uncle Abner, Joab's brother offers twice (16:9[30] and 19:22) to liquidate the insubordinate Shimei. David rejects this offer both times with disgust. The same Abishai previously suggested that David kill his adversary when he snuck into the camp of King Saul with David (1 Sam 26:8–11). Here, too, David is appalled at the suggestion. It seems that we are dealing with the same author in both cases. This shows how pretentiously the narrator uses the term משיח (1 Sam 26:9, 11; 2 Sam 19:22). This also indicates that the two stories of anointing (Saul: 1 Sam 9:1–10:16; David: 16:1–13) must be part of the same textual stratum. The note about David's anointing by the elders of Israel in 2 Sam 3:3 does not explain the use of the term משיח יהוה in 19:22. Our narrator seems to want to express clearly that David prevented further action whenever the sons of Zeruiah (a common reference to Joab and Abishai) asked for permission to kill Saul, *the anointed*, himself or a member of his house.

This is also true for the case of Shimei. David even swears to him: "You will not die" (2 Sam 19:24). How can we possibly connect this oath to David's

---

Erzählsystem der Samuelbücher (BWANT 158; Stuttgart: Kohlhammer, 2002); Alexander A. Fischer, *Von Hebron nach Jerusalem: Eine redaktionsgeschichtliche Studie zur Erzählung von König David in II Sam 1–5* (BZAW 335; Berlin: de Gruyter, 2004).

30. Shimei is described with a drastic metaphor—a "dead dog"—that otherwise occurs in the David narratives in 1 Sam 24:15 (in the middle of the so-called narrative of David's rise, where David uses this term to describe himself to Saul!) and in 2 Sam 9:8.

recommendation to Solomon not to leave Shimei unpunished (1 Kgs 2:8–9)? Shortly before his death, David interprets his oath to mean that *he* would not kill Shimei; Solomon, however, is not bound by the oath. The narrator probably did not see this as sophistic cynicism but rather as correct behavior, since he even reports how Shimei transgressed the house arrest imposed on him by Solomon, thus bringing the death sentence upon himself (2:42–46). This member of the house of Saul had forfeited his life many times and eventually paid the price. His death is much less a blemish on David (and Solomon) than any other death in the house of Saul.

An even brighter light falls on David from another member of Saul's house: from the crown prince Jonathan and his family. According to the biblical text, David was bound to Jonathan in close friendship. Jonathan "loved" David from the first time they met (1 Sam 18:1, 3; 20:17; 2 Sam 1:26), as did the princess Michal (1 Sam 18:20, 28), King Saul himself (16:21), as well as all of Saul's servants and "all of Israel and Judah" (18:16). Jonathan's love for David is described as so great that he defended David against his suspicious father, risking his life in the process (1 Sam 20). In the end, Jonathan hands over his right to the throne to David (23:17). Thus, Jonathan appears as the perfect vehicle to transfer the kingship from Saul to David. He appeared on the scene as a glorious warrior against the Philistines, which helped his father, but also pushed him into the background (1 Sam 14). As a selfless mediator he stood between his father, the current king, and his friend, the future king, never denying his loyalty to the one or his love for the other. As a loyal son, he finally dies at his father's side, thus vacating the stage for David (1 Sam 31).

David shows his gratitude for Jonathan's love in a moving song of lament (2 Sam 1:26) and keeps his promise never to harm a descendant of Jonathan (1 Sam 20:14–16, 42). The narrator develops this motif with great care: he tells us in great detail how David grants to Jonathan's physically handicapped son Meribaal the lands of his grandfather Saul (!) and provides him with a place at the king's table (2 Sam 9); he tells us how Meribaal hopes for kingship over Israel (!) following Absalom's rebellion, leaving open whether this is actually true or mere slander (16:1–4); he tells us how Meribaal denies these allegations upon David's return and proclaims his loyalty to David (19:29). The legitimation of the transfer of power from Saul to David could not be described with greater clarity. David rewards Meribaal by abstaining from punishment and merely dividing his land holdings in half!

David's noble behavior toward members of Saul's house matches his behavior toward King Saul himself. Even when the old king raged against him, David never lifted a hand to harm him. Twice David even spared the king when he had the chance to take his life—against the advice of his comrades (1 Sam 24; 26). The description of Saul is even more telling of how much the narrator abhors simple black-and-white evaluations.

Readers of 1 Samuel have always been uncertain whether to understand Saul as a negative or a tragic figure. True, Saul commits heinous deeds: he throws his spear against unsuspecting individuals, is prepared to execute insidious murders, allows a massacre among defenseless priests (1 Sam 18:11, 17–26; 19:10; 20:13; 22). In all this, however, he seems driven by demons rather than someone who is totally evil. The text states clearly that an "evil spirit from YHWH" had come upon Saul (16:14, 23; 18:10; 19:9). David's breathtakingly good fortune is a potent source for jealousy and premonition (18:9; 20:31). Saul pursues David with manic determination. Only two people can temporarily detract him from his obsession: Jonathan (19:6) and David himself, when he delivers unquestionable proof of his own loyalty (24:17–22; 26:21, 25). It is very moving to see the king cry on this occasion (24:17)—whether out of desperation over his own evil or because of the nobility of David.

Saul is not an evil person; he simply does not seem to be able to be good. His death is symptomatic for his life when Philistine archers corner him and drive him to suicide. Could a portrait of the archrival of the founder of the Judahite dynasty possibly be more empathetic from a Judahite point of view?

Our narrator does not stop at describing the fate of Saul's house during the reign of David. He also describes how the people of northern Israel resisted David's rule on the one hand but felt drawn to it on the other hand.

This begins already with the above-mentioned "love" of Israel (and Judah) for the young David. When David later flees his home country to escape Saul, his relationship to Israel continues to surface. Achish of Gath believes that he "has become odious to his people, to Israel," whereas in truth he has battled with the enemies of his people (1 Sam 27:12). David does not participate in the final battle that Israel loses against the Philistines, even though he is a vassal of the Philistines (1 Sam 29). Following this defeat, which he mourns with a moving song of lament, he seeks to win the loyalty of the people of Jabesh in Gilead, Saul's most loyal supporters outside of Benjamin (2 Sam 2:4–7). When Abner and Eshbaal nevertheless attempt to continue Saul's kingship, David resists this movement with great moderation (2 Sam 2) and immediately enters into negotiations when they are initiated by Abner (2 Sam 3). He is not responsible for the murders of Abner and Eshbaal (2 Sam 3–4), and when the elders of Israel come to him in Hebron in order to anoint him, he does not demand unconditional surrender but agrees on a mutual contract (5:3).

Thus the double monarchy of Judah and Israel is installed. The north remains a clearly defined independent unit that David treats with respect and that nonetheless continues to cause him troubles. Once he relocates his residence to Jerusalem, he transfers the ark—an old *Israelite* cultic artifact—to the capital; the text emphasizes that the elect of *Israel* assist him in this transfer (2 Sam 6:1). When Saul's daughter Michal, who has once again become his wife, attacks him because of his behavior during the procession, he retorts: "YHWH has chosen me instead of your father and instead of his whole house in order to appoint me as *nagid* over *Israel*" (6:21). Thus he clearly defines the status of Israel and of the house of Saul under his own rule. The obstinate Michal does not bear any children from David, thus ending up with a fate somewhere between Meribaal and Shimei.

The whole of Israel is represented in the final sentence of the summary on David's wars and victories: "David was king over all of Israel, and David administered justice and equity to all his people" (2 Sam 8:15). He guaranteed peace and order for Israel not only on the outside but also on the inside. It was not without tragedy that a son of David, Absalom, would be the source of dissent. Absalom proclaimed that David was not a just ruler but that he, Absalom, would administer justice and equity—and thus "he stole the hearts of the men of Israel" (15:6). The soon-erupted rebellion was, at least according to the biblical description, carried out primarily by (northern) Israel. "Israel and Absalom" camped in Gilead before the decisive battle (17:26); David's army moved against "Israel" (18:6); after his victory, David refrained from pursuing "Israel," and "all Israel fled to its tents" (18:16–17; 19:9b); in the end, the northern Israelites themselves said that they would have anointed Absalom king (19:11).

Soon after Israel and Judah enter into a strange competition to determine who will have the honor of first welcoming the returning David and reappointing him king. It is no coincidence that the respective passages (2 Sam 19:9b–16, 41–44) frame the scenes of David's second encounter with the Saulides Shimei and Meribaal (19:17–31) and introduce the narrative on the rebellion of Sheba ben Bichri (20:1–22). This *revolutionary* (אִישׁ הַבְּלִיַּעַל), a Benjaminite (20:1), initiates the secession of the north with his famous outcry: "Every man to his tents, Israel!" "So all the men of Israel withdrew from David and followed Sheba the son of Bichri, but the men of Judah followed their king" (20:2). It seems that the northern tribes do not want to install a different kingship but intend to return to a nonmonarchic polity. David crushes these ambitions immediately, not by means of the Judahite militia but through the mercenaries under Abishai and Joab. Joab murders Amasa on this occasion, whom Absalom has appointed general and whom David has chosen to be Joab's successor (17:25; 19:14). Thus the Judahite camarilla eliminates everything that opposes them from the north.[31] A bloodbath is prevented when Joab succeeds with the aid of a "wise woman" in capturing Sheba.

Thus order returned to northern Israel for a while. The Solomon traditions describe a network of provinces that the king established in the north in order to raise taxes (1 Kgs 4:7–19). In this context the text does state that "Judah and Israel" were numerous and happy under Solomon's rule (4:20), but we soon hear that the king demanded "conscripted labor from all of Israel" for his large construction projects (5:27)—the very topic that led to the collapse of the double monarchy. Is it mere coincidence that Sheba's battle cry is repeated almost literally when this secession takes its course (12:16; cf. 2 Sam 20:1)? This time Israel actually did go "to its tents" (1 Kgs 12:16) and dared "to rebel against the house of David until this day" (12:19).

It can hardly be doubted that we are dealing with one and the same author in all of the passages described above. The author who related the destruction of the united monarchy with anger and sadness also related the beginnings of this monarchy under (Saul and) David, including the various crises that shook its beginnings. His message can be summarized as follows. The kingdom of Saul commanded respect but was doomed to failure from the beginning. David was the right man to lead Judah and Israel to previously unknown heights. The transfer of power from the north to the south did not occur without pain: especially the house of Saul had to suffer. David, however, was not responsible for this suffering, but rather independent subjects, violent foreigners, or members of the house of Saul themselves were responsible. Israel repeatedly rebelled against David's rule to its own disadvantage. After David, however, the oppression of the north became so strong that it led to a collapse of the united monarchy under Rehoboam.

We could imagine the creation of such a message shortly after the demise of the divided kingdom in Judah, but the pain in Judah over the loss of the north was so great[32] and its dependency on Israel so oppressive[33] that such a

---

31. Amasa (with respect to his father Ithra) is named in 2 Sam 17:25 explicitly as an "Israelite." Following 1 Chr 2:17, the later tradition (and often textual criticism!) made him an "Ishmaelite." This is wrong. First, the proto-Arabic Ishmaelites inherited the Midianites not before the late period of monarchy. Second, the variation by the Chronicler is understandable, because he could not imagine that an "Israelite" in the time of David was a foreigner whose identity had to be declared. See Ernst Axel Knauf, *Ismael: Untersuchungen zur Geschichte Palästinas und Nordarabiens im 1. Jahrtausend v. Chr.* (2nd ed.; ADPV; Wiesbaden: Harrassowitz, 1989), 12–13.

32. Compare the many notes on military conflicts between the south and the north in 1 Kgs 14–15.

33. We have to think only of the oppressive superiority of the Omride dynasty that has Judah appear almost as a vassal of the north (see 2 Kgs 3; 9). This leads to the immedi-

generous attempt at reconciliation as we find in this narrative history could hardly have been written during this time. A further aspect is the literary and historical horizon represented by these texts. The language is highly artistic and is already influenced by prophetic material.

Thus it seems prudent to date these texts to the eighth, perhaps even the seventh, century. The north experienced similar and even worse oppression from the Assyrians than they had experienced from the Philistines. In the end, the north was once again defeated and lost its king. The land was at the disposal of foreign conquerors. We can meanwhile account for a large movement of refugees from the north to the south in connection with the events surrounding 722 B.C.E. This explains well the incorporation of northern Israelite traditions (e.g., Saul's rise, reign, and death) into the historical narrative described here. This would also explain the persuading apologetics that aim to protect the house of David from the suspicion of having not only observed the collapse of the north but of actively having participated in it,[34] including even the murders of kings.[35] If these assumptions are correct, then the moral of the history of the early monarchy is quite clear: You of northern Israel have nothing to fear from the house of David but much to hope for! Let us all admit our previous mistakes and set aside unjustified suspicion and deep-seated mistrust in order to start a new future together!

III.2.4.3. On the Portrait of David in This Narrative History

The portrait of David in the books of Samuel is strongly but not exclusively determined by his interaction with Saul and the house of Saul as well as by his relation to the Israelite north. We now turn to other facets, starting once again with the redactional layer in 2 Sam 11–12 and 1 Kgs 1–2. From there we will be able to follow thematic lines that connect to other textual material. Interestingly enough, most of this material is found in what formerly

---

ate Judahite support of the anti-Omride campaign of Jehu (2 Kgs 11).

34. We should remember that Judah and Israel were actually at war with each other during the so-called Syro-Ephraimite war (734/3 B.C.E.; see 2 Kgs 16:5–9; Isa 7:1–17). The fact that in Isa 7:17 the division of the kingdom is described as the most tragic event in the history of Israel and Judah shows that this time period was characterized by intensive discussion about the unity of and conflicts between the two brother states since 926 B.C.E.

35. Perhaps the nervousness displayed in the northern sanctuary of Bethel as a reaction to the critical speeches of a Judahite prophet named Amos (Amos 7:10–17) is connected to such apprehensions. Murders of kings and violent transitions from one ruler to the next seemed to have been an integral part of the Israelite system, increasing greatly toward the end.

has been called the succession narrative. The narrative of Amnon, Tamar, and Absalom in 2 Sam 13 is especially close to the expanded narrative of Bathsheba, David, and Uriah in 2 Sam 11–12.

Nathan tells David a parable, and David believes that it is a judicial case. In this parable Nathan tells of a poor man and his only lamb, "who ate (אכל) from his portion, drank (שתה) from his cup, and lay (שכב) in his bosom" and who was "as a daughter (כְּבַת) to him" until the rich neighbor came and "took (לקח) her and prepared her for his guest." There are several allusions to the previous David-Bathsheba-Uriah affair; this already includes the name of the woman that begins with בַת but also the fact that David "took her" (לקח)[36] and "lay with her" (שכב, 2 Sam 11:4), as well as the fact that her husband then refused to go to her to "eat," to "drink," and to "lay with" her (אכל, שתה, שכב, 11:11). All this has already been observed and matches the clever intention of the parable and can be seen as evidence for the high artistry of the narrator of this parable to fit his new text into the previous narrative context. We also observe narrative connections to the other side, to the affair of Amnon, Tamar, and Absalom. The lovesick Amnon entices Tamar to come to his house by claiming that his recovery is dependent on receiving something to "eat" from her hands (אכל, 13:5, 9, 11); Amnon "lies" on his bed and eventually with Tamar (שכב, 13:5, 6, 8, 11, 14).

There are other linguistic aspects connecting the Bathsheba and Tamar narratives: both women "go"—seemingly unsuspecting—to the man who will take them (בוא אֶל, 2 Sam 11:4; 13:10, 11); both come after David has "sent" for them (שלח, 11:4; 13:7), just as he will "send" Amnon to Absalom's feast and thus to his death (13:27). David is just as "enraged" over Absalom's violent act as he is over the violence of the rich man in the parable (חרה [אף] מאד, 13:21; 12:5). With this last passage we have once again arrived at the redactional layer of 2 Sam 11–12.

Verbal allusions connect these texts with material in the entire corpus of the books of Samuel. We notice very courtly language, such as in the description of Bathsheba in 2 Sam 11:2 (as a טוֹבַת מַרְאֶה מְאֹד), Tamar in 13:1 (יפה), Absalom in 14:25 (אִישׁ־יָפֶה), or Adonijah in 1 Kgs 1:6b (טוֹב־תֹּאַר מְאֹד). Saul already had been described as טוֹב (1 Sam 9:2), David as עִם־יְפֵה עֵינַיִם וְטוֹב רֹאִי (16:12), as אִישׁ תֹּאַר (16:18), again as עִם־יְפֵה מַרְאֶה (17:42), and Abigail as טוֹבַת־שֶׂכֶל וִיפַת תֹּאַר (1 Sam 25:3).

---

36. In 2 Sam 11:4 we read, "And he sent messengers and took her," whereas 12:4 intensifies the expression: "And he took [the lamb] away." The slight change in meaning is an interpretation of the first text.

It seems that our redactor did not merely rework the old Bathsheba-Solomon narrative but also connected this narrative to the whole corpus of the books of Samuel, combining it especially with the Amnon-Absalom story so that the text now reports on four sons of David, of which only the youngest, Solomon, survives. If we include the fact that the old Bathsheba-Solomon novella already reported the death of the other son of David, Adonijah, then we clearly see that this redactional layer deals in 2 Sam 11–12 and 1 Kgs 1–2 with the topic of the succession to David's throne (instead of assuming an old contemporary succession narrative). Our final narrator, who was already concerned with the legitimacy of the transfer of power from Saul to David, was also concerned with justifying the transfer of power from David to Solomon. We notice with dismay, however, how David is more and more deeply involved with the brutal and bloody events in his house that are described in the subsequent narratives up to Solomon's enthronement. The old narrative of the Bathsheba-Uriah scandal had set the tone for this description. Our redactor could not or would not eliminate the dark shadows that fell upon his hero in these texts. On the contrary, by continuing with the story of Amnon and Absalom and then again of Adonijah and Solomon, he showed how David's crime led to a series of calamities. Nathan's prediction, that "the sword will never depart from the house of David" (2 Sam 12:10a), was relentlessly and gruesomely fulfilled.

The old Bathsheba-Solomon story is the literary origin for this story of woe. The final narrator did not want to spare his readers this material. It seems he believed that even these dark aspects could not destroy the image of the great king David but that they would provide him with profile and credibility. No one is perfect, not even a great king, not even David. Even David must submit to prophetic judgment and repent of his crime when he has gone wrong. By doing this, David is a model even as a sinner for all humans who would never claim to be infallible.

But David is not only a paradigm on the negative side; the biblical portrait especially presents him as a paradigm on the positive side. This is true of all the stories of David. With the sole exception of the affair of Bathsheba and Uriah, David's behavior is exemplary, even when he is subject to adversity and temptation. Toward his sons Amnon, Absalom, and Adonijah, David is torn between strictness and love—and who can hold it against him, especially after what has happened? He deals correctly, even generously, with the insubordinate Benjaminites. He responds relentlessly and cleverly to the attacks against his kingdom. He allows himself to be persuaded by the wise woman of Tekoa, sent by Joab, but he is not tricked by her. He keeps his distance from the violent Joab and Abishai but is unable to control them; his attempt to replace Joab with Amasa ends with the murder of the latter. There

are many parallels to David's wrestling with the house of Saul: enemies fall
from David left and right, but we can see no fault of David's; sometimes he is
even clearly innocent.

The most moving example is the death of his son Absalom. The narrative
goes to great lengths to show that David was not responsible for this but suffered greatly as a result. Both the wise woman of Tekoa as well as the narrator
promote empathy for Absalom in an attempt to rehabilitate the crown prince
after his fratricide. David is much too unsuspecting to notice how Absalom
intrigues against him, finally starting a rebellion out of Hebron. He must flee
in great haste, but he does not forget to prepare the ground in Jerusalem for
Absalom's eventual failure—but not death. On the eve of the decisive battle
in the hills of Ephraim (in which David does not participate, not of his own
volition but rather due to the request of his soldiers!), he insistently admon-
ishes the troop leaders to spare the life of his son (2 Sam 18:1–5).[37] Once the
news of his son's death does reach him, he is overwhelmed by raging grief
and abysmal sadness that could hardly be described with more staggering
impact (19:1–5).

Let us briefly look at one of the artfully constructed individual scenes
that make up the Absalom narrative. Following the victory of David's troops
and the death of Absalom, two messengers compete to reach David, knowing full well that they have to convey simultaneously a message of joy (בשׂר)
and of death. When the arrival of the first messenger, Ahimaaz ben Zadok,
is reported to David, he exclaims, "This is a good man, and he comes with
a message of joy" (2 Sam 18:27). Adonijah will later receive the messenger
Jonathan ben Abiathar (in the Absalom narrative, quasi Ahimaaz's twin; see
2 Sam 15:27; 17:15–22) with almost the same words when he comes with
the latest news from Jerusalem—and this messenger will also convey a message of doom (1 Kgs 1:42). Who would doubt that these two scenes belong
together: 1 Kgs 1 revised by the narrator and 2 Sam 18 composed by that
same narrator?

The messengers themselves are worthy of detailed examination. Ahimaaz
reports to Joab with the words: "I want to run and tell the king the good news
that YHWH has delivered him from the hand of his enemies" (2 Sam 18:19).
Later he reports the victory to David with the words: "Blessed be YHWH your
God, who has delivered up the men who lifted their hand against the king"

---

37. It is impossible to remove this scene from the text as a secondary addition. Even
the simple soldier who sees Absalom hanging from the tree by his hair knows of the king's
order to spare him (18:12–13), and once David has come to his senses after the death of
his son, he sits "in the gate" watching the army parade by him, just as he did before the
battle (cf. 18:4 to 19:9).

(18:28). He avoids David's inquiry into the well-being of Absalom. The second messenger answers this inquiry with intentional vagueness, but clear enough for David: "May the enemies of my lord the king be like this young man [Absalom]" (19:32). The terminology used here is well known from other Davidic narratives. אֹיֵב is a central term in a long passage from the so-called narrative of David's rise. Early on Saul becomes "the enemy of David for all times" (1 Sam 18:29); with all his might he tries to take David's life. When his daughter Michal helps David escape, he barks at her that she allowed his *enemy* to flee (19:17). It is only natural that David's comrades (24:5; 26:8) as well as Saul himself (24:20) believe that David, too, seeks to take the life of his "enemy" Saul. They are taught that this is not true: David spares Saul twice and thus does not become guilty of turning into the enemy of the anointed king. This is exactly Saul's crime, and thus Jonathan's statement is ambiguous when he says that "Yhwh will eliminate the enemies of David" (20:15–16). The rich but foolish Nabal, whom David also considers his "enemy" (25:22), becomes a case example for what God does with the enemies of his anointed: in the end, God strikes Nabal "so that he dies" (25:38). It is also ambiguous when Abigail, the wife of Nabal, expresses the wish to David that God "may throw away the life of your enemies" (25:29); she is directly referring to her husband and to Saul—and, as we now see, also of Absalom. The lives of all of David's enemies are ended, but David did not have to raise his hand against them. This is the lesson that the wise Abigail teaches David and that he follows for the rest of his life: that he should not "fall into blood guilt" and that he may not help himself "against his enemies with his own hand" (25:26). We thus observe a thematic and verbal connection that is present in the entire scope of the David material.

The motif of David's innocence that is so important for the narratives of David's rise is also a basic element in the Absalom story: David was innocent of the death of his rebellious son. With great nobility of character he tried to spare him—just as he abstained from punishing Meribaal and Shimei and tried to thank old Barsillai for his loyal friendship. All of these texts are part of *a single* textual layer, the final layer of the whole narrative. This final redactional layer thus follows a pro-Davidic tendency. This was never in question for the texts that were considered part of the so-called narrative of David's rise. It is also true for the material in the so-called succession narrative (and not only for the secondary additions to this material!). If the material in these two collections does seem to be colored differently, if the portrait of the younger David seems brighter than the portrait of the older David, then this may be the result of the different materials used by the final narrator. But who is to say that this narrator saw these different colors as a problem? He was not a writer of propaganda but rather a thoughtful individual who wanted to show that no person, not even a king, not even Saul, Solomon, or David, is more than human. The narratives know of only one transcendent character, to whom we will turn now.

III.2.4.4. On the Image of God in the Narrative

Gerhard von Rad, following Leonhard Rost, once emphasized the infrequent, but in his view decisive, passages in the so-called succession narrative containing theological evaluation. According to our observations, two of these passages belong to the redactional layer of the Solomon-Bathsheba story and thus to the narrative history on the early monarchy: "It was evil in the eyes of YHWH what David had done," namely, the adultery and the murder of Uriah (2 Sam 11:27b); and "YHWH loved Solomon" from the moment of his birth (12:24bβ).

We already mentioned that *love* (אהב) is of central importance in the so-called narrative of David's rise; it is no coincidence that God himself is now the one who loves the future king—and that this is mentioned precisely in the context of Solomon's highly problematic birth.

The terms *good* and *evil* are also guiding themes in the so-called history of David's rise. We already encountered several passages: "What man finds his enemy and allows him to go on a good way?" (David does! 1 Sam 24:20[38]). David's enemies desire *evil* for the king (25:26, said of Nabal by Abigail), whereas Abigail prophecies that "evil will not be found in you as long as you live" (25:28). Only once did David actually treat someone in his path, namely, Uriah, as his enemy, doing great evil to him. This promptly calls YHWH on the scene to foretell through Nathan: "Behold, I will let evil rise up against you in your house" (2 Sam 12:11). The old Bathsheba-Solomon novella already spoke of *evil* but in a very different context. David relayed the message to Joab that it should "not be evil in your eyes" (11:25) to sacrifice a few men (including Uriah) at Rabbah Ammon. This cynical statement must have upset the narrator of our narrative history, who thought intensively about good and evil,[39] so much that he responded with an appropriate answer: "It was evil in the eyes of YHWH what David had done."

This statement is closely connected to the third theological comment in 2 Sam 17:14. When Hushai presents Absalom with his poisoned advice, "Absalom and all the men of Israel said, 'The counsel of Hushai is better [!]

---

38. Saul adds the wish, "May YHWH award you with good [!] for what you have done to me today."

39. The following passages were most likely written by him: 1 Sam 24:12; 25:21, 30, 31; 26:18; 2 Sam 3:36, 39; 16:12; 1 Kgs 1:42, 47.

than the counsel of Ahithophel,' for Yʜwʜ had appointed to defeat the good [!] counsel of Ahithophel, to the intent that Yʜwʜ might bring evil [!] upon Absalom." Some scholars have tried to classify this statement as a secondary addition—with plausible source-critical arguments that nevertheless fail to describe the text convincingly. As soon as we give up the need to separate a "negative" old succession narrative and a "positive" secondary redaction, we recognize that the Absalom narrative is pro-Davidic (and thus Absalom-critical) from the beginning. If this is the case, there is no reason why we should separate this pro-Davidic commentary (and thus Hushai's entire speech) from the original narrative.

The Hushai episode is closely connected to the appearance of the wise woman of Tekoa who persuades David to allow Absalom to return to Jerusalem following his murder of Amnon and his subsequent escape. (No one can guess at this point that this return will lead to Absalom's rebellion.) The woman answers David, who clearly perceives that Joab is behind this clever charade, with a large compliment, "My lord has wisdom like the wisdom of the angel of God to know all things that are on the earth" (2 Sam 14:20). We have already mentioned that the final narrator in his redaction of the Solomon-Bathsheba narrative uses the guiding theme of wisdom to connect to the Solomon traditions (1 Kgs 2:6, 9). In this context, we should emphasize that this motif is connected to David. In 2 Sam 19:28, Meribaal says of David, "My lord, the king, is like the angel of God—do what is good [!] in your eyes." The soldier who discovers Absalom hanging in the tree but is hesitant to kill similarly says that "nothing remains hidden from the king" (18:12–13).

The final narrator, whose hand we readily recognize in these passages, also emphasizes his theological evaluation of David in his commentaries in the narrative of Solomon's ascent to power. The respective passages show their full importance only when we read them in the context of the entire narrative history on the early monarchy. Benaiah—of all people!—gets to say the following to Solomon: "As Yʜwʜ was with my lord the king, he may also be with Solomon!" The statement of God's presence with the king occurs throughout the narratives of David's rise, and this topic is reactivated here in the context of the narratives on Solomon. The short notes on God's loyalty to his promise similarly have a long prehistory. Already Abigail prophesied to David, "Yʜwʜ will certainly build my lord a steadfast house" (1 Sam 25:28). Nathan had promised this directly to David, "Yʜwʜ wants to build a house for you" by raising one of David's descendants "and confirming his kingdom" (2 Sam 7:11b, 12).[40]

---

40. According to my analysis (*David, Saul und die Propheten*, 118–28) this passage belongs to the pre-Deuteronomistic material in Nathan's prediction, more precisely to the

Solomon introduces his command to execute Adonijah with the solemn words: "As Yhwh lives, who has established me and placed me on the throne of David my father and who has made me a house, as he promised" (1 Kgs 2:24). The final sentence of the narrator reads: "The kingdom of Solomon was firmly established in the hand of Solomon" (2:46). We can breathe a sigh of relief with our narrator: the commotion surrounding the succession of David has come to a good ending—*hominum confusione dei provisione* ("In human confusion God's foreknowledge is found").

---

textual stratum that incorporated a formulaic prophetic enthronement speech into the present historical context by the pre-Deuteronomistic narrator of the David story.

IV. Theological Conclusions

IV.1. The Early Monarchy and Biblical History

The narratives about Israel's first kings, Saul and David, the queens Michal, Abigail, and Bathsheba, the crown princes Jonathan, Amnon, and Absalom, the prophets Samuel, Nathan, and Gad, about the turmoil surrounding the establishment of the first state, and about the actions, speeches, and silences of God during this important time are among the most beautiful in the Bible, even in all of world literature. How does the Bible describe and evaluate the origin and history of the early Israelite state as well as the actions and sufferings of the various groups that participated in it—including God?

If we understand 1 Sam 1–1 Kgs 12 to be a part of the Deuteronomistic History, stretching from Deuteronomy to the end of the books of Kings, from the conquest of the land to the loss of the land, then we realize that the early monarchy is a unit all its own. It has a clear beginning and a clear ending, is structured by common themes, and is thus separated from the book of Judges (i.e., the time of the tribes), on the one side, and the continuation in the books of Kings (i.e., the time of the divided kingdom), on the other side.

After describing how the tribes of Israel were caught up in a vortex of blood and chaos, the book of Judges ends with the sentence, "In those days there was no king in Israel. Every man did what was right in his eyes" (Judg 21:25). These were indeed horrendous deeds that were right in the eyes of the people of Israel! The next sentence, the first sentence of the first book of Samuel, describes a new beginning, "There was a single man [אִישׁ אֶחָד] from Ramathaim-Zophim from the hills of Ephraim and his name was Elkanah.... and the name of his wife was Hannah" (1 Sam 1:1). *Sunt nomina omina* ("Do the names predict the things")? "El-kanah" means "God created," and "Hannah" means "He (God) was merciful" (probably a shortened form of Hani-El). God emerges from the chaos of the period of Judges—not in person, but through this man and this woman. Elkanah will prove himself to be a mild and loving (yet not especially helpful) husband, very different from the men who were the subject of the end of Judges (Judg 19–21). Hannah is a strong and determined woman, not merely the victim of male action and violence, like so many women during the end of the period of the judges. This man and this woman conceive … no children. Everyone in ancient Israel, every woman, every child, knew that many stories of important Israelite leaders begin like this; as listeners we wait for him who is to come. So Hannah desires and "prays for" this child with great intensity. The verb *ša'al* ("to pray for, ask, request") is the central motif of 1 Sam 1, and it appears on occasion as a passive participle: *ša'ul*, "the requested one"—*Ša'ul* was the name of Israel's first king. But perhaps in contrast to the reader's expectation, Hannah does not give birth to a Saul but to a Samuel, a name that is also reminiscent of *ša'al*, but only indirectly. The one who now appears on the scene is not yet the future king; he is the one who will prepare the way for the king, who will prepare the kingship. His appearance signals that God has listened, not merely to this couple's desire for a child but also to the desperate hopelessness of Israel. God makes a new beginning possible by giving Elkanah and Hannah to Israel, Samuel to Elkanah and Hannah, and Saul through Samuel to Israel.

Samuel is the central character of the first half of the first book of Samuel. His first counterpart is Eli the priest, who is something like Israel's last "judge" or "deliverer," except that he fails miserably. Samuel succeeds him and finishes what Eli was not able to finish (1 Sam 1–7). In the end, Samuel (or better, God through Samuel) lifts Saul onto the throne. Samuel assists Saul through guidance and warning; without Samuel, Israel would have stumbled into the new era without help and guidance (1 Sam 8–12). Saul, who succeeds at first, thanks to Samuel's assistance (1 Sam 11), fails completely by not following Samuel's instructions perfectly. Samuel immediately receives instructions to reject the one whom he (better, God) elected (1 Sam 13–15).

We thus reach a turning point, but once again Samuel (better, God) opens a path out of this disaster. Following God's orders, Samuel anoints the young David as Saul's successor. This is the beginning of the complex and exciting story that Jan P. Fokkelman refers to as the "The Crossing Fates" in his extensive interpretation of these texts. David's ascent surpasses Saul but follows a very convoluted path through dark valleys and many detours to a preordained end—much like the story of Joseph in Genesis.

The ending of 1 Samuel describes Saul's tragic death (1 Sam 31) in opposition to this hopeful new beginning; Samuel has already passed away (25:1). What looks like a new ending is in truth merely an interruption, even a necessary transition: Saul must exit the stage so David can now fully occupy its center. Thus 2 Sam 1 once again reports the death of Saul, but now in David's presence, who immediately initiates many precautions that are to prevent the death of the first king from becoming a catastrophe for Israel and to ensure that this event will be the start of a glorious career. After only a few chapters, David already wears several crowns, achieves one victory after another—only to stumble over the Bathsheba-Uriah scandal (2 Sam 10–12) and to fall into a deep abyss that he will never fully escape. This is the beginning of a difficult and painful journey: the great king is no longer able to control his own family or prevent large-scale rebellion. In the end, it will cost him his most promising son, Absalom (the third son who dies prematurely; a fourth will be executed on orders of Solomon).

Before this occurs, before Solomon ascends the throne of his father David and thus starts the long chain of the Davidic dynasty (i.e., before the transition from the founding of the Israelite state to the history of the two states in Israel), the ending of 2 Samuel marks an important cadence: David steps off the stage that he commanded with such competence, even though it became more difficult toward the end. In the first chapter of 1 Kings we encounter a weak, almost spiritless old man who is inundated by the events around him (*almost,* for the old man's will moves the story once more toward the next important step). In 2 Sam 21–24 David is still the unrivaled protagonist, even if his actions are no longer as unquestionable as they once were. Two important narratives frame this section: the story of the execution of seven members of the house of Saul (2 Sam 21); and the story of the public census and the subsequent plague sent by God (2 Sam 24). In both cases David is not a particularly shining role model; instead, he appears to be driven and humiliated. Both narratives frame a sequence of various lists: lists of heroic acts and lists of heroes (21:15–22; 23:8–39). David is not the subject of any of these actions. On the contrary, the victory over the giant Goliath is credited to someone else (21:19). David, however, is the subject of the two texts that stand at the center of this collection in 2 Sam 22 and 23:1–7. Here he is portrayed as a poet and man of prayer. There is only one other biblical character who sings two songs at the end of his life: Moses (Deut 32; 33). The great statesman David stands at the side (or, shall we say, in the shadow of?) the great man of God—a rather impressive ending for a truly amazing political career!

Prepared long in advance by none other than the divine hand itself, Solomon now succeeds David and assumes his legacy. Even if the original text in 1 Kgs 1–2 still shows traces of the horror that accompanied this transfer of power, the redacted text emphasizes the joy that God's promise of a Davidic dynasty is now being fulfilled. Solomon's head and hands are no longer bound by war; his reign can start from the high standard established by David. Solomon no longer has to fight for anything; he must only accept what is presented to him as a gift: divine wisdom and anything else a king might hope for (long life, riches, superiority over all enemies, 3:13). He thus organizes his new state with great insight and success. The climax and goal of his reign is the construction of the temple that stands not only in the center of Jerusalem but also in the center of the Solomon narratives in 1 Kgs 5–8. A house, *the* house for YHWH: this is Solomon's life task. But where we find light, we also discover shadows. Solomon, gloriously equipped with all the attributes necessary for this task, falls into hybris and disloyalty to his God (1 Kgs 9–11); he transgresses the central commandments of the Deuteronomic law of kings (Deut 17:14–20).

The end of Solomon's glorious reign is already hinted at in 1 Kgs 11, and it comes with a bang in 1 Kgs 12: announced and even incited by YHWH, the northern Israelite tribes strive for freedom from the yoke of Solomonic rule. The monarchy that was united under David and Solomon falls apart immediately after Solomon's death; the history of the united kingdom of Israel becomes the history of the two small kingdoms: Israel and Judah. The monarchy takes its first step down the declining path that will end first in the destruction of the northern kingdom, then of the southern kingdom.

Thus the early monarchy in the Deuteronomistic History is an era of unparalleled success and blinding glory, but also an era full of danger and strife, temptation, and transgression. Neither David nor Solomon are superhuman. There is only one who is enthroned in heaven, and he observes with compassion and love, but also with sadness and anger, what is done by and to his people of Israel.

Aside from this basic evaluation of this era, the texts between 1 Sam 1 and 1 Kgs 12 deal with certain specific topics that are already important for the early, pre-Deuteronomistic textual layers. These topics are important for the self-understanding, worldview, and theology of Israel (and not just Israel!). We will address some of these topics in the following, not so much because they were important *during* the early monarchy but because their importance was exemplified *by means of* the early monarchy. The narratives of the early state in Israel had not only etiological meaning (in the sense of explaining the origin and early development of the state) but also paradigmatic meaning: the history of Israel's first kings provides an excellent framework to reflect on topics of central importance that continue to be relevant.

IV.2. STATE RULE AND DIVINE RULE

Becker, Uwe. "Der innere Widerspruch der deuteronomistischen Beurteilung des Königtums (am Beispiel von 1.Sam 8)," in *Altes Testament und christliche Verkündigung: Festschrift für Antonius A.H. Gunneweg zum 65. Geburtstag* (ed. Manfred Oeming and Axel Graupner; Stuttgart: Kohlhammer, 1987), 246–70. **Boecker,** Hans

Jochen. *Die Beurteilung der Anfänge des Königtums in den deuteronomistischen Abschnitten des 1. Samuelbuches: Ein Beitrag zum Problem des "Deuteronomistischen Geschichtswerks"* (WMANT 31; Neukirchen-Vluyn: Neukirchener, 1969). **Crüsemann,** Frank. *Der Widerstand gegen das Königtum: Die antiköniglichen Texte des Alten Testamentes und der Kampf um den frühen israelitischen Staat* (WMANT 49; Neukirchen-Vluyn: Neukirchener, 1978). **Dietrich,** Walter. "Martin Noth and the Future of the Deuteronomistic History," in *The History of Israel's Traditions: The Heritage of Martin Noth* (ed. Steven L. McKenzie and M. Patrick Graham; JSOTSup 182; Sheffield: Sheffield Academic Press, 1994), 128–52. **Eslinger,** Lyle M. *Kingship of God in Crisis: A Close Reading of 1 Samuel 1–12* (BiLiSe 10; Decatur, Ga.: Almond, 1985). **Müller,** Reinhard. *Königtum und Gottesherrschaft* (FAT 2/3; Tübingen: Mohr Siebeck, 2004). **Veijola,** Timo. *Das Königtum in der Beurteilung der deuteronomistischen Historiographie: Eine redaktionsgeschichtliche Untersuchung* (AASF B/198; Helsinki: Suomalainen Tiedeakatemia, 1977). **Vette,** Joachim. *Samuel und Saul: Ein Beitrag zur narrativen Poetik des Samuelbuches* (Beiträge zum Verstehen der Bibel 13; Münster: LIT, 2005).

In discussions on the founding and development of the Israelite state, religion undoubtedly played an important role. Israel's name contained a divine element even before the state was established. Already early on YHWH, "the one from Sinai" (Deut 33:2; see Judg 5:4), became involved in the history of El with Isra-El. The experience of YHWH's acts of liberation, such as the exodus of a group from Egypt or the victory over the Canaanites (Judg 5) may have led to the honoring and worship of YHWH in Israel while simultaneously creating a group identity and lasting desire for freedom.

On the other hand, the loss of freedom and the experience of bondage must have been understood as challenges to faith in the liberating God YHWH. How could it happen that the people of YHWH threatened to destroy themselves through inner chaos, civil war, and conflict with external enemies such as the Philistines? Faith in YHWH must have taken major damage when the sacred ark, which a tribal league had taken into battle against the Philistines at Ebenezer, was lost. The fact that YHWH easily held his own while in enemy country was a small comfort. Israel's immediate reaction to the severe political and military devastation at the turn of the millennium was the establishment of the monarchy. This, too, did not take place outside of Israel's faith in YHWH. The biblical texts, however, also let the request for a king collide with trust in YHWH. After the previous disasters, it was perfectly understandable that the Israelites requested a king from Samuel "to rule us and to fight our battles" (1 Sam 8:20). But were these tasks in Israel truly the tasks of kings? Were these tasks not the responsibility of judges and liberators appointed by YHWH and equipped with his spirit? The biblical narratives portray with great skill how Samuel was highly successful in this double role just before the people requested a king (1 Sam 7). In a rapid revision of history, the text tells us of a second battle at Ebenezer—and this time a "stone of help" can be erected as a monument to an overwhelming victory against the Philistines. Regarding Israel's ongoing internal turbulences, the text in 7:15–17 expressly states that Samuel administered justice in a circle of cities and remained judge over Israel to the end of his life.

We thus take the step into the new era in Israel with mixed feelings. Did Israel need the monarchy? Yes and no. Were the judges (a noncentralized form of leadership) truly inadequate? Yes and no. It seems as if Israel continually deliberated these questions. The books of Judges and Samuel can be seen as a dialogue, or better, a multivoiced conversation on what type of society was truly appropriate for the people of God.

On the one hand, there are those who favor a noncentralized social organization. This includes the traditions of the judges and liberators, which speak of these leaders in glowing terms. These texts describe glorious heroes; we encounter legendary leaders of Israel's early history. A pious interpretation understood all these actions to be guided by God's spirit; the divine spirit fell upon his chosen, and it allowed a woman to sing a jubilant song of praise (after she had roused Israel's men to engage in victorious battle). Israel was Yнwн's people; he protected and guided them even during the most turbulent times. Attempts and temptations to turn these liberators into kings for life were either rejected or failed (Judg 8–9).

In 1 Sam 8; 10:17–27; and 12, we hear Deuteronomistic voices from a much later time that are highly critical of the monarchy. The request for an earthly king meant the rejection of the heavenly king and becoming like all other people, thus gambling away God's election. If this people was to have a king at all—and only a deficient faith could see the need—then this king would have to be someone who follows God's instructions, transmitted by Samuel, to the letter. Otherwise this new development would lead to a great catastrophe. Saul never lived up to these high expectations, David and Solomon only in part, not to mention later potentates. All this means that statehood, at least as a monarchy, was a very precarious form of existence for Israel. (This youngest textual layer was probably created shortly after the exile, when Judaism wrestled with the shape of the polity to be established. There were messianic hopes and desires, but there were also many critical voices based on Israel's previous experiences in history. These voices of warning gained the upper hand, most likely encouraged by the Persian overlords; as a result, Israel did not establish a state for a long time.)

There is, however, also the other side, the side open to statehood and monarchy. This side is also present from the earliest textual layers onward: What type of polity may it have been that could not guarantee Israel's internal stability and external security? As much as the great acts of the individual liberators were to be praised, they never were able to establish permanent order; new enemies kept appearing on the horizon from all directions, even from within Palestine. These continual attacks with all the suffering that went with them had to last long enough for Israel time and again to remember its God, who then sent a new liberator. The quality of these heroes seemed to decrease as time passed. All of them were undoubtedly heroes, but they also unfortunately had other qualities: Ehud was an assassin; Gideon succumbed to the temptation of idolatry; Barak was incapable of gathering all of Israel behind him; Jephthah was wrapped up in family tragedy and civil war; Samson was a well-known womanizer and hooligan; and Eli was a leader without vision and strength. Even Samuel was not without blemish: he was unable to prevent his sons from going astray (1 Sam 8:1–3), and his behavior toward Saul was not always truly transparent. Even the former tribal leaders, the so-called "lesser judges" (Judg 10:1–5; 12:7–15), were unable to prevent the increase of bloody chaos in Israel (Judg 12:1–6; 17–21). The worst of it was the fact that judges were unable to provide adequate protection from Israel's main enemy, the Philistines. Samson died at their hands (even if he killed many of them in the process), Eli and his sons died through Philistine influence, and even during the days of Saul they were able to move unchecked straight through the mountain regions of Israel to loot wherever and whenever they desired. They established a monopoly in iron (1 Sam 13–14) and succeeded in destroying Israel's first dynasty (1 Sam 31).

All this is combined with the fearful question: What kind of God allows this to happen to Israel? Is he unable—or rather, unwilling—to spare his people turmoil, error, and suffering? Is he mean-spirited and vengeful? How else could the (in truth, quite petty) crimes of two sons of a judge lead all of Israel into bloody and tearful disaster (1 Sam 2–4)? Could it be that the decentralized organization of the polity, which according to the biblical text was solely guided by God, was unhealthy for Israel? Was the request that the people presented to Samuel to have a king and to "be like all other nations" (8:5) not only understandable, but necessary?

Recent redaction-critical analyses have shown that only parts of the Deuteronomistic layer in 1 Sam 7–12 were shaped by the radical evaluation present in 8:7 and 10:19, that the request for a king was not just the rejection of Samuel but also the rejection of the God of Israel. The Deuteronomistic authors did incorporate the early glorious stories of Saul and David, and they also postulated God's own involvement in creating the state and establishing its first kings (8:22; 10:24; 12:13; 15:10; 2 Sam 7:17–29). The older preexilic traditions were clearly shaped by a high opinion of the early monarchy. They took the positive acceptance of the monarchy for granted and praised this institution highly. The state was seen as a natural development in the course of history that turned away much calamity from Israel. Internal and external problems had to be dealt with, and the monarchy was the only institution capable of doing so.

Thus the institution of the monarchy has two faces in the biblical texts: to a certain degree, it is capable of dealing with problems of stability and security, but it is also shaped by the immanent tendency to destabilize itself. The state, which back then could only be thought of as a monarchy, is at best a necessary evil. The era before the state, which after all lasted for two centuries, was not principally a time of dark anarchy; it also had its positive side: a high degree of autonomy for the people; public gatherings and communal decisions and responsibilities (even if the results were not always positive); and a less hierarchical, more segmentary form of leadership by constantly alternating judges from various tribes. In a sense, these elements describe an early form of democracy and separation of powers. The important areas of economics, jurisdiction, and religion were not gathered in the hands of a central power. Only during war were all these forces combined—but again only on a regional level. Everyday life seemed to develop in a family or township, in any event a decentralized context.

It seems that this beginning of Israelite history continued to influence developments during statehood. The people of Israel never became passive subjects. It is quite telling that this people did without statehood for several centuries. The first king was a man without his own power base and with very limited powers. Under his rule, Israel continued to decide much of its own fate. According to the biblical traditions, Saul collided not only with the Philistines but also with divergent claims in his own house and kingdom (we only have to think of Jonathan and David or the Gibeonites). In all of Saul's reign, YHWH's own authority remained supreme. In the case of the wars against the Philistines and the Amalekites, the people wrestled not only with an external enemy but also with the question of internal authority: Should the king be allowed to act according to his own political-military insight, or should the final decision remain with YHWH and his prophet?

With the second king, David, power and religion did not drift apart to this degree: David took both into his own hands. In an ingenious religious and political move, he transferred the forgotten and dishonored ark of YHWH to his newly established residence and placed it at the center of cultic procedures (2 Sam 6; see also 2 Sam 24). He, whom we are told was elected by YHWH, elected YHWH to be the personal God of his dynasty. This was an action with wide-reaching consequences. The successes of this most successful of all Israelite and Judahite kings were credited to the actions of YHWH and vice versa: this man did not owe his success to his own prowess but to YHWH. The name of YHWH was connected to the house of David and vice versa. From now on, the attitude and the actions of all Jerusalem kings could be measured by the relation to YHWH; their successes as well as their failures could be explained from this point of view.

The Bible already makes an example of the founder of the dynasty. The prophet Nathan, sent by God, once promises David and his whole house that YHWH's presence and grace will be with them (2 Sam 7) and once proclaims YHWH's anger and judgment after the king has become an adulterer and a murderer. From now on, dark shadows accompany the reign of the previously successful monarch. He is no longer able to control his sons' lust for power and blood, and finally the fires of two large rebellions burn the land. We gain the impression that the people—especially the people of northern Israel—gathered under Absalom and Sheba (2 Sam 15–19; 20) to rise against their king and that the king was able to stay in power only by waging war alongside his mercenaries against his own people.

David's succession was arranged internally: a palace intrigue and the royal guard ensured that Solomon won the race. His opponent Adonijah seemed to have been favored by the Judahite population—and also could have had the God YHWH, honored by this people and represented by the priest Abiathar, on his side. Solomon, however, also had important religious supporters: the prophet Nathan and the priest Zadok. They anointed him, most assuredly in the name of YHWH, as king (1 Kgs 1). YHWH had become the specific God of this specific dynasty. The bill was paid a generation later. Following a failed rebellion during Solomon's lifetime (1 Kgs 11:26–28, 40), all the northern tribes seceded from the Jerusalem monarchy immediately after Solomon's death; the first northern Israelite king, Jeroboam I, established two state sanctuaries in Dan and Bethel in direct competition to the Jerusalem sanctuary of YHWH. He referred to the God honored in these new sanctuaries as *Elohim* (perhaps originally as El? or even as YHWH?), "who had led Israel out of Egypt" (1 Kgs 11:28).

The north now constituted its own monarchy, but this monarchy was unstable and remained at the mercy of turmoil and political unrest. Centrifugal forces kept gaining the upper hand against the attempts at centralization and stabilization (we only have to think of the continually changing capital cities during the beginning and of the various short-lived dynasties). In the more centralized Judahite south, the rural population also developed a high sense of personal freedom and autonomy, but it remained loyal to its dynasty at all times (following 1 Kgs 1, see also 2 Kgs 11; 22–23; Mic 3).

Thus the foundation was laid in Israel and Judah for limited loyalty to the monarchy. The centrally ruled state may have been better equipped to solve certain problems than any decentralized system. It was, however, always in danger of mutating into a tyrannical system in which the people lost their autonomy and YHWH his place. It seems that this danger was not seen with greater clarity anywhere else during antiquity than in Israel; there is much to be said for the suggestion that this clarity and insight was directly connected to faith in YHWH. No human institution had the right or the power to compete with YHWH, to limit his freedom or the freedom of his people. If anyone attempted to do so—whether Israelite or Judahite or even the much more powerful kings of the ancient empires—then sooner or later they had to deal with an incredibly self-confident and freedom-loving people and their faith in the God YHWH, who consequently developed from a regional mountain God to the God of the entire world. The Bible clearly addresses all the smaller and greater rulers of this world as responsible to the God who established himself as the liberator of the oppressed from the very beginning: either as warning to those in power or as hope for those oppressed.

IV.3. ELECTION AND REJECTION, TRAGEDY AND BLESSING

Barth, Karl. *Kirchliche Dogmatik* (4th ed.; Zürich: Evangelischer Verlag, 1959), 2.2:404–34. **Berges,** Ulrich. *Die Verwerfung Sauls: Eine thematische Untersuchung* (FB 61; Würzburg: Echter, 1989). **Deist,** F. E. "David, a Man after God's Heart? An Investigation into the David Character in the So-Called Succession Narrative," in *Studies in the Succession Narrative, OTWSA 27 (1984) and OTWSA 28 (1985): Old Testament Essays* (ed. W. C. van Wyk; Pretoria: n.p., 1986), 99–129. **Dietrich,** Walter. *David: Der Herrscher mit der Harfe* (Biblische Gestalten 14; Leipzig: Evangelische Verlagsanstalt, 2006). **Dietrich,** and Christian **Link.** *Die dunklen Seiten Gottes: Willkür und Gewalt* (4th ed.; Neukirchen-Vluyn: Neukirchener, 2002). **Donner,** Herbert. "Die Verwerfung des Königs Saul," in idem, *Aufsätze zum Alten Testament* (BZAW 224; Berlin: de Gruyter, 1994), 133–64. **Exum,** J. Cheryl. *Tragedy and Biblical Narrative: Arrows of the Almighty* (Cambridge: Cambridge University Press, 1992). **Gunn,** David M. *The Fate of King Saul: An Interpretation of a Biblical Story* (JSOTSup 14; Sheffield: JSOT Press,1980). **Hentschel,** Georg. *Saul: Schuld, Reue und Tragik eines "Gesalbten"* (Biblische Gestalten 7; Leipzig: Evangelische Verlagsanstalt, 2003). **Klein,** Johannes. *David versus Saul: Ein Beitrag zum Erzählsystem der Samuelbücher* (BWANT 158; Stuttgart: Kohlhammer, 2002). **Knierim,** Rolf. "Die Messianologie des ersten Buches Samuel," *EvT* 30 (1970): 113–33.

The biblical description of the early monarchy is shaped mainly by the polarity between Saul and David. Until the middle of 1 Samuel, the first king of Israel determines the events while increasingly becoming darker and darker. He has a falling out with YHWH's prophet Samuel (1 Sam 15), after which the "spirit of YHWH departs" from him and "an evil spirit from YHWH" tortures him (16:14). At this moment, the second main character steps onto the stage: first as a young shepherd boy (16:1–13), soon as a young warrior (16:15–23), then as the glorious vanquisher of Goliath (1 Sam 17). Both characters stand in front of us, as if in a spotlight: the rejected king, dark, bitter, without hope; and the elect young man, glorious, full of vigor, victorious.

Saul and David have entered into cultural memory as hero and antihero.[1] The Bible itself stands at the beginning of this development. The figure of Saul with his family is more and more relegated to the background during the course of the books of Samuel, and he disappears completely in the books of Kings. In contrast, David with his house is clearly the main protagonist of the books of Samuel, and his dynasty remains a constant focus of the entire history of the monarchy. The book of Chronicles elevates David to sainthood while reporting of Saul only his death (1 Chr 10). No prophet, no wisdom teacher ever mentions Saul; no psalm is attributed to him. He is not mentioned in the "Praise of the Fathers" of Jesus Sirach nor in the New Testament. If Christian kings and emperors refer to any biblical king, it is to David and his dynasty, not to Saul. More telling than words are works of art. When sculpting the ideal human being, Michelangelo naturally used David, not Saul. The central east window of the English Selby Abbey depicts the kings of the house of David (created probably during the time of Edward III, with a clear reference to English royalty): from David (actually Jesse) all the way to Jesus (and Joseph), including Solomon, Rehoboam, and all the others, even the highly questionable kings Manasseh, Jehoiachin, and Herod Antipas. Saul, however, is nowhere to be seen.

Johann Kuhnau, composer and direct predecessor of Johann Sebastian Bach as Thomaskantor in Leipzig, published his "Musicalische Vorstellung Einiger Biblischer Historien / In 6 Sonaten / Auff dem Claviere zu spielen / Allen Liebhabern zum Vergnügen" with Immanuel Tietzen in Leipzig in 1700. According to the preface he tried to express some of the biblical portraits and stories in sound. These pieces are fine examples of program music. The pieces do not recite the biblical stories (at most they only contain a brief reference in a foreword); instead, they try to communicate the subject matter through musical means only. The second of the six sonatas is titled "Der von David vermittelst der Music curirte Saul" (Saul, Cured by the Music of David). The two movements, superscribed with "Sauls Traurigkeit und Unsinnigkeit"

---

1. There are a few examples to the contrary in reception history. We must credit Jewish exegetes who did write much about the pious (and sinful!) David, but sometimes also in a positive sense about Saul. See J. Klein, "Streben nach Sündlosigkeit als Mangel— Sündenverstrickung als Vorzug eines Herrschers: Gedanken zur Taldmudstelle b.Joma 22b," in *König David, biblische Schlüsselfigur und europäische Leitgestalt* (ed. Walter Dietrich and Hubert Herkommer; Fribourg: Universitätsverlag; Stuttgart: Kohlhammer, 2003), 229–38.

(Saul's Sadness and Madness), and "David's erquickendes Harffen-Spiel" (David's Revitalizing Harp-Playing) can be seen as the musical expression of the topic "election and rejection."

In his introduction to this trio sonata, Kuhnau describes how he imagines Saul:

> The eyes roll and flicker, casting sparks, so to speak. The face is contorted, removing all semblance to human features. The stormy ocean of the heart throws waves of froth from the mouth. Jealousy, envy, hate, and fear attack him with vigor. ... In short, where God is absent and the enemy present, all evil finds its home. ... As God uses individuals to perform wonders, he sends him a glorious musician, the excellent King David, and equips his harp-playing with great power. When Saul sweats in the hot bath of sadness, David performs a piece of music and revives the king, granting him peace.[2]

The contrast between election and rejection is seen in the music even more clearly than in this introduction. A glance at the score shows that Saul's raving is expressed in wild, choppy, syncopated phrases, David's music in linear lines and harmonious chords (see fig. 16). What the eye cannot see and the modern piano cannot perform is the mean tone temperament of Kuhnau's "Clavier." In contrast to modern well-tempered tuning, mean tone temperament creates very different tone colors based on the tone of the respective key. By setting Saul and David in different keys with a different number of accidentals, Kuhnau creates a very audible distinction between the horrors of the one rejected and the trust of the one elected.

This sharp contrast between election and rejection that determines the commonly held evaluation of David and Saul does not match the texts of the first book of Samuel. These texts do try to persuade the reader that Saul had to go and that David had to come. At the same time, however, they create unease and dissent because of the basic inequality of the starting positions of

---

2. German: "Die Augen verkehren sich / und springet / so zu reden / ein Feuer Funcke nach dem andern heraus: Das Gesichte siehet zerzerret / daß man die wenigen Reliquien menschlicher Gestalt fast nicht mehr erkennet: Das Hertz wirfft als ein ungestümes und wütendes Meer den Schaum durch den Mund aus. Mißtrauen / Eiffer / Neid / Haß und Furcht stürmen hefftig auff ihn zu. ... Wo Gott abwesend / und der böse Feind gegenwärtig ist / da muß freylich eine Behausung alles Übels sein. ... Dieweil aber Gott bißweilen durch Menschen Wunder zu thun pfleget; So schicket er ihm einen herrlichen Musicum / den vortrefflichen König David / und leget auff sein Harffen-Spiel eine ungemeine Krafft. Denn wenn Saul / so zu reden / in der heissen Bad-Stube der Traurigkeit schwitzet / und David nur ein Stückgen musiciret / so wird der König gleich wieder erquicket / und zur Ruhe gebracht."

Figure 16: From Johann Kuhnau's sonata "Saul, Cured by the Music of David"—above: "Saul's Sadness and Madness"; below: "David's Revitalizing Harp-Playing"

these two individuals. The one is covered in good fortune, whereas the other is burdened with misfortune. The rise of the one seems as unstoppable as the fall of the other. Why does David exude such assurance and Saul such resignation? Is Saul truly so much worse than David? Why does God discriminate against Saul and favor David? Does he reject without reason; is he arbitrary, even cynical?

A few comments on the biblical understanding of election and rejection are warranted. Election is not exclusive; there is no principle that there can be one only who is elect, that the election of the one must lead to the rejection of the other. The belief that Israel was elect did not, in fact, lead to the idea that all non-Israelite peoples were *rejected* and thus subject to divine punishment. God moves against powers and people who oppose his good will. The fact that God has an elect people or elect individuals does not necessarily presuppose that God stands against all those who are not elect. His positive decision for an individual or a group does not presuppose that he has decided against all others. Saul's rejection thus was not a precondition for David's election, in the sense that God, having decided on the one, now had to reject the other.

Our ideas on the theological topic of election and rejection are often, unfortunately, based on very physical concepts, such as a magnet with two related but opposite poles or two connected tubes: if the water level rises in one toward election, it falls in the other toward rejection. The individuals and groups on either side can really do nothing about this fact: they are dealing with natural laws that result in a downward movement to correspond with an upward movement somewhere else. God's action becomes a natural law, a force prior to and independent of human action. Such thinking has determined much of the disastrous defining of the relation between Israel and the church. If God has chosen to elect a new people, this must mean that he has rejected those who were previously elected. Either them or us; then it was them, now it is us. This is the basic paradigm of anti-Judaistic concepts of the Christian inheritance of God's election. Saul and David become the personified paradigms for this natural law necessarily determining God's actions.

Such mechanistic thinking is completely outside the worldview of the Hebrew Bible. At first David is not even chosen; Saul is! When Saul is lifted to the throne, he is (at least according to Samuel) the one *chosen by Yhwh* (1 Sam 10:24). Then Saul is *rejected*, by this very Samuel, who again feels compelled by God to do so (15:26; see also 13:13–14). We thus see that a person or group cannot be elected and rejected simultaneously. Whoever is rejected can no longer be elected. We also see that only one who has previously been elected can also be rejected. Thus there is no direct opposition between election and rejection but rather a somewhat elliptical relationship.

Immediately after Saul's rejection, the narrative turns to David, even though his introduction is still hidden from public view (1 Sam 16). The kingship (and the election to be king) is not torn away from Saul right away and given to the other, to David. The one rejected will remain king for a long time, an almost painfully long time; the one elected will be treated as one rejected. God's decision to reject Saul does not immediately release energies that flow into one another. Saul retains his historical mandate; he is given the opportunity to prove himself. The term בחר ("to elect") occurs in connection with David only after Saul has failed completely and his kingdom has fallen to David. David himself now speaks of his election and negates any lasting claim to power by the house of Saul—but he does not speak of Saul's rejection (2 Sam 6:21).

In the context of the two figures Saul and David, their election and rejection, we must also address various temporal shifts and changes in subject matter that do not create a roughly hewn portrait but rather a picture with many subtle changes. This was examined with great sensitivity by a scholar whose use of the Bible is well known but not always appreciated by exegetes: Karl Barth. In his *Church Dogmatics*, especially in the section on the nature of God, he uses Saul and David as paradigms for the relation between rejection and election. Neither of the protagonists deserves one or the other from the outset and without reservation. From the beginning, the figure of Saul is ambivalent: the people are on his side, but their request for a king is questionable from the start. God has a plan for this first king, and thus Saul is without a doubt God's elect! But he is also the personification of Israel's large ambition and lack of faith. Saul has only to show "microscopic" traces of this combination of ambition and lack of faith to suffer immediate rejection. His small transgressions show that he was brought into office within a context not set by God but by the ambition of the people. Saul would have had to be completely different from his people to compensate for this basic blemish of his kingship. But Saul is not completely different, and he thus has to step aside. David now takes his place. He is also no heavenly being, not at all. He has his weak points, and he soils himself with blood guilt (worse than Saul ever did!)— yet God does not take his election away. Why not? Because he was not *first* desired by the people of Israel but chosen by God. His kingdom came from God, and he retained his kingdom only because of God. He was lifted from nothing; he was pursued and threatened; he was deeply caught in sin; he experienced his limits again and again. Thus, David has a "Saul-side" just as Saul has a "David-side." Both are imperfect and limited, even though the mixture is different in each case. Neither of these kings is a truly perfect human. They and all Old Testament rulers are merely placeholders for he who is to come: Christ. In him, in his death on the cross, God takes the rejection onto himself and settles with the "Saul-side" of human rule; in his resurrection he fulfills the "David-side" in human nature. Because the history of the Israelite monarchy is the prequel to the story of Jesus Christ, the election outweighs rejection, grace outweighs judgment. God's work of salvation leads from Saul to David to Christ.

Barth's reading of the Bible shows certain similarities to the growing field of "literary criticism," in which texts are read as a whole and analyzed according to their various intertextual facets. The focus is not on the question of how the text came to be, its historical context, and the concrete intentions of its authors, but on the artistic composition and intention of the final text. This approach has not (yet) become common in German-language research, but it is highly developed in an English context. Regarding the David and Saul stories, the two most important contributions were made by David M. Gunn and J. Cheryl Exum.[3] They are completely focused on the final biblical text. Gunn reads the final text as a very specific theological tragedy. For him, the opposition between rejection and election is the motor of the entire narrative. The reader knows from the beginning that Saul's rule is ill-fated; the reader experiences how Saul is rejected and how Samuel quickly chooses a successor with God's help. Saul does not know who this successor will be, only that someone will replace him. In tragic irony, Saul brings his own opponent into his court and finds him to be an indispensable assistant. His suspicions slowly increase, however, and his affection for the young David turns into distrust and finally hate. Whatever he does to eliminate or even liquidate David, it turns against him and works in David's favor. In the end, he fails—not because of David or the Philistines, not because of himself, but because of God. It is none other than God who forces the kingship on him and who then seeks to take it away again. It is God who turns fate against him and who leads him into one precarious situation after another, using the king's first mistake as grounds for his rejection. Saul, according to Gunn, is the victim of God's arbitrariness and impatience. David, on the other hand, can do whatever he wants and remains God's favorite. As readers, we understand that Saul resists this injustice and his unforgiving fate, doing horrible things in the process. We might be willing to forgive, but God is not. David is not really the one who is being pursued: Saul is continually subjected to God's persecution. God relentlessly stays on his heels and does not rest until he is destroyed.

Gunn presents all this not as his own but as the Bible's evaluation of Saul and David; not his own but the Bible's portrayal of God contains so many dark elements. In Gunn's view, the Bible itself leads its readers to a criticism of religion through its positive and subversive portrayal of Israel's first king and his divine enemy. Exum, who works within the same exegetical framework as Gunn, argues that Gunn has an all too one-sided evaluation of where the Bible lays blame: God the perpetrator, Saul the victim. But Saul, at least as much as God, is portrayed as an ambiguous character. His fall is brought on for two main reasons: God's animosity against the kingdom, or better, against *Saul's* kingdom; and Saul's "turbulent personality" (Exum 1992, 41). God works toward Saul's failure—and finds in Saul his most able assistant. According to

---

3. J. Klein (who is also open to diachronic questions) has also made a recent contribution in German.

Exum, the biblical authors find positive elements in this combination: Saul carries the punishment for Israel's sin of requesting a king. His ruin expunges this guilt and prepares the way for a new beginning—with David.

This is a very important insight. The narrators do not get stuck with Saul's appalling fate but use this dark background to present the saving history of David. Both opposing tendencies belong to the same portrait that the Bible draws of the creation of the monarchy in Israel. The founding of the state, Israel's existence not only as a people of God but also as a nation, contained several threatening aspects but also positive and hopeful elements. The dark aspects had to be dealt with in Saul's story so that the hopeful elements could break through in the reign of David and his house. Despite all first appearances, Saul thus plays a positive and constructive role in God's historical plan by personifying the rejection of a type of kingship not accepted by God. The founding of a state as such is not a source of temptation and ruin; such a state could well be a gift and an opportunity! The temptation and ruin lay within the acceptance of such a state as a source of salvation in competition with the salvation given by God to his people.

Just as the life of an individual person contains elements of guilt and tragic sin, the state also is not fully immune to these elements. Evil lurks at every corner, even in the shape of the basically harmless and likeable character of Saul. Goodness, however, is, thank God, also present, represented here by the character of David, who despite all his shortcomings was blessed by God. Rolf Knierim suggested that the David-Saul narratives develop their own "messiology."[4] This messiology is defined in positive and negative terms, but not in a clear separation, as if Saul represents the dark side and David the light side. In the end, however, only one of the two is able to do justice to God's high expectations for the kingship as intended by him. The other makes more and more mistakes and finally fails completely. Until his untimely end, however, Saul remains the anointed, and God allows him to retain his power to pursue and drive away the other, the true anointed. David never appears as

---

4. The term "messiology" is most often associated with messianic expectations of later times connected to the figure of David. This is hardly a concern of the books of Samuel. First indications may be present in 2 Sam 7 and especially in the reception history of this chapter (see Michael Pietsch, "Dieser ist der Sproß Davids...": Studien zur Rezeptionsgeschichte der Nathanverheißung [WMANT 100; Neukirchen-Vluyn: Neukirchener, 2003]). On the topic of messianism connected to David, see Dietrich and Herkommer, König David (therein the essays by M. Karrer, C. Thoma, M. Voigts, E.-J. Waschke, and R. J. Werblowsky) as well as the summary comments in Walter Dietrich, David: Der Herrscher mit der Harfe (Biblische Gestalten 14; Leipzig: Evangelische Verlagsanstalt, 2006), 329–57.

one of limitless power, even during the high point of his career. This is basically how we can describe the Bible's double portrait of David and Saul.

In their attempt to understand and explain the factual events, the transfer of power from the once-anointed Saul to David, the narrators explain it as not only tolerated but enacted by God. They have little difficulty with the concept of *election*. Saul could easily be as elect as David (and he was). Election is not based on personal achievement or specific character attributes. Saul never could have earned his election, and even David was no superhuman with a right to remain elect for all times. Election is always unmerited. The Bible, however, sees rejection as fully warranted by human behavior. The narrators thus have problems with Saul and David. With David, reasons for rejection were very clear, but he was not rejected; instead, he died in old age after fulfilling his glorious life's work, knowing that his descendants would continue his work. Saul died in misfortune in battle, and his house had no future; in other words, he must have been rejected—but why? The biblical authors searched for answers (we could say, desperately) for why God may have turned away from him. They found no worse reasons in the traditions handed down to them than what we now read in 1 Sam 13 and 15 (and we should honor them for not inventing any horrible misdeeds to surpass these). They wanted to lead their readers to think about why Saul experienced God's blessing and protection only in small measures but David in abundance.

The biblical narrators seem to have had a difficult time creating a clear and concise picture of the God who stands behind the very unclear and even unjust transfer of power from Saul to David. They do not stand alone with this problem. Time and again biblical texts raise the issue of God's justice in the face of clear injustices suffered by human beings.[5] As (most?) other biblical authors (such as the authors of the lament psalms, of the books of Jeremiah and Job), they hold fast to the supposition that God's gracious hand is at work even when human eyes and a human sense of justice are no longer able to perceive it. The painful and tragic experiences that Saul and even David have to suffer are a challenge to, but not a contradiction of, a faith in a God who does not send us misfortune but salvation. God's grace does not take effect in the life of each individual, such as with Saul; other individuals, however, such as David, and the people of Israel as a whole, experience how God's saving grace does break through in the end.

---

5. See Walter Dietrich and Christian Link, *Die dunklen Seiten Gottes*, vol. 1: *Willkür und Gewalt* (4th ed.; Neukirchen-Vluyn: Neukirchener, 2002); and vol. 2: *Allmacht und Ohnmacht* (2nd ed.; Neukirchen-Vluyn: Neukirchener, 2004).

This is the faith of the narrators of the books of Samuel, a faith shared by those who continued to tell the history of the early monarchy throughout the monarchy until its catastrophic end in the collapse of the two states Israel (722 B.C.E.) and Judah (587/6 B.C.E.). This does not mean that these individuals and this people were never thrown into severe doubt when the darkness of fate came upon them. Such doubts were created especially by the Babylonian exile and—if the jump forward in time may be permitted—the Holocaust in the twentieth century. Yet even in ghettos and in concentration camps, Jews stood by their faith in a God who continued to hold on to them in all suffering. The promise of the Bible is not the absence of suffering; its promise—and this we see in the portraits of Israel's first kings and its inseparable mixture of blessing and tragedy—is the presence of God with his people, with all peoples, leading them to a good goal and accompanying them with his presence.

IV.4. MEN AND WOMEN

Berlin, Adele. "Characterization in Biblical Narrative. David's Wives," *JSOT* 23 (1982): 69–85. **Clines,** David J. A., and Tamara C. **Eskenazi,** eds. *Telling Queen Michal's Story. An Experiment in Comparative Interpretation* (JSOTSup 119; Sheffield: JSOT Press, 1991). **Exum,** J. Cheryl. "Bathsheba Plotted, Shot, and Painted," *Semeia* 74 (1996): 47–73. **Horner,** Tom M. *Jonathan Loved David: Homosexuality in Biblical Times* (Philadelphia: Westminster, 1978). **Naumann,** Thomas. "David und die Liebe," in *König David, biblische Schlüsselfigur und europäische Leitgestalt* (ed. Walter Dietrich and Hubert Herkommer; Fribourg: Universitätsverlag; Stuttgart: Kohlhammer, 2003), 51–84. **Nicol,** George G. "The Alleged Rape of Bathsheba: Some Observations on Ambiguity in Biblical Narratives," *JSOT* 73 (1997): 43–54. **Schroer,** Silvia, and Thomas **Staubli.** "Saul, David und Jonathan—Eine Dreiecksgeschichte?" *BK* 51 (1996): 15–22. **Thompson,** J. A. "The Significance of the Verb *Love* in the David-Jonathan Narratives in 1 Samuel," *VT* 24 (1974): 334–38. **Trible,** Phyllis. *Texts of Terror: Literary-Feminist Readings of Biblical Narratives* (OBT 13; Philadelphia: Fortress, 1984). **Valler,** Shulamith. "King David and 'His' Women: Biblical Stories and Talmudic Discussions," in *A Feminist Companion to Samuel and Kings* (ed. Athalya Brenner; FCB 5; Sheffield: Sheffield Academic Press, 1994), 129–42.

There are hardly any other texts in the Bible that center so explicitly and so intensively on the relationship between men and women as the narratives on the early monarchy. As this topic is not only of theological significance for the Bible but also of importance to all people of all times, we are justified in spending some time on this issue.

We should start with the relationship between men. Throughout most of our texts, this relationship is one of competition, of adversity, of battle. According to the stylistic paradigm of Hebrew narratives, individual scenes are made up of the relationship between two men: David and Saul; Eli and Samuel; Samuel and Saul; David and Goliath; David and Nabal; Joab and Abner; Joab and Asael; David and Eshbaal; David and Uriah; Amnon and Absalom; Hushai and Ahithophel; David and Absalom; Joab and Sheba; Adonijah and Solomon. It is interesting (and somewhat shocking) that all of these and many other stories end with the death of one of the opponents. The most important relational paradigm between men seems to be: you or me. The world of men is full of speechlessness, lack of emotion, and violence. This at least seems to be true for the early monarchy. Is this archaic or archetypical?

We should, however, not describe thi·.gs in black-and-white terms. Most of the male relationships that end in deaun also contain certain touching features. Eli and Samuel are not merely competitors for the highest spiritual office. Eli values his student highly and accepts without envy that he has contact with YHWH, whereas YHWH no longer speaks to him. When Samuel reports the contents of the theophany to Eli, foretelling the approaching death of the old priest, Eli accepts the verdict without protest. David and Saul are not merely rivals for the highest position in the state. Saul needs David (as music therapist, as mighty warrior, even as a son-in-law), and David honors and spares Saul (even when Saul is willing to kill him, 1 Sam 24; 26). Both refer to each other as father and son—in this situation quite a depressing relational attribute. David and Uriah are not merely the rivals for the beautiful Bathsheba. Uriah is a loyal and honorable, perhaps somewhat naive and inflexible, officer and thus receives the death sentence while David tries everything to shift the parenthood of the child conceived in adultery to him and thus save his life. David and Absalom are mortal enemies and yet remain father and son: Absalom when he regains his father's favor after his murder of Amnon, when he hesitates immediately to pursue and kill his father, rejecting Ahithophel's probably correct advice; and definitely David when he reacts to the news of Absalom's death.

These are not simply portraits of barbaric, violent men. They respect each other, but they become tragically connected and cause each other much suffering. Perhaps we can use the relationship between Nathan and David as a case example. In 1 Kgs 1 Nathan appears as an opportunistic accomplice of the power-hungry Solomon. But is Solomon not the symbol of God's grace to the house of David amidst the purgatory fire of the Bathsheba-Uriah scandal? Was Nathan not the one who initiated this purgatory? He pronounced a death sentence against the king, or rather led the king to pronounce this death sentence himself, but then he shifted the death sentence to the child conceived in adultery. In the matter of the temple construction, Nathan was not a willing oracle but resisted the tit-for-tat mentality of the king by establishing a special covenant between king and God within the context of the covenant between YHWH and Israel. He thus prevented any attempt of the divinely blessed king to control the deity. On the other hand, he made a promise to the king that God would bless the dynasty as long as the kings acted in accordance with God's guidance. Nathan is no doubt devoted to the king and the royal house, but he nevertheless remains the speaker for God and the people.

There are also stories of true friendship between men. David is described as a leader who was able to inspire his followers, to gather them behind him and to turn them into friends who would risk their lives for him. Joab was such a follower, as well as his brother Abishai, the "two sons of Zeruiah" (whoever opposed them was flirting with death). When David must escape from Jerusalem, this painful farewell briefly highlights another friendship: David and Ittai, the Philistine commander of a mercenary unit. David allows him to remove himself and his men from this dangerous situation. The answer, however, is not the answer of a mercenary: "Wherever my lord the king shall be, whether in death or life, your servant will also be there" (2 Sam 15:21). This place will be a place of life—but a place of death for Absalom and numerous Israelites; Ittai will have contributed his share to these deaths.

The story of the love between David and Jonathan is a special example of friendship between men. No other story in the Bible describes such a friendship with such warmth and sympathy, whereas Greek literature is full of such stories. David himself created a lasting tribute to his friendship by composing a moving lament for the fallen friend. In this lament, he praises his love as greater than a woman's love (2 Sam 1:26). At an earlier point, the texts narrate how Jonathan willingly transferred his claim to the throne to his friend, merely asking that his descendents be treated well (1 Sam 20:12–17; 23:16–18). David made this promise and kept it (2 Sam 9; 16:1–4; 19:25–31).

Were there homosexual elements in the friendship between David and Jonathan? Writers (e.g., Stefan Heym and Allen Massie) as well as exegetes (Horner, Schoer, Staubli) are quite certain about this issue; most exegetes deny it (who knows for what reasons). The biblical texts allow us both viewpoints. The fact that David had many wives and children and that Jonathan had at least one son does not mean that a homosexual relationship, especially in their younger years, would have been impossible. In the context of the history of the suffering of homosexuals, one might well desire that the Bible portray homosexual relationships with sympathy at least in this case, but we cannot allow this motivation to determine our exegesis (the same is true for the opposite point of view that denies the Bible could ever portray homosexuality in a positive light). Given the general negative attitude toward homosexuality in the ancient Near East, it would be very difficult to assume that the narrators described David and Jonathan as a homosexual couple if they were intent on creating a positive description. It would have been very easy to suppress or modify such traditions (if they ever did exist!). In addition, the verb אהב, most often translated as "to love," has a wide scope of meaning: the erotic-sexual attraction of lovers; the nonerotic friendship between individuals of all genders; the altruistic love and charity that determines the actions of both Jews and Christians (Lev 19:18!); as well as the grateful-deferential love of the faithful toward their God (Deut 6:5!) or of the vassal to his lord (see Thompson 1974). It is difficult to determine which of these facets were most important to the narrators in their description of the love between Jonathan and David. This much, however, is true: the David-Jonathan stories do not support the discrimination against same-sex relationships that is common in Christian circles, most often by making reference to the Bible.

The Bible is clear on one point: the relation between David and Jonathan is not described as a relationship between equals. Jonathan appears as the one who gives, David as the one who takes. Only after Jonathan's death does David give back some of the love he received from his friend to Jonathan's descendents (2 Sam 9). In the context of the transfer of power from Saul and his house to David and his house, Jonathan's affection for David serves primarily the purpose of portraying David as Saul's legitimate successor. The reader is supposed to understand that friendship and selfless love, not hate and murder, were present at the birth of the Davidic kingship.

We now turn to the relation between men and women. Here we will see two main tendencies: the one portrays women as the victims of men; the other describes women as powerful and self-confident individuals. It is a striking feature of these texts that both tendencies are interwoven in the description of almost all the female characters.

Hannah (1 Sam 1-2) is victim to the patriarchal view that women are valuable only when they produce children, especially sons. Surprisingly enough, it is a woman, Hannah's co-wife Peninnah, who causes Hannah pain by emphasizing this fact, while her husband, Elkanah, appears as a loving, understanding, but also completely helpless individual. Hannah finally dares to go to the sanctuary alone and bewail her fate to God—only to be yelled at by Eli the priest. Right then, perhaps encouraged by her faith in God's grace, she rises to tell the priest that he is wrong. Eli immediately retracts and gives her a divine promise. Hannah later becomes pregnant and gives birth to a special son who will become Eli's successor and Israel's leader. Hannah has become strong, and she sings a song that finds no equal in strength and hope (1 Sam 2:1-10). With this song, which also foretells the advent of a king, Hannah becomes a prophet and provides us with an anticipatory interpretation of the monarchy. This is a trumpet call at the very beginning of the books of Samuel, sounded by a woman!

Then there is Michal, Saul's daughter and David's first wife. Even though she is a self-confident, powerful individual, this woman is ground up by these men as if caught between two millstones. The texts introduce her with the sentence: "Michal, the daughter of Saul, loved David" (1 Sam 18:20). This statement is completely unique in the entire Bible (with the sole exception of the Song of Songs), yet it is only the trigger for a perfidious murder scheme: Saul uses Michal, the woman who loves, as bait to lead David into the Philistine trap. David, however, not only brings one hundred Philistine foreskins as demanded, but two hundred to earn Michal's hand in marriage (18:21–27). We are not told what Michal thought of this price. She now appears as a resolute wife and opposes her father. When Saul tries to kill David, she hides him and helps him to escape, risking her own life in the process. David shows no gratitude for this devotion: he disappears to Philistine territory, perhaps forever, and her father "gives" her to another man (most likely without asking her). Many years later (it is astonishing how the Bible follows biographies over long periods of time and with great sensitivity), once Saul is dead, David demands his wife back from Saul's general Abner, who is willing to defect to David's side. Once again, she is taken away, and we do not discover what she thinks or feels; we are told only that her current husband bewails her departure. Then there is the final scene (2 Sam 6:20–23): as a proud and cold woman, very much the royal princess and daughter of Saul, she confronts David with his supposedly unworthy behavior during the ark procession. David does not take this accusation lying down but responds in kind. In the end, she does not have children from him—either because he or because she does not want to.

Finally, there is Bathsheba, the wife first of Uriah, then of David (2 Sam 11–12). Many interpreters, artists, and exegetes (always men, such as Stefan Heym or George Nicol) have blamed her in part or in full for David's affair with her. The text does not expressly state that she was innocent. The narrator tells us that David saw her from the roof of his palace while she was washing herself. We are not told why she was washing herself in a way that the king could see her. We are also not told what she thought and felt when she was called to the king and learned of his intentions: "He lay with her" (11:4). Male imagination loves to fantasize that Bathsheba would have enjoyed this encounter, even pushed for it. The text says nothing of the sort. When she becomes pregnant, David has her husband taken from the front lines in order to shift parentage onto him, but Uriah does not go to his wife. Once again, we are not told whether Bathsheba was party to the failure of this clever plan (Jerusalem was only 100 by 400 meters in size!). Both men continue the story on their own, and the narrator does not reveal whether Bathsheba (or her husband) ever fully understood what was going on. One thing is certain: the text does not indicate Bathsheba's guilt with a single word, whereas it speaks of David's guilt with great clarity. Bathsheba is like the lamb led silently to slaughter. First her husband dies, then her child—we are told nothing of her emotions. Then she gives birth to Solomon. Much later—perhaps twenty years later—she reappears, perhaps incited by the prophet Nathan (1 Kgs 1–2). Now she displays unyielding strength and engages in questionable but understandable action. She fears for the life of her son and for herself and thus participates in the elimination and finally the liquidation of the rival Adonijah. Who is Bathsheba? Is she a clever and unscrupulous schemer from the beginning or a victim of royal power and male violence who is able to enjoy revenge for this humiliation once the opportunity arises?

The Bathsheba story becomes somewhat clearer when we read it in connection with the Tamar story (2 Sam 13). Tamar, Absalom's sister, is clearly the victim of a brutal rape. Despite her youth, she is a strong and intelligent woman, but these assets are of no help to her. Once she falls prey to her brother Amnon, who lusts after her and can no longer escape his advances, she tries to reason with him, both prior to the rape and even after. But he is stupid and dull-witted, first out of lust, then out of hate (13:15 presents us with the abysmal description of the sudden switch from lust to disgust). Instead of seeking a legitimate relation with her, in which she could live with honor, he coldly throws her out of the house. Her brother Absalom responds to her screaming injustice by holding back and lurking: he sees not her plight but rather the chance to eliminate his older brother in a somewhat legitimate fashion. The story ends with murder (of the brother) and madness (of the sister).

David should have seen this tragedy coming, but he does nothing to prevent it. On the contrary, he enables many of the events by *sending* first Tamar to her rapist and then Amnon to his death (2 Sam 13:7, 27)—just as he *sent for* his victim Bathsheba and *sent* Uriah to his death (11:4, 14). Amnon desires to *lay with* his half-sister and *lays with* her against her will, just as David *lay with* Bathsheba (11:4; 13:11, 14). This means that we are not dealing with a father who helps a son but with one rapist who helps another, more unconsciously than with conscious intention. Both licentious men mirror each other by refusing to take responsibility for their actions until they have dragged others into their doom. If the (female?) biblical narrators spread all this out before our eyes without explicitly commenting on it, then we are confronted with a silent but screaming outcry against the violence done to women by men.

IV.5. VIOLENCE AND ABSTINENCE FROM VIOLENCE

Beauchamp, Paul, and Denis **Vasse.** "La violence dans la Bible," *CaE* 76 (1992): 5–63, esp. 43–47. **Dietrich,** Walter. "Die Erzählungen von David und Goliat in I Sam 17," *ZAW* 108 (1996): 172–91. **Dietrich.** "Die zweifache Verschonung Sauls durch David (I Sam 24 und I Sam 26)," in *David und Saul im Widerstreit: Diachronie und Synchronie im Wettstreit: Beiträge zur Auslegung des ersten Samuelbuches* (ed. Walter Dietrich; OBO 206; Fribourg: Academic; Göttingen: Vandenhoeck & Ruprecht, 2004), 232–53. **Dietrich.** "The Mark of Cain: Violence and Overcoming Violence in the Hebrew Bible," *Theology Digest* 52 (2005): 3–11. **Dietrich,** and Moisés **Mayordomo.** *Gewalt und Gewaltüberwindung in der Bibel* (Zürich: Theologischer Verlag Zürich, 2005). **Exum,** J. Cheryl. "Rizpah's Vigil and the Tragic End of the House of Saul," in idem, *Tragedy and Biblical Narrative: Arrows of the Almighty* (Cambridge: Cambridge University Press, 1992), 109–19. **Jensen,** Hans J. L. "Desire, Rivalry and Collective Violence in the 'Succession Narrative,'" *JSOT* 55 (1992): 39–59. **Levenson,** Jon D. "1 Samuel 25 as Literature and as History," *CBQ* 41 (1978): 11–28. **Schenker,** Adrian. *Der Mächtige im Schmelzofen des Mitleids: Eine Interpretation von 2 Sam 24* (OBO 42; Fribourg: Universitätsverlag; Göttingen: Vandenhoeck & Ruprecht, 1982).

The biblical stories about the early monarchy are full of violence and war. The beginning of this story is made by the request for one "who will go before us to fight our battles" (1 Sam 8:20). This is the life task of the first king, Saul. The final summary of his rule states, "He fought against all of his enemies: the Moabites, the Ammonites, the Edomites, the [Aramean] king of Zobah, and the Philistines" (14:47). Some of these battles are described in great detail. Saul qualified himself for the position with a grand victory over the Ammonites east of the Jordan (1 Sam 11). Most of his energy was drained by the never-ending conflict with the Philistines (1 Sam 13–14; 17–18), which in the end cost him his life and the life of his sons (1 Sam 31).

Saul was surpassed by another who was even more successful in war: David came to Saul's court as a young warrior and was given the post of the king's weapon carrier (1 Sam 16:14–23). His first great accomplishment was the victory over the Philistine hero Goliath (1 Sam 17). He soon advanced through the ranks to become an officer and the commander of Saul's mercenary troops; Israelite women praised the two heroes of war: "Saul defeated [or killed?] thousands, David tens of thousands" (18:7; 21:12). With his troop of four to six hundred, David served the Philistine ruler of Gath as "trouble shooter" against Israel. He used this position to perform raids of all types against southern Palestinian tribes (27:8–12; 30). Once established as king of Hebron (2 Sam 2:1–3), he destabilized the rule of Saul's son Eshbaal over Israel with continual border conflicts (2 Sam 2–4), finally extending his own kingdom to include the north (5:1–3). As in the case of Saul, the text also contains a summary of David's wars and victories. This summary is somewhat more extensive and includes a much wider military and political horizon (2 Sam 8). David also fought against the Ammonites, the Moabites, the Edomites, the Philistines, and the king of Zobah as well as other Aramean kings; he succeeded in establishing an empire from the Negev in the far south all the way to Syria. In addition to these wars against outside enemies, there were civil wars: against the rebellious prince Absalom (2 Sam 15–18) and against the separatist leader Sheba (2 Sam 20). All this is part of the biblical narrative, which thus portrays the early monarchy as a time of bloody conflict.

The biblical texts are also full of acts of individual violence. Many narratives deal with a conflict between two opponents in which one loses his life: David and Saul; David and Goliath; David and Nabal (1 Sam 25); Amnon and Absalom (2 Sam 13); David and Absalom (2 Sam 14–19); Hushai and Ahithophel (2 Sam 17); Joab and Amasa; Joab and Sheba (2 Sam 20); Adonijah and Solomon (1 Kgs 1–2). Most appalling is the violence committed by men against women. Saul's daughter Michal, introduced as a woman of love and the savior of her husband, is ground up between male power struggles (1 Sam 18:20–27; 19:11–17; 25:44; 2 Sam 3:14–16; 6:16, 20–23). Bathsheba is a silent victim of male lust and desire (2 Sam 11). Tamar speaks words of wisdom, but men speak to her only in harsh commands, as her father sends her to her half-brother, who rapes her and throws her out; her brother uses her to justify fratricide (2 Sam 13).

Most disconcerting is the fact that God himself participates in many acts of violence. In the summaries mentioned above we read twice that God "helped David wherever he went" (2 Sam 8:6, 14). Was it thus God's will that David lay the defeated Moabites on the ground and measured them: "two lines to be put to death and one line to be spared" (8:2)? Saul's victories over Israel's enemies were also won with God's consent; in fact, God made them possible. Saul could defeat the Ammonites after "the spirit of God came upon him" (1 Sam 11:6). Jonathan's foray against the Philistine post succeeded because God "gave his enemies into his hands" (14:10). This foray does not remain a fringe episode but rather triggers a major victory for Israel because at the right moment "the earth shook and a trembling of God" paralyzed the Philistines (14:15). Most disturbing is God's command to Saul: "Now go and smite Amalek, and utterly destroy all that they have; do not spare them, but kill both man and woman, infant and suckling, ox and sheep, camel and ass" (15:3). Saul is rejected at the end of this story—not because of performing the commanded genocide but because he did not execute the genocide completely.

Saul's rejection seems to start a game of very subtle divine violence. God seems to be playing with Saul. The king knows that "another who is better than he" will replace him (1 Sam 15:28). Readers discover who this other is in the very next chapter, when God sends Samuel to Bethlehem to anoint young David (16:1–13). David is thus also informed. Saul, however, does not know who his opponent is. An unequal confrontation develops. It is almost as if a one-sided mirror separates the two rivals: David can see through the glass and observe how his rival grows more and more nervous, striking out in all directions. He can always bring himself to safety in time while allowing Saul to strike at ghosts. Saul only *suspects* who stands behind the mirror, but he cannot *see* his opponent, only himself. Everything he does works against him: hateful and reconciling actions. Saul does not stand a chance. This strong man resembles a bull penetrated by two arrows: the arrow of election and the arrow of rejection. God has shot both arrows and seems to watch dispassionately how his victim moves closer to his end the more he tries to resist. Shortly before the decisive battle against the Philistines, Saul attempts to seek contact with God one last time, using all sorts of cultic procedures. God, however, remains silent (28:6). When Saul then contacts the dead Samuel by means of a necromancer, he succeeds only in having Samuel rise briefly from the dead in order to repeat his crushing judgment and pronounce a devastating oracle: "Tomorrow you and your sons will be with me" (28:19). This is exactly what happens.

We must acknowledge these facets of the description of humans and God contained in the biblical texts. Do they not sow a seed that bears horrible fruit at least in the reception history of these texts?

On the other hand, we must state that the biblical portrait of the early monarchy also contains very different elements. If military successes are credited to the help of God, then human military prowess is not only honored but also put into perspective. The very first narratives of military conflict in the books of Samuel show paradigmatically that the issue of security is not dependent on military might and violence but on the will and the actions of God. If the Israelites believe that the ark guarantees them divine presence and thus military invincibility, they are quite mistaken (1 Sam 4). It is also mistaken to assume that Israel and its God are lost merely because the battle and thus the ark are lost. God realizes his mighty presence in the middle of Philistine territory without any assistance from Israelite soldiers: idols collapse and a plague spreads throughout the country until the Philistines allow the ark to return in a triumphal victory procession—what irony!—to the territory of Israel and Judah (1 Sam 5–6). There is only one who wields true power: God. If humans attempt to emulate this, they will meet their doom sooner (Israel) or later (the Philistines).

Shortly thereafter Samuel—notably not a general but a priest and prophet—achieves a glorious victory over the Philistines (1 Sam 7). When the Philistines dare to interrupt Israel during a large worship service, Samuel offers a sacrifice and prays, and God "thunders mightily," driving the enemies apart and allowing the Israelites to "defeat them as far as below Beth-car" (1 Sam 7:10–11). Wherever this place may be, this battle definitely did not occur. The biblical narrators created this battle in order to show who was responsible for defeating the Philistines and who was not—also in the case of Saul and David.

As often as the texts tell of Israel's victories over its enemies, it also emphasizes that the aggressors attacked Israel without reason. Before Saul defeats them, for example, the Ammonites besiege the Israelite town of Jabesh without reason and threaten the inhabitants with brutal violence even though they are willing to negotiate and surrender (1 Sam 11:2). In the time of David, the Ammonites once again initiate a battle (2 Sam 10). The same is definitely true for the Philistines, who are always the ones to move against Israel (1 Sam 4:1 LXX; 7:7; 17:1; 28:1; 2 Sam 5:17). The description of the setting of the first battle between the Philistines and Saul in 1 Sam 13:17–20 is a case in point. Philistine raids occur in the middle of Benjaminite territory, and no one can prevent this, for "no smith was to be found throughout all the land of Israel, for the Philistines said, 'Lest the Hebrews make themselves swords or spears'; therefore, every one of the Israelites went down to the Philistines to sharpen his plowshare, his mattock, his axe, or his sickle." Who could hold it against Israel that it did not stand up against such oppression?

All this is concentrated into a parable in the narrative of David and Goliath (1 Sam 17). Goliath is the personification of arrogant, aggressive, and seemingly invincible power. The entire Israelite army, including King Saul, is paralyzed with fear. Then the shepherd boy David appears on the battlefield. Saul first tries to prevent him from engaging in single combat, then tries to equip him with the best possible armor: his own (which strikingly resembles Goliath's armor). David rejects all this and defeats Goliath with a sling and Goliath's own sword. The emphasis of the narrative is not on these actions but on the speeches of the opponents. Goliath repeatedly "mocks the armies of the living God" (17:10, 26, 36) and "curses David by his god" just before the stone hits his forehead (17:43). David, on the other hand, gives the following high-spirited speech before he flings the stone: "You come to me with a sword and with a spear and with a javelin, but I come to you in the name of YHWH of hosts, the God of the armies of Israel, whom you have defied. This day YHWH will deliver you into my hand … and all this assembly will know that YHWH saves not with sword and spear; for the battle belongs to YHWH" (17:45–47). The message to the readers could not be clearer: God makes sure that the enemy's violence is broken and Israel's existence secured; Israel is helped not by force but by faith.

Finally, the Amalekites. In 1 Sam 30 they appear as nomadic marauders, and David recaptures what they have looted with full moral justification. The war of extermination in 1 Sam 15, on the other hand, is motivated entirely by theological and not material reasons. According to 15:2, God wants to "punish what Amalek did to Israel in opposing them on the way, when they came up out of Egypt." This text activates the tradition that the Amalekites attacked Israel (Exod 17) soon after it passed through the Red Sea and found water and food for the first time in the desert (Exod 14–16). According to the biblical text, this attack threatened to become not only a massacre among the exhausted Israelites but even a genocide, destroying the people of God completely. This genocide was prevented, *not* by Israel's military strength, but by Moses' prayer. The fundamental importance of this battle matches the fundamental importance of the command to Saul, "Go and utterly destroy Amalek" (1 Sam 15:3). The text no longer refers to the actual Amalekites—they hardly existed any longer during the time when 1 Sam 15 was written—but to the personified antithesis of the people of God, to the power of evil in general that must be destroyed at all costs. The presence of such a text in the Bible is certainly problematic; it would be a serious misuse of the text, however, if one transferred its content from its theological context to a realistic military context and use it to justify genocidal fantasies or anti-Jewish sentiments.

What is true for the political arena is also true for individuals. Violent people have no future; God will find means to break their violence—by force, if necessary.

Let us start with the most obvious examples. In the books of Samuel, Joab and Abishai, the "two sons of Zeruiah," appear as the very personification of violence (Abishai: 1 Sam 26:8; 2 Sam 16:9; 19:22; Joab: 2 Sam 3; 11; 18; 20). David is portrayed as nonviolent in direct opposition to these two men; he repeatedly laments that he does not have the means to control the sons of Zeruiah. In the end, David at least issues orders and Joab receives his due punishment (1 Kgs 2:5–6, 28–34—these orders also allow Solomon to get rid of one of the most important supporters of his rival Adonijah; see 1:7, 41).

Amnon is murdered by Absalom after his rape of Tamar (2 Sam 13:23–29). This may satisfy our need for justice, but it is in truth nothing but a private lynching and fratricide. One violent act cannot be redeemed by another violent act; this leads only to more injustice and most often more violence. Absalom must indeed escape from his father's wrath and go into exile. It is possible that the idea of a rebellion came to him during this time. Thus the spiral of violence continues to escalate. Absalom's rebellion, prepared with great care, is successful at first, but then the son falls into his father's clever trap of leaving a secret network of supporters behind in Jerusalem. The Bible does not miss the opportunity to state that "Yhwh had ordained to defeat Absalom" (2 Sam 17:14). It is well known what happened to the rebel Absalom.

Lurking behind the violent crown princes is the shadow of their father—he too is a violent man. David, however, was allowed to grow old and die a peaceful death. He too was broken but in a much more subtle way. His mourning over the death of his oldest son Amnon lasts for a long time (2 Sam 13:36); he is torn by frantic grief over the death of his second son Absalom (19:1–5). Even before these two, however, there was the death of another child: the child conceived in adultery with Bathsheba—here, too, his pain was immense (12:15–23). It is no coincidence that David is struck by this fate once he has reached the high point of his power (2 Sam 5–10). He now possesses unlimited power over his subjects, such that he can even take Uriah's wife and then his life (2 Sam 11). No one is able to call him to account—except for God and his prophet. The mighty ruler must submit himself to God's judgment (2 Sam 12), and in each of the subsequent deaths of his sons he will know why they happen and who stands behind them. Only as a ruler who was brought to his knees by the power of God—thus probably the connection of Ps 51 to David!—can David become the prototype of a ruler who is agreeable to God and the precursor for the expected Messiah.

In deliberate contrast to David, who fell deeply but was not abandoned by God, the Bible portrays Saul as one who barely stumbles at the beginning but continues to fall deeper and deeper, finally plunging into the abyss—not because the narrators saw him as a much more violent man than David but because he, unlike David, continued to fall into acts of violence and could no longer be held back. Saul is portrayed as a basically reticent and modest person. If there ever were a ruler in Israel who did not make a grab for power, it was Saul (1 Sam 9–10). Ancient Jewish exegesis even blames him for this feature: his love of power was not developed enough for one who wanted to rule. Then the conflict between Saul and Samuel ensues, and once Samuel has told him of his rejection, he becomes sick and increasingly violent. His spear—his personal landmark—threatens David twice and once even his own son Jonathan (18:11; 19:10; 20:33). He sees traitors among his closest followers (22:6–8), opposes a prophetic group around Samuel with force (19:18–24), and finally massacres an entire family of priests (1 Sam 21–22). He pursues his rival David through the entire Judean desert "like one who hunts a partridge in the mountains" (26:20). He finally drives David out of the country, which turns out to be a grave mistake (24:9–23; 26:13–25). When the Philistines prepare for their final battle against Israel, Saul is missing his most effective and proven warrior (1 Sam 29). Abandoned by God and his most capable general, Saul is lost; thus it follows a certain logic when he throws himself on his own sword in the end (1 Sam 31). This ending could not have been different. Saul had turned into a manic and dangerous character. He is also an example of the fact that individuals who do not turn from violence will necessarily fail in the end.

Apart from breaking violence with violence, the narratives about the early monarchy also tell of another way to fight against violence: again and again they tell us of instances of deliberate abstinence from violence.

Let us begin once again with military examples. When the troops of Saul's successor Eshbaal encounter the troops of David, a bloody battle ensues, with many casualties. Eshbaal's men start to lose ground and are in danger of being overwhelmed. At this moment, Abner shouts to the opposing general Joab: "Shall the sword devour forever? Do you not know that the end will be bitter? How long will it be before you bid your people turn from the pursuit of their brethren?" Joab answers, "As God lives, if you had not spoken, surely the men would not have given up the pursuit of their brethren until the morning." He then blows the trumpet, and the battle is ended (2 Sam 2:26–28).

We find a similar situation in the Sheba narrative in 2 Sam 20. This northern Israelite separatist is driven to the far north by Joab's troops, where he seeks refuge in the city Abel-beth-maacah. When Joab besieges the city, a wise woman addresses him from the city wall and asks, "Do you seek to destroy a city and a mother in Israel? Why will you destroy the heritage of YHWH?" Joab answers, "Far be it from me, far be it! I will not swallow up or destroy!" He is interested only in Sheba; if Sheba is surrendered, he will immediately leave the city (20:18–21). Soon after this, Sheba's head flies over the wall. Joab blows the trumpet, his army retreats, and the city is spared.

When Absalom flees to a neighboring Aramean kingdom following his murder of Amnon, David thinks about leading his army there (2 Sam 13:39 is probably best translated as: "then King David planned to go out against Absalom"). Joab wants to prevent this, but he does not dare to address the king directly; instead, he sends a "wise woman" from the Judahite town of Tekoa. This woman proves as clever as Nathan during the Bathsheba-Uriah scandal. She creates a fictional judicial case that David decides mildly and with great wisdom—and she then shows him that this decision and his treatment of his son are closely related (2 Sam 14). David allows himself to be persuaded, and Absalom is allowed to return. Bloodshed is prevented.

Even when bloodshed occurs, we gain the impression that the narrators are denouncing war instead of glorifying it. This is especially clear in the narrative about the war against the Ammonites that forms the background for David's adultery and murder. When Uriah, the bothersome husband, is killed as planned and with him several other soldiers, David cynically sends a message to Joab that he should not worry about the whole incident, "for the sword devours now one and now another" (2 Sam 11:25). Anyone who reads this line will remain suspicious about any glorification of war and heroic death.

The Bible justifies the fact that Solomon, not David, built the temple in Jerusalem with the statement that David was a warrior (2 Sam 7:10–13, which stands *before* the large war narratives in 2 Sam 8 for a reason; see also 1 Kgs 5:17–18; 1 Chr 22:8; 28:3). It seems that war and worship do not go well together. The temple builder Solomon is presented as a ruler of peace. Under his scepter "Judah and Israel were as many as the sand by the sea; they ate and drank and were happy" (1 Kgs 4:20); "Judah and Israel lived in safety, from Dan to Beer-sheba, every man under his vine and under his fig tree, all the days of Solomon" (5:5 Eng. 4:25). Thus Solomon can rightfully say that God has given him "peace on all sides, no adversary [literally, *satan*!] and no evil occurrence" (5:18). It is only *now* that the preparations for temple construction begin. It seems that the description of the early monarchy reaches its climax not in war and victory but in peace.

In this context we should mention a small but interesting fact. In the first list of David's officials, Joab is mentioned first and Benaiah, the commander of the mercenaries, in fifth place (2 Sam 8:16–18). In the second list, Joab is still mentioned first, and Benaiah has climbed to second position—two military men at the head of David's cabinet (20:23). Under Solomon, only Benaiah remains, and he occupies the fourth position (1 Kgs 4:2–4). Does this not indicate that the army and war lost their predominance under Solomon?

The vision of peace pursued by the biblical texts already starts with David. In the supplement to the David narratives in 2 Sam 21–24 we encounter a story that is highly significant in this context. David comes up with the idea—according to the present text, due to an evil inspiration by God (24:1)—to count "all the tribes from Dan to Beer-sheba." Joab, the military leader, is appointed to perform this census; David thus clearly desires to find out what his military power is. After initially refusing, Joab and his men start the process and report after exactly nine months and twenty days: "in Israel there were 800,000 valiant men who drew the sword, and the men of Judah were 500,000" (24:9). If these numbers were not hopelessly exaggerated, they would have greatly pleased the king; instead, "his heart struck him after he had numbered the people, and David said to Yhwh, 'I have sinned greatly'" (24:10). As punishment, God sends a plague that kills "seventy thousand men from Dan to Beer-sheba" in a very short time. Only extreme cultic measures succeed in turning away God's wrath and stopping the angel of death. This is a bizarre story that is clearly critical of war and military power.

Two stories shall be mentioned at the end that show how women—notably once again women!—are able to break the escalating spiral of violence among men and create peace.

When the wealthy stockman Nabal refuses to pay the protection money demanded by the outlaw David, David rides with several hundred men to

Nabal's homestead, determined to kill everything "that pisses against a wall" (1 Sam 25:22), a vulgar expression of male violence. It is only thanks to the initiative of the beautiful and intelligent Abigail that a bloodbath is prevented. Her gifts, her charming appearance, and especially her clever speech bring David back to reason. God himself, she says, wants to prevent him from "falling into blood guilt"; God will "certainly establish a sure house" for the king, and it should not become "an offense and stumbling block" that the king "shed innocent blood" (25:*26–31). David changes his mind and retreats with his men. Soon after, Nabal is struck down without David's involvement, and David can marry the widow. David learns that he must not eliminate his opponents by force but must leave such actions to God. Recent exegesis (Levenson, Dietrich 2004) has shown in detail how this narrative is woven into its present context: in 1 Sam 24 and 26, David spares Saul. The first time David already has a knife in his hand but only cuts off a piece of Saul's cloak—and even this burdens him with a guilty conscience. The second time he acts with complete nobility and largesse and does not even touch Saul. The three narratives together form a triptych on the subject of violence. The centerpiece is the glorious figure of Abigail, who teaches David an incredibly important lesson: a truly great king can abstain from using violence.

The other narrative is the story of Rizpah, one of Saul's concubines (2 Sam 21). At first she is the helpless victim of male lust for blood and revenge. Her two sons (and five further descendants of Saul) die because the inhabitants of the city of Gibeon and King David believe that this is the only way to turn away God's wrath and end the famine that has come over the land. The background of this narrative is also composed of accounts that still have to be settled between the Gibeonites and David with the house of Saul. The narrator dispassionately reports the mass execution and then emphasizes Rizpah's reaction: she publicly defends the corpses of her sons against wild animals until she is allowed to give them a proper burial. Only then—not after the killing of her sons—does the desired rain fall. The reconciliation with God seems to have been brought about not by the act of violence but by Rizpah's act of love.

The biblical description of the early monarchy does not limit itself to tracing the path of violence that runs through this time period. It also composes subtle but clearly recognizable scenes in which violence is limited and avoided. The message is clear: the promise is not connected to acting out violence but to overcoming it.

Index of Names and Subjects

INDEX OF BIBLICAL REFERENCES

Printed in the United States
92634LV00003B/76-198/A